DRAWING **PLAN GRAPHICS** ON THE COMPUTER

DRAWING **PLAN GRAPHICS** ON THE COMPUTER

C. Carlyle Rood, RLA, LEED AP

To My Family.

ISBN: 978-0-615-34344-0

CONTENTS

FOREWORD

I could tell there was something special about Carlyle early on. When we hired him, we had been struggling for years to improve our computer-generated plan graphics. We wanted to produce computer plan graphics that were consistent with (or better than) the hand-drawn plans we were proud of for so many years.

Our clients had grown accustomed to loose, creative, variable hand graphics. These drawings were particularly appropriate for conceptual plans. They gave artistic form and meaningful organization to the client's ideas without appearing to say "this plan is fixed, finished, or finalized, prior to your further input."

We wanted our computer-drawn graphics to appear like these hand-drawn graphics. Our early computer-drawn plan graphics lacked the three-dimensional form, depth, and subtlety of our hand-drawn plans. They were composed mostly of contrasting black lines and simple, flat, solid colors.

After we hired Carlyle, it wasn't long before he was showing us how we could incorporate all of the characteristics of the hand-drawn plans we and our clients were accustomed to. He used a variety of techniques he had either developed or discovered to create plan graphics superior to the plans we had been able to produce—even by hand. Not only did Carlyle's techniques allow us to create the artistic subtlety we desired, but also to achieve a consistency throughout our design staff regardless of their individual talent or experience drawing on the computer. We were even able to produce renderings with the characteristics of more sophisticated techniques such as air-brush, water color washes, silk screens, etc. Furthermore, when our projects progressed to the final steps, Carlyle's techniques were equally appropriate and adaptable to more sophisticated final presentations—especially for use in marketing, but also for all other varieties of graphic communication.

It is gratifying to see that Carlyle has translated his considerable talent, skill, and knowledge into this clear and concise instructional book. It is sure to enable many design professionals across many disciplines to improve their skills and presentations to discerning clients.

Thank you Carlyle,

J. Edward Pinckney, FASLA
10 January 2010

PREFACE

I think computer graphics should look better. I am not sure what happened after computers were introduced to design professionals; but, clearly something was lost in translation. Most computer drawings simply do not possess the same clarity or artistry of hand-drawn graphics.

Curiously, something else happened after computers were introduced to our profession: hand-drawn graphics diminished in quality too! Some of that can be attributed to fewer professionals drawing by hand; but, even professionals that used to draw well simply are not as good as before. Why is that?

I think the primary reason for this is because instruction books for computer graphics have taught us to be incompetent. The first shortcoming of these books is that instead of sharing the fundamental principles, strategies, and techniques for drawing well, instruction books have focused entirely on using a specific brand of software to draw. So we become experts at using a specific computer application. We learn to conform our work to the limitations of that software (or, at least its instruction). And as we become accustomed to drawing like this on the computer, we begin to draw just as modestly by hand too. A second shortcoming is that, even if we understand the fundamentals for drawing well, we do not have enough practical step-by-step examples demonstrating them. Understanding these fundamentals is important obviously; but, sometimes we just want to see explicitly how something is drawn.

An artifact of this is a lot of mediocre drawings on the computer. And then a conflict naturally arises within the office: a war waged between two factions of professionals—those that champion the artistry and elegance of hand-drawn graphics and those that champion the efficiency and flexibility of computer drawings.

Well, it does not have to be this way. We can draw better. In this book, we learn how. First, we will address and dismiss some common myths and misconceptions about drawing on the computer. Then we will look at some examples of what computer plan graphics can, and should, look like. Next we will learn principles, strategies, and techniques for drawing well on the computer—skills that you can apply to any computer graphics software on the market. And finally, we will look at some practical, explicit, step-by-step drawing examples using the most familiar and popular graphics software in use today, Adobe Photoshop.

I wrote this book for design professionals, particularly landscape architects. I encourage you to read this book and apply its teachings. If you do, I am confident that you will be more effective communicating your designs and you will enjoy your work more.

ACKNOWLEDGMENTS

I read a lot of books. Often, I read more than one book at a time. My night stand is littered with them. And I do not just read them—I study them. Open one of my books, and you will find copious notes in the margins. You will see words circled. You will find questions (and hopefully their answers) scribbled throughout. Rarely will you find a page without some sort of notation or comment.

But one section of every book always seems to remain in mint condition, and that is simply because I do not read it: the Acknowledgments. Well, that is going to change. Having just endured writing my first book, I recognize just how important the contribution of others is. This book simply would not be as good without their help. They deserve acknowledgment and I hope you take the time to read the following paragraphs.

Jeanie and Edwin Jones allowed this book to happen. I began writing it in their home. They made certain that I had the time to write it. They ensured that I had the funds to finance it. They purchased the software required to develop it. They even bought a printer so that I could review my progress—three of them, actually. Anywhere I plugged in my laptop, it seems, I would find Edwin unpacking a new printer.

Several design professionals made important contributions to this book. Edward Pinckney, FASLA, has allowed me to share numerous drawings produced while working for his firm, Edward Pinckney/Associates Ltd. in Bluffton, South Carolina. Michael Riley, golf course architect, allowed me to reuse some of his grading and design plans to produce several golf course renderings. Mike also helped review and proofread several portions of the book. And lastly, Christina Moore Bryant, RLA, meticulously scoured the entire manuscript. The quality and utility of this book can be debated; but, it is indisputable that this book is far better than it was before Christina reviewed it. I want to thank all of these professionals for their contributions to this book.

1 TEN MYTHS (AND TRUTHS) ABOUT COMPUTER GRAPHICS

Before jumping into the principles, strategies, techniques, and examples in this book, it might be helpful to dispel some common myths about computer graphics. Some of these myths have been repeated so frequently that they are now accepted as fact. Too often, I have seen people use these myths to discourage others and themselves from using computer graphics.

If you are introducing computer graphics to your office, you may very well find yourself confronted with these objections. This can be especially frustrating—particularly if the decision makers are inexperienced using computers to draw or draft. If so, then you will certainly want to be equipped with the answers to these myths.

TEN COMMON MYTHS ABOUT COMPUTER GRAPHICS

1. If you can draw well by hand, then you do not need to learn how to draw on the computer.
2. You have to be a computer expert to draw well on the computer.
3. It takes years to develop the skills required to draw well on the computer.
4. It takes specialized software to view or print a drawing created on the computer.
5. Computer graphics software is too expensive.
6. Drawing on the computer is slower than drawing by hand.
7. Computer graphics should look realistic.
8. Every drawing on the computer should be its own masterpiece.
9. Computer graphics should always be drawn in color.
10. If it looks good on the computer screen, then it will look good when it is printed.

Myth 1: If you can draw well by hand, then you do not need to learn to draw on the computer.

> **Truth 1:** Learning to draw on the computer will make you a more effective designer, whether you draw well by hand or not.

The ability to draw by hand is one of the most useful skills you can possess as a designer. There is a flexibility and creativity permitted when drawing by hand that is difficult—if not impossible—to replicate on the computer. In fact, even if you become an expert at drawing and drafting on the computer, I would still encourage you to draw and sketch by hand as often as possible. This is especially true as you develop an idea during the conceptual phases of your project.

That being said, if you develop the skills to present your work graphically on a computer, you will be more effective at communicating your designs—including your hand-drawn designs. Why is that? Well, to begin with, you will be able to present your message in more ways to more people. For example, after you have scanned your drawing and saved it in a digital format, you will be able to:

- Drop your drawing into an elegant frame or template.
- Add an attractive title and label your drawing more clearly.
- Reduce or enlarge your drawing to a more convenient size.
- Enhance or amplify the color of your drawing.
- Erase undesirable elements from your sketch or add more detail.
- Print or plot your drawing on more attractive paper.
- Drop your drawing into a visual presentation.
- Integrate your design drawing into a narrative.
- E-mail your drawing.
- Transfer your drawing to a remote computer.
- Archive your drawing for later use.

The list goes on. You are going to be a more effective communicator because you are allowed to deliver your message in more ways.

Myth 2: You have to be a computer expert to draw well on a computer.

> **Truth 2:** Both computer experts and novices can learn to draw well on a computer.

Experience using a computer is an advantage, certainly. The more familiar you are with a specific computer application, the more efficient you will be using it. For example, the more you know about the menus, tools, filters, and functionality of Adobe Photoshop, the faster and more creative you are going to be using it. That is just common sense.

But familiarity with an application and computer experience are not prerequisites to drawing well on a computer. In fact, there are two fundamental reasons why your previous experience and expertise may actually work against you.

The first reason expertise is not necessarily helpful is because software and computers are improving and developing so rapidly that much of your so-called expertise may already be obsolete. Consider the following questions:

- Are you using the same computer that you did five years ago?
- Are you using the same operating system that you did five years ago?
- Are you using the same version of your word processor that you did five years ago?
- Do you expect to continue to use this computer, operating system, or word processor for another five years?
- Do you intend to upgrade any of the software you currently use in the near future?

Though I would not expect everyone to answer the above questions the same way, I do hope by answering these questions you recognize that the computer and software that you use regularly will almost certainly change in the near future—if it has not already.

If you have been using computers regularly, then you have already been adapting to these changes. Some of these new habits are so subtle that we hardly recognize we are changing.

Other times, these "upgrades" can be so jarring and revolutionary that they are frustrating to endure. But, we endure them ultimately because we understand that eventually we will be better at what we enjoy doing.

The second reason expertise is not necessarily helpful is because you can be biased by your own experience. For example, I have been using Adobe Photoshop for well over a decade. I was asked once to show someone else—a far less experienced person—how I did a certain task within Photoshop that we did routinely at our company. I told him about the utility of the task and why it was important. I walked him through the steps required. I pointed out the common pitfalls and how to avoid them. And ultimately, I produced the effect I wanted. Afterwards, I asked if he understood how to reproduce what I had just done and if he had any questions.

An awkward silence followed my presentation. Was he confused? Did I go to fast? Finally, I asked him what was troubling him. "Well," he answered, "isn't there a filter that does that already?"

Embarrassed and somewhat indignant, I challenged him to "Show me!" Patiently, he sat down at my desk and produced precisely the same drawing—only he did it within a few seconds! Now it was my turn to be awkwardly silent.

And that can be one of the pitfalls of experience. The longer you do something, the easier it is to become complacent and fall into routines. The intent of this book is not to help you acquire experience drawing on the computer. The intent is to broaden your skills and cultivate a habit of growth. Whether you have a great deal of computer expertise or not, this book will teach you strategies and skills that will allow you to grow as a communicator and designer.

Myth 3: It takes years to develop the skills required to draw well on the computer.

> **Truth 3:** You will be able to draw well on the computer, quickly, by learning and applying the techniques taught in this book.

Like many myths, there is an element of truth to this one. If you devote a modest amount of time, every day for a few years, working to develop your skills, then you will certainly improve. You will not be very good at first; but, through trial-and-error, you will eventually figure out how to do things correctly.

If drawing well on the computer is your life's ambition, then this might be a plausible route. After all, employing this strategy will probably take a lifetime before you have the skills required to draw well! There are so many mistakes to be made, that you can occupy the rest of your lifetime learning to overcome each one.

I do not expect you to have the time or patience to spend years developing your computer graphics skills. Even if you did, there is really no point in that sort of commitment. You can acquire the same skills far more quickly. I am going to teach you specific strategies and techniques to help you draw well now. In many cases, I will explicitly tell you how to draw a subject using today's most popular graphics programs. But more importantly, I will teach you fundamentals of drawing that you will be able to apply during the remainder of your lifetime, regardless of the software you use.

Myth 4: It takes specialized software to view or print a drawing created on a computer.

> **Truth 4:** You will be able to share your work whether your audience has the same software or not.

The graphics software that allows you to draw well on the computer is highly specialized. They are complex programs, and the underlying technologies they utilize are often proprietary. But your audience will not be required to use the same software to view your document that you used to create it.

And thank goodness, for that. Most computer graphics software is expensive. And while it is justifiable to purchase those programs if you intend to use them to produce special documents, it would be unfair to expect your clients to foot the same sort of bill just to look at your work.

Be assured that every computer graphics application will allow you to produce your work in a universally accepted format that your audience can view and print from.

Myth 5: Computer graphics software is too expensive.

> **Truth 5:** Used appropriately, computer graphics software is a profitable investment.

Computer graphics software is expensive—very expensive. However, when is it too expensive? Certainly computer graphics software is too expensive when you do not use it. If the software is not useful for doing your job, then it is too expensive. As long as your software allows you to provide a useful service or product, then its expense can be justified.

If you learn to use your computer graphics software effectively, then you are going to be better at your job, you are going to provide more value to your clients, you are going to get paid handsomely for your work, and you are going to earn more money than you spent.
So there are two reasonable conclusions we should reach: (1) If purchasing computer graphics software will allow you to generate more money than you will spend, then it is not too expensive; and (2) If you have already purchased the graphics software, then you better learn how to use it to justify that expense.

And if you are still not convinced it is a good value, or if you are uncertain it will be useful for your job, then do not buy it. Did I just say that? Am I really asking you to buy my book, but not buy the software I am teaching you to use? Yes, you heard me right.

Most software companies recognize how expensive their software is. That is why they are willing to loan it to you for a while—often for free. They figure that you will learn how to use it, get accustomed to its ease, and perhaps even become dependent on their product to do your job! Visit their website. They almost certainly have a trial version of their product. It may not have all the functionality of the retail version and it usually expires after a certain amount of time; but, you will learn whether it will be useful or not.

This is also a useful practice when considering whether to upgrade, later. You will have a chance to learn whether the new functionality of an upgraded program justifies an additional investment.

Myth (and Truth) 6: Drawing on a computer is slower than drawing by hand.

If you have been told that drawing by hand is faster or more efficient than drawing on the computer, then I can assure you of one thing: They are wrong. And if they are especially emphatic or vigilant in convincing you that they are right, then they almost certainly have a stake in whether you draw by hand—that is, they want to sell you something. Conversely, if you have been told that drawing on the computer is faster or more efficient, I can assure you just as confidently of another thing: They are wrong, too.

I have argued both sides of this argument, and I have tested both sides of this argument. I have concluded that the only truthful thing you can say is that sometimes drawing by hand is faster and more efficient, and sometimes drawing on a computer is. And if you are really that preoccupied with which is better, then you miss the point of this book altogether. I do not want you to stop drawing by hand. I am not trying to replace your markers, pens, and pencils. I just want you to be better at communicating your ideas. I think learning how to draw on the computer will help accomplish that.

You are going to learn when you should choose one method over the other. You will learn that just from the day-to-day experience of doing your job. As you will see later, though, if you find yourself doing a similar task again and again, it is usually good to do it "once" on the computer, and then refine or revise it as required. But, let us defer that argument for now.

It suffices to say that by the time you have finished this book and learned to apply its principles, you are going to be better equipped to decide when it is appropriate to draw on the computer, and when it is not.

Myth 7: Computer graphics should look realistic.

> **Truth 7:** Realistic drawings often waste your time and compromise your message.

Many software applications are available now that will allow you to create photorealistic renderings of your design. In fact, I have seen drawings that were almost indistinguishable from photographs. I have even seen realistic movies that simulated flyovers of a design project years before construction ever began. The technology and expertise required for this sort of modeling is remarkable; but, so are the results.

Some of the software used in the illustrations throughout this book have comparable capabilities, too. And when afforded this capability, there is a tremendous temptation to make your drawings life-like. If you find yourself being drawn down this path, then please resist it. I do not have anything against photorealistic drawings. There are occasions when it is useful, or even necessary, to draw realistically. But there are two reasons I want you to avoid it: (1) Time that could have been spent refining your design is wasted trying to make your drawing realistic; and (2) The message behind your drawing often gets obscured.

Drawing a photorealistic rendering takes time—and a lot of it. The models you are required to construct are complex. The detail required is substantial. The textures and images available to you are seldom comprehensive enough to complete your drawing. Often, you are required to construct and assemble your own library of textures, patterns, and images. Lighting and shadow models require constant refinement and correction. Eventually, if you are fortunate, you will finally be able to complete your drawing.

Of course, the first and greatest temptation I have when reviewing a photorealistic rendering is to try to find what does not fit. And when you find that item that does not fit—and there is always something—it can become a tremendous distraction every time you see it.

It is much like a scene from one of my favorite movies, an Alfred Hitchcock thriller called *North by Northwest.* There comes a point in the movie when Roger Thornhill (played by Cary Grant) is shot by Eve Kendall (played by Eva Marie Saint) in a crowded cafeteria at the base of Mount Rushmore. It is a tremendously suspenseful and climactic scene. Regrettably, it was pointed out to me that, right before Eve fires the gun, a child in the background can be seen putting his hands over his ears to protect them from the sound of the imminent gunshot.

I guess the scene took multiple takes before they got it just right. The child, quite naturally, began covering his ears after the first take. Nonetheless, whenever I see this scene, I inevitably watch the child covering his ears rather than watching Eve shoot Roger.

And that is why I am not a big fan of photorealistic drawings. Inevitably, you spend hours producing a scene where everyone ultimately ends up looking at the kid (the flaw in your drawing) instead of the gunshot (your design).

Myth 8: Every drawing on the computer should be its own masterpiece.

Truth 8: Most of your drawings should look harmonious with previous work.

I recognize that there is an inherent impulse when designing to create a uniquely artful rendering of that design. You want your design to stand out from others—including your own previous work. This is a natural and familiar impulse for many of us. Even the suggestion that a drawing should be standardized, homogenous, or uniform generates an instantaneous and reflexive resistance. How can anyone be truly creative with these sorts of constraints?

And yet that is exactly what I am going to propose that you do when using the computer to draw. I want you to standardize when possible. I want you to construct your drawings using the same fundamental components. I want you to consistently apply the same techniques. I want you to structure your drawings uniformly.

Why would I want to impose these constraints? Why would I deliberately try to limit the methods, tools, and limitless flexibility afforded you? The answer is because standardization can liberate design. To begin with, documents that are organized consistently are easier to edit, and thereby inherently more flexible to alter. Standardization facilitates participation by more team members, thereby broadening the design input and critical feedback. Templating avoids redundancy and omissions, thereby reducing errors. Standardization permits reuse and recycling, thereby jump-starting design and permitting greater refinement. And lastly, standardization allows everything you present to seem harmonious and appropriate together.

Therefore, if you want your designs to be more flexible, refined, accurate, correct, consensus-building, and harmonious, then standardization is a more desirable route.

Myth 9: Computer graphics should always be drawn in color.

Truth 9: You should spend most of your time designing—not drawing on the computer.

If you use color appropriately and effectively in your drawings, it will almost certainly communicate a more positive and persuasive message about your design. Color stimulates. Color activates. Color invigorates. But, often, color does not sell. Why not?

The most common reason why computer graphics should not be done in color is because we choose our colors so poorly. When colors are selected carelessly, it not only detracts from the drawing, it distracts from your design. A poorly colored drawing can make your work seem juvenile and incompetent.

Another reason why color is not as effective is because your audience often cannot see it. No, I am not talking specifically about color blindness—though that is a legitimate concern. I am talking about the fact that many of the people who will evaluate your design will not see your work as you originally presented it. So often your work will be copied or scanned without color. It is very difficult to differentiate reds from greens from blues, et cetera, after they have been copied in black-and-white. Be sure that you are not depending on color to communicate your message.

For these reasons, time spent coloring a drawing would probably be better spent refining your design. That being said, if you follow the techniques taught in this book, then you will not only have more time available to refine your design, but you will have time to use color appropriately and effectively to communicate that enhanced design.

Myth 10: If it looks good on the computer screen, then it will look good when it is printed.

> **Truth 10:** To make your design presentable on both a computer screen and a printer, you need to plan your drawing deliberately.

If you invest the time to make your drawing attractive, harmonious, and beautiful as you draw it on your computer screen, then you should be able to expect your drawing to be attractive, harmonious, and beautiful once it is printed. This is a legitimate expectation. Unfortunately, this is not always the case.

Colors are constructed in entirely different ways by your computer and your printer or plotter. Your computer screen uses light. Your printer uses ink. Because they use different components, they cannot build precisely the same thing. That being said, there is no reason you cannot make your design presentable and effective regardless of which medium you choose. You will simply have to plan and organize your drawing to allow this to happen. This book will teach you the techniques required to make this happen.

TEN TRUTHS ABOUT COMPUTER GRAPHICS

1. Learning to draw on the computer will make you a more effective designer, whether you draw well by hand or not.
2. Both computer experts and novices can learn to draw well on a computer.
3. You will be able to draw well on the computer, quickly, by learning and applying the techniques taught in this book.
4. You will be able to share work created on the computer whether your audience has the same software you used or not.
5. Used appropriately, computer graphics software is a profitable investment.
6. Drawing on the computer is faster, and sometimes slower, than drawing by hand.
7. Realistic drawings often waste your time and compromise your message.
8. Most of your drawings should look harmonious with previous work.
9. You should spend most of your time designing—not drawing on the computer.
10. To make your design presentable on both a computer screen and a printer, you need to plan your drawing deliberately.

2 EXAMPLES

Having just dispelled many of the common myths about drawing on the computer, and prior to discussing the specific principles, strategies, and techniques for drawing well, it may be helpful to see some good examples of plan graphics drawn on the computer.

When you complete reading this book, you should have the skills and experience required to recreate all of these drawings. Hopefully, some of the drawings on the following pages will motivate you to learn and apply the techniques discussed in this book.

I created some of the examples specifically for this book. That is, some of the examples were intended to demonstrate specific techniques I wanted to teach. But the preponderance of the drawings were prepared for clients. They are drawings that were submitted to planning commissions to earn approval for development. They are drawings that were presented to banks and investors to secure financing for large-scale projects. They are drawings that were marketed to prospective homeowners. Which is to say that they are authentic, real-world examples of using the computer to produce plan graphics.

Though I was primarily responsible for rendering these drawings, recognize that most of the following examples benefitted from the expertise and skill of many talented people. And while I am proud of the contribution I made to each of these drawings, the greatest amount of credit belongs to other design professionals. Specifically, I want to acknowledge and thank the professionals at the firms of Edward Pinckney/Associates Ltd. and Michael Riley Design for their contributions to these renderings.

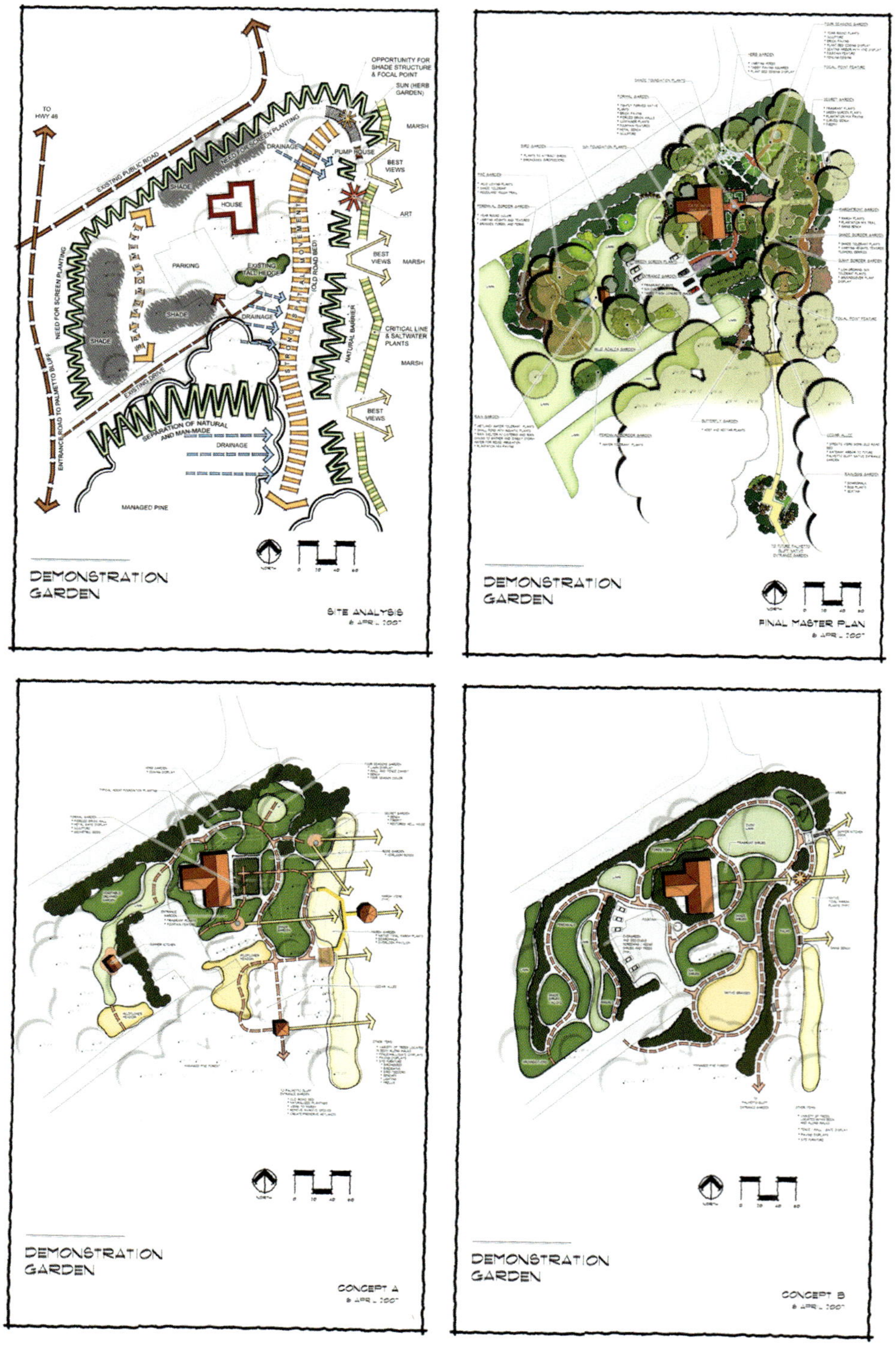

Figure 2-1. Demonstration Garden (clockwise, from upper left) Site Analysis, Conceptual Master Plan, Concept B, and Concept A.

Edward Pinckney/Associates Ltd.
Bluffton, South Carolina.

Originals
24" x 36"
200 pixels per inch
Scale: 1" = 10'-0"

Software
Autodesk AutoCAD
Adobe Photoshop

About This Rendering
These plans were developed to propose alternative designs for a demonstration garden at a residential development.

The plans get progressively more detailed and formal as the design process progresses. The site analysis, for example, is deliberately loose and sketchy. The master plan, however, is far more detailed—building on the two proposed concepts.

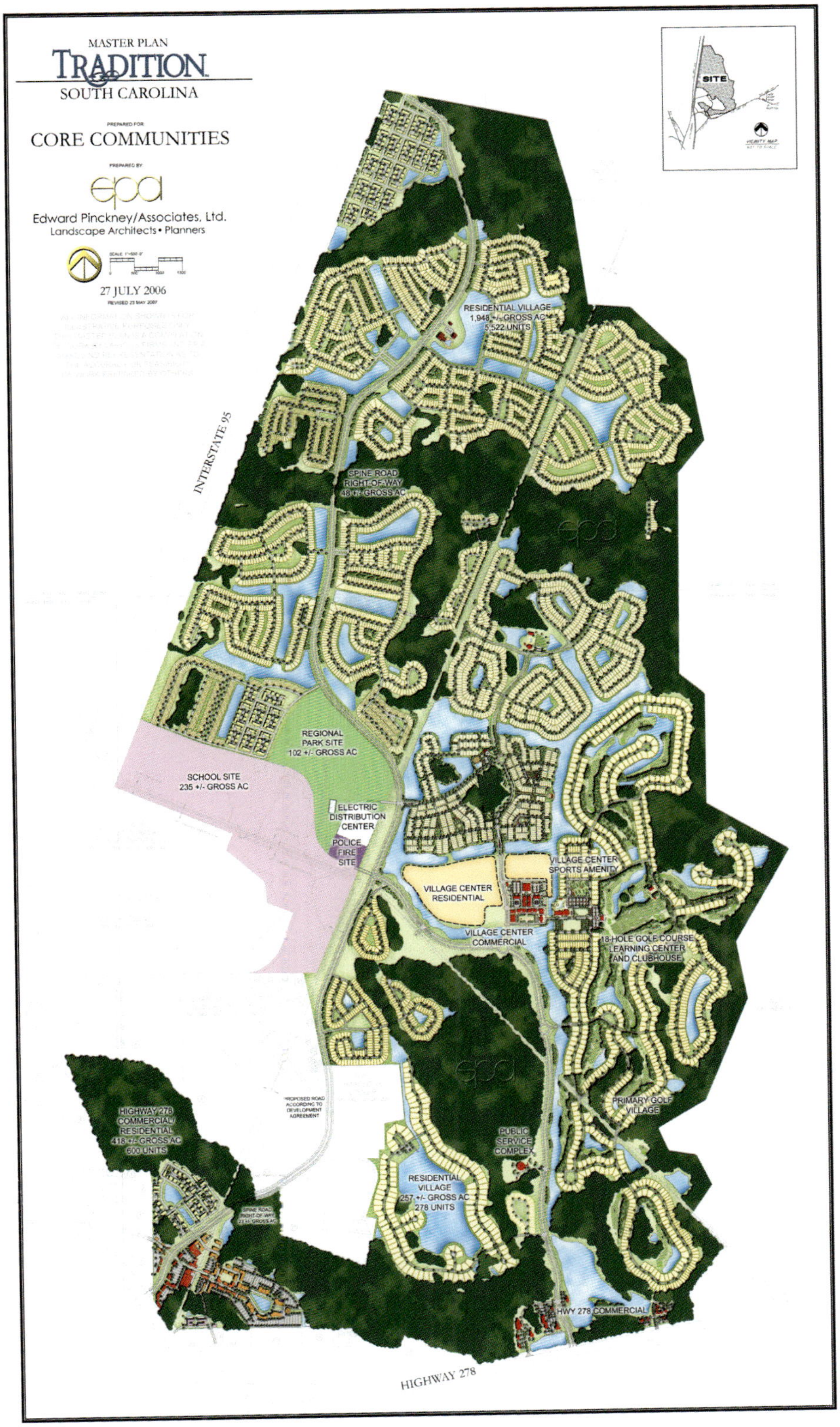

Figure 2-2. Master Plan.

Edward Pinckney/Associates Ltd.
Bluffton, South Carolina.

Original
36" x 72"
200 pixels per inch
Scale: 1" = 500'-0"

Tools
Autodesk AutoCAD
Adobe Photoshop
Markers and Pens

About This Rendering

This is a master plan for a multi-use development and includes civic, commercial, institutional, single-family residential, multi-family residential, and golf course developments.

This rendering is a composite of almost a dozen separate drawings, including hand-drawn portions.

This project was designed, approved, and developed in different stages. Therefore, it was important that (a) different sections remained independent drawings for separate submittals, and (b) those unique drawings could be integrated back into this comprehensive plan to maintain the overall vision.

Figure 2-3. Parking Lot Concepts.

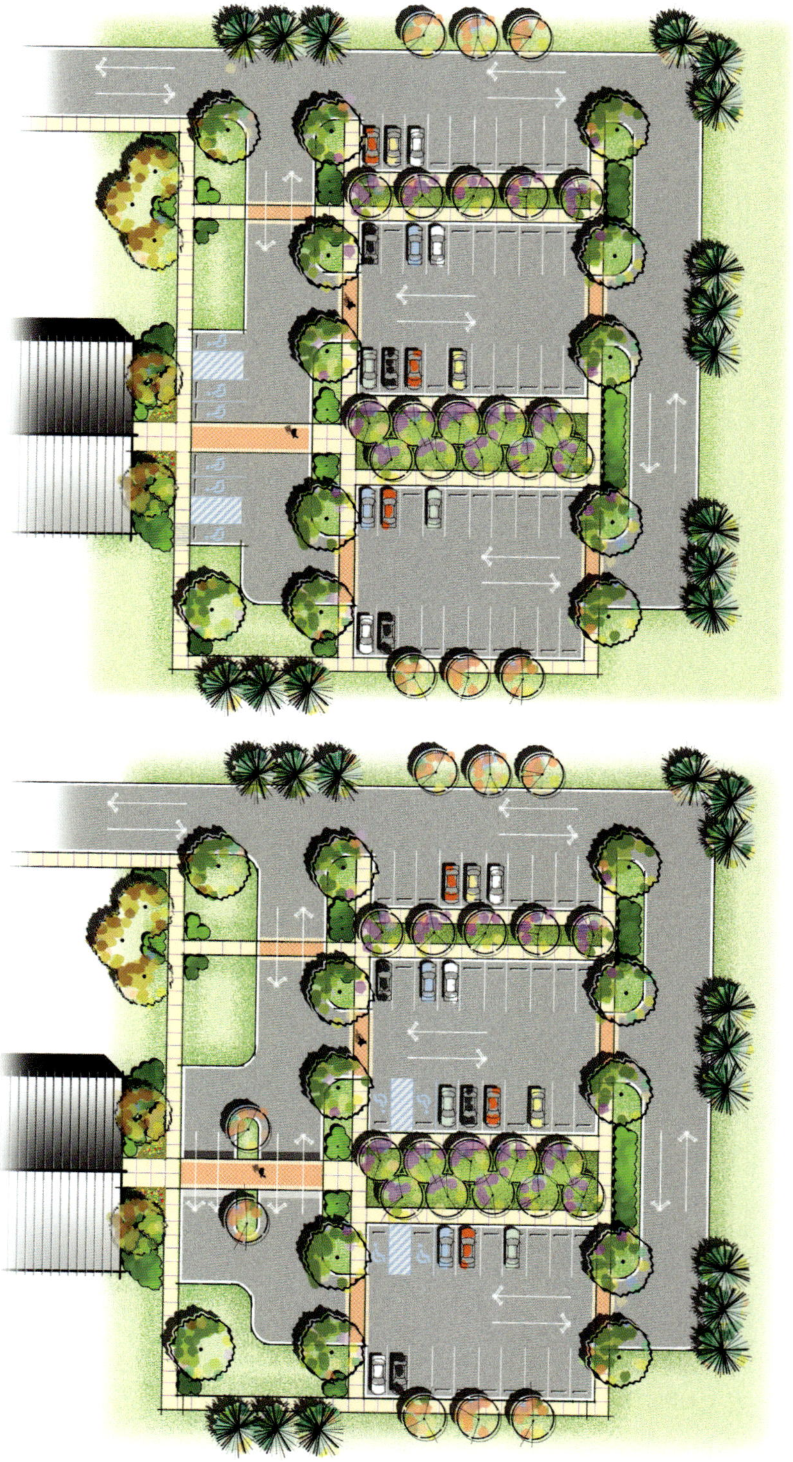

Originals
8" x 10"
200 pixels per inch
Scale: 1" =20'-0"

Software
Adobe Photoshop

About This Rendering
These drawings illustrate two different concepts for a parking lot. Obviously, a great deal of the bottom drawing was recycled from the top drawing.

Rapidly developing new designs from previous work is one of the most useful features of computer graphics.

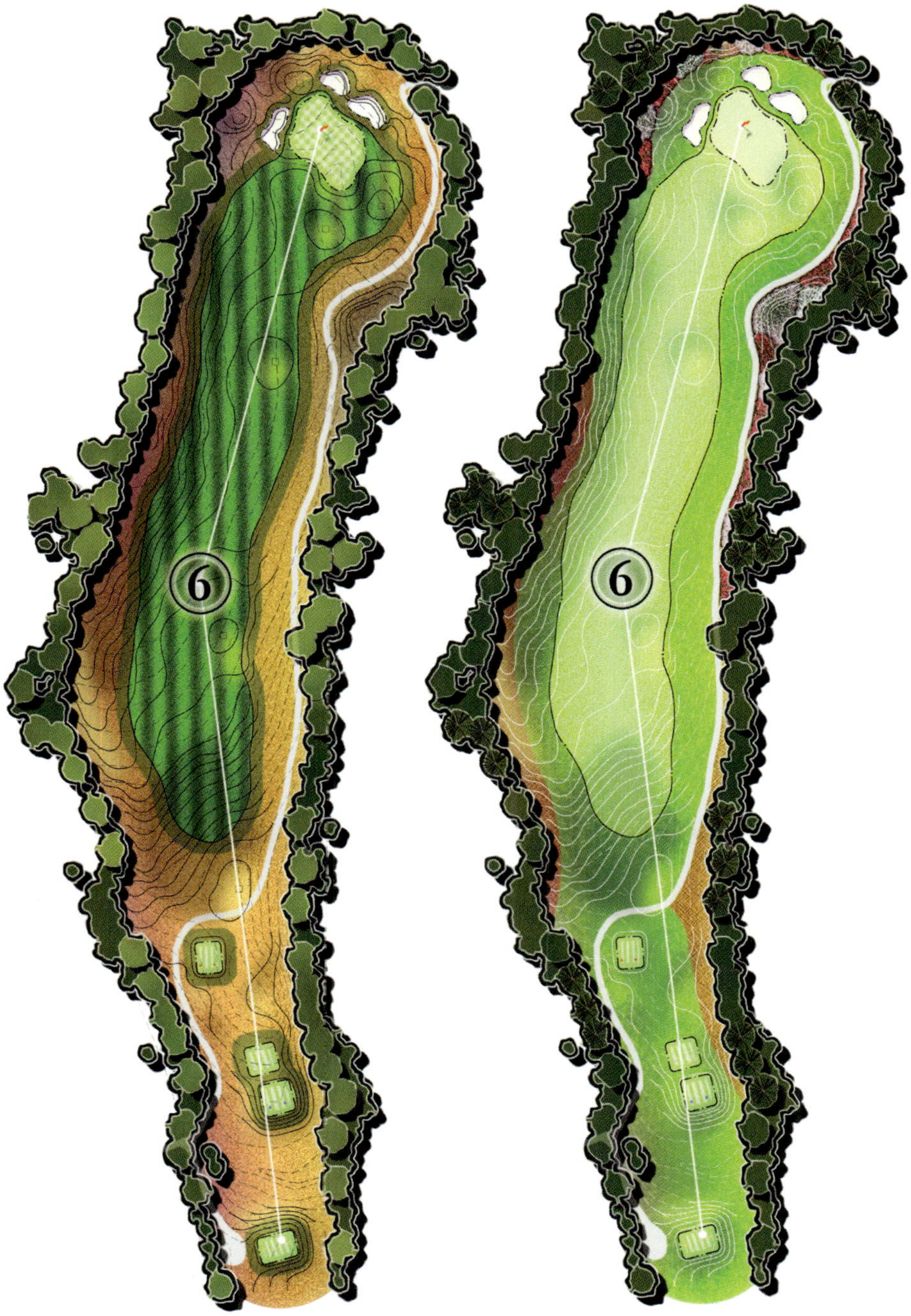

Figure 2-4. Golf Rendering Study.

Golf Design Source
Michael Riley Design LLC.
Marietta, Georgia.

Originals
11" x 17"
200 pixels per inch
Scale: 1" =100'-0"

Software
Autodesk AutoCAD
Adobe Photoshop

About This Rendering
This drawing was created to prototype different rendering techniques for golf courses.

The topography and other golf design line work was traced in AutoCAD from a scan of a blueprint.

Trees and color were added within Photoshop.

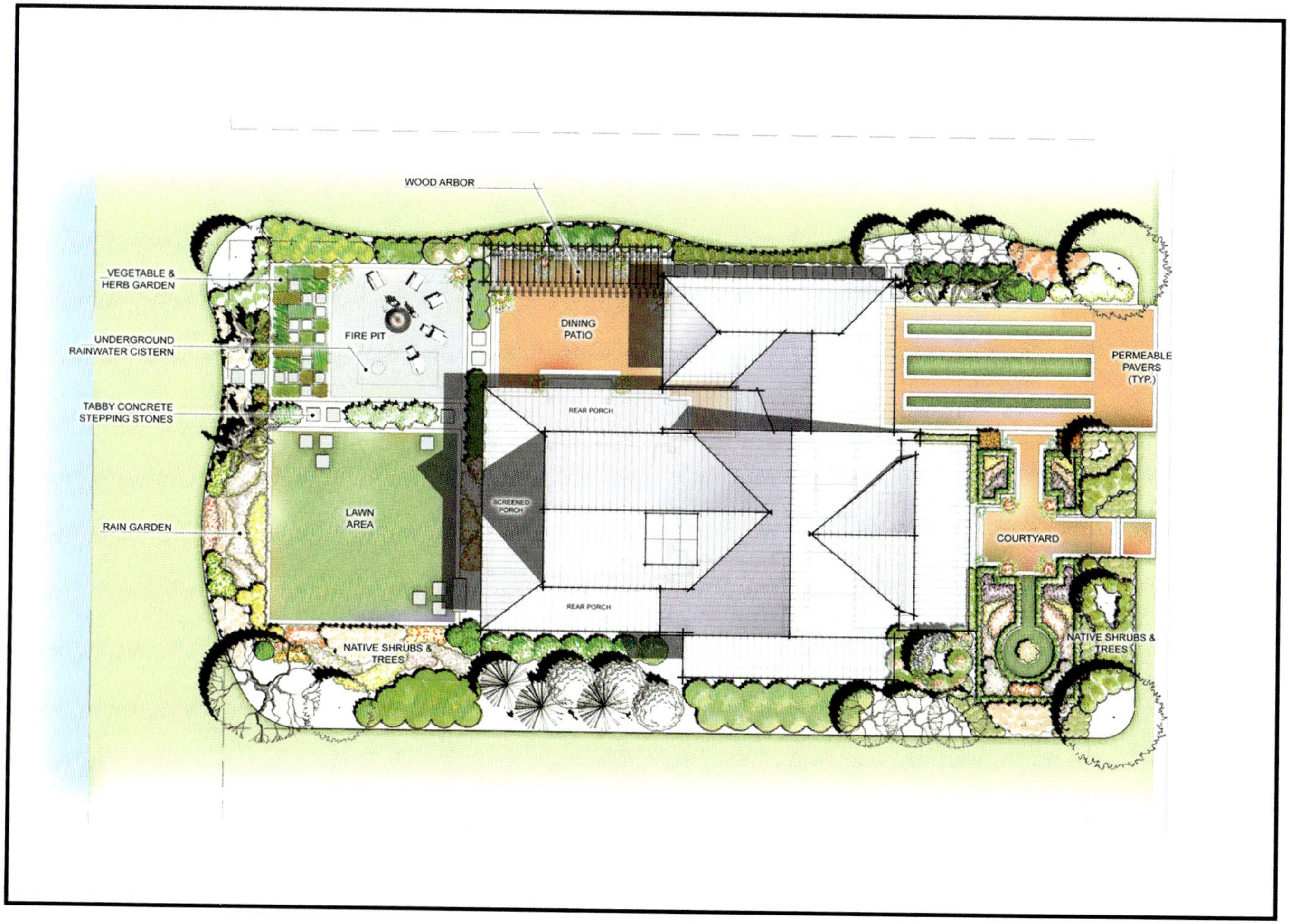

Figure 2-5. Conceptual Hardscape and Planting Plan.

Edward Pinckney/Associates Ltd.
Bluffton, South Carolina.

Original
36" x 24"
200 pixels per inch

Tools
Autodesk AutoCAD
Adobe Photoshop
Markers and Pens
SketchUp

About This Rendering
This rendering is a composite of several drawings, including those drawn by hand.

Because of the complexity of the roof, a primitive, 3-dimensional model of the home was created within SketchUp to see how shading and shadows would appear.

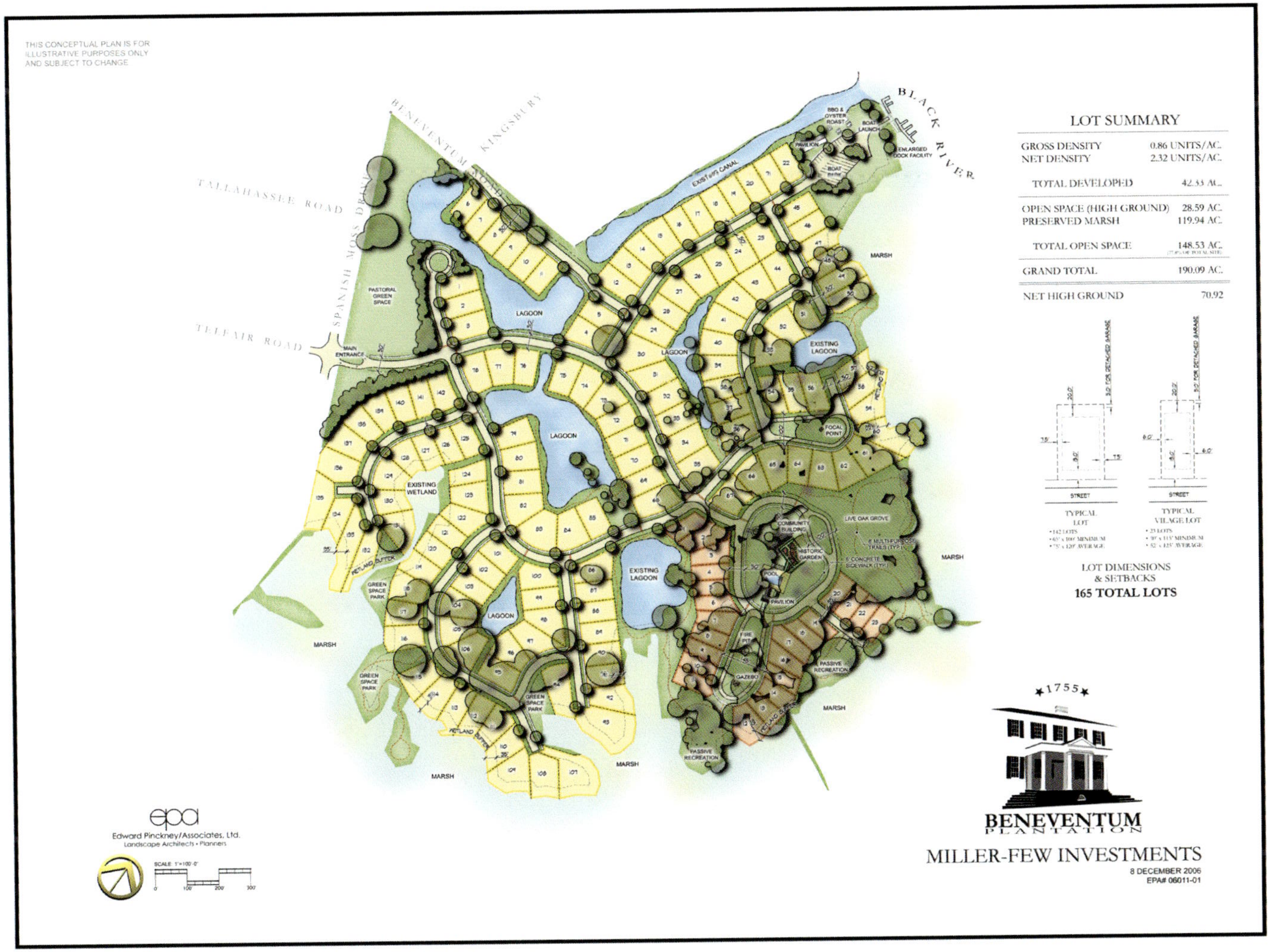

Figure 2-6. Conceptual Master Plan.

Edward Pinckney/Associates Ltd.
Bluffton, South Carolina.

Original
42" x 30"
200 pixels per inch
Scale: 1" = 100'-0"

Tools
Autodesk AutoCAD
Adobe Photoshop

About This Rendering
This is an early conceptual master plan for a residential community. Like so many preliminary drawings, it was begun before all information about a site was collected.

For example, the appearance and composition of the adjacent marshes and remnant rice fields were unavailable; therefore, their representation is very abstract.

A comprehensive tree survey, however, was available. So even though an aerial photograph was not provided, a reasonable representation of the existing tree canopy was possible.

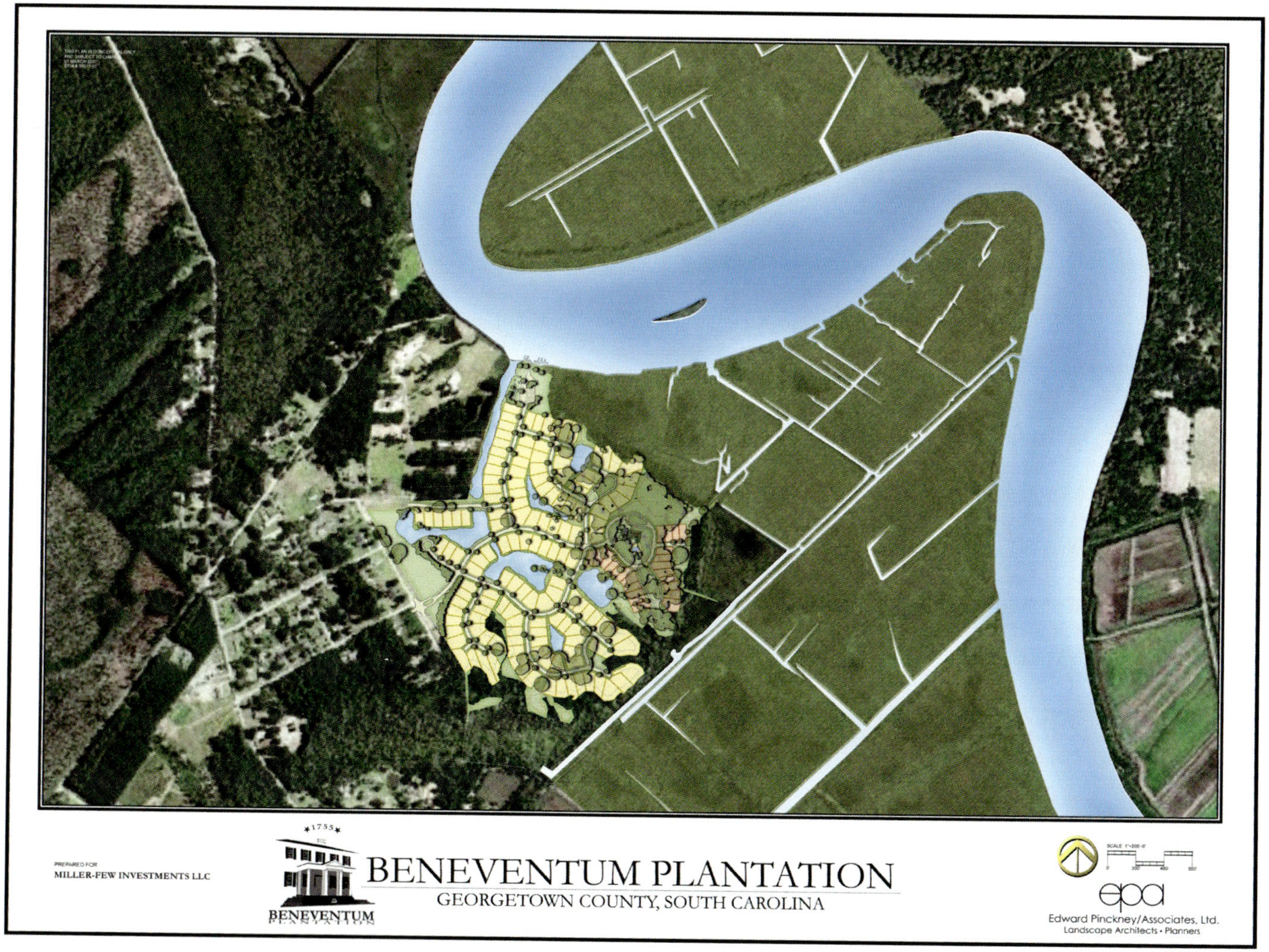

Figure 2-7. Conceptual Master Plan superimposed over an aerial photograph.

Edward Pinckney/Associates Ltd.
Bluffton, South Carolina.

Original
48″ x 36″
200 pixels per inch
Scale: 1″ = 200′-0″

Tools
Autodesk AutoCAD
Adobe Photoshop

About This Rendering
This rendering recycles the conceptual master plan from Figure 2-6. An aerial photograph from a U.S. Geological Survey was purchased to demonstrate the site's proximity to existing neighborhoods and the Black River.

Though the aerial photograph was very informative, the river and remnant rice fields—major assets to the property—did not look artful. Therefore, these elements were rendered again in Photoshop.

To lend some authenticity, though, the transparency of the rice fields was diminished to allow the aerial photograph to show through modestly.

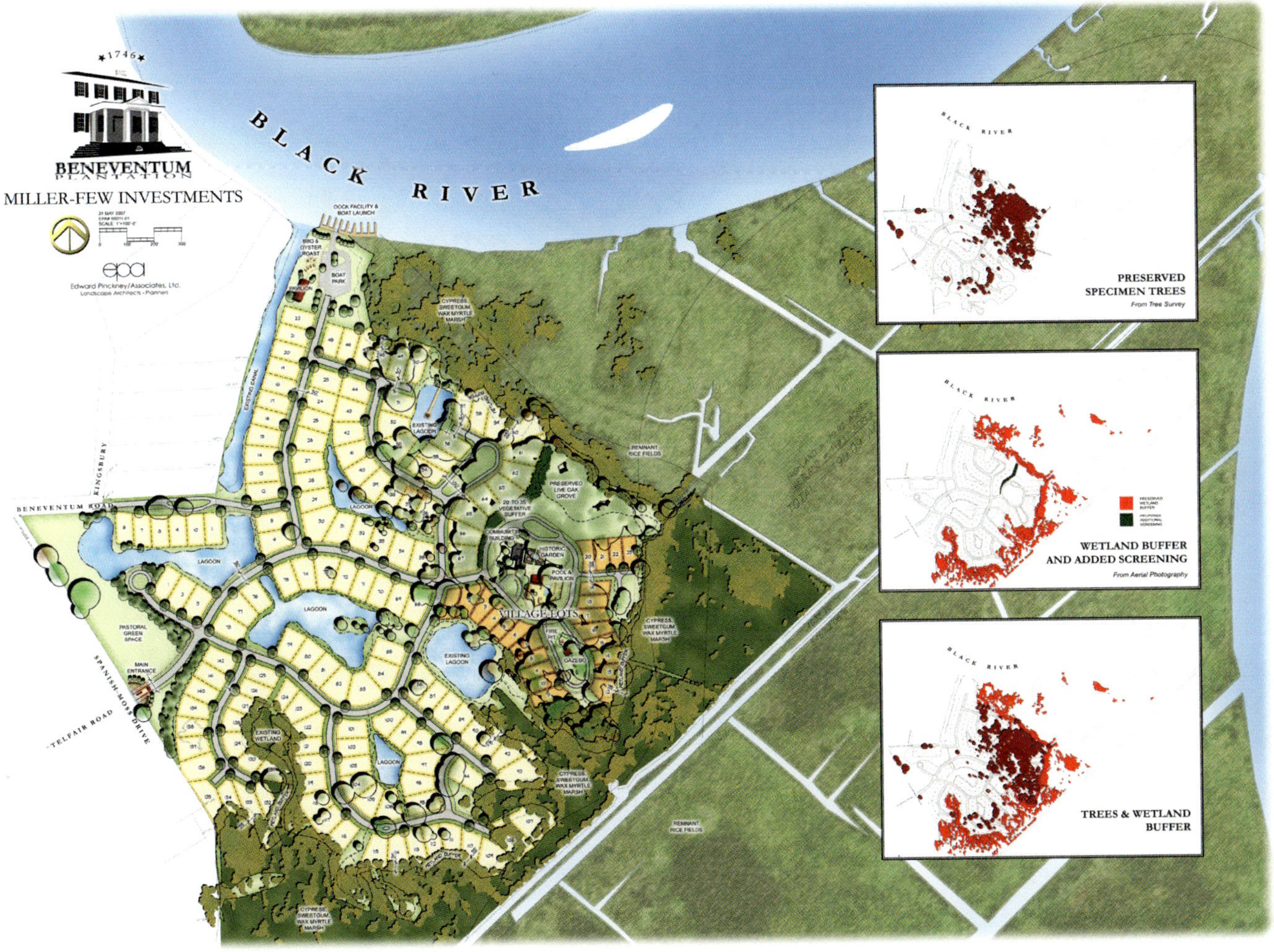

Figure 2-8. Conceptual Master Plan and Tree Survey Exhibits.

Edward Pinckney/Associates Ltd.
Bluffton, South Carolina.

Original
48" x 36"
200 pixels per inch
Scale: 1" = 100'-0"

Tools
Autodesk AutoCAD
Adobe Photoshop

About This Rendering
This rendering builds on the conceptual master plan from Figure 2-7.

The aerial photograph from the previous drawing, however, has been turned off. Nonetheless, the aerial was used to locate and draw existing cypress, sweetgum, and wax myrtles within the remnant rice fields. This was useful because it was important to emphasize the protection of, and buffer provided by, existing trees on the site.

This drawing also includes exhibits showing preserved specimen trees, added screening, and wetland buffers.

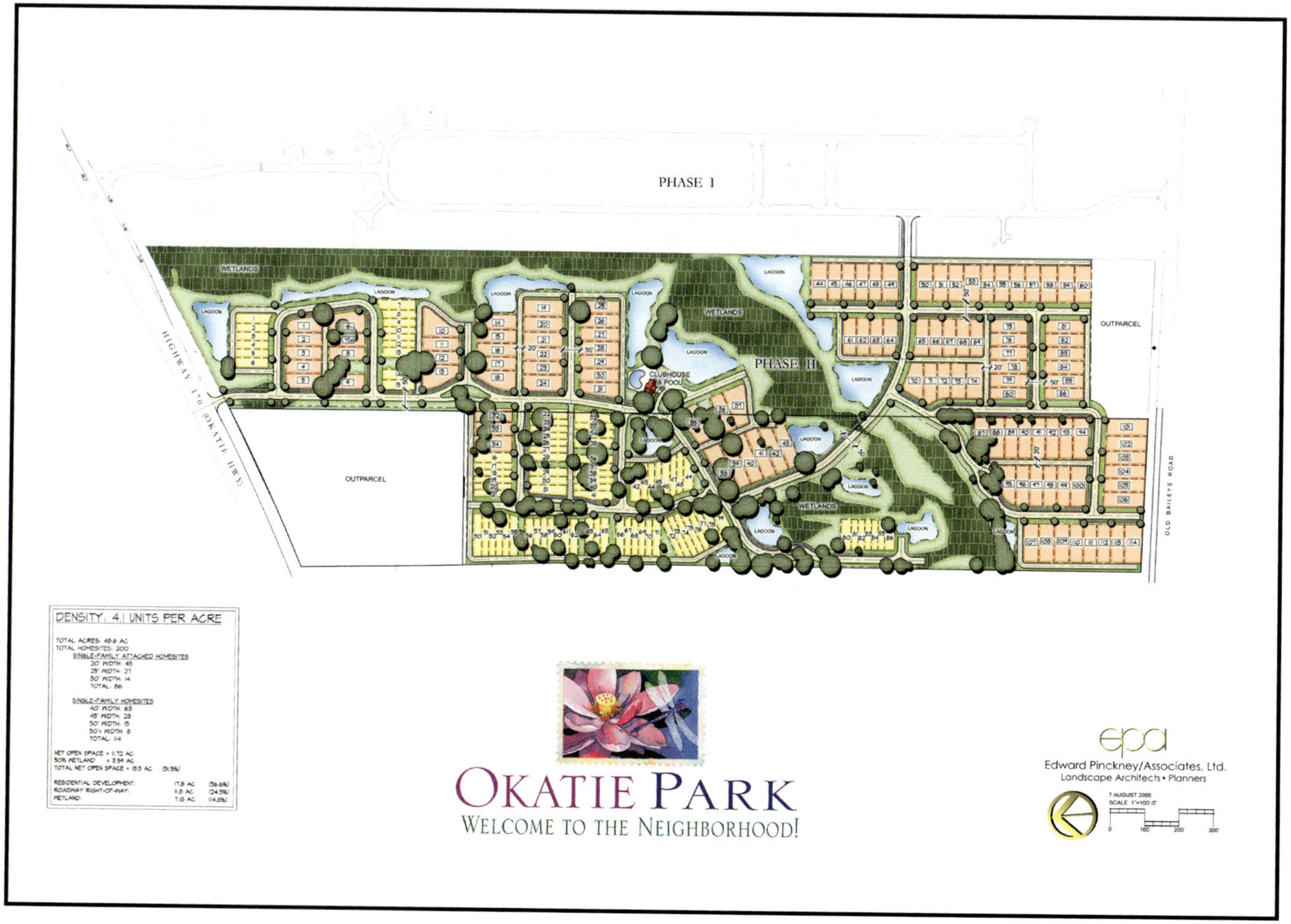

Figure 2-9. Conceptual Master Plan.

Edward Pinckney/Associates Ltd.
Bluffton, South Carolina.

Original
36″ x 24″
200 pixels per inch
Scale: 1″ = 100′-0″

Tools
Autodesk AutoCAD
Adobe Photoshop

About This Rendering
This rendering is a conceptual master plan for a proposed residential community.

In this case, the preponderance of labeling was done within AutoCAD. The logo for the community was provided by the client.

Notice that the trees and wetlands are drawn abstractly rather than realistically.

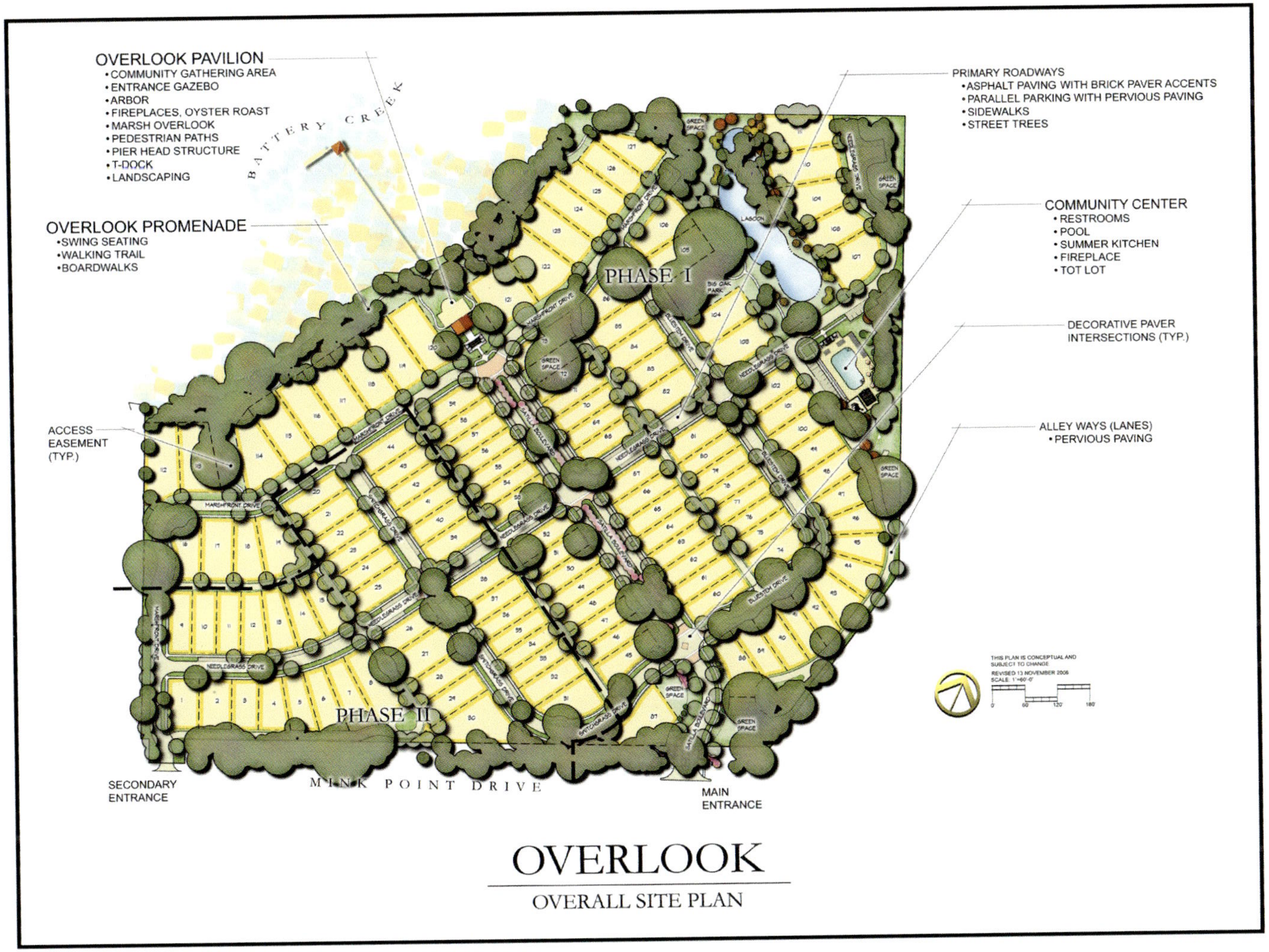

Figure 2-10. Conceptual Master Plan.

Edward Pinckney/Associates Ltd.
Bluffton, South Carolina.

Original
36” x 24”
200 pixels per inch
Scale: 1” = 60’-0”

Tools
Autodesk AutoCAD
Adobe Photoshop
Markers and Pens

About This Rendering
This rendering is a conceptual master plan for a proposed residential community.

Existing trees have been scaled and drawn from a tree survey.

The hand drawn rendering of the marsh adjacent to Battery Creek was recycled from a previous, conceptual plan.

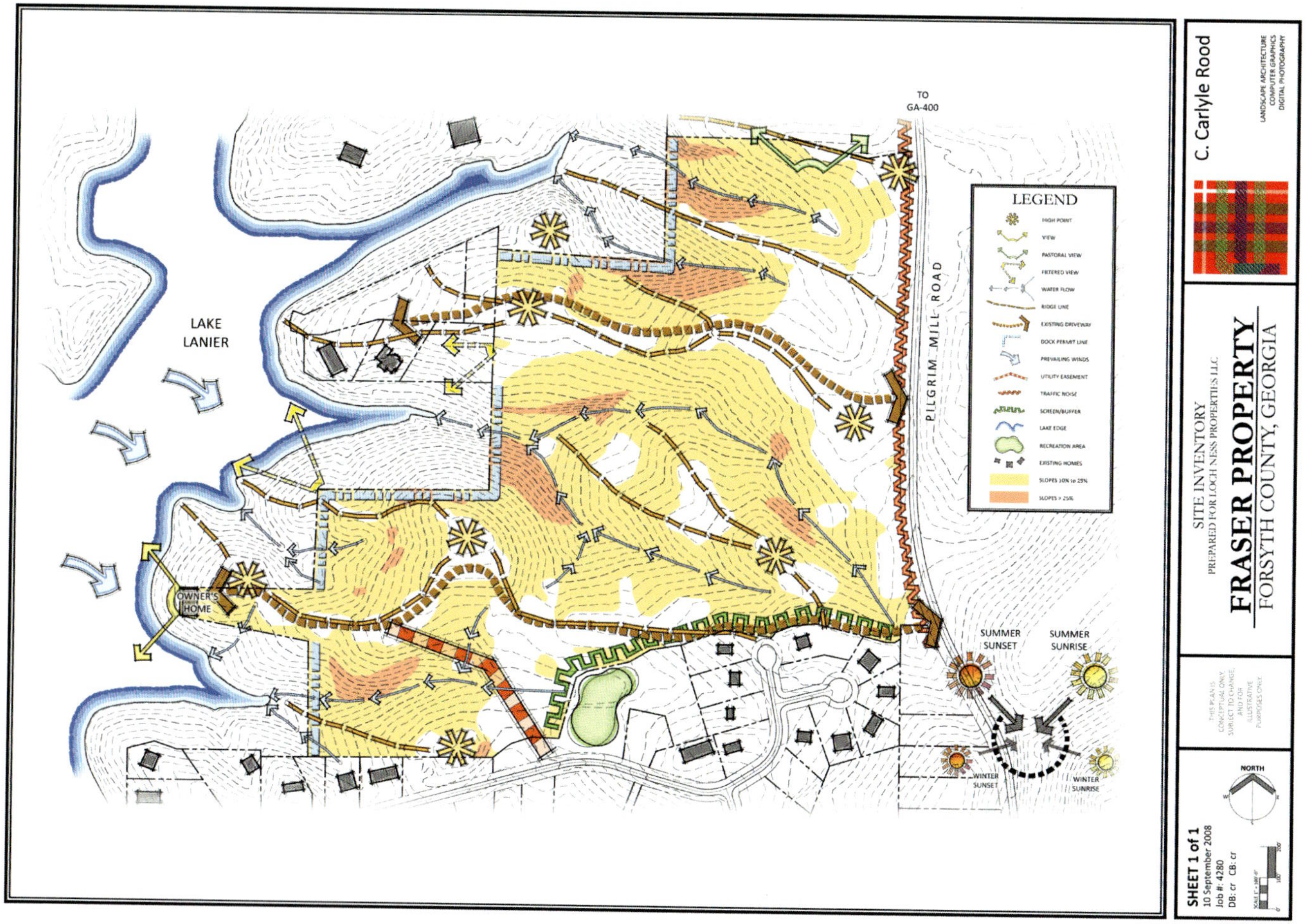

Figure 2-11. Site Inventory.

Original
36″ x 24″
200 pixels per inch
Scale: 1″ = 100′-0″

Tools
Autodesk AutoCAD
Adobe Photoshop

About This Rendering
This rendering is a site inventory for a proposed residential neighborhood.

There are no hand-drawn graphics in this rendering.

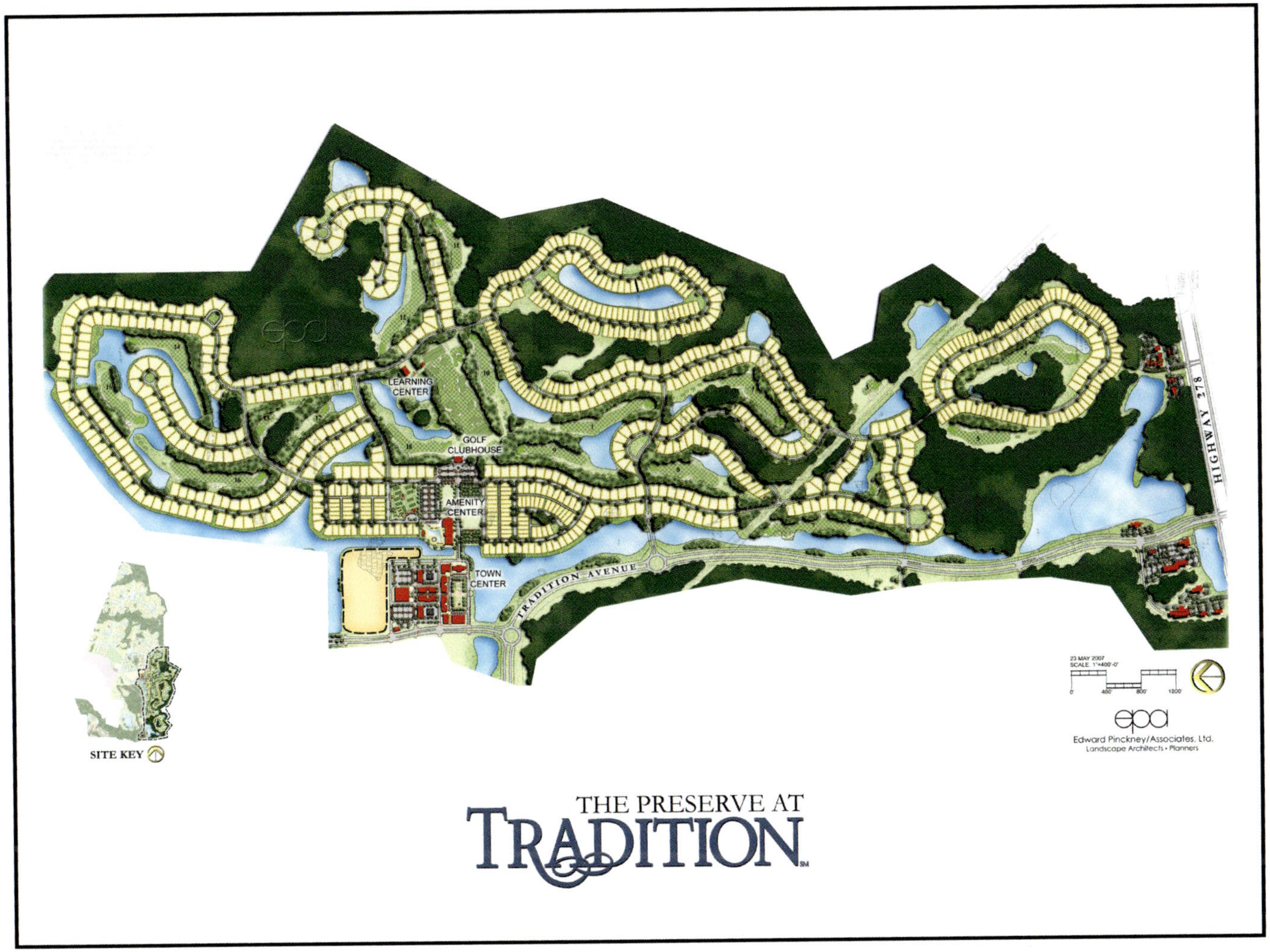

Figure 2-12. Master Plan.

Edward Pinckney/Associates Ltd.
Bluffton, South Carolina

Original
48" x 36"
200 pixels per inch
Scale: 1" = 400'-0"

Tools
Autodesk AutoCAD
Adobc Photoshop

About This Rendering
This rendering is a master plan for a residential golf community.

You may recognize that this drawing was incorporated into the overall plan shown in Figure 2-2. In fact, notice that Figure 2-2 was used in this drawing for the Site Key.

3 LEARNING PRINCIPLES

After browsing the summary of learning principles, below, the temptation will be to jump ahead to the more practical strategies, techniques, and step-by-step examples. That would be a great pity because unless you apply the principles discussed in this chapter, you will simply not be as effective or successful as you are capable of being. You may still have a rewarding career. You may still be able to provide a stable and secure income for your family. You may still get promotions, recognition, and accolades. But, you will not be as good as you are capable of being.

I know this because at one time or another during my career, I have violated every one of these principles and have suffered because of it. And even though I recognize, now, how integral and necessary all of these principles are to my success, I often still struggle to embrace them all completely. That being said, when I am at my best—when I am the most effective—I am always doing these things.

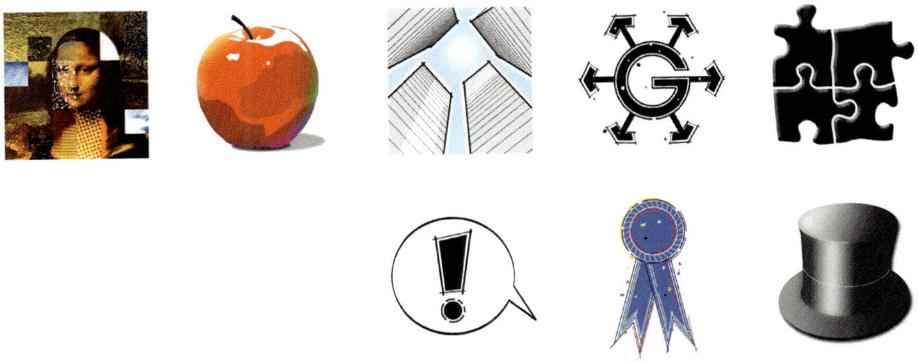

Figure 3-0. Learning Principles: Row 1 (left to right), Emulate Others; Teach Others; Be Confident and Humble; Share Your Goals; Seek Interdependence. Row 2, Accept Criticism, Ignore Critics; Credit Others; Be Honest.

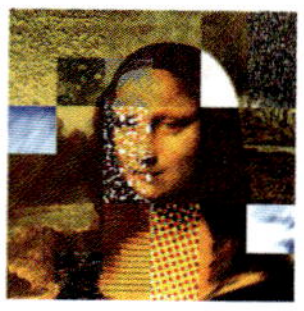

Emulate Others

The fastest way to learn how to do something well is to emulate others that already do that task well. To acquire expertise, you need to seek experts. If you want to draw well, seek others that draw well. If you want to be an excellent architect, seek excellent architects. If you want to be a good spouse or parent, seek good spouses and parents. They are good at what they do for a reason. Rarely is someone successful merely by happenstance and good fortune.

Nor is it an accident that the most successful people are usually willing to share why they are successful. Often, they will go out of their way to share their insight with you. If you admire someone's work, seek them out and let them know. You will accomplish two very important things. First, you will reinforce for that person the motivation to make more things that you may appreciate. Second, you will likely benefit when they reciprocate your positive feedback and share their experience and advice with you.

You will not always be able to meet everyone you want to emulate. Not everyone you admire will be a contemporary of yours. For example, you simply will not be able to sit down with Leonardo da Vinci, Frank Lloyd Wright, or Claude Monet. You may, however, collect a treasury of books, journals, photos, and drawings authored by, or written about, these artists.

Similarly, you should collect examples of work from your peers. Maintain a file of these documents for your reference. Some of these examples you may want to emulate later, and others may be used simply for inspiration.

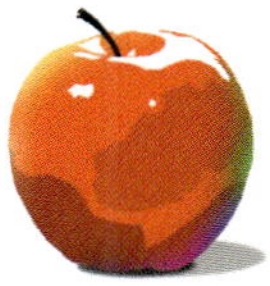

Teach Others

Teaching others has many practical benefits. Teaching helps you learn more. Teaching requires you to review and inventory your own knowledge. That self-assessment will help you identify your strengths and weaknesses. You will recognize where improvement is necessary. You will reinforce positive habits for the long-term. You will get better—and you will be better at it for longer.

Teaching others also allows your good work to be done by others. Regardless of how efficient and resourceful you are, there is a finite amount of work that you can accomplish by yourself. However, by teaching others you can equip them to accomplish the work you value. This certainly expands the scope of your influence.

Lastly, teaching others is rewarding. People are appreciative when you help them. They are enthusiastic about learning. They are encouraged by your interest in them. That sort of enthusiasm and encouragement is contagious. It will infect your work and make you more excited to do it, as well.

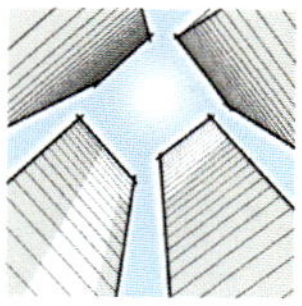

Be Confident & Humble

Confidence should not be confused with arrogance. Confidence is an artifact of being comfortable with, and assured of, your skills. You recognize what you are capable of accomplishing, so you are assured of the outcome. Confident people are humble, though. They are open to criticism and appreciate that others can help them get better.

Arrogance, though, is the result of an unjustified perception of self-worth or a disdain for others. Arrogant people can be useful, talented, and productive; but, there is a ceiling to that utility, talent, and productivity. They are limited because they either will not accept the help of others, or those that can help are repelled by their behavior.

Arrogant people think they are the best at what they do—and they are wrong. Confident people think they can get better at what they do—and they are right.

Share Your Goals

Write down your goals. Read them regularly. Most importantly, though, be sure to share your goals. Others may be interested in helping you achieve those goals. They may even share your goals. You may meet your next employer, client—even partner—this way.

If you already have a job, your employer should be interested in your goals. Your boss should be preparing you professionally to reach those goals and monitoring your progress toward them. If your employer is not interested in your goals, then this is certainly a sign that you should share your goals with someone else—perhaps at a competing firm.

Sharing your goals also adds urgency to completing them. When people are aware of your ambitions, they will encourage you and remind you to stay the course. If people have an expectation for you to fulfill a goal, this can be tremendously motivating. You will want to validate their expectations. Conversely, if someone is especially discouraging, it can be just as rewarding to invalidate his expectations. Not only that, you may awaken a critic to his potential by modeling more positive behavior. You will have realized your goals, while inspiring others to generate their own.

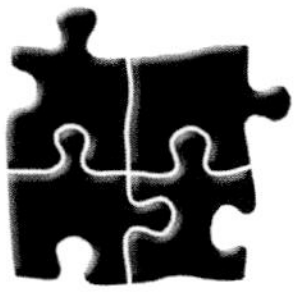

Seek Interdependence

It is not realistic for you to become an expert at everything, nor should you try to do everything yourself. In fact, the more tasks you attempt to do, the more mediocre you will be at each task. Certainly, you should try to do everything to the best of your ability. But to do your best, you must not try to do everything at once.

Instead, learn what you are most effective at doing and seek people that have skills that can complement those strengths. Form teams within your company, and alliances with people outside, that will allow everyone to use their strengths more effectively. This sort of interdependence will allow each of you to be far more effective as a whole than you would have been independently.

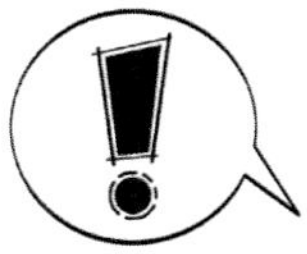

Accept Criticism; Ignore Critics

Actually, almost no one struggles to accept constructive criticism. When advice is offered in a thoughtful, sympathetic, and optimistic tone, criticism can actually be encouraging.

Regrettably, most criticism is not intended to be constructive. Sometimes criticism is offered so that the critic can merely demonstrate how knowledgeable he is. Sometimes criticism is intended to diminish your status, and thereby elevate the critic by comparison. Other times it is just offered as a cheap way for the critic to seem clever or funny. That being said, you can still get good advice from people with the wrong motives. To do so, you need to accept their criticism while ignoring the critics themselves.

Believe it or not, you have an opportunity to improve almost every time someone is critical of your work. Rarely is a criticism entirely without merit. There is always something within it that you can use to improve—even by the smallest measure. So your goal should be to separate the criticism from the critic. Divide the useful advice from the hurtful, and sometimes malicious, person offering it. Learn to accept the criticism gracefully—even gratefully—from the most vicious critics.

Two things usually happen when you accept criticism in this way. First, and more important, you get better. That is always something you can be comfortable accepting. Second, and more curiously, your critics will become more constructive. Why is this? Because you have embraced and valued their criticism, because they will recognize that you have improved because of it, and because they will feel some ownership in your progress, they will suddenly become more interested in developing your talent. They will begin to perceive your success as a reflection of their input, so they will enjoy success for themselves by proxy. They will want you to follow their advice again. As a result, they will begin to share their criticism more diplomatically and constructively.

Additionally, it is just as important that you accept praise correctly. If someone compliments your work, be thankful certainly, but also remember to ask why it was effective. It is important to learn what works from your admirers too.

Catalog your compliments just as you would catalog the work you like by others. Not only will it be a useful resource to reinforce what has worked before, it can also be a source of encouragement and enjoyment when you read through those positive comments again. Besides, you may need that encouragement as you try to accept the less constructive criticism mentioned before.

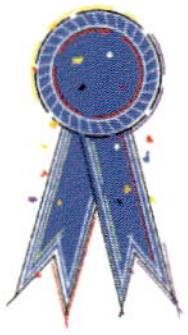

Credit Others

You work very hard to produce your creative designs. You deserve the right to be credited for that work. You have earned this recognition. For the same reasons, you need to credit others.

If you want to use other people's work, then ask for their permission. If they do not give you permission to use it, then do not use it. If they give you permission, then give them credit. This seems obvious, but remarkably this protocol is violated regularly. In all cases, it is unethical to use another's work without his permission. In many cases, it is illegal too.

This is especially a problem in the era of the Internet. So often people presume because work is posted on a web page, then it is permissible to use that work at their discretion. The argument is made that because the work is posted publicly and often it is available to browse for free, it must be assumed to be part of the public domain and, therefore, the public's property and free to use. This is absolutely untrue. Understand that copyrights are often automatic and do not require formal registration. Copyrights grant exclusive rights to the copyright holder. If you do not understand what those exclusive rights are, then you should definitely seek legal guidance before using someone else's work without his permission. Copyright law is beyond the scope of this book; but, common sense and common courtesy suggests that you should get permission to use the work of others.

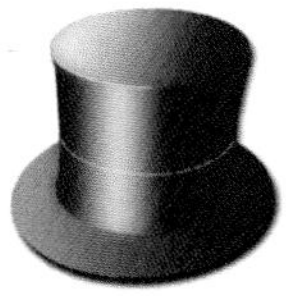

Be Honest

If you did not find the last principle patronizing, then you may find this one to be. Certainly everyone understands that it is important to be honest.

But honesty is a little more complex than merely being factual. Honesty also speaks to your intentions. In fact, you can present something honestly without that presentation being entirely accurate or truthful. For example, if your intent is to demonstrate the elegance of a landscape design, then it is perfectly legitimate to artificially remove parked cars and pedestrians from a photograph of that design. After all, parked cars and pedestrians are not intrinsic to the landscape design. They are included in the photograph only because of unfortunate timing. In this circumstance, the honesty of the presentation is not affected by your editing.

Now imagine you have a photograph of a distressed home. You edit this photograph to remove the graffiti from the garage door, you replace garbage cans with flower pots, and you obscure a hole in the roof with an ornamental specimen tree. If your intent is to sell this home as is, then this is fundamentally dishonest. On the other hand, if your intent is to solicit funds to restore this home, this is perfectly legitimate. Without such an illustration, it may be difficult or impossible to imagine such a distressed home after restoration. Presenting a viable restoration is useful and fair.

Now it is easy to distinguish whether the previous examples are presented honestly or not. In fact, they were deliberately selected to be obvious. The real world of ethics is more ambiguous. Good people can disagree about what is ethical or unethical, and they can make compelling arguments to defend both positions. The point really is that you are going to face more difficult decisions in the future. The software you will use is powerful. It will allow you to manipulate designs and photographs arbitrarily. Whether you decide to use these tools honestly is entirely up to you.

4 GENERAL STRATEGIES

In the previous chapters, we dispelled some common myths about computer graphics and we discussed some fundamental learning principles. So by now you should have a greater understanding about what computer graphics is and is not, and you should be more receptive to learning the strategies and techniques required to succeed.

In this chapter, and the chapters that follow, we will progressively learn more and more specific information. That is, we will introduce the broadest and most generically applicable strategies first, then we will discuss more specific techniques, and then we will apply these strategies and techniques in explicit step-by-step examples.

This chapter will introduce you to the most general strategies that will lead to better computer graphics. These strategies are universal, so they apply to all computer graphics applications. Therefore, if you embrace these strategies, you will be more productive regardless of the tools you use.

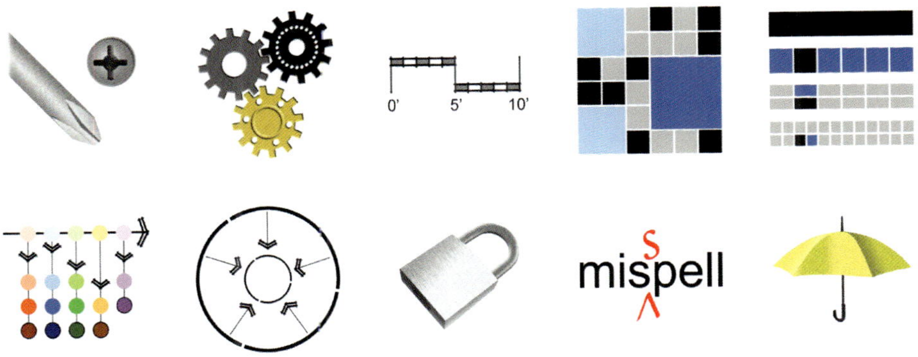

Figure 4-0. General Strategies: Row 1 (left to right), Choose the Appropriate Tool; Standardize; Draw to Scale; Draw Proportionally; Divide and Conquer. Row 2, Draw Sequentially; Begin Big, Then Reduce; Know Where You Are, Limit Where You Can Go; Check Spelling; Back-Up Your Work.

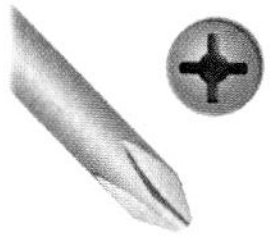

Choose the Appropriate Tool

You should select software that is specifically designed to accomplish your task. This seems like an obvious strategy; but, I see it violated frequently.

One reason we do not always choose the correct tool is because we have a natural inclination to use tools that we are already familiar with. Instead of seeking the most appropriate tool, many of us just begin with the tools we are accustomed to using. One of two things usually happens when we do this. Either we waste time accomplishing our task, or we produce inferior work. Do not fall into this trap. Be open to using new and unfamiliar software. Instead of trying to fit the task to the software you understand, spend your time defining the problem you want to solve and then finding the most suitable software for your solution.

Another reason we do not always choose the correct tool is because we are misled. Be wary of software products that are marketed as all-in-one solutions. Though they may be able to perform all the tasks that they claim, it is unlikely that they do all of these tasks as well as software designed specifically for each task. Instead, seek out software that can work collaboratively with other software. Such software will be able to import files within their framework, or export their work into a format that other products can use. Often collaborative software will be marketed as a suite of products that work together or independently.

The following is a list of software applications that I use regularly. The list is not comprehensive, nor is it intended to be. There are many other applications that are capable of accomplishing the same tasks. These are simply tools that I use frequently, and the tasks that I find them most useful for.

SOFTWARE APPLICATION	MOST USEFUL FOR
AutoCAD	Drafting, Leaders, Labeling, Measuring
Photoshop	Photo Editing, Sketchy Drawing
Illustrator	Precise Drawing
InDesign	Layout, Publishing
SketchUp	Loose 3-Dimensional Modeling
Flash	Animation
Word	Word Processing, Tables
Excel	Spreadsheets, Calculations

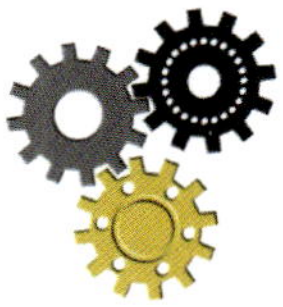

Standardize

In the previous chapter, I discussed some of the motivations to standardize how you draw on the computer. Standardization allows you to edit drawings and refine designs more quickly, efficiently, and collaboratively. Standardization ensures harmony and cohesiveness in your presentations. Standardization encourages sharing, reuse, and refinement. Templating—which is simply standardizing a document's structure—can avoid redundancy and omissions, thereby reducing errors.

So then, what should you standardize? What documents should be templated? The short answer is that you should standardize everything that you do regularly and repetitively. You want to standardize things you do regularly because these are things that you will be required to do frequently. You want to standardize repetitive tasks so that you only have to do the most fundamental things once, and then recycle and refine as required. Conversely, there is no benefit to standardizing a task you rarely will repeat, and there is no way to template any activity that cannot be repeated. The following is list of items—though incomplete—that you should consider standardizing:

- Methods
    - Folder and file locations
    - Folder and file naming conventions
    - Naming conventions for layers, variables, and constants
    - File back-up procedures
- Techniques
    - Color palette
    - Fonts and labeling
    - Line hierarchy, line weights
    - Image dimensions and resolution
    - Shadows
- Document Information within Templates
    - Logo presentation
    - Company contact information such as name, address, phone, and e-mail
    - Scales, north arrow, sheet names and numbers
    - Page titles
    - Common page or sheet dimensions
    - Disclaimers

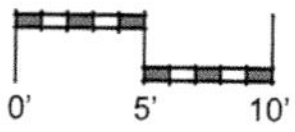

Draw to Scale

When drawing on the computer, you should always be aware of the scale you are using. The scale you use will affect the choices you make regarding line weight, page size, hatching, labeling—you name it. Anything that will be a part of the ultimate presentation will be affected by the scale you choose.

If you are using a computer-aided drafting program (such as AutoCAD), you should always draw at a scale of 1:1. Whether you are drawing in decimal, architectural, or any other units, the scale should never deviate from 1:1. Drawing at any other scale will almost certainly invite errors of proportion. Because lines, shapes, and forms are expressed as mathematical functions rather than bytes of data, the size of your file will not be affected by choosing another scale. So there is not any advantage to using another scale.

If you are using a raster-based graphics program (such as Photoshop), the size of your canvas and its resolution will affect the size of your file. A letter-sized document will have a far smaller file size than a 30" x 42" document. To make larger-dimensioned documents a more comparable file size to smaller-dimensioned documents, you will have to reduce the resolution of the document tremendously. By reducing the document's resolution, you thereby reduce the clarity of the drawing as well. The scale you select, therefore, will directly affect whether your drawing will fit within the dimensions of your canvas and whether your drawing will be clear enough to understand. Consider how the three unique scales in Figure 4-1 affect the size and detail of the building.

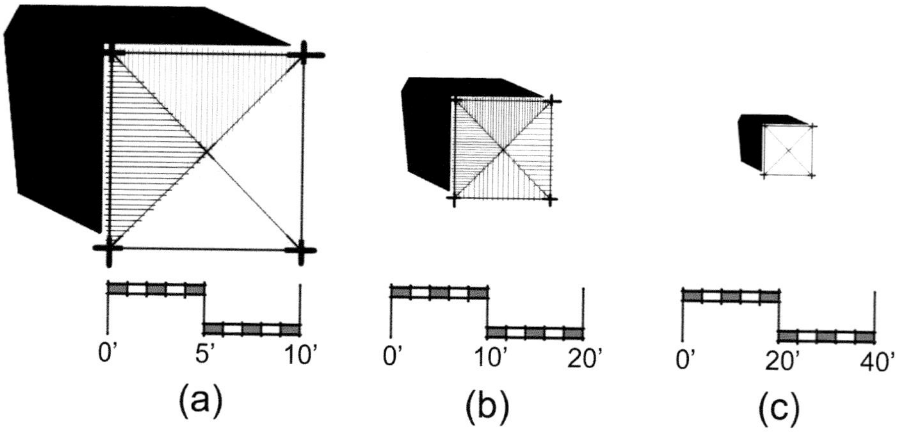

Figure 4-1. All buildings are the same size, 10' x 10'. (a) Scale: 1"=10'-0". (b) Scale: 1"=20'-0". (c) Scale: 1"=40'-0".

When selecting a scale, you should use standard scales appropriate to your profession. Common scales include 1:1, 1:4, 1:8, 1:12, 1:16, 1"=20'-0", 1"=30'-0", 1"=40'-0", 1"=50'-0", 1"=60'-0", 1"=100'-0", and 1"=200'-0".

Draw Proportionally

When speaking of drawing proportionally, we mean that we draw everything in sizes that are relative to each other rather than a specific unit of measure. So instead of considering how large we should draw two trees with regards to a specific measurement, we will draw the first tree in proportion to the second tree—such as twice as big, half as big, the same size, or something to that effect.

When you draw objects proportionally to one another, they will seem harmonious regardless of the scale you select. Consequently, you can reuse proportionally drawn objects in drawings with different scales simply by adjusting their dimensions. This can be very useful when creating a composite drawing from many separate images.

When we define a line hierarchy, we are drawing proportionally. We are communicating the importance of a line by adjusting its line weight relative to other line weights. A bold, thick line is intended to stand out when compared to a lighter, thinner line. Of course, if the distinction between line weights is too subtle, then the hierarchy is lost. While line weights of 1, 2, 3, 4, and 5 are clearly unique from one another, the lines may not be distinct when compared to each other. So the line weights need to be selected relative to one another to ensure that the hierarchy is clear. For example, line weights of 1, 3, 6, 12, and 18 are clearly more distinct relative to each other—despite the fact that we have not even defined the units of measure we are using.

Consider the proportions of the circle diameters and line weights in Figure 4-2. Notice how well the circles correspond in (b) when compared to (a).

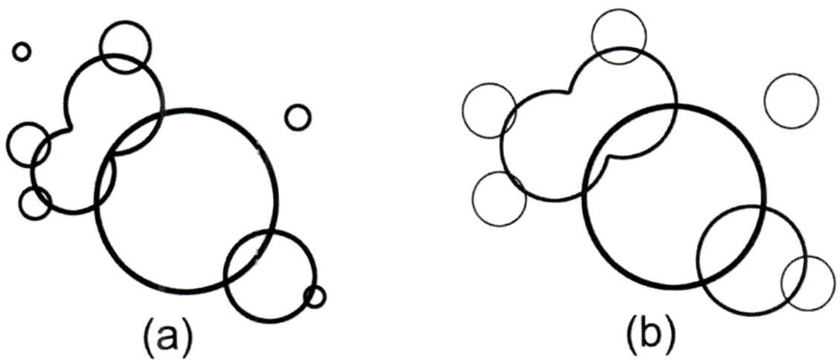

Figure 4-2. (a) The circle diameters are arbitrary and random. The line weights, though different, are too similar to be distinct. (b) The circle diameters and line weights are proportional to one another.

Divide and Conquer

Drawing a comprehensive illustration can be a daunting task. Drawings can take several days to complete. Sometimes you will be required to start before the design is complete. Sometimes you will not be the only person editing the drawing. Whatever the obstacles, it is always best to divide the construction of a drawing into smaller tasks.

Dividing a large drawing into many, smaller tasks simplifies its construction. It allows you to work on separate portions of a drawing independently and congruently. You do not even have to be working within the same file. You can consolidate the multiple files later. This is especially useful as the file size becomes cumbersome. You can work quickly within several smaller files rather than plodding through one enormous file.

Likewise, the independence of tasks allows others to help you construct a drawing. There is no reason why a drawing should require only one author. Instead, divide tasks among multiple people to complete the drawing more quickly.

Lastly, by breaking down a drawing into smaller pieces, you allow modifications to be made more easily. You will be able to edit within a smaller portion of the drawing, and thus affect less of the previously drawn work.

Draw Sequentially

The order you draw in may make a difference. To draw sequentially means that you convey as much information as possible as early as you can. Consider the drawing in Figure 4-3. This site inventory requires 95 steps to draw all of the information we need, excluding the legend, labels, and title block.

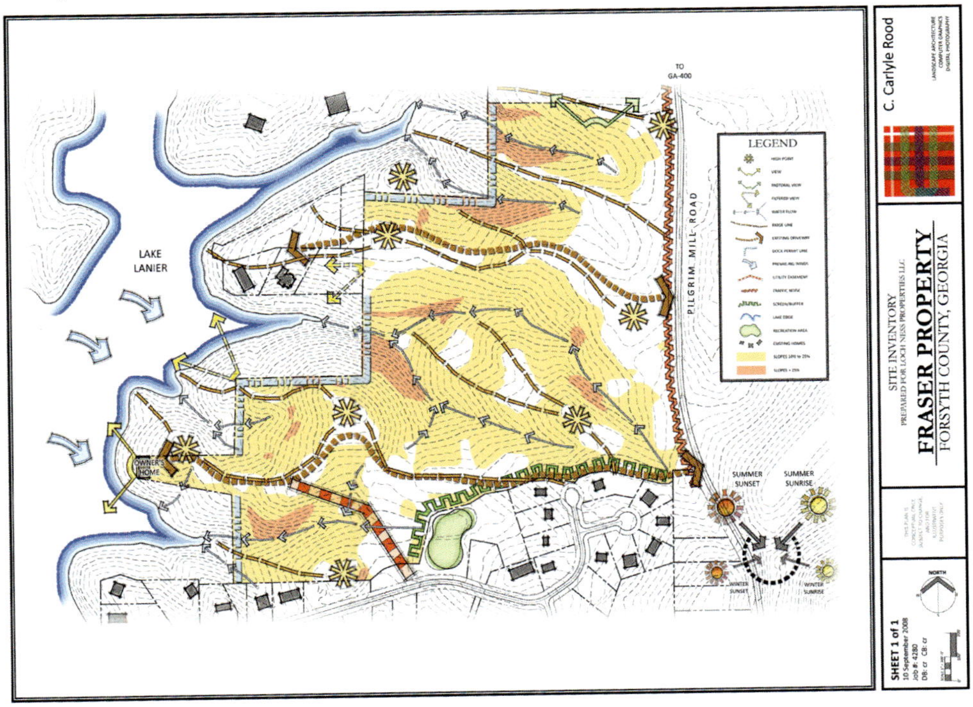

Figure 4-3. This is how the site inventory should look after completing all steps.

Now consider Figures 4-4 and 4-5 on the following page. In both drawings, we have completed about half of the 95 steps; however, the amount of information conveyed is entirely different. The drawing in Figure 4-5 is clearly more informative. Which drawing do you want to be working on when your client shows up unexpectedly?

Figure 4-4. This is how the drawing may look after completing half the steps. Naturally, about half the site inventory is drawn completely.

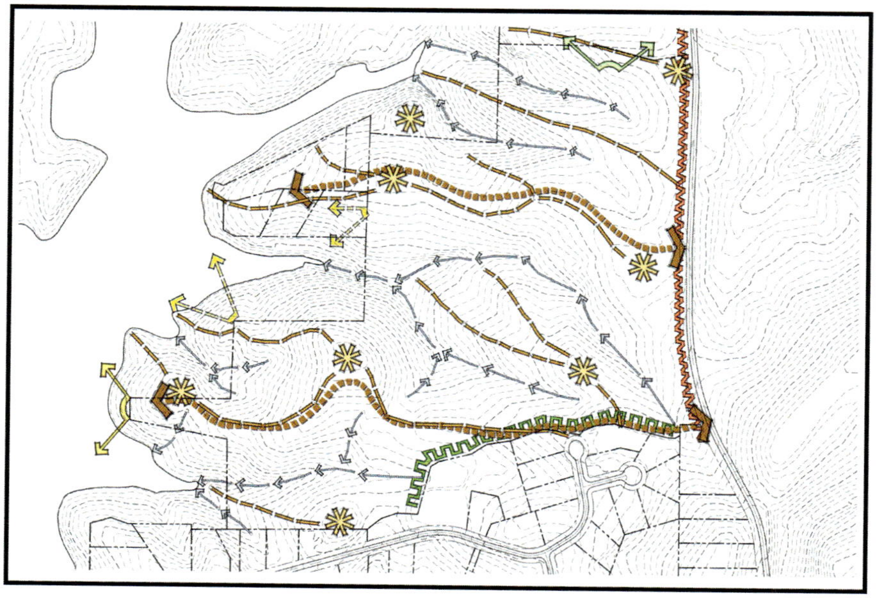

Figure 4-5. This is how the drawing may look after completing half the steps, as well. Notice, however, that the entire site inventory has already been drawn—though not refined yet.

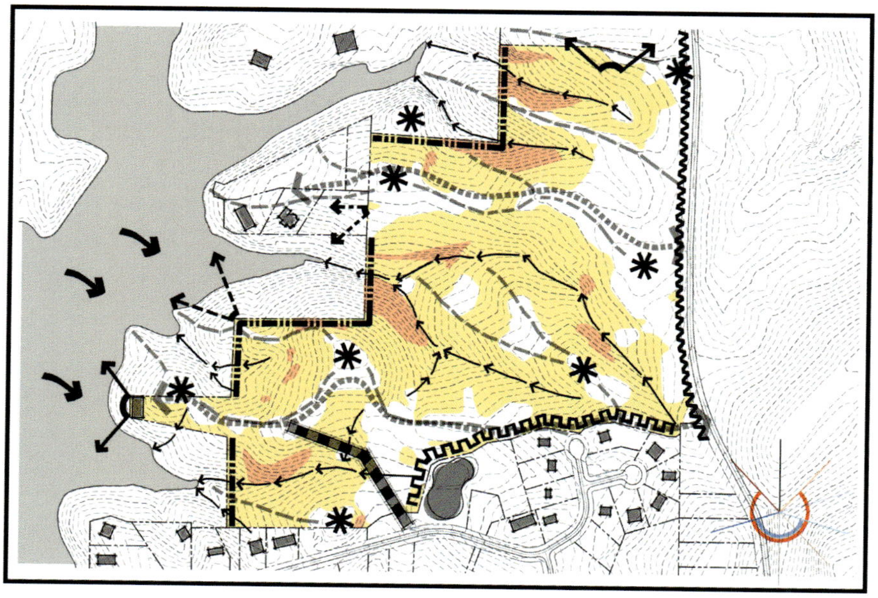

Table 4-6. This table summarizes the information conveyed within each drawing. Though incomplete, the drawing in Figure 4-5 clearly contains far more information.

FIGURE 4-4	FIGURE 4-5
High points	High points
Ridge lines	Ridge lines
Water flow	Water flow
Traffic noise	Traffic noise
Screen/buffer	Screen/buffer
Views	Views
Existing driveways	Existing driveways
	Prevailing winds
	Lake edge
	Utility easements
	Recreation areas
	Existing homes
	Slope inventory
	Dock permit line
	Solar orientation

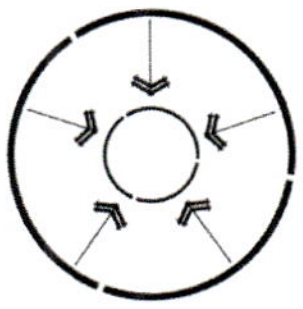

Begin Big, Then Reduce

If you have ever walked into a showroom with a line of new televisions along the wall, you have probably noticed that the smaller televisions seem to have sharper picture. Though all the televisions are fed the same picture, the smaller televisions are shrinking the image to fit within their dimensions while the larger televisions are stretching the image to fit theirs. It is only natural that the smaller televisions will seem sharper than the larger ones.

Drawings done on the computer work the same way. When you begin by drawing on a large canvas, then reduce its scale to fit a smaller document, your work should remain clear and vivid. In fact, a reduced drawing often seems sharper than the original. Conversely, when you begin working on a small canvas, then expand its scale to conform to a larger document, clarity and vividness are lost. This is true regardless of the resolution you use (though less dramatic the greater the resolution).

Consider how scaling up and down affects the trees drawn in Figure 4-6. The original drawing of the tree is on the far left. In the center is the tree after being reduced in width and height by 50 percent. Though smaller, the tree remains sharp. On the right is the tree after being enlarged 200 percent from the center image. Now compare the trees on the far left and far right. Though both images are the same size, the original drawing is clearly sharper.

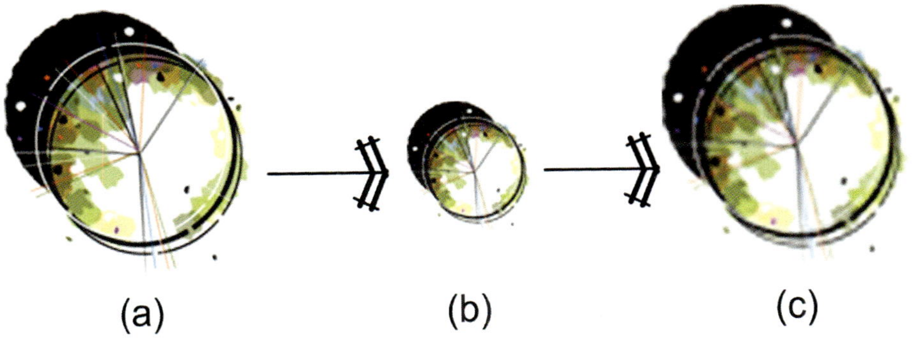

Figure 4-6. (a) This tree was originally drawn at 200 ppi. (b) Reduced by 50%. (c) Enlarged by 200%.

Regardless of how well your drawing looks when reduced, you must pay special attention to the size of the lettering you use, too. Often your labeling can become unreadable when reduced—especially if it has been scaled down for display on the computer only. You will either need to choose a larger font in your original drawing, or you will need to re-label your drawing after it is reduced.

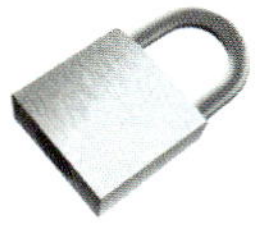

Know Where You Are; Limit Where You Can Go

Computer graphics and other documents are often organized and constructed from smaller parts. For example, a drawing in Photoshop is a composite of different layers of drawings, as illustrated in Figure 4-7. A document in Word is made up of styles, paragraphs, bullet lists, headings, etc. If you learn what parts are available, you can assemble more dynamic graphics and documents. That makes sense because the more parts you have to build with, the more things you can build from them.

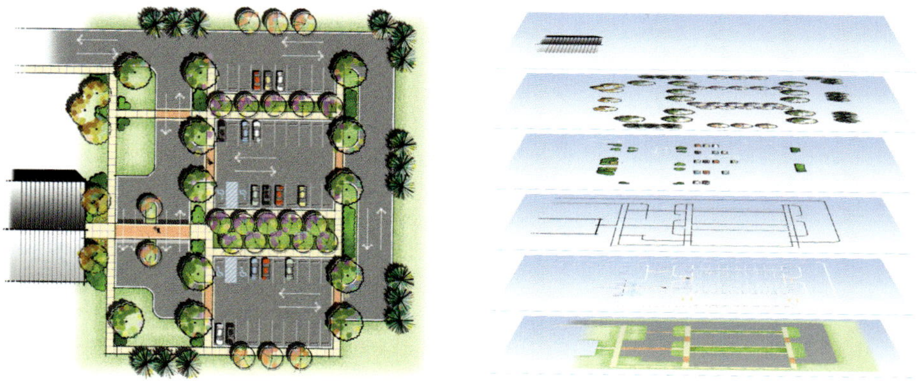

(a) (b)

Figure 4-7. (a) This rendering of a parking lot is actually a composite of many layers of drawings. (b) This is a conceptual representation of how the drawing on the left can be created by stacking layers of drawings.

On the other hand, you are not required to break down your work into these composite parts. You can create a Photoshop drawing with only one layer. You can create a Word document simply with the default text—manually changing the fonts, emphasis, and other attributes as required. By doing so, however, you end up doing more work to accomplish less, you limit what you can create, and you diminish your ability to modify it later. When everything is assembled in one piece, it becomes more and more difficult to manage. It is a lot like making spaghetti sauce and then trying to remove the tomatoes afterwards.

Of course, you are not limited to the number of parts you use either. Conceptually, you could create a Photoshop drawing composed of thousands of brush strokes—each on a unique layer. While that is a simplistic exaggeration, it is not uncommon to find that your drawings become very complex and unwieldy. It is easy to lose track of what you have done. It becomes more important than ever to "Know where you are (and limit where you can go)."

For the moment, let us discuss how to use this technique within Photoshop's context of layers. Photoshop is not the only application that uses layers.

Conceptually, if not by the same name, other applications use the same idea. It will be simpler, however, to discuss this technique by using a specific example, though the techniques can be applied elsewhere.

One of the easiest ways to know where you are is to name the layer you are in. It is not important what you name a layer; but, the name should mean something to you. For example, instead of naming successive layers {A, B, C, D, E}, it would be more helpful to name those layers {trees, shrubs, groundcovers, buildings, roads}.

Of course, even if you give every layer an appropriate name, your drawing could still become unwieldy as you draw more and more layers. When this happens, it is useful to group layers together. In the previous example, it might make sense to group the layers {trees, shrubs, groundcovers} into a folder called Landscape.

Lastly, once you are satisfied that you know where you are (from naming and grouping layers appropriately), you still need to limit where you can go. Organizing your layers will not mean anything if you begin to draw trees on a layer for buildings or you draw roads on a layer for shrubs. To limit where you can draw, lock the layers that you are not using. This will ensure that you draw only where you intend to. When you are done, lock the layer you just worked in, select another layer, unlock it, and then work as before.

By naming and grouping layers, you will always know where you are. By locking and unlocking layers, you will always work where you intend to. As a consequence, your drawings will be more dynamic, easier to modify, and less error-prone.

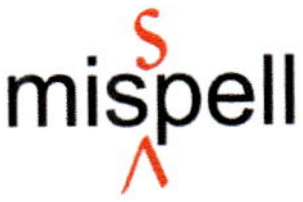

Check Spelling

Nothing will diminish your credibility more quickly than misspelled words. Nearly every software application that allows you to add text will also allow you to check your spelling. Take advantage of this utility. It only takes a few moments; but, it can save you an eternity of embarrassment.

Back Up Your Work

Almost everyone seems to learn this rule the hard way. It hardly matters how it happens. Whether your hard drive crashes, a virus infects your computer, your network goes down temporarily, a disgruntled employee erases files, or some other calamity, it will eventually be necessary to restore your work from a backup. It is simply unrealistic to think you can prevent every potential catastrophe. You do not have to, either; but, you should take the steps to mitigate such damage when necessary. The easiest and most effective way to accomplish this is to back up your work regularly.

At a minimum, all files that have been created or edited during the week should be backed up. I usually choose to back up my files every Saturday. At the end of every month, you should back up all files—whether edited or not.

You should copy files just as they appear on your computer. That is, if a file is stored in a specific folder, then that file should appear on your storage media within a folder of the same name. This will make it easier to find your files, later. After all, there really is no benefit to backing up a file if you cannot find it later.

Store your backup files somewhere else. There is no point to archiving files on the same computer as the original files. If your computer fails, then you will lose both your originals and your backups. Your monthly (full) backups should not even be on the same premises as your originals. Instead, select another place to store your files. You could copy your files to a DVD. You can save them to another computer. You can store them remotely by copying them over the Internet. There are many alternatives. The point is to move your backups somewhere distinct, but where they are still accessible.

How often do I back up files? Aside from regular weekly and monthly back-ups, I copy my work every time I make material changes to a document; that is, whenever I make changes that I do not want to be required to make again. And if I am going to make changes that are difficult or impossible to change back, then I will archive a version of my work before making the changes. Sometimes you will simply wish you had never made a change to begin with. In these circumstances, it is nice to be able to return to the status quo by stepping back to a previous version.

5 LINES & LINE WEIGHTS

This chapter provides techniques for the foundation of all your drawings—lines. While labels, color, shadows, and shading are all very important, all of their techniques are intended to amplify and complement your line work. You can still communicate a design effectively without using labels, color, shadows, or shading. It is nearly impossible, however, to draw effectively without using lines properly. The techniques discussed in this chapter are listed in the table, below.

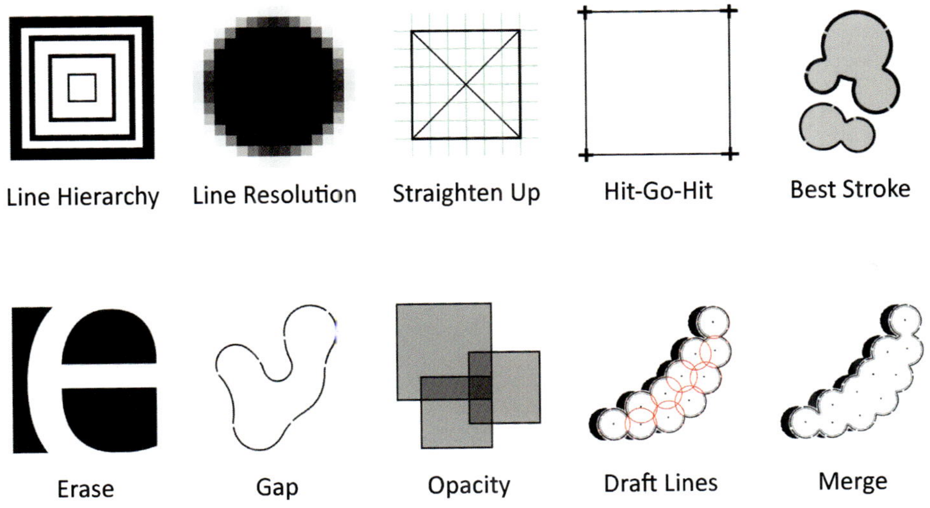

Figure 5-0. Techniques for lines and line weights.

The most important techniques you will learn relate to line weights: Line Hierarchy and Line Resolution. If you take the time to understand and use a line hierarchy, you will be able to create striking, elegant, orderly drawings. Understanding how the resolutions of your monitor and printer affect your line work will ensure that your message reaches your audience.

The remaining techniques will help you draw more accurately (Straighten Up), quickly (Best Stroke, Erase), and artfully (Hit-Go-Hit, Gap, Opacity, Draft Lines, Merge).

Line Hierarchy

The first thing you should establish before you begin drawing is a line hierarchy. By defining a line hierarchy, I mean that you define the line weights (line thickness) you intend to draw with. You should be using the same line weights for items of similar importance in your drawing. Generally, thicker lines should be used for the most important parts of your drawing—the parts you most want to stand out. Conversely, thinner lines should be used for supporting line work such as hatching, leaders, and accents.

Below, in Figure 5-1, is an example of a commonly used line hierarchy. In fact, if you are accustomed to using computer-aided design (CAD) applications, you may recognize this hierarchy. It has been standardized collaboratively by the ISO (International Organization for Standardization) and the DIN (German Institute for Standardization).

Figure 5-1. (a, b) The ISO/DIN line weight color coding system for computer-aided design. (c) Approximate pixel width at 200 pixels per inch for the line widths expressed in column b. (d) Line width expressed in a unit of measurement called points. This is also roughly equivalent to pixel widths at 72 pixels per inch.

It is not necessary to adapt a previously defined standard; but, you should make an attempt to define some sort of hierarchy for the sake of clarity and consistency. My own preference is to draw at 200 pixels per inch using the following brush widths in Figure 5-2.

Figure 5-2. Example of a line hierarchy when drawing at 200 pixels per inch.

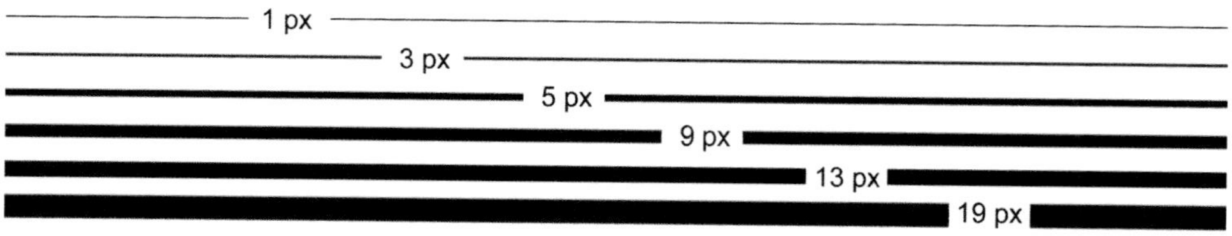

Line Resolution

A computer screen is composed of tiny dots of light called pixels. Depending on the dimensions of your computer screen, your computer is able to display a certain number of pixels per inch (along the width and height, respectively). Though computers screens vary, you may presume most monitors are capable of displaying at least 72 pixels per inch (ppi). These hundreds of thousands of pixels of light are arranged to present an image on your computer screen.

Your printer, however, can print far more pixels (or dots of ink) per inch. Consequently, you can print an image far more accurately to paper than you can if you merely displayed it on your monitor. This is because the resolution of the printer is much greater than the resolution of the monitor. In other words, the denser the pixels are packed together, the greater the resolution. And the greater the resolution, the sharper it will appear when printed.

A problem arises because we draw while looking at a computer screen—a screen that is not necessarily capable of displaying what we intend to print, later. As a result, you need to be keenly aware of the resolution you are drawing with. If your resolution is not great enough, then you may be disappointed when you print your drawing. Consider the three sets of lines in Figure 5-3. Each set was drawn using the same width brushes; however, the results when printed are strikingly different.

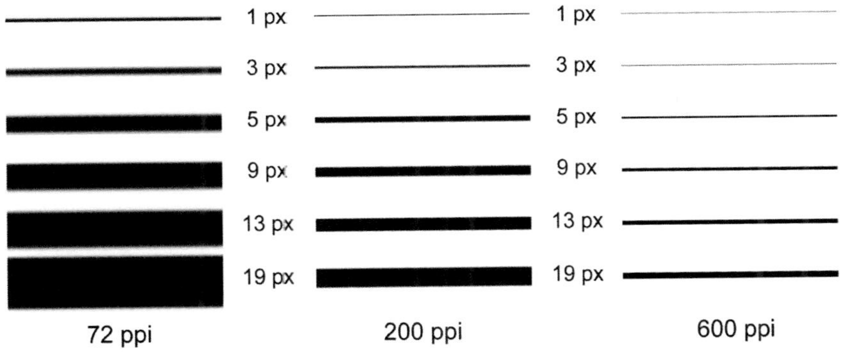

Figure 5-3. As the resolution increases, the lines become thinner and sharper.

Therefore, you need to select a resolution that is great enough to display what you want, and then you need to choose brush sizes that are appropriate to that resolution. (Sometimes you will be able to select sizes using measures that are independent of resolutions; e.g., points and picas. For many of the most useful graphic tools, however, the unit of measurement required is pixels.) Generally, I prefer to draw with a resolution of 200 ppi. I prefer to edit photos with a resolution of at least 300 ppi. You may choose to use these resolutions, or you may prefer others depending on your task.

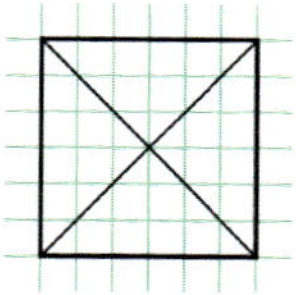

Straighten Up

When drawing by hand, if you are left to your own devices, you simply will not be able to draw a straight line. With practice, you may be able to approximate a straight line. But you will never draw a perfectly straight line without the benefit of a straight edge, such as a ruler or parallel glider.

Regrettably, the same is true when drawing on the computer. Left to your own devices, you simply will not be able to draw a straight line without help. Fortunately, computers have straight edges too. Both the drawings in Figure 5-4 use these faux straight edges. Whether using predefined grid systems or defining your own guidelines, you will be able to draw straight lines consistently and accurately.

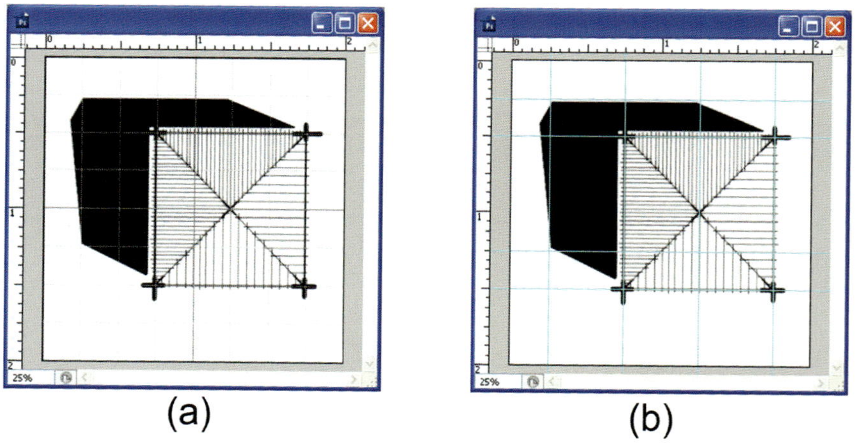

Figure 5-4. (a) Predefined grid systems permit you to begin and end your strokes on fixed points, thereby allowing you to create straight lines. (b) Many applications let you define your own guidelines, as this drawing illustrates.

In addition to grids and guides, many applications also allow you to draw straight lines using keystrokes. In Photoshop, for example, you can hold down the [Shift] key to draw straight lines on either the x- or y-axis. Whatever the application, there is almost certainly a way to draw straight lines. Learn how to use these aids. You would not hesitate to use a straight edge when drawing by hand. Neither should you hesitate to use a straight edge on your computer.

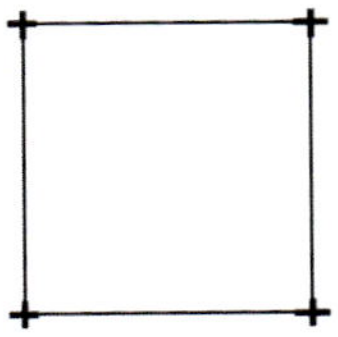

Hit-Go-Hit

If you are accustomed to drafting by hand, then you know all about the hit-go-hit technique. It is a very simple and effective way to draw. It creates a straight line while also emphasizing the ends of that line. Consider the strokes (in red) as illustrated in Figure 5-5. You draw to an endpoint (hit), then reverse back to another point (go), and then reverse back and stop abruptly (hit).

Figure 5-5. Rather than just drawing from one point to another, the hit-go-hit technique reinforces the end points by reversing the strokes back over the ends of the line.

The strokes are simple, yet they create a very elegant line with obvious end points. This effect is even sharper when similar lines intersect. Regrettably, this is a very difficult stroke to emulate on the computer. The precision available on the computer actually works against you. Computers prefer to draw things accurately. You ask a computer to draw a line from point A to point B. It does. Now it is ready for another task.

Computers do not appreciate the term approximate. Of course, design is inherently approximate. Often when we draw on the computer, we are trying to articulate an abstract idea rather than a specific methodology. Hence, a hit-go-hit line implies a certain flexibility that a precise line simply cannot.

Therefore, to convince a computer to draw just as arbitrarily, we have to manipulate its drawing variables just as arbitrarily to mimic the same things. Unfortunately, the manipulation of these variables must be somewhat extreme, as illustrated by Figure 5-6. Notice how, even though the flow of ink from the brush is diminished by half, the end points are still difficult to distinguish in the line work at the top. It is not until we reduce the flow by seventy-five percent that we recognize the end points distinctly.

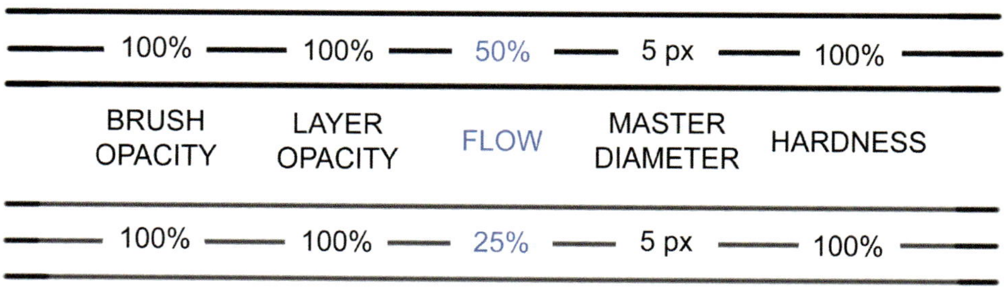

Figure 5-6. All lines are drawn at a resolution of 200 pixels per inch. Until the brush flow (rate of ink dispersal) is reduced to 25%, the endpoints of the line are nearly indistinguishable.

Diminishing the flow rate this much is somewhat drastic. Consider how this flow rate affects line weights, as illustrated in Figure 5-7. Though the end points are emphasized, the lines themselves seem understated because of the exaggeration of the flow rate.

Figure 5-7. All lines are drawn at a resolution of 200 pixels per inch. Notice how the reduced brush flow rate of 25% diminishes the sharpness of the line work.

I have found that the benefits of emphasizing a line's end points do not justify the sacrifices that must be made to the line itself—at least not with the radical adjustments required and illustrated, in Figure 5-7. Instead, I try to recreate the same effect by drawing two lines and erasing the center of the thicker line. Some examples of this method are illustrated in Figure 5-8.

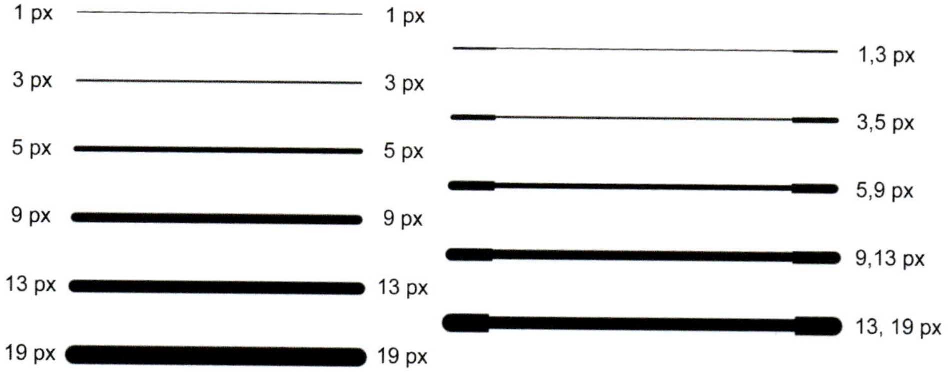

Figure 5-8. You can mimic a hit-go-hit line by drawing two lines and erasing the center of one of them.

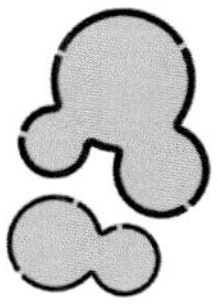

Best Stroke

Most graphics applications have tools that allow you to construct complex lines and shapes. They may have you select points to draw to and from. They may let you construct a path that you want a line to follow along. They may allow you to explicitly specify a width, length, radius, or the like. The precision permitted by these tools is remarkable.

But often you will not require this sort of precision in your drawings. You may just want to get a quick, loose drawing down. In these circumstances, it is often faster and easier to simply draw a solid form and then have your software draw an outline along its edges. Figure 5-9 illustrates this technique.

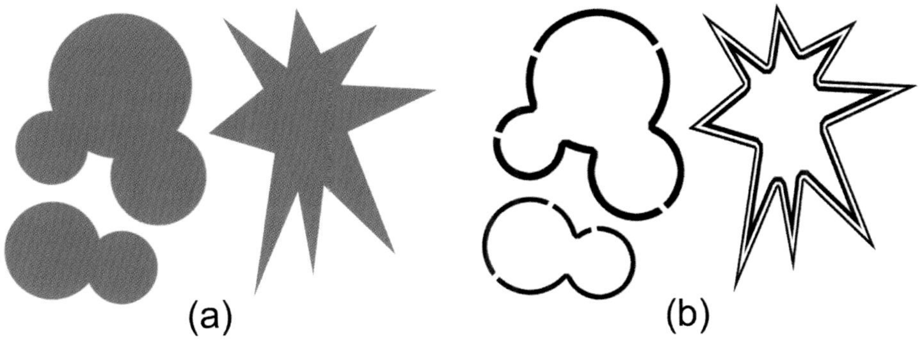

Figure 5-9. The lines illustrated in (b) were constructed by drawing an outline around the simple, solid forms shown in drawing (a).

When you decide to make your stroke does matter. Consider how different the outlines of the trees seem in the two drawings in Figure 5-10. In the left drawing, the stroke was performed after the tree masses were distorted by a filter. Consequently, the stroke is uniform around the outline. In the right drawing, the stroke was performed prior to the distortion. This gives the outline a distorted and irregular form, as well.

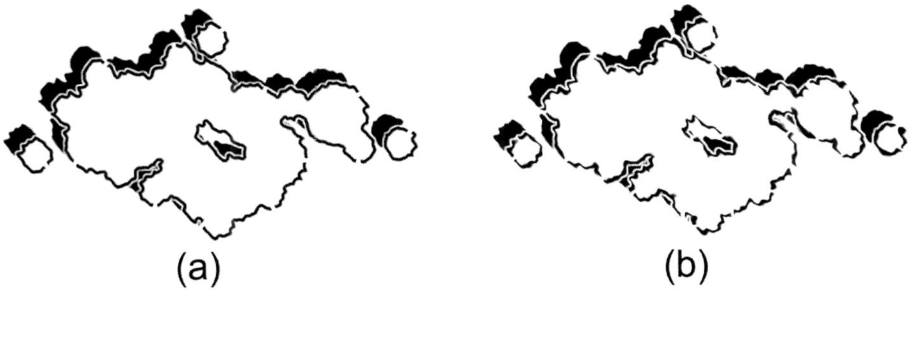

Figure 5-10. (a) The outline of the trees was added after distorting the tree mass. (b) The outline of the trees has been distorted with the same filter used to manipulate the tree mass.

Erase

This technique complements the Best Stroke technique. Like before, you can construct lines quickly by simply drawing an outline along the edges of a simple, solid form. But instead of creating your simple forms from only brush strokes, you also use an eraser to add negative space. Figure 5-11 illustrates how a tree symbol is constructed by merely erasing from a simple circle.

Figure 5-11. To create the elegant tree symbol in (c), you merely have to erase from the edges of a simple circle (a) and then draw along its outline (b,c).

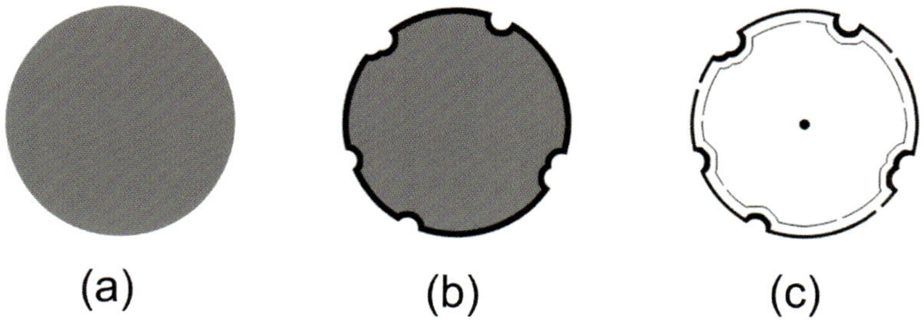

A corollary to this technique is to use one simple form as a mask for another simple form. This will allow you to create more complex drawings quickly, as illustrated in Figure 5-12.

Figure 5-12. The drawing in (c) was created by erasing the form in (b) from the original square.

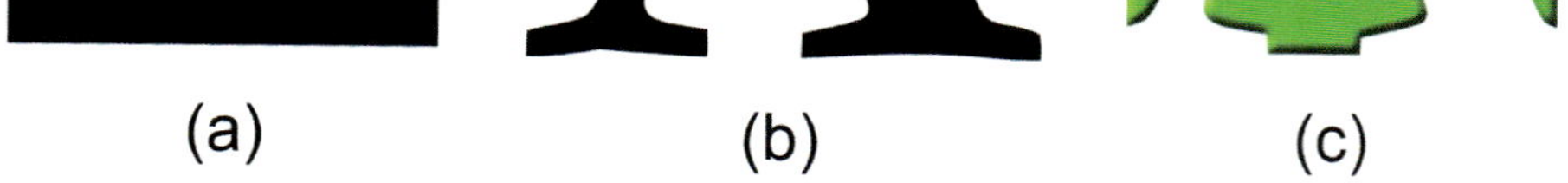

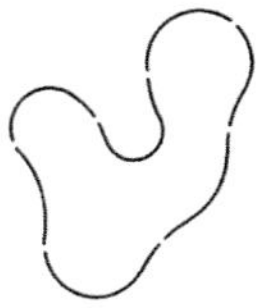

Gap

In this technique you break up curvilinear lines with small gaps. This gives your line work a looser impression. Your gap should be at least as wide as your line weight. In Figure 5-13, for example, the gaps were made with an eraser width of 7 pixels, while the lines were made with a brush width of 5 pixels.

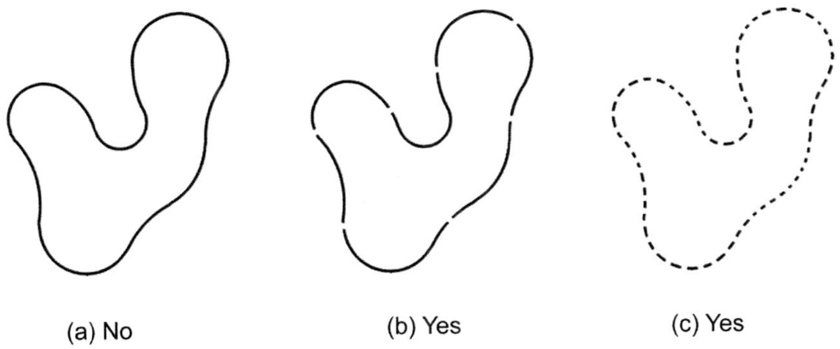

Figure 5-13. (a) An uninterrupted line around an organic form is static and stale. (b) By breaking up curvilinear lines, the form seems more loose and flowing. (c) Because this line is interrupted by so many gaps, it may be inferred that this form is either proposed or to be removed.

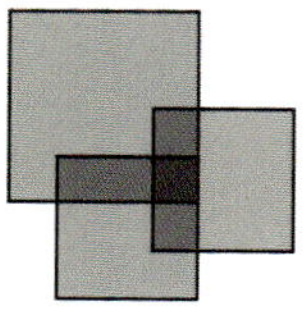

Opacity

If a line is fainter, then perceptually it may seem thinner or less important. If you have already used the minimum line width permitted by your software, or if you want to de-emphasize a line without drawing it again, a useful technique is to simply reduce the opacity.

If you have already drawn the line, then you will have to reduce the opacity of the layer that the lines appear on. If you have not drawn your line, then you can either reduce the opacity of your brush, or you can reduce the opacity of the layer after drawing your line. As Figure 5-14 illustrates, adjusting either of these properties will produce the same result.

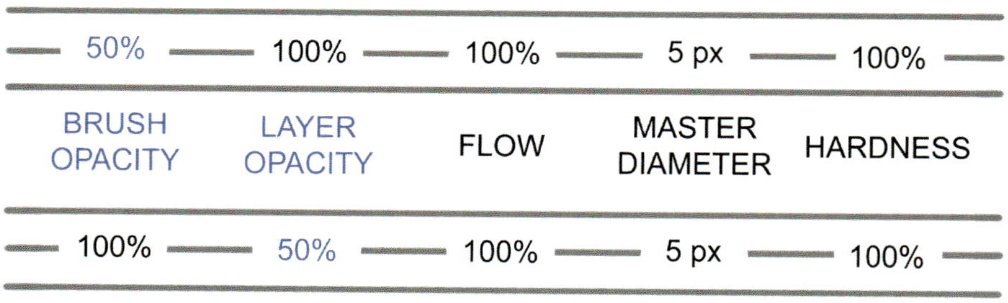

Figure 5-14. Though different properties have been adjusted, the result is identical.

I always prefer to reduce the layer opacity. This is because I like the flexibility of being able to adjust the layer opacity later if I change my mind. Once I have drawn a line with an opacity less than 100%, I am stuck with the result.

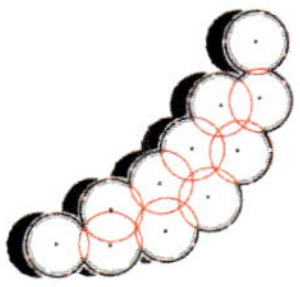

Draft Lines

When drawing by hand, it is sometimes helpful to lightly draw lines to help guide your work. Often you will either erase these lines later or simply draw over them. Of course, when using a computer this is unnecessary. The software already allows you to use grids and guidelines. Nonetheless, you may want to consider adding these lines to give your drawing that folksy, hand-drawn appearance as illustrated in Figure 5-15.

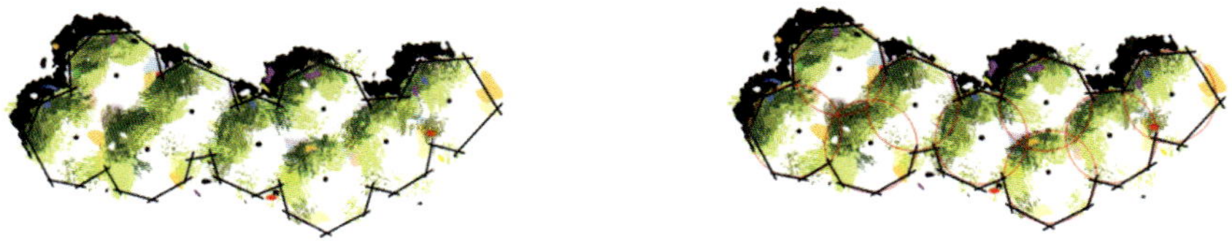

(a) (b)

Figure 5-15. The red circles in drawing (b) are reminiscent of the drafting guidelines that frequently appear in hand-drawn renderings.

When drawing landscape plans, I often include these draft lines because it helps me count the number of units within a grouping of plants and it reinforces the spacing of the plant layout.

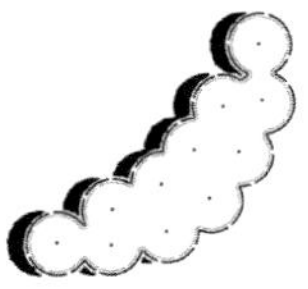

Merge

If items are grouped together and overlap, then you should consolidate them into one cohesive unit. In the era of computer-aided design (CAD), this technique is violated frequently. It has become acceptable to merely clone a symbol and place copies on top of one another. This is a shame because clarity is lost in the jumble of symbols. Consider how much clearer the symbols on the right are than the symbol on the left, in Figure 5-16.

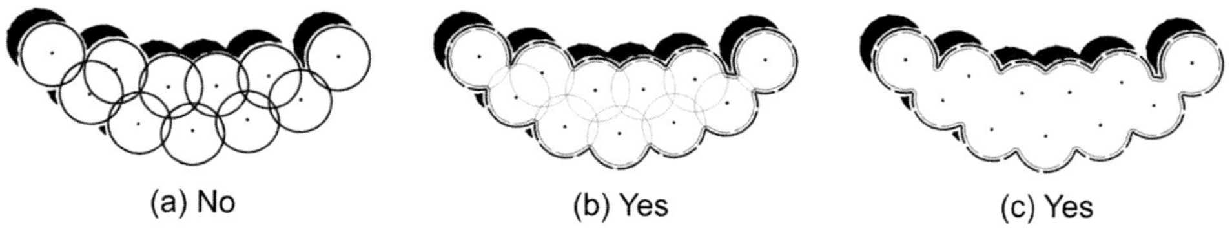

Figure 5-16. (a) Overlapping symbols create a jumbled mess. (b) If you want the symbols to maintain their distinction, then consider de-emphasizing the overlapping lines. (c) This drawing emphasizes the whole rather than the parts.

Additionally, if you clone symbols to reuse throughout the drawing, then some effort should be made to make them seem unique. Consider how, in Figure 5-17, the tree symbols were altered so that they still seem similar, but are no longer identical.

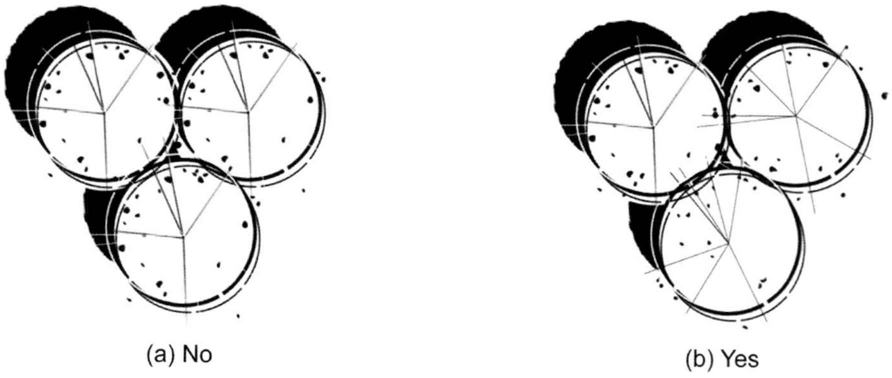

Figure 5-17. (a) These symbols are identical. (b) These symbols obviously represent the same kind of tree; but, they are not identical.

6 LABELS

Labeling your drawing is often the most effective way to communicate your design. Sometimes your audience may not be able to comprehend a design without a diagram or drawing; however, most often you can articulate your design far more precisely with words. This chapter introduces techniques to help you label your drawing quickly and effectively.

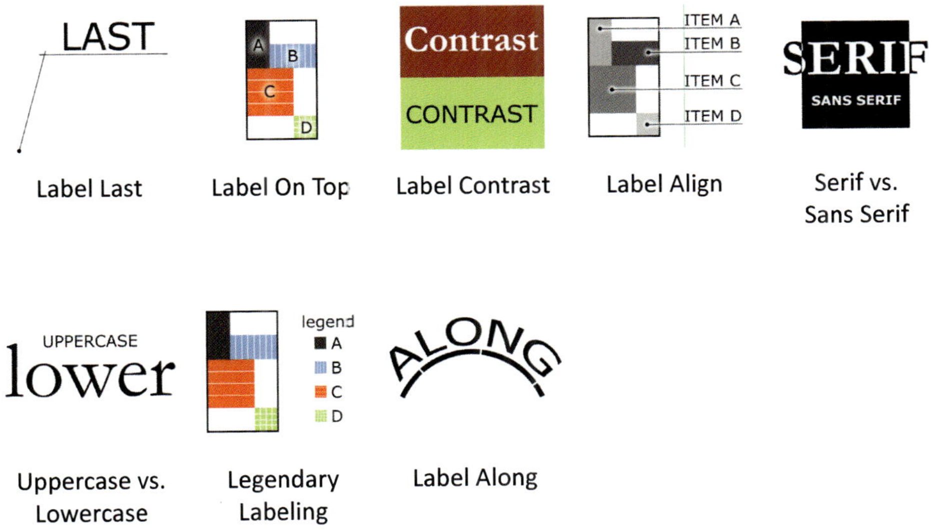

Figure 6-0. Techniques for labels.

Techniques regarding font selection are covered (Label Contrast, Serif vs. Sans Serif, Uppercase vs. Lowercase); but, the preponderance of techniques cover how labels should be ordered and arranged (Label Last, Label On Top, Label Align, Legendary Labeling, Label Along).

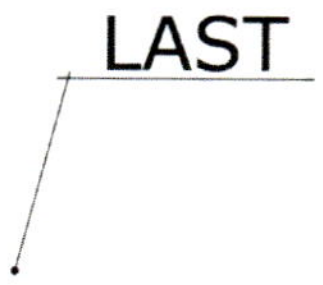

Label Last

Labeling is time consuming. As a result, I recommend labeling last. But by "last," I mean only that you wait to label until after you have learned where everything on your drawing will be. I do not mean that labeling should be the last thing you do.

Consider the evolution of the drawing in Figure 6-1. As early as the first drawing in the sequence, you have already learned where everything is. Though the drawing will be refined considerably before it is complete, you have already conveyed enough information in your drawing to justify labeling it.

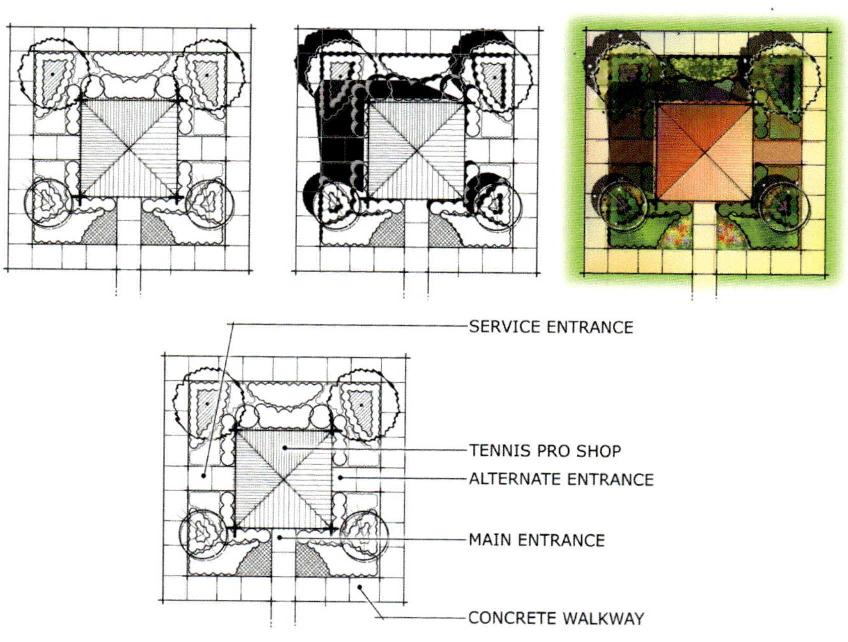

Figure 6-1. After you have learned where everything will ultimately be, it is time to label.

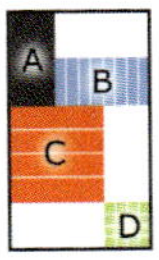

Label On Top

The message behind this technique is two-fold. One, labels can be placed directly on top of the items they denote. This is much more direct than drawing a leader from an item and labeling it on the side of your drawing. When space permits you to label directly on—or next to—an item, then you should consider doing it. Two, your labels should be physically separate from, and placed on top of, your drawing. This will allow you to make modifications to your labels without requiring you to edit the drawing itself. Consider how the drawings illustrated in Figure 6-2 utilize this technique.

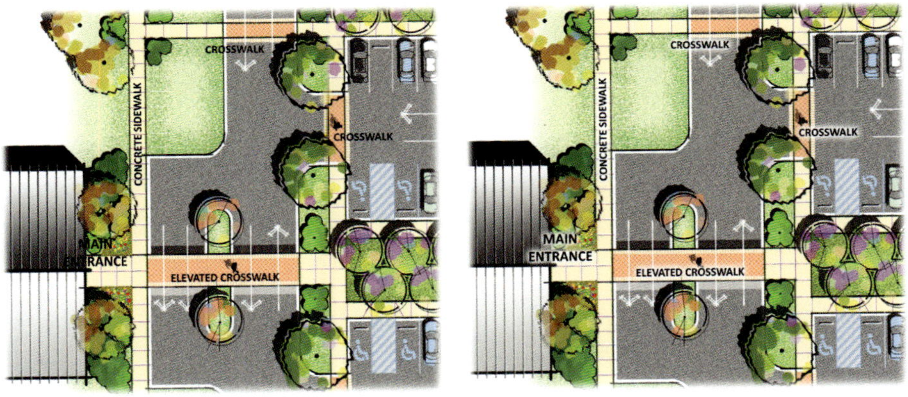

(a) (b)

Figure 6-2. (a) Though the labels are on top of the drawing, the black text seems to merge with the black line work. Perceptually, the labels are no longer on top. (b) By adding a white glow around the labels, the text clearly is on top.

When considering the illustrations in Figure 6-2, one should also note the items that have been labeled without text—the handicap parking spaces and traffic flow. These symbols communicate more effectively than labeling with text. The handicap spaces are represented just as they may be painted when constructed. The traffic flow symbols are deliberately more schematic because I do not want to imply that these arrows actually appear on the pavement.

Also, in keeping with the Label on Top principle, there are not any cars parked in the handicap spaces. When drawing a parking lot, you should never park cars in handicap spaces (whether you have a permit or not). Handicap spaces are frequently a core requirement of building codes, so you do not want to obscure this information from the people reviewing your drawing for compliance.

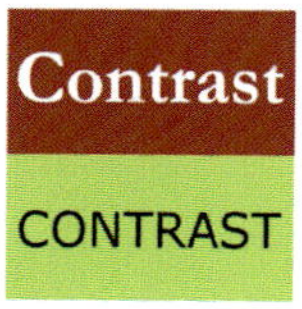

Label Contrast

This technique encourages you to select a font color that contrasts with your drawing. It is remarkable how often text is difficult or impossible to read because the background is too similar. If your drawing justifies a label, then that label should be clearly readable. Figure 6-3 illustrates some good—and bad—examples of how to contrast labels with dark and light backgrounds.

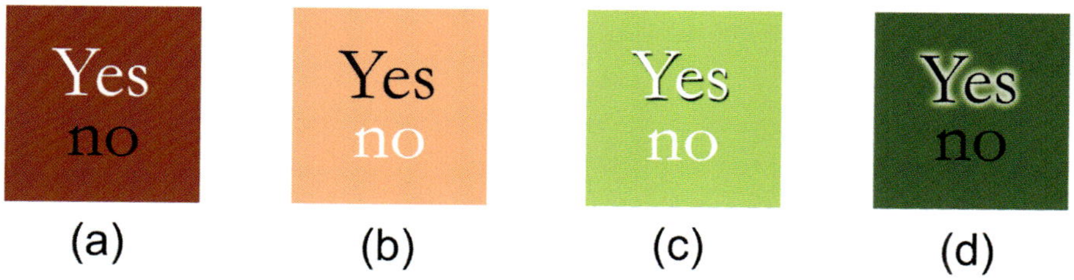

Figure 6-3. (a,b) Choose light colors for text on dark backgrounds, and dark colors for text on light backgrounds. (c) When using light colors only to label, consider giving the text a shadow to create contrast. (d) When using dark colors only to label, consider giving the text a light glow to help it stand out.

Conversely, if you do not want your labels to stand out, then you should use light colors on light backgrounds and dark colors on dark backgrounds. Believe it or not, there are circumstances when you do not want your text to stand out. You may have information you want to relate that is relevant, but that is not as important or as vital as other information. In these cases, you want the information to be available, just not as vivid as other information. Just be certain that there is enough contrast that the labels are still readable. For example, in Figure 6-3 above, the second line of text ("no") is readable in all cases; but, it is clearly not as dominant as the first line of text ("yes").

Though you can use any font color to label, I use white and black almost exclusively. Most often, I will use black with a white glow around it, as illustrated in Figure 6-3(d).

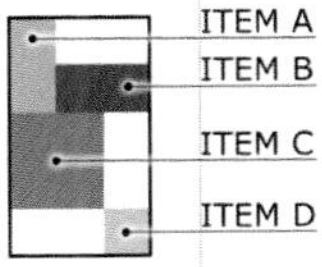

Label Align

When possible, align your labels so that your audience can review information quickly—without darting their eyes all around the drawing. Though the illustration in Figure 6-4 contains only five labeled items, the reader is still required to hunt for information.

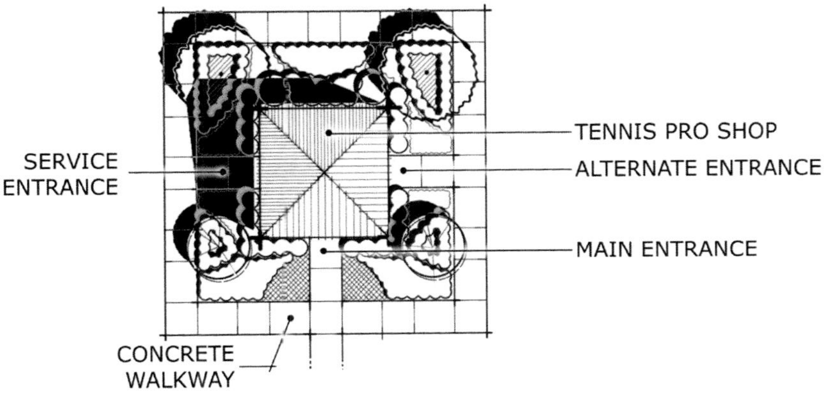

Figure 6-4. (a) Arranging labels haphazardly requires your audience to look in multiple places to find all the information.

Contrast that with Figure 6-5, where all information is aligned in one convenient column.

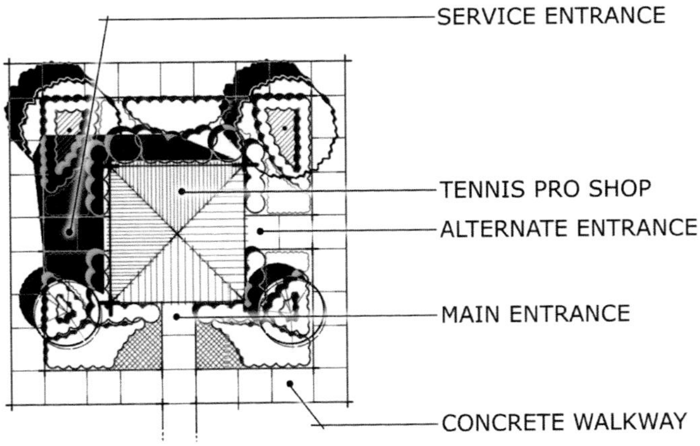

Figure 6-5. By aligning the labels, all information can be read quickly.

Often it is not possible to align all the information in one column. This might be because there is not enough space, or because an element of your drawing is substantially apart from the others. Nonetheless, an effort should be made to align as much as practical. Also, it may be helpful to align text labels and leaders in one area, and align measurements in another.

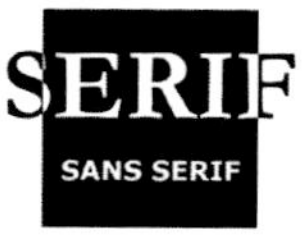

Serif vs. Sans Serif

If a font is sans serif, it merely means that it does not have the ornate extra strokes that make letters more interesting. For example, in Figure 6-6, the letters in column (a) are serif, while the letters in column (b) are sans serif. Notice how elementary the strokes are for the sans serif letters in Figure 6-6(b).

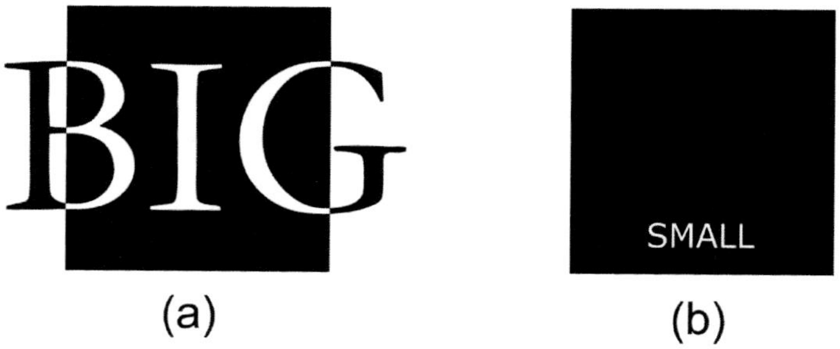

Figure 6-6. (a) This is a serif font called Garamond. (b) This is a sans serif font called Verdana.

Generally, most people will read serif fonts more quickly and easily than sans serif fonts—particularly small print. The smaller a font gets, the more useful using a serif font will be. Printed materials—like books, magazines, and brochures—usually benefit from using a serif print because of this ease of comprehension. However, there is one important exception: the computer. Because of technical limitations, computer monitors struggle to present serif fonts when they get very small. For this reason, I always recommend using a sans serif font when your typeface is small.

In this era of e-mail, it is not uncommon to find that your drawings are scanned and forwarded by electronic mail to any number of recipients. Especially frustrating, is the carelessness that your drawings will be reduced and diminished so that they are a more convenient size for e-mail. For this reason, I always use sans serif fonts for small fonts (or for drawings that will likely be reduced dramatically and, therefore, be much smaller). It is a counter-intuitive practice given the customary benefits of serif fonts; but, it is very practical solution when you can not depend on your original work being presented as you intended.

UPPERCASE
lower

Uppercase vs. Lowercase

Generally, reading uppercase letters takes longer than reading lowercase letters. When reading short labels or titles, this disparity is barely evident. When reading long narratives, however, the difference becomes more noticeable. That being said, the difference can be so slight that the use of uppercase versus lowercase becomes more a matter of custom than necessity. Therefore, consider the examples provided in Figure 6-7 as a guide rather than a rule.

LARGEST TITLES & HEADINGS

TITLES & HEADINGS

Subtitles

Genus species 'Cultivar'

LABELS FOR LEADERS IN CAPS

Avoid using script, especially CAPS.

TINY TEXT IN UPPERCASE, SANS SERIF FONTS.

Figure 6-7. Bold letters are most appropriate for headings and titles. When headings are especially big, I often will make the first letter of each word larger. Italics and scripts are difficult to read and should be avoided.

The only hard rule is that long narratives should always use predominantly lowercase letters. Make sure it is not too difficult to find the beginning of the next line after you have read to the end of the previous line. You may even consider breaking the narrative down into columns of paragraphs.

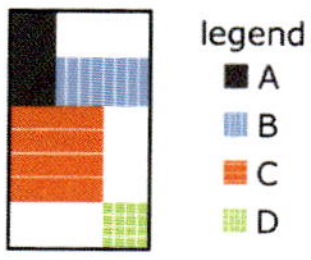

Legendary Labeling

When appropriate, it is often helpful to summarize items within a legend—or key—rather than labeling them directly. This is especially true when your drawing is schematic or functional. Figure 6-8 illustrates an example of a legend that could be used for the site inventory in Figure 4-3.

Figure 6-8. Above is an example of a symbolic legend for a site inventory diagram.

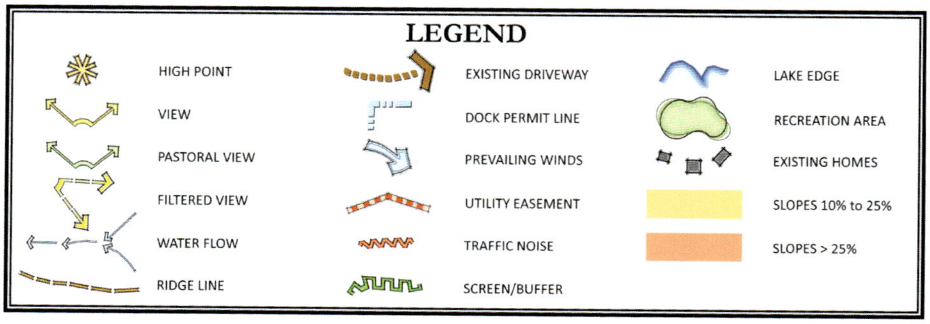

In some cases, a legend is sufficient enough that you will not need to ultimately label the drawing itself. In most cases, however, a legend should merely be used to supplement items already labeled. Unless your drawing is especially symbolic, or space for labeling is severely limited, you should consider labeling most items even though they also appear in the legend.

When constructing a legend, be certain that the symbols in your key are large enough and distinct enough that they clearly represent what appears in your drawing. So often a legend becomes useless because the symbols are too small to correlate with the actual drawing.

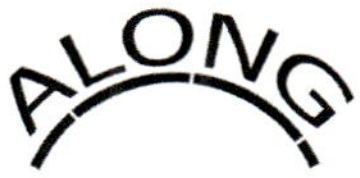

Label Along

If you are not careful, your labels can contradict your drawing. For example, notice how the street labels in Figure 6-9 affect your perception of the road layout. In the left drawing, the angular street labels create an implicit triangle. Subconsciously, your mind perceives the roads will meet at an angle. In the right drawing, the street names bend with the curves in the road. The labels actually reinforce the road design.

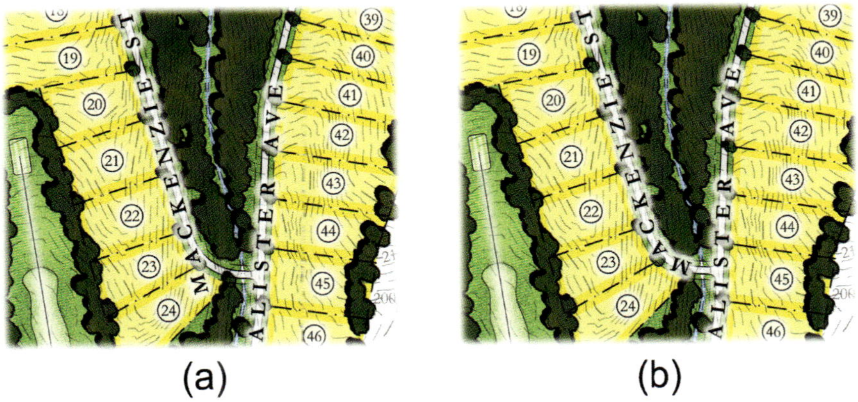

Figure 6-9. (a) The street names have been rotated; but, they do not follow along the road. (b) Because the street names bend with the road, the curves are emphasized.

Be sure that all labels are readable from two sides of the drawing (at most). Consider how the labels are aligned in Figure 6-10. In the drawing on the far left, the paper must be rotated 360 degrees before all labels can be read. The next two drawings can be read more quickly.

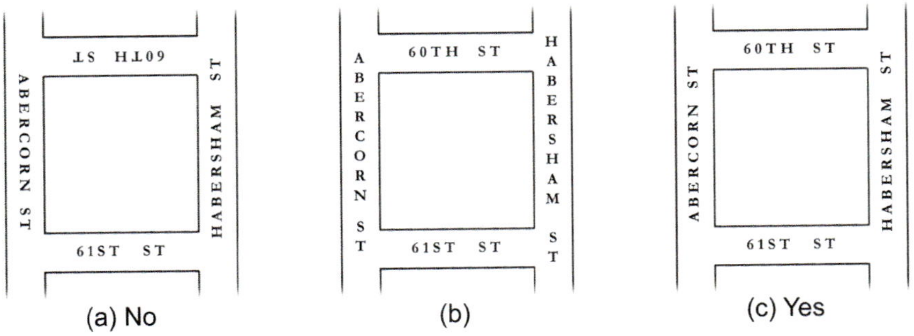

Figure 6-10. (a) Must be rotated 360 degrees to be read. (b) No rotation. (c) One rotation.

7 COLOR

This chapter introduces many techniques that will allow you to use color more effectively in your drawings. Many of the techniques utilize the concept of a color palette, and all may be used concurrently. That is, all the techniques complement one another.

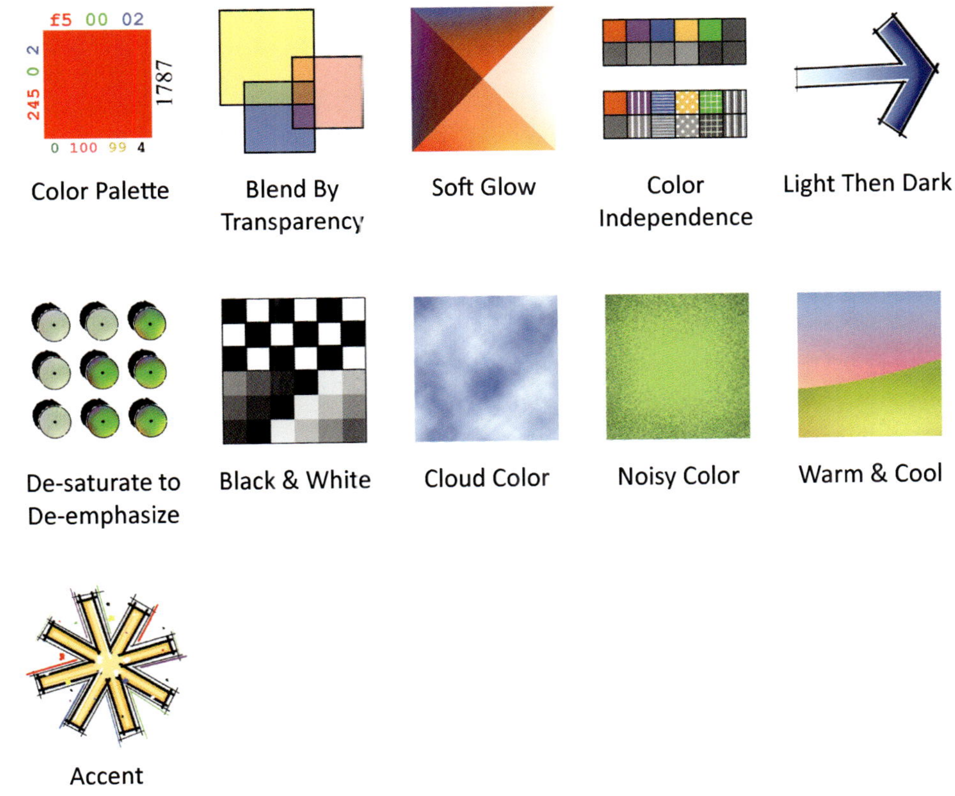

Figure 7-0. Techniques for using color.

Before jumping into each of the techniques, however, it will be helpful to understand how color is composed—both on your computer screen and, afterwards, when it is plotted or printed. Each way is unique, and the medium you choose for displaying your work may affect the colors you choose.

In the simplest terms, your computer screen usually displays color by mixing different intensities of red, green, and blue light. Colors created like this can be expressed mathematically in a format called RGB, which you have probably already guessed stands for Red, Green, Blue.

Many colors can be composed by varying the intensity of each. Yellow, for example, is composed of high intensities of red and green light, and less (little or no) blue light. Each intensity of red, green, and blue has an associated value between 0 and 255 (or #00 to #FF in hexadecimal). The higher the value, the more intense the light is. White, for example, has the maximum value of 255 for red, green and blue light (or #FFFFFF in hexadecimal). Black has the lowest value of 0 for red, green, and blue light (or #000000 in hexadecimal). When all is accounted for, 16,777,216 unique color combinations can be created.

Regrettably, printers and plotters require ink—and not light—to display your drawing. Because few colors can be constructed from red, green, and blue ink, your printer requires another format to draw your illustrations correctly. Instead, colors are composed from different amounts of cyan, magenta, yellow, and black ink. Hence, we have CMYK format. CMYK expresses values of cyan, magenta, yellow, and black for each, ranging from 0 to 100 (percent). Consequently, there are 104,060,401 combinations possible.

Now, if you are doing the math at home, you know that 104 million (CMYK) is greater than 16.8 million (RGB). That intuitively means that not every color combination can be expressed mathematically in both formats. But, it is not time to panic yet. It is our good fortune that our eyes and brains can only distinguish between a substantially smaller number of colors anyway.

So, why all the fuss? What difference does it make which format we use when either format can already construct millions of colors we can not distinguish anyway? Well, the short answer is that it does not matter which one you use. But what is relevant are two important consequences of this disparity of formats:

1. What you see on the computer screen may not look like what you print.
2. What you draw by hand and scan may not look the same on the computer screen.

Therefore, whenever you work with color, you need to recognize that what you see is not necessarily what you get. Be vigilant. Make test prints of your work. Verify that your message is not compromised by poor color. Make allowances and changes when necessary. Be patient and good luck.

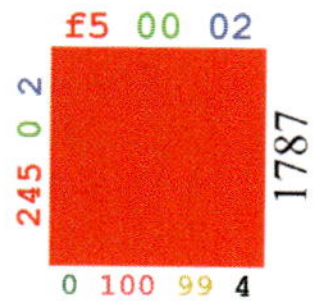

Color Palette

In Chapter 4, we discussed the importance and utility of standardization. Of all the things to standardize, a color palette may be the most useful.

At a minimum, you should specify a base set of colors to serve as a foundation for all of your drawings. Certainly, you may use colors beyond your defined palette; however, you need a minimal set of familiar colors that will always appear in your drawing. This will allow all of your drawings to maintain a consistent and harmonious feel—whether you end up reusing or recycling them later or not.

I actually began constructing my computer color palette from the set of markers I commonly used when drawing by hand. I simply scribbled a sample of each marker on a white background, scanned the drawing, and sampled the colors directly from the scan—making subtle changes when necessary.

Whether you already use a common set of markers in your office or not, there are spectrums of colors that should appear in all palettes (as demonstrated by Figure 7-1). Reds, yellows, and blues should be present along with the colors derived from their combinations: oranges, greens, and purples. Additionally, a more subtle and expansive palette of grays should range from white to black. Lastly, you should augment your palette with some rich, vivid accent colors.

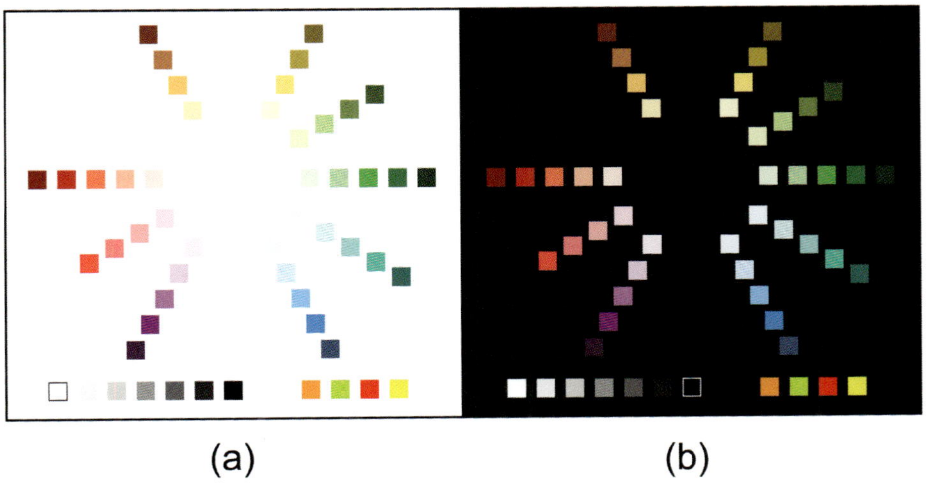

Figure 7-1. (a) As these axes demonstrate, the colors are derived from red-yellow-blue and combinations thereof. Additionally, a gray spectrum and accent colors are present. (b) Recognize that your palette may be more, or less, effective on a darker background.

On the following pages, I have included the color palette which I used for the illustrations used throughout this book. While you may find this color palette to be helpful in your own work, understand that it is not intended to be a universally accepted standard. These are simply colors that I have grown accustomed to using. Instead, recognize that this palette is provided simply as an example of how you could document and construct your own color palette.

To make sense of the palette as displayed in Figures 7-3 and 7-4, you will first want to consider the legend provided in Figure 7-2. Each color square has values you may use to express the color for your graphics application. Some graphics applications prefer colors to be expressed as combinations of red, green, and blue light. Others prefer you to express colors as combinations of cyan, magenta, yellow, and black ink. Others may allow you to select a Pantone® color directly. Therefore, I like to include the values for the most common formats in my palette.

It is worth noting that the values that appear are equivalent; but, they are not identical. For example, if you converted from RGB to CMYK mode, the new CMYK values will be similar to, but not exactly, the values in the chart. In fact, even if you converted from RGB to CMYK mode and then back again, you would not necessarily get your original RGB values again. This is just one of the quirks of trying to express colors as combinations of either light or ink. Regardless, the values provided are similar enough that you can be assured that they will look good together whether displayed on your computer or plotted on your printer.

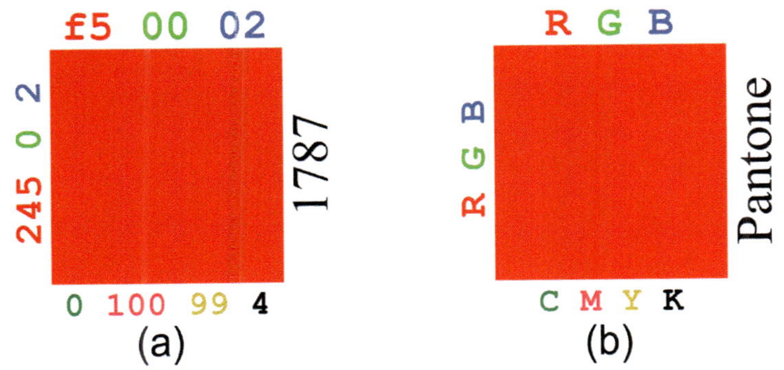

Figure 7-2. (a) This is an example of the color information as presented in the palettes on the following pages. (b) This is a legend for the color information, clockwise from top: Red, green, and blue hexadecimal values; Pantone number; Cyan, magenta, yellow, and black values; Red, green, and blue decimal values.

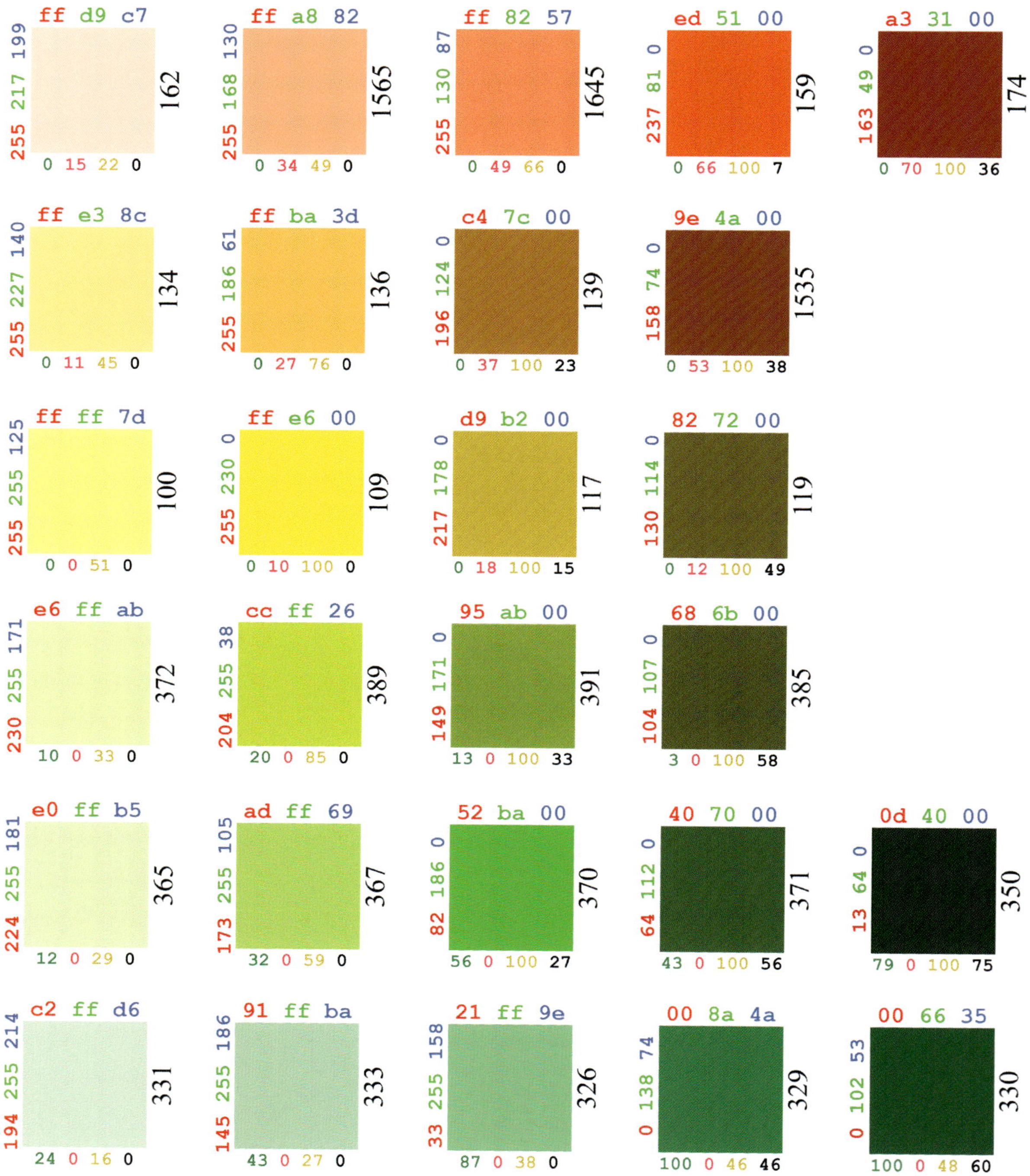

Figure 7-3. This is an example of a color palette (Page 1 of 2).

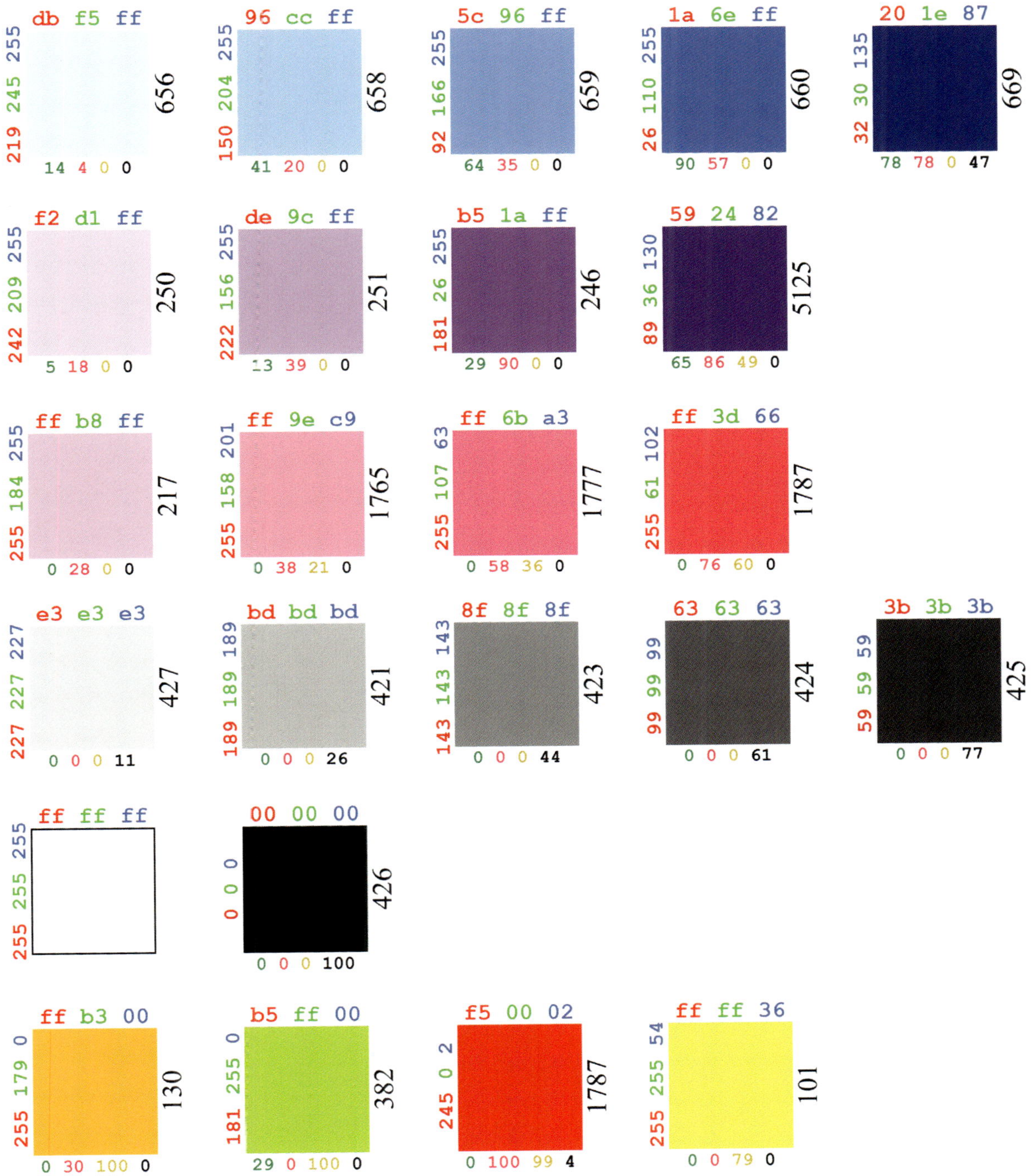

Figure 7-4. This is an example of a color palette (Page 2 of 2).

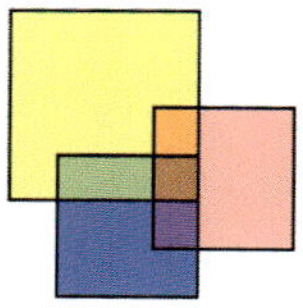

Blend By Transparency

To create more complex and interesting colors, use transparency to allow colors to show through and blend with each other. Draw colors on different layers and then adjust the layer opacity to your preference. Consider the two renderings in Figure 7-5. In the first rendering, colors merely overlap one another. The most dominant colors in this drawing are the last ones drawn, simply because they cover up previous strokes. Contrast this with the latter drawing, where every layer blends with each other. The colors in this drawing complement one other, rather than compete with each other.

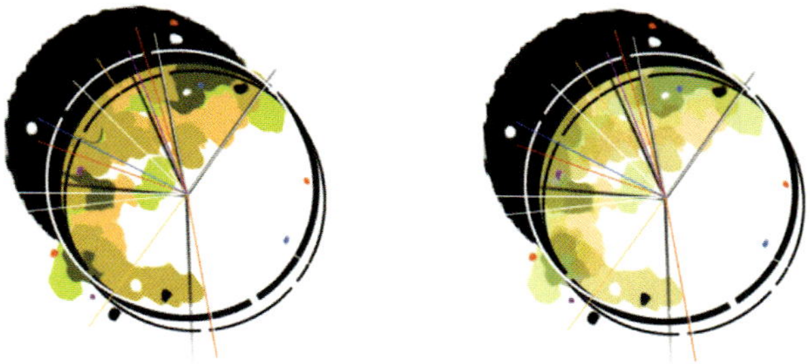

(a) No (b) Yes

Figure 7-5. (a) Because all layers have an opacity of 100 percent, the last brush strokes cover up previous strokes. (b) By varying the transparency of all the brush strokes, the colors blend with each other, creating new colors and greater complexity.

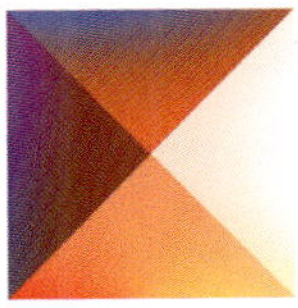

Soft Glow

A quick and simple way to add a subtle touch of color and depth to a drawing is to use a technique I call soft glow. Basically, I take a big, soft brush and just touch the edges of the selected part of my drawing. I will use purples and blues on dark portions of a drawing. I will use yellows on the lightest portions. And I will use reds and oranges on the midtones. See how the purple, especially, livens up the drawing in Figure 7-6.

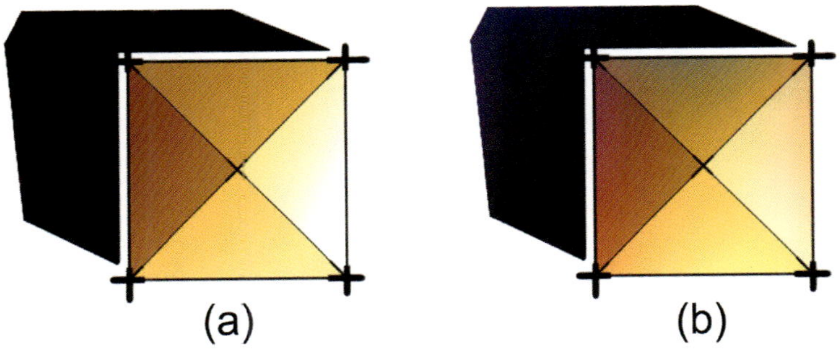

Figure 7-6. (a) This drawing uses simple gradients to shade the roof. (b) This drawing adds hues of purple and blue to the darkest parts of the roof, and hues of red and orange to the midtones and lightest parts of the roof.

This is an especially useful technique when you are trying to make separate elements in a drawing appear more harmonious. For example, I might add a touch of green glow to a pond if a tree overhangs the water. Conversely, I may also add a blue hue to the edge of that tree. By sharing properties, both the water and overhanging tree will seem more integrated.

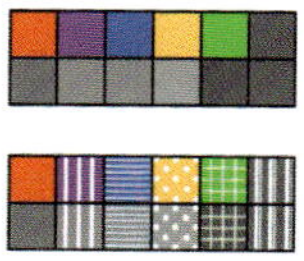

Color Independence

This technique requires that you use color to enhance your message, but not depend on color to convey your message. That is, be certain that your drawing communicates the same message whether you use color or not.

Consider Figure 7-7, which illustrates one of the hazards of depending on color. In the top row, the designer differentiates unique species of trees by using different colors. The bottom row, however, is how the original drawing appears once it has been photocopied.

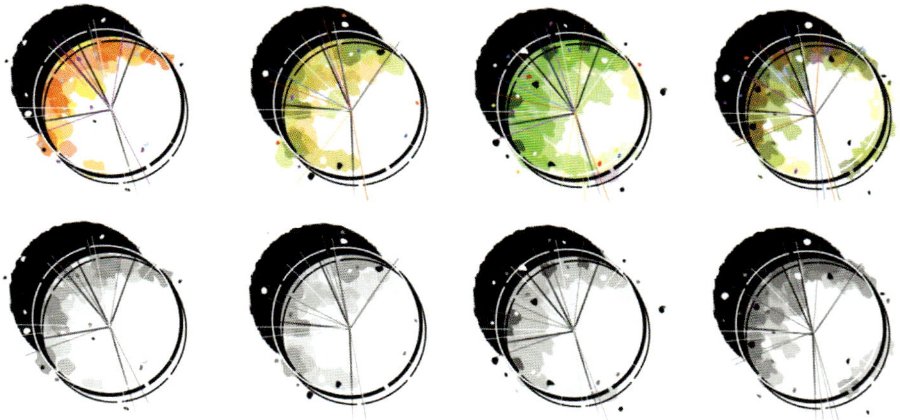

Figure 7-7. Once the top row is photocopied (as shown in the bottom row), the trees are indistinguishable.

Alternatively, consider the drawings in Figure 7-8. Though all the trees use comparable colors, their symbols clearly distinguish each tree from the other.

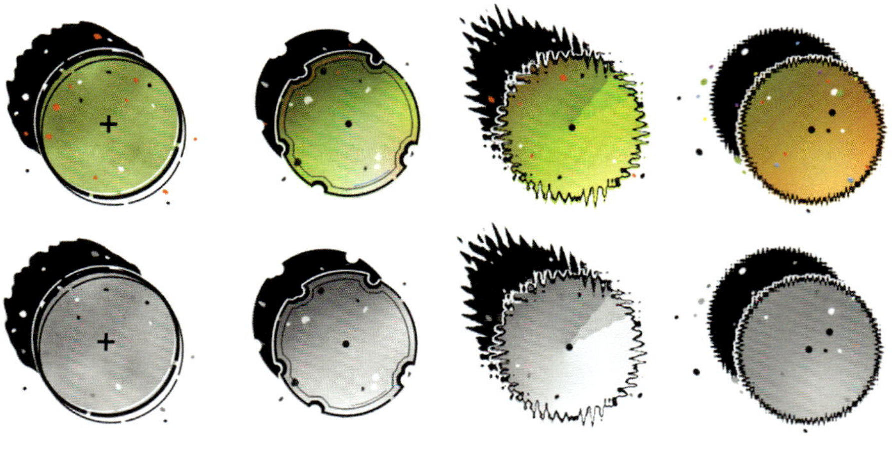

Figure 7-8. By using unique symbols, your message is conveyed with or without color.

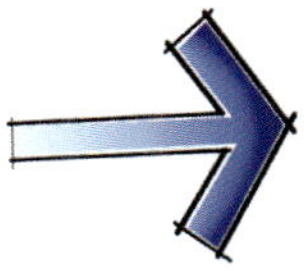

Light Then Dark

This technique encourages you to construct complex color combinations by successively adding darker and darker layers of color. Consider the progression of drawings in Figure 7-9. You begin by adding a foundation of subtle, light colors. Next you add a range of midtones—especially the most prevalent colors. In our example of a symbol for a tree, the midtones are logically dominated by greens. Lastly, the darkest midtones and most vivid accent colors are added.

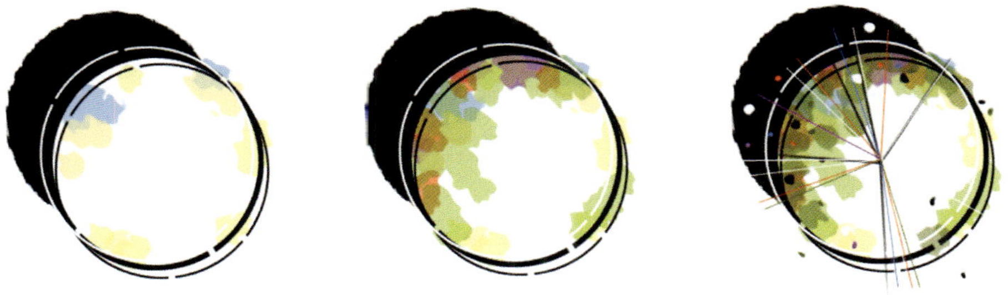

(a) (b) (c)

Figure 7-9. (a) Foundation colors are light. (b) Midtones. (c) Darker colors are added last, with rich, sharp accents on top.

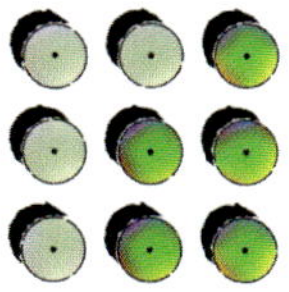

De-saturate to De-emphasize

Often, you will need to tailor your drawing for a specific audience. Instead of creating an overall impression, you will need to call attention to a specific element within your drawing. When this is necessary, I find this technique to be especially helpful. Basically, I will de-emphasize the portion of the drawing that I want to ignore by removing its color. This will allow the portions I want to emphasize to stand out by contrast, as in Figure 7-10.

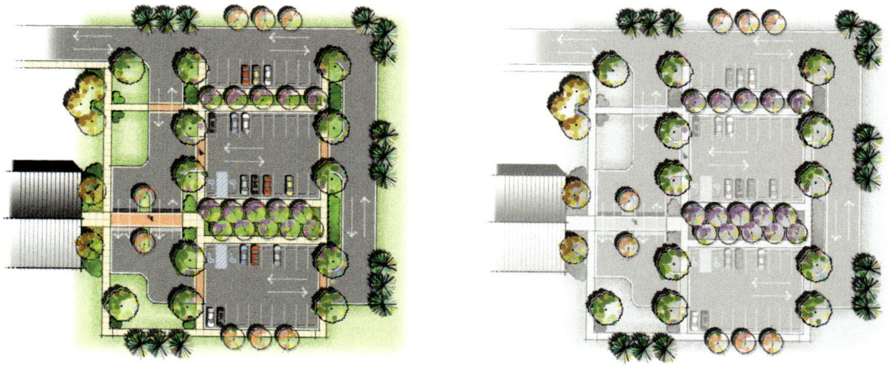

(a) (b)

Figure 7-10. (a) This rendering is intended to convey an overall impression of the parking lot design, hence the consistency of saturation. (b) Trees are clearly intended to be the focus of this drawing.

Often, after I have de-saturated the undesirable elements within a drawing, I will also turn down their opacity—thereby making that portion of the drawing lighter too. I did this in Figure 7-10(b), as well. This is because I want to maintain the contrast even if someone were to photocopy my color drawing in black-and-white. Note how the drawing in Figure 7-11(b) still maintains its contrast despite the absence of color.

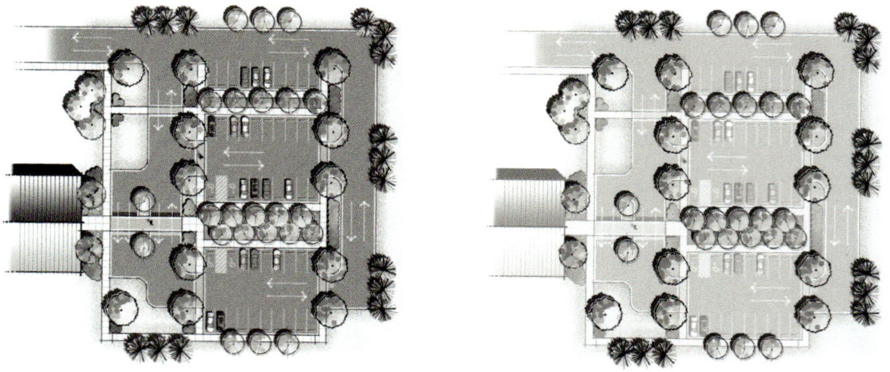

(a) (b)

Figure 7-11. Both illustrations demonstrate how the drawings in Figure 7-10 might appear if they were photocopied in black-and-white.

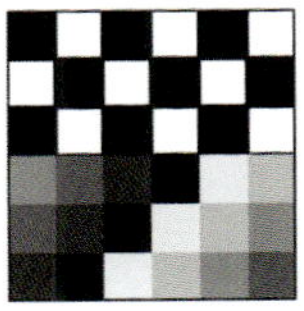

Black & White

This technique recognizes that black-and-white is not synonymous with monochrome. Just because a drawing is absent of color, it does not mean that the drawing is black-and-white. Consider the drawings in Figure 7-12. Though neither drawing utilizes color; the black-and-white (black line) drawing on the left is clearly sharper and more striking than the monochromatic drawing on the right. Because a more limited range of colors (grays and whites, primarily) is used in the drawing on the left, the contrast is greater.

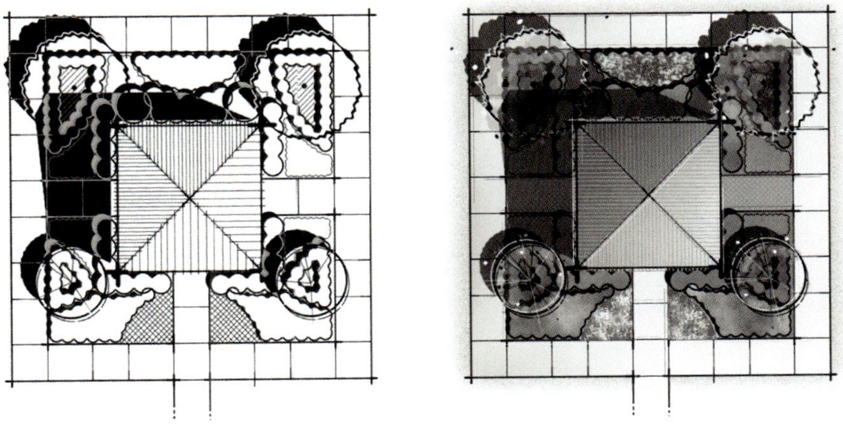

(a) Black Line (b) Monochrome

Figure 7-12. (a) This drawing is composed primarily of two colors—black and white. (b) This drawing is monochromatic. It is composed of a spectrum of shades of gray.

Of course, we rarely create monochromatic drawings, as in Figure 7-12(b). More often, our work is displayed as a monochromatic drawing simply because someone has photocopied our original color rendering. This is especially common during the most preliminary stages of design.

Whether you decide to render your drawing in black-and-white (black line) or not should probably depend on the likelihood your audience will alter your work. And I do not just mean whether it is likely your drawing will be photocopied, as above. If your design is preliminary and is certain to be modified, you should not invest much time adding color to your renderings. Instead, invest that time considering other design options.

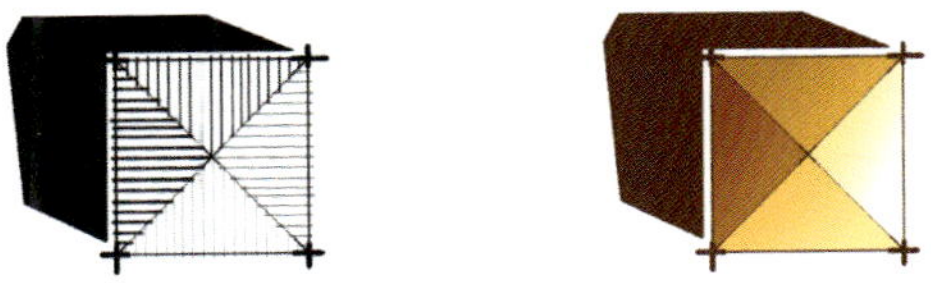

(a) Black Line (b) Monochrome

Figure 7-13. Though the drawing on the right is not black-and-white, it is still monochromatic because is utilizes a range of only one color—brown.

Cloud Color

This is a useful technique for adding color to tree masses or water bodies—or any other parts of a drawing that take up a lot of space. The larger the item is that you are coloring, the greater the danger that the item will take on a flat and dull appearance if colored uniformly. In these circumstances, you can give your drawing more depth by having your uniform spaces take on the appearance of clouds or cotton, as in Figures 7-14 and 7-15.

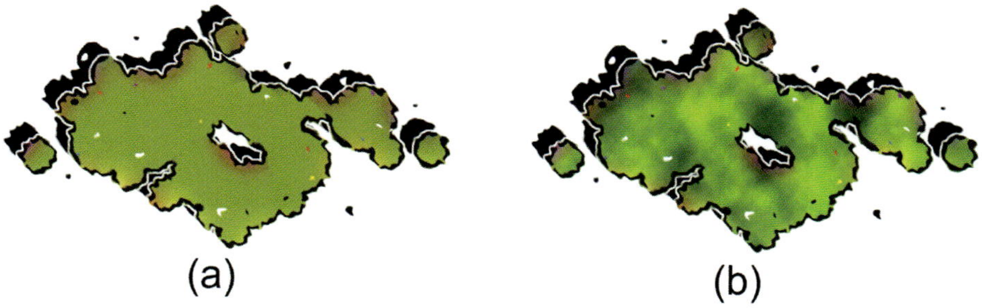

Figure 7-14. (a) Because these trees are painted uniformly, they seem flat and dull. (b) By taking on a cloud-like appearance instead, the trees have more depth and interest.

The software I use regularly actually has a filter that does exactly this; however, you can emulate the same effect by painting with a soft brush too.

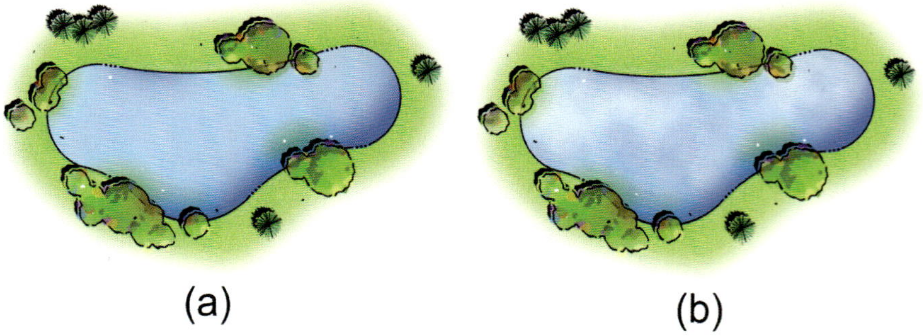

Figure 7-15. (a) A solid blue paint fill. (b) Clouds reflect off the surface of the water.

Noisy Color

Like Cloud Color, this technique is useful for uniformly painted spaces. It especially lends itself to grass, sand, and other fine textures. Consider the two drawings in Figure 7-16. In the left drawing, the grass has simply been painted with a uniform green color. In the right drawing, two filters have been applied to the green grass. The first filter "spatters" paint drops along the edges of the grass. The second filter adds "noise" throughout the drawing—sort of like the hissing screen you see when a television can not receive a channel.

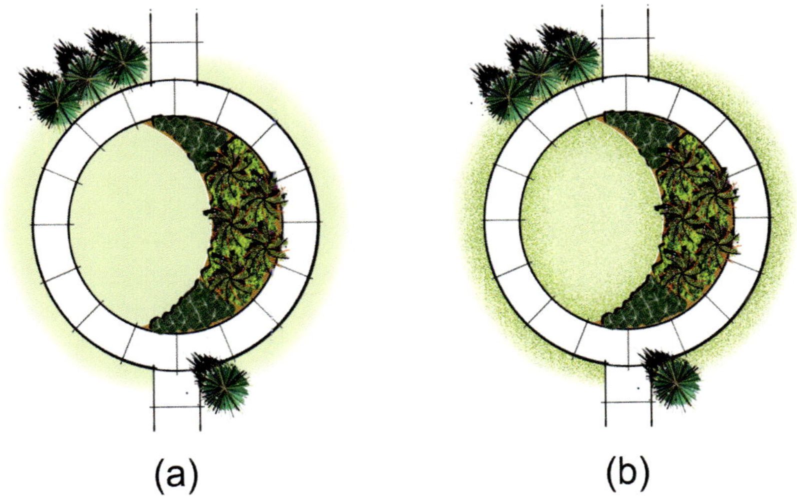

Figure 7-16. (a) The grass seems flat and dull when drawn uniformly. (b) The grass edges are accentuated by the stippling, and the dots give the grass texture.

If your graphics software does not have filters to create these effects, you can likely recreate a similar look by painting with a rough, noisy paintbrush.

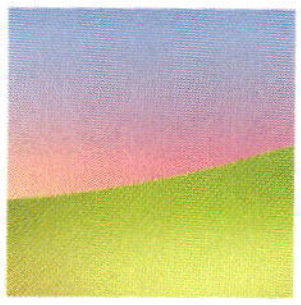

Warm & Cool

In this technique, you juxtapose warm colors with cool colors. This creates a pleasant conflict that allows all colors to take on a greater intensity. For example, consider how the sky interacts with the rolling hills in Figure 7-17. Even in this simplistic illustration, there is a definite back-and-forth interaction between the cool and warm colors.

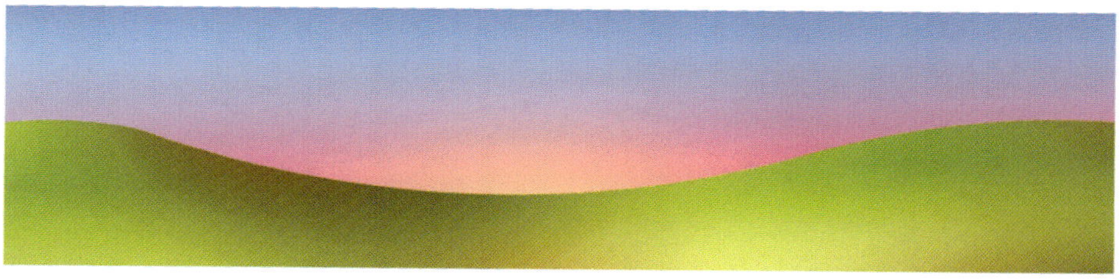

Figure 7-17. The warm colors of the ground plane juxtapose with the cool colors of the sky.

Of course, how does one distinguish a warm color from a cool color? Well, unfortunately, it is somewhat arbitrary. If I were to borrow the swatches from the color palette discussed earlier, I might divide the colors as shown in Figure 7-18. Reds, yellows and oranges are intuitively warm colors, just as blues, purples, and magentas are intuitively cool. Notice, however, that shades of green appear throughout both sets of colors. The greens with red and yellow tinges appear with the warm colors, while the greens with a blue hue appear with the cool colors.

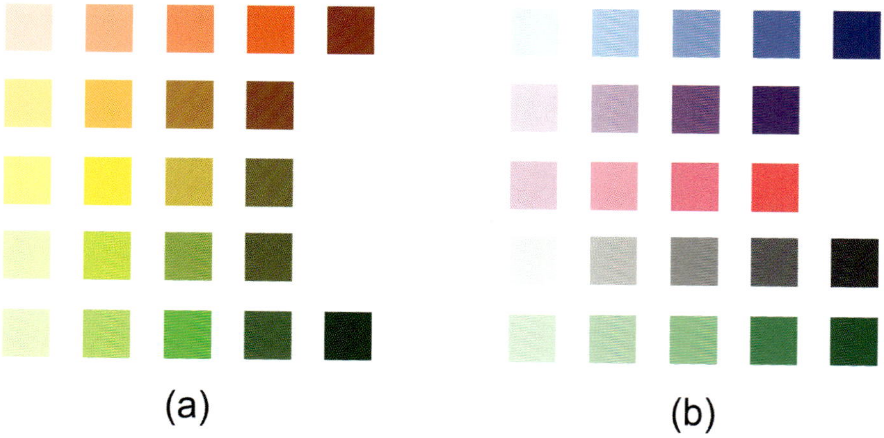

Figure 7-18. (a) These are examples of warm colors. (b) These are examples of cool colors.

One of the things I like to do is pair a warm color with a cool color directly, as in Figure 7-19. Notice how pleasant the color combinations work with each other. This is especially true of colors that appear on the opposite ends of the spectrum (e.g., red-green, yellow-purple, orange-blue).

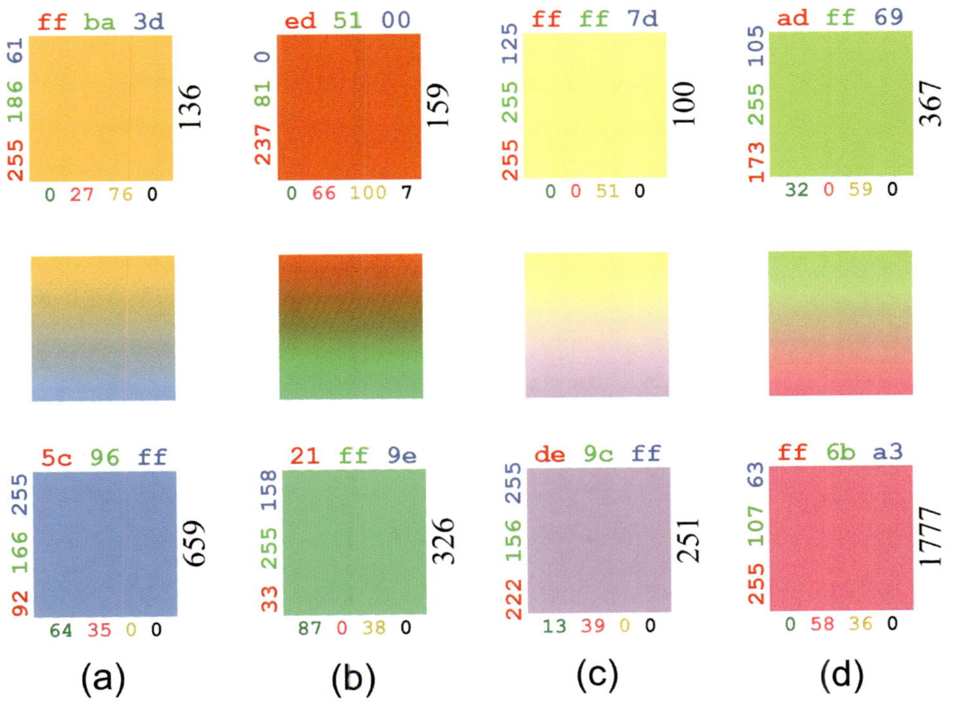

Figure 7-19. The first row is comprised of warm colors. The third row is comprised of cool colors. Notice how well the warm and cool colors appear together, particularly in the opposite spectrum color pairs in (a) orange-blue, (b) red-green, and (c) yellow-purple.

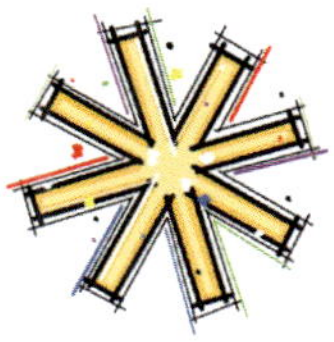

Accent

This technique uses the boldest and most vivid colors in your palette; yet, the intent is to use these colors in the most subtle way possible. To accomplish this, you need your brush strokes to be on one (or both) of two ends of the spectrum: either (i) sharp and thin, or (ii) soft and broad. Figure 7-20(b) illustrates both. Notice that thin, vivid strokes of red, purple, blue, and yellow sharpen the drawing, while also giving the building a subtle hint of color. Notice, also, that accent colors of blue and purple are used to enhance the gradient shading (utilizing the Color Glow technique).

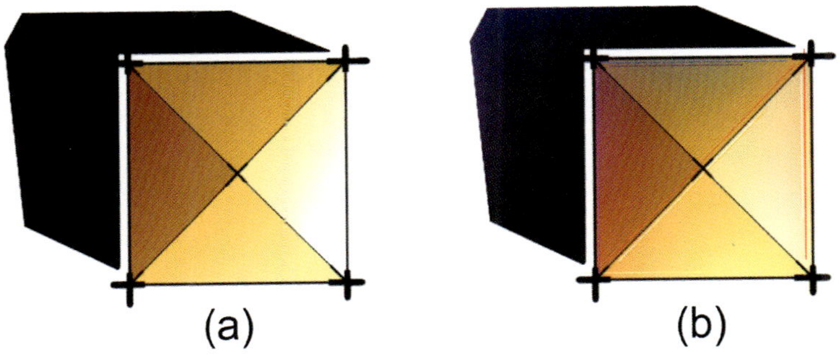

Figure 7-20. (a) This building has no accent coloring. (b) Accent colors are used with both sharp, thin strokes, as well as with the Color Glow technique.

Often, your audience may overlook your accent coloring at first—especially from a distance. Nonetheless, your illustrations will take on an energy and vitality that they would not possess otherwise. Consider how, in Figure 7-21, the drawing on the right seems to divert your attention from the drawing on the left.

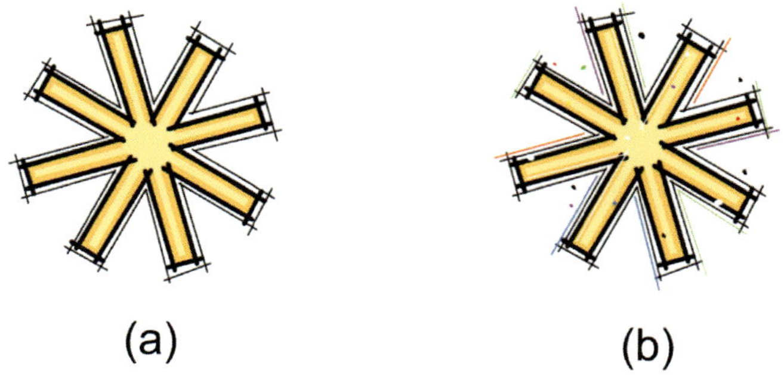

Figure 7-21. (a) This symbol does not use accent coloring. (b) Notice that the edges of the asterisk have been accentuated with thin strokes of red, blue, and purple.

When using uniform, dark colors it is especially effective to accent with fine, sharp, light colors. Notice how in Figure 7-22(b) the needles of this coniferous tree are suddenly sharper and more spindly because of the accents.

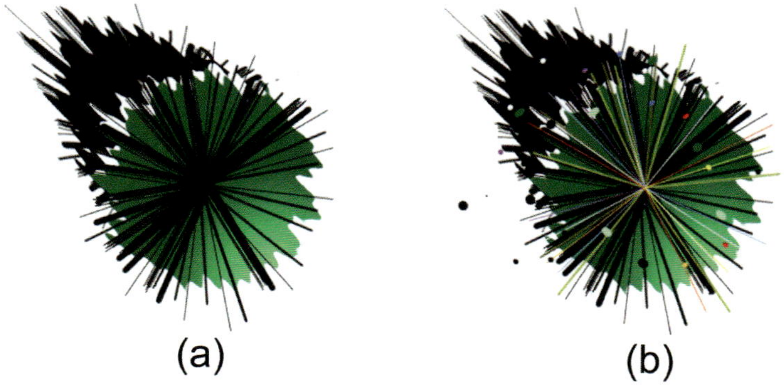

Figure 7-22. (a) This tree does not have accent coloring. (b) Sharp streaks of accent colors invigorate this evergreen tree symbol.

8 SHADOWS

Shadows are fundamental to good plan graphics. Not only do they enhance your drawing aesthetically, they also enhance your ability to effectively communicate your design. Because shadows allow a drawing to take on a 3-dimensional quality, valuable information about a design (e.g., height, depth, form, orientation) can be expressed more elegantly. Shadows can express movement, or the absence thereof, very simply and succinctly. Shadows can also either amplify or soften edges. Shadows do not just make your drawing more attractive. They make your drawing more effective.

Regrettably, shadows are frequently the last item added to a drawing, when time is most scarce. Often that means that shadows are drawn casually and carelessly—as well as incorrectly! That is a great shame because shadows are one of the most powerful ways to communicate ideas through your drawing. Do not wait until the last second to draw shadows. Instead, embrace the following techniques for drawing shadows in this book and you will almost certainly become a more effective communicator.

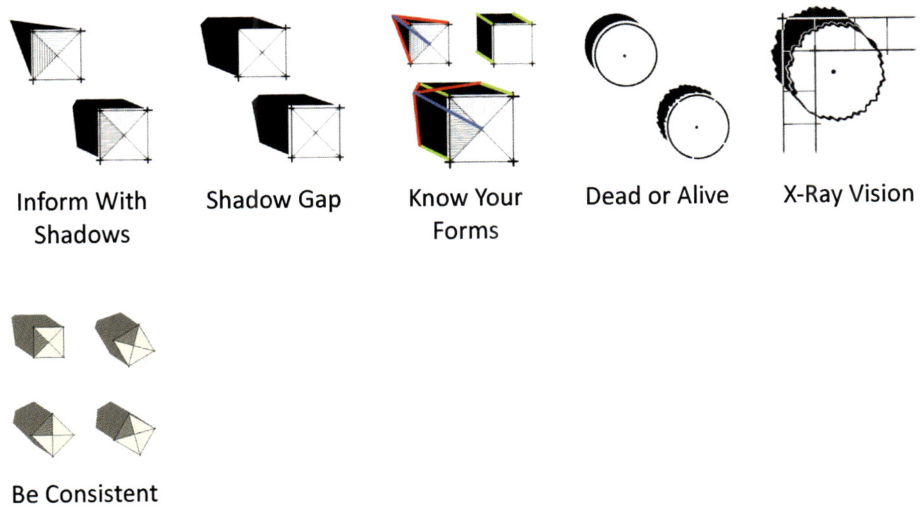

Figure 8-0. Techniques for drawing shadows.

Before diving into each of these techniques individually, however, it may be helpful to discuss some general concepts about shadows. Understanding these fundamentals will facilitate learning the techniques that will follow.

Shadows are affected by a number of variables, including the time of day, the time of year, the location on earth, as well as the form of the object casting the shadow. The mathematical functions to calculate shadows are quite complex—deriving solutions using inputs like the solar azimuth (arc of the horizon), solar altitude (angular distance of the sun to the horizon), latitude, longitude, and time zone. Fortunately, understanding these functions is not necessary for our purposes. There are calculators available that can do the math for us. What is important, however, is recognizing how these variables affect shadows.

Generally, the sun rises in the east and sets in the west (see Figure 8-1). The longest shadows are cast in the morning and evening, while the shortest are cast during mid-day (see Figure 8-2). Seasonally, the longest shadows are cast during the winter, while the shortest are cast during the summer.

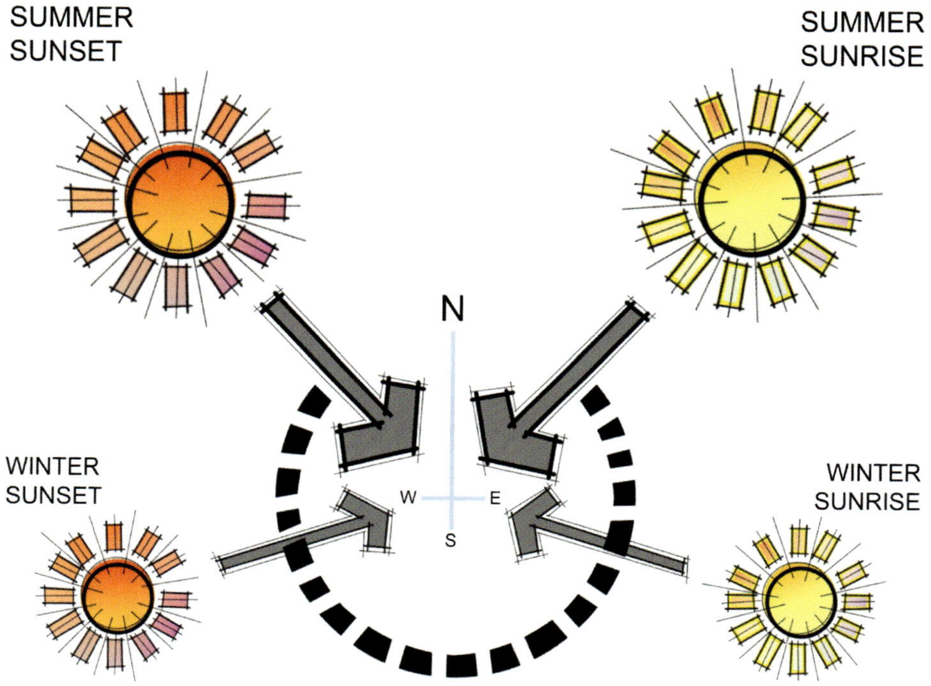

Figure 8-1. This is an abstract representation of the sun's movement throughout the day. This particular solar pattern represents Atlanta, Georgia.

Therefore, to create the most dramatic effects, it would make sense to show shadows cast during the winter solstice (around December 22) in the early morning or late evening. The least effective shadows would be cast around noon during the summer solstice (around June 21). A useful compromise is to use shadows cast during the spring or autumn in the early evening or morning.

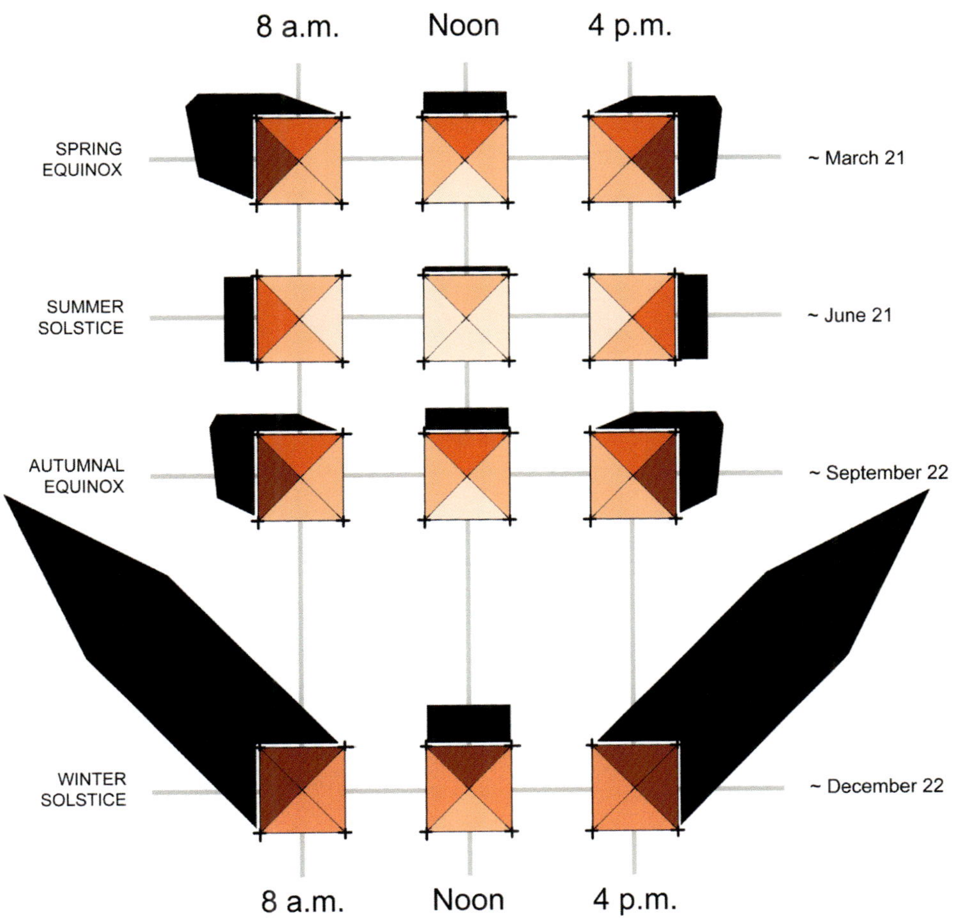

Figure 8-2. These shadows are representative of how shadows may look at different times of the day and year in Atlanta, Georgia.

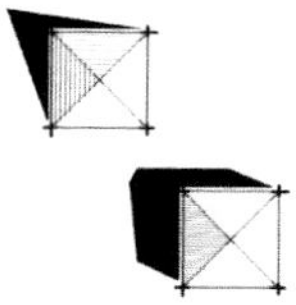

Inform With Shadows

Shadows give your drawing depth. Shadows engage your audience. Most importantly, however, shadows inform your audience. When drawn correctly, shadows reveal an object's height, form, and orientation.

Consider the following two forms in Figure 8-3: a pyramid and a building. Though both forms are nearly identical in plan view, their shadows inform the viewer that these are unique forms.

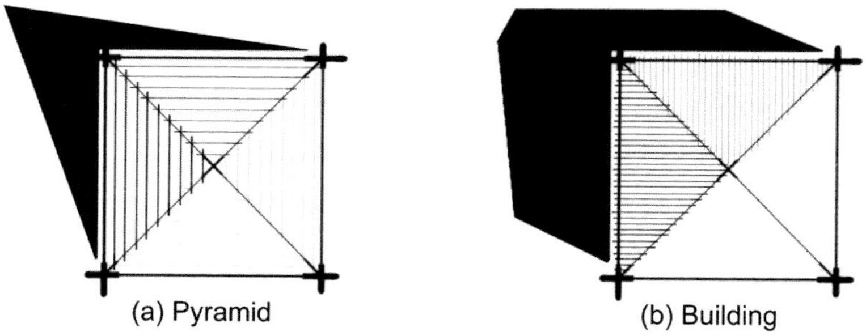

Figure 8-3. Shadows should inform the audience about an object's height, form, and orientation.

Without shadows, your audience will have to guess what you have drawn. For example, if you omit the shadows, as in Figure 8-4(a), how will the viewer know what form the building is? Is the roof pitched? Is the roof divided and flat?

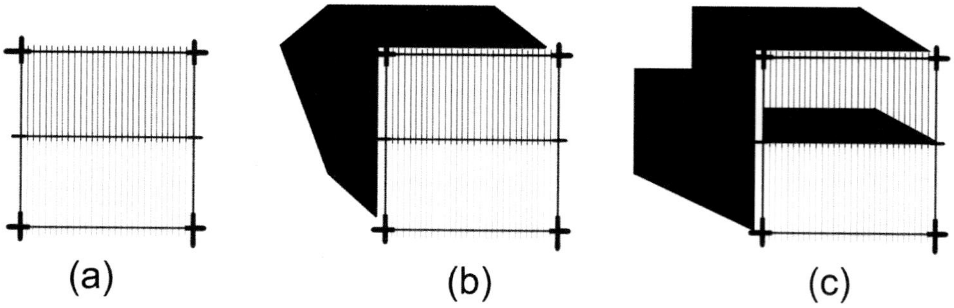

Figure 8-4. (a) Omitting shadows can create ambiguity. (b) From this shadow, the viewer can infer this building has a pitched roof. (c) From these shadows, the viewer may infer that the front of the building is higher than the rear, and both roofs are flat.

Because shadows are so informative, you must ensure that they are drawn correctly. When you are careless drawing shadows, you may accidentally mislead your audience. A common mistake is to draw the same shadows around all trees. For example, an evergreen tree with a pyramidal form should appear with a pointed shadow as in Figure 8-5(b).

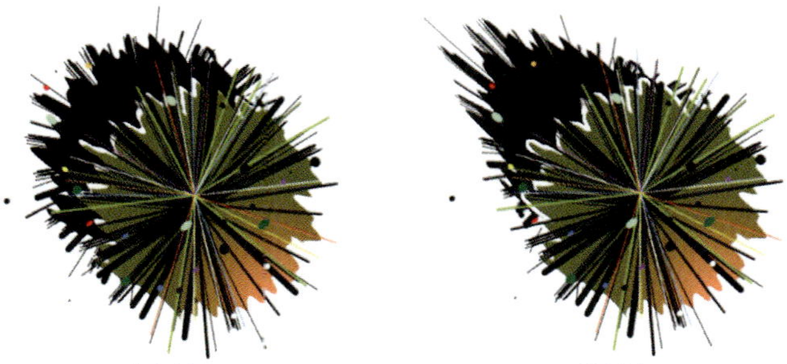

(a) No (b) Yes

Figure 8-5. Be sure your shadow matches the form of your trees. Pyramidal trees have pointed shadows, as in (b).

Shadows inform your audience about the height, form, and orientation of elements within your drawing. Shadows help differentiate unique elements that may appear similar in plan view. Shadows should be drawn carefully and correctly to ensure the audience is not accidentally misled.

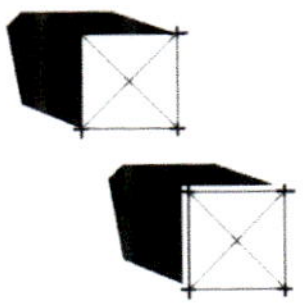

Shadow Gap

Shadows are boldest when drawn in black. Unfortunately, using black sometimes obscures other meaningful elements of your drawing, especially edges and lines. It can make edges and corners seem dull and passive. Black shadows can begin to dominate, rather than accentuate, a drawing.

To overcome this, you can either select another color for your shadow, or add a gap between your object and its shadow. The fastest way to change a shadow's color is to merely change its opacity, as shown in Figure 8-6(b). Now you can see the line work clearly, though you have only changed the properties of the shadow. Alternatively, you can change the color of the shadow altogether. Purple and dark blue are especially useful colors for shadows. They are dark enough, and vivid enough, to accentuate your drawing without competing with your rich, black line work. The most dynamic of solutions, however, is to add a gap between your object and its shadow, as in Figure 8-6(c). Whether you draw a white line over your shadow, or erase part of the shadow, is a matter of preference.

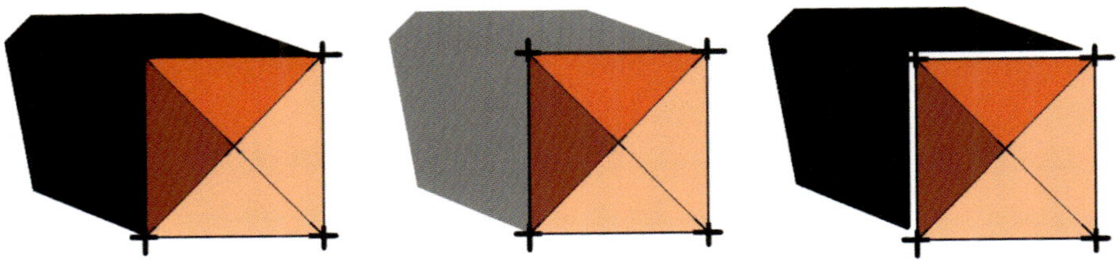

(a) No (b) Yes (c) Yes

Figure 8-6. (a) The shadow obscures the edges of the building. (b) By using a lighter shadow, the edges of the building are more evident. (c) A gap between the building and the shadow allows the building edges to be visible.

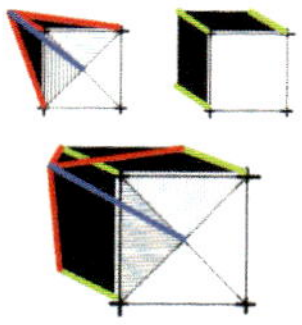

Know Your Forms

Drawing shadows can be intimidating, at first. Though few people struggle drawing simple shadows of basic forms (like cubes, spheres, or pyramids), many find it frustrating to draw more complex and challenging shapes. Fortunately, complex objects are merely aggregates of smaller, simpler forms. If you can master drawing shadows for the more common, elementary shapes, then you will be able to construct more complex shadows by accumulating these simpler shadows.

For example, consider the building in Figure 8-7. This simple building form may be constructed by stacking a pyramid on top of a cube.

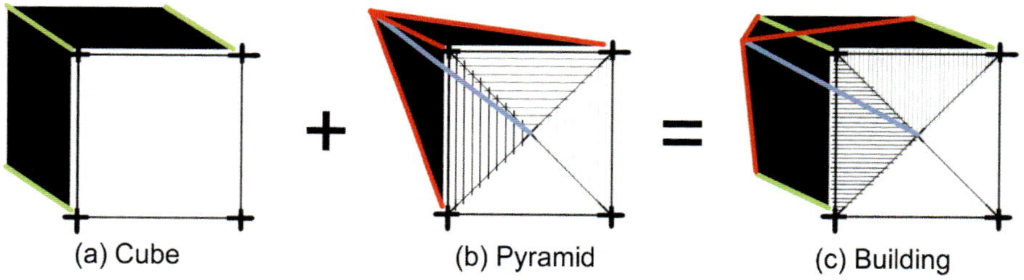

Figure 8-7. The shadow of a simple building can be assembled from the shadow of a cube and a pyramid.

Notice that you do not merely stack the pyramid's shadow on top of the cube's shadow. Instead, the ends of the red line segments (from the pyramid's shadow) will shift to reach the ends of the green line segments (from the cube's shadow). The distinction is subtle; but, it is important.

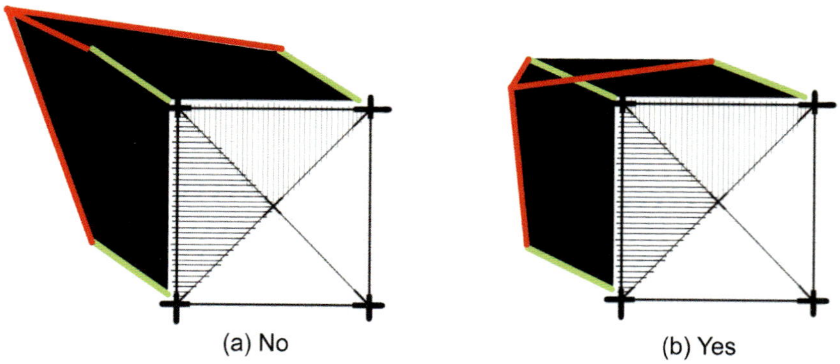

Figure 8-8. Though you may create a building form by stacking a pyramid on top of a cube, you may not create its shadow by stacking a pyramid's shadow on top of a cube's shadow.

It is common to reuse similar forms in many drawings. It may be helpful to create a simple reference sheet with commonly used shapes and their corresponding shadows, as in Figure 8-9.

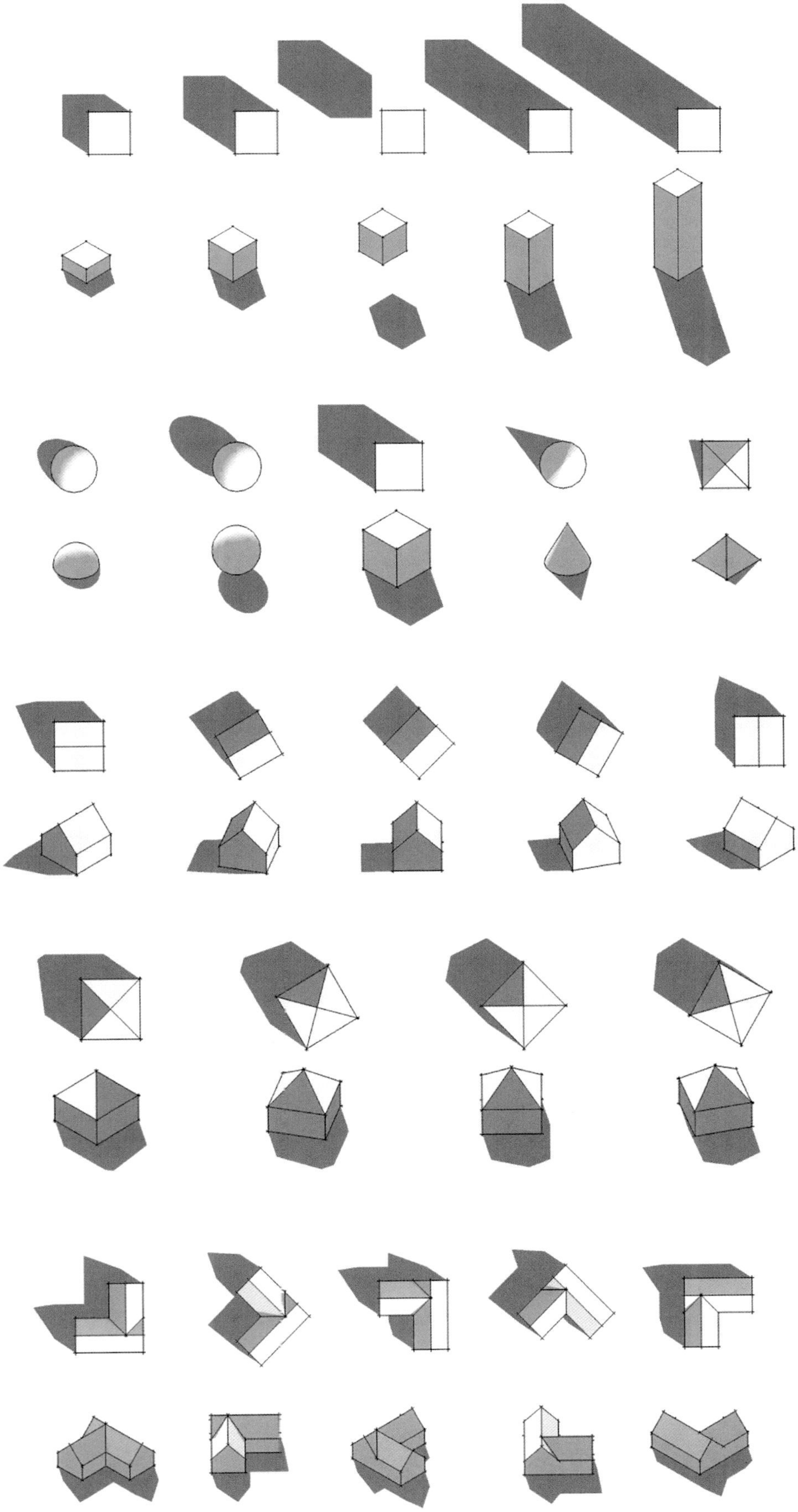

Figure 8-9. Examples of basic forms and their corresponding shadows, in alternating rows of plan view and isometric view.

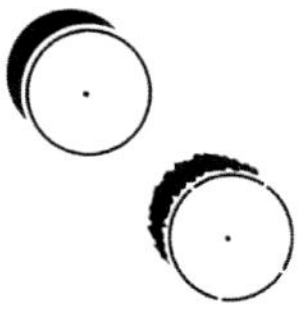

Dead or Alive

Living elements should seem active and dynamic. Conversely, inanimate elements should seem static and fixed. Their shadows should express this, too.

For example, trees are living organisms. Trees grow. Their leaves rustle in the wind. Though their movement is subtle and limited, trees are dynamic nonetheless. Shadows of trees should communicate this activity. Therefore, a sharp, precise shadow edge, as in Figure 8-10(a), would be inappropriate for a tree. Instead, a tree's shadow should be somewhat irregular and loose, as in Figure 8-10(b).

Similarly, a building's architecture is precise, so its shadow should be just as sharp. An irregular shadow might suggest the building is moving—and this certainly would not be a desirable characteristic for a building.

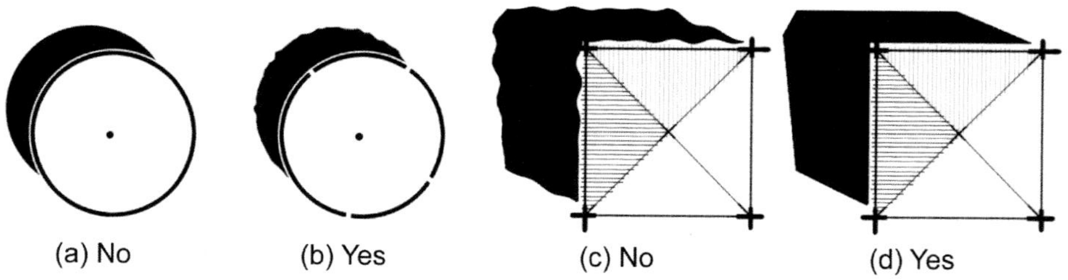

Figure 8-10. (a) This shadow may be appropriate for a table, but not for a tree. (b) The irregular edge of this shadow is more appropriate for a tree. (c,d) Buildings are static and rigid; therefore, their shadows should be similarly sharp and concise.

An exception to this rule may be when you are drawing highly conceptual drawings, where your line work is deliberately sketchy and loose. Conceptual drawings are inherently dynamic anyway. Design choices are intended to be flexible at this point, so shadows can be just as informal whether depicting inanimate elements or not, as in Figure 8-11.

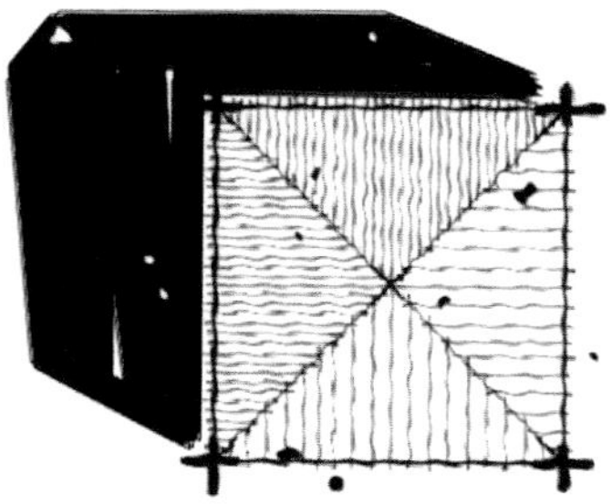

Figure 8-11. Informal sketches may have more irregular shadows.

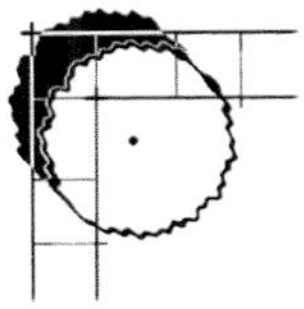

X-Ray Vision

Occasionally, shadows can hide important information within your drawing. Consider the two drawings in Figure 8-12. Much of the landscaping within the drawing on the left is hidden—and an entrance to the building is obscured entirely! Obviously, this is undesirable.

A useful workaround is to provide your audience with "X-ray vision." In a black-and-white rendering, that would mean inverting the part of the drawing that appears within the shadows, as in Figure 8-12(b).

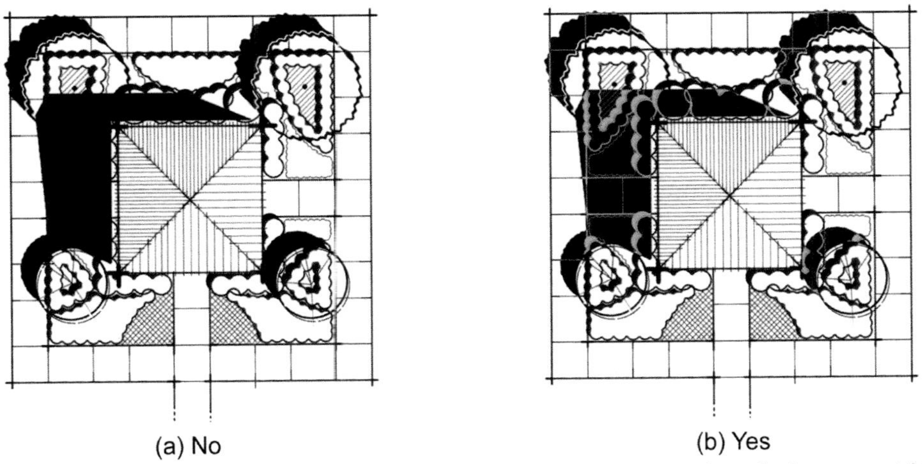

Figure 8-12. (a) Information is lost when the shadow obscures part of the drawing. (b) Information is restored by inverting the part of the drawing within the shadow.

An astute observer will notice that the shrubs still have shadows, though they are within the building's shadow. You might ask, "How can a shadow be cast within a shadow?" Well, the short answer is that it can not! Nonetheless, I have discovered that many people will overlook this defect—and often they prefer it. Perhaps this is because the scale of the shrubs will diminish without the false shadows anchoring themselves to the legitimate shadows. Whatever the reason, it is merely a preference and you may certainly choose to omit the phony shadows.

Providing X-ray vision for a color rendering is far easier. Simply change the opacity of your shadow to allow the drawing underneath to show through, as in Figure 8-13(b). While this may mean that you have some shadows that are lighter or darker than others, this inconsistency is justified by the information revealed.

Figure 8-13. (a) Though you can see the detail in the shadow by inverting the design, the absence of color is distracting. (b) For a more harmonious drawing, change the opacity of the shadow to allow the color to show through.

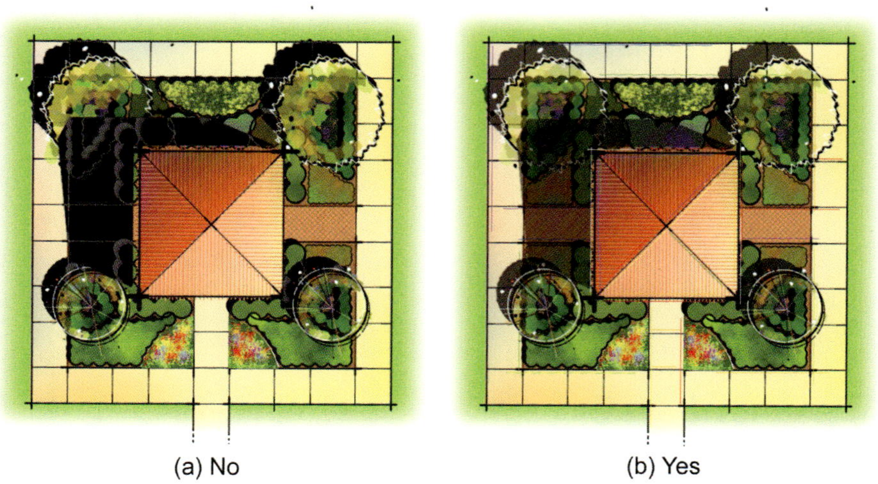

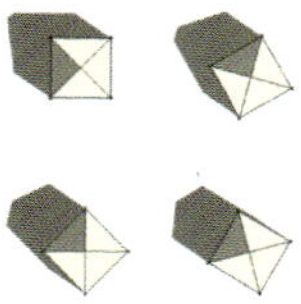

Be Consistent

When drawing shadows, be certain that all elements within your drawing share the same sources of light. In particular, if your drawing depicts an outdoor scene during daylight, be certain that all shadows represent the same source (the sun) at the same time of day. Be consistent.

Taller buildings should cast longer shadows than shorter buildings. Trees should have broader shadows than shrubs. Buildings and trees should cast shadows in the same direction. While all of these edicts are obvious, they are frequently overlooked. This is especially true when you are reusing elements from one drawing and dropping them into another.

As much as possible, draw using the same solar orientation, during the same time of year, at the same time of day. This will allow you to reuse elements of your drawings, later, without worrying whether they will match your new drawing.

Figure 8-14. Because all of the drawings are depicted with similar light conditions, it creates a more harmonious and accurate drawing.

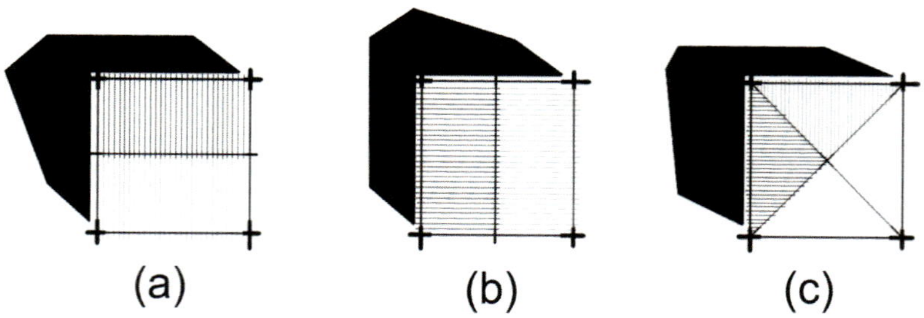

9 SHADING

Just as shadows are a useful technique for giving your drawing a three-dimensional feel, shading also gives a drawing a special depth and vitality. Shading is a complementary technique to shadowing, and neither technique is as effective without the other.

Just as with drawing shadows, you must be aware of the source and direction of light. If you are outdoors during the day, your source of light is obviously the sun. When indoors, you will have to recognize where your light sources are and consider how that light may reflect off those surfaces. Regardless of whether you are indoors or outdoors, however, all of the following techniques can be used to shade surfaces within your drawing.

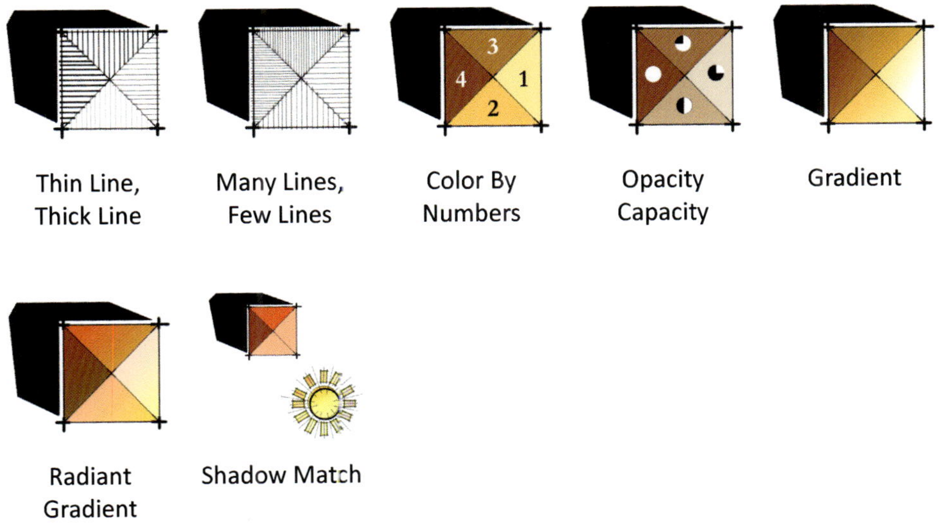

Figure 9-0. Techniques for shading drawings.

Of course, you can still use stippling, hatching, crosshatching, and scribbling as effective ways to shade surfaces within your drawing. You only need to select the appropriate paintbrush and draw. The techniques above, however, especially lend themselves to computer graphics and they will allow you to shade surfaces more quickly and efficiently.

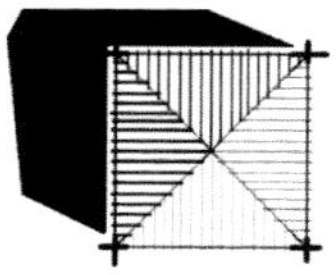

Thin Line, Thick Line

A simple and elegant way to provide shading is to vary line weights. The darker you intend an item to be, the thicker and bolder you draw your lines. Conversely, the lightest areas should be drawn with thinner lines. Notice how, in Figure 9-1, portions of the building roof seem richer and darker where the line weight is boldest. This is accomplished despite the fact that the all lines are drawn the same distance apart from one another.

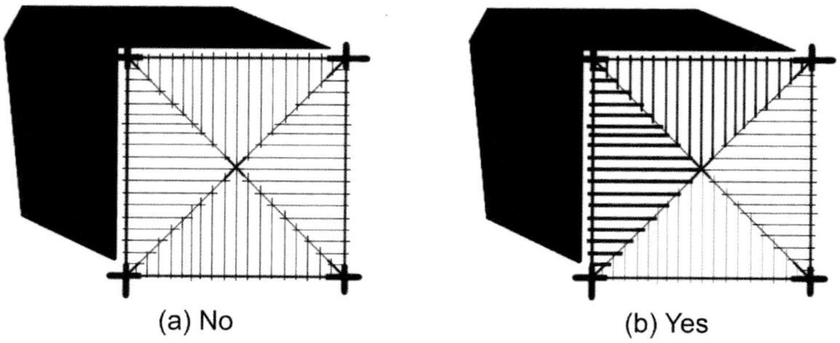

Figure 9-1. (a) Without shading, the surface of the roof seems flat and ambiguous. (b) By varying line weights, the roof takes on a 3-dimensional appearance.

This is a useful technique when you need to draw objects before you are certain where the sun will be. You may simply draw the pattern for the roof as in Figure 9-1(a). Once you learn where the shadows and shading should be drawn, you can simply draw over the corresponding lines with a bolder brush or pen, as in Figure 9-1(b).

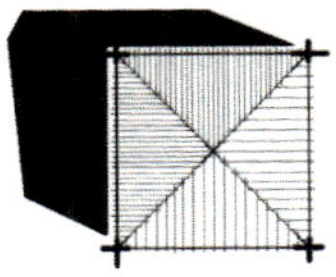

Many Lines, Few Lines

Another simple way to shade objects is to vary the number of lines you use when shading. The farther apart lines are, the lighter that area will appear. Notice how the building roof in Figure 9-2(b) seems more 3-dimensional than the roof with uniform line spacing.

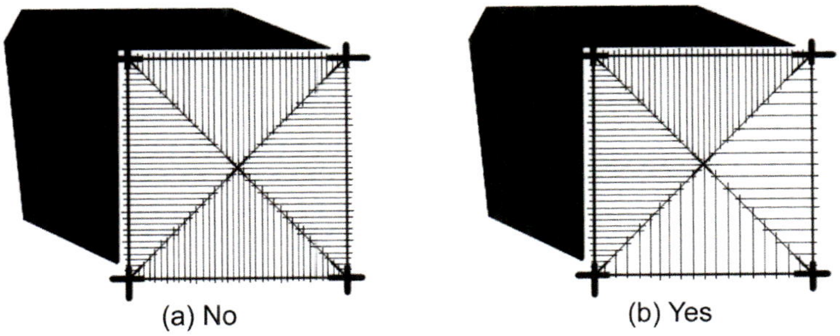

Figure 9-2. (a) This building roof is uniform and ambiguous. (b) By varying the spacing between lines, this building roof pops up.

This is also a useful technique when you are uncertain whether the orientation of the building or the sun's angle will change. To space the lines farther apart, you merely need to draw the lines as in Figure 9-2(a) and then erase as required.

Notice, however, that this technique must be adapted when you use lighter lines on a darker background. Darker backgrounds require lighter and more abundant lines to make their surface seem bright. This is entirely the opposite of using dark lines on a light background, as demonstrated in Figure 9-3.

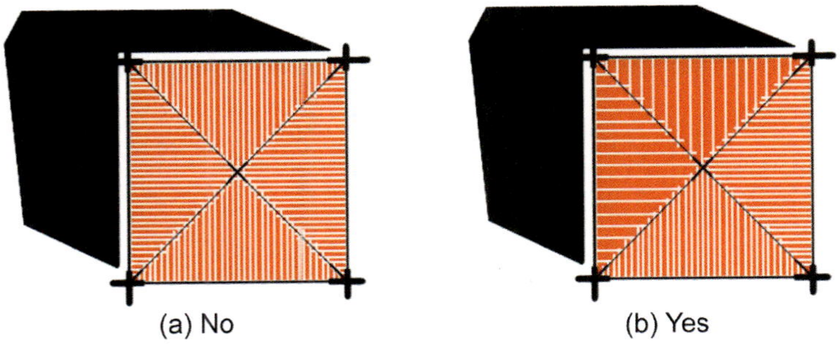

Figure 9-3. Lighter lines on a dark background have the opposite effect of darker lines on a light background.

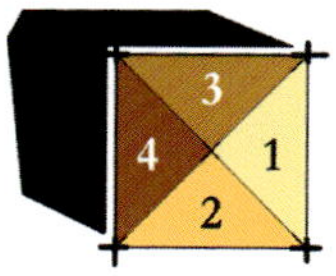

Color By Numbers

This technique utilizes the concept of a color palette, introduced earlier in the book. Basically, you shade your building just as you did with your first coloring books as a child. Simply choose colors from your palette as illustrated in Figure 9-4.

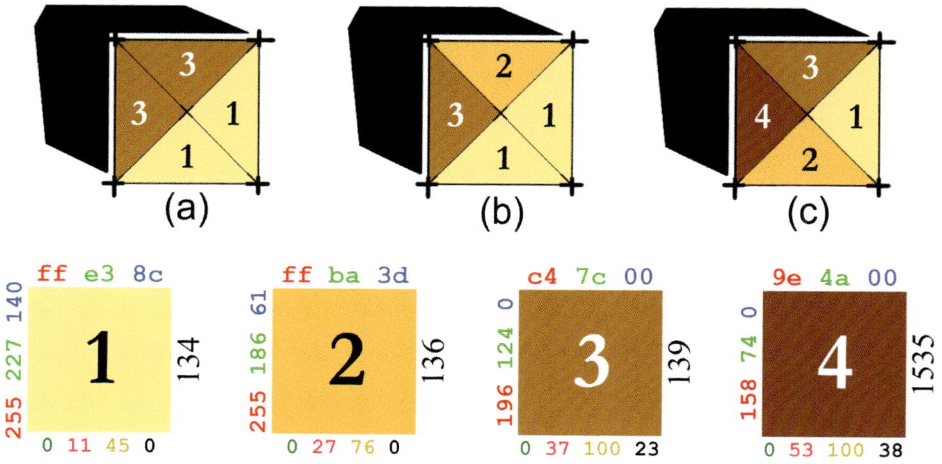

Figure 9-4. (a) Good shading. (b) Better shading. (c) Best shading.

In the above example, I have selected four shades of brown from the corresponding row in my color palette. Of course, you could choose from any row in the palette and get comparable shading, as in Figure 9-5.

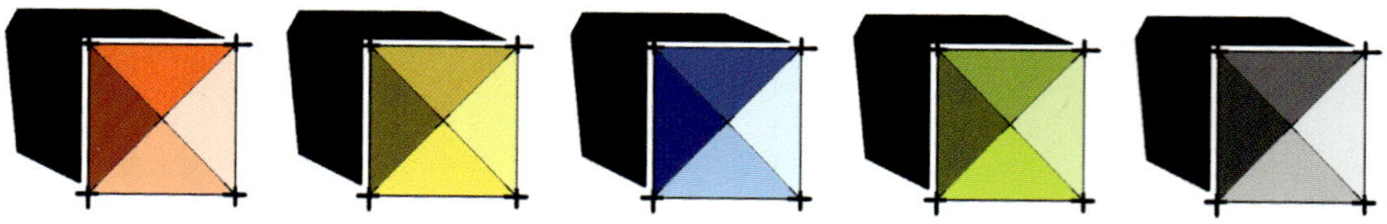

Figure 9-5. This technique can be applied using any set of colors.

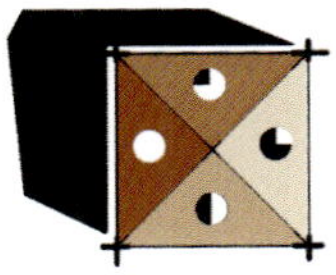

Opacity Capacity

As an alternative to the previous technique, you can change the opacity of one color rather than using two to four distinct colors. Notice in Figure 9-6 that all the buildings use the same base color, a dark brown. You are simply changing the opacity of the base color. The advantage of this technique is that you can alter your shading later without repainting, flipping, or rotating previously colored layers.

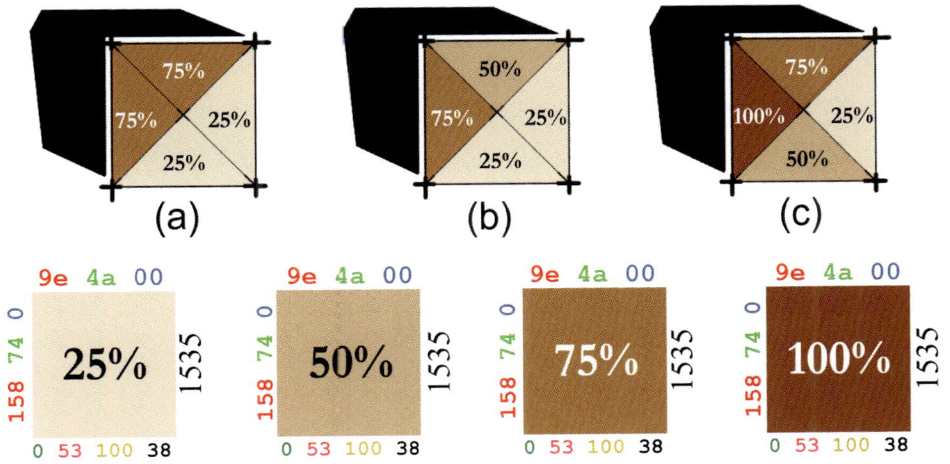

Figure 9-6. (a) Good shading. (b) Better shading. (c) Best shading.

This technique has two distinct disadvantages, however. First, as you reduce opacity, colors often become less vivid and warm. Colors begin to look dull and flat. Second, as your layer becomes more transparent, objects under your drawing begin to show through. This can be very frustrating if you're pasting your drawing on top of another background. In this case, you will either have to erase under your transparent layers, or you will need to paint white over the layers peeking through.

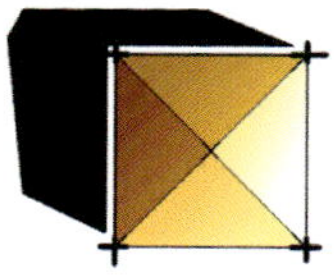

Gradient

The most attractive shading is accomplished when you use gradients to create subtle transitions from darker to lighter colors. This is effectively the "Color by Numbers" technique; but, you are using a gradient fill rather than a solid fill. Consider the shaded buildings in Figure 9-7.

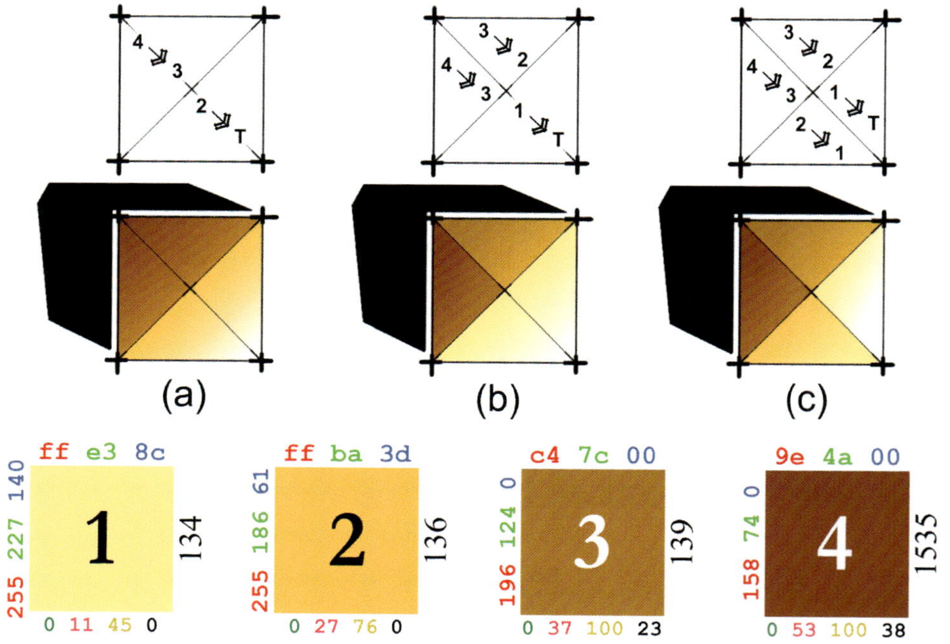

Figure 9-7. (a) Good gradient shading. The 'T' is for the "transparent" color; but, you could use white too. (b) Better gradient shading. (c) Best gradient shading.

Because each of these buildings uses transparency in one of their gradients, the base color simply fades as it reaches the edge, and the white background shows through. Alternatively, you could transition to white and create a similar effect. This might be more suitable if there are undesirable elements on the background that you do not want to show through the roof.

On edges where the gradients meet, the colors should be unique. If the colors are identical, then the edge will disappear. Also, be sure that your gradients go from dark to light in the same direction on every face. A common mistake is to draw light-to-dark then dark-to-light on adjacent faces—thus diminishing the edge and making your drawing look awkward. Figure 9-8 illustrates this error.

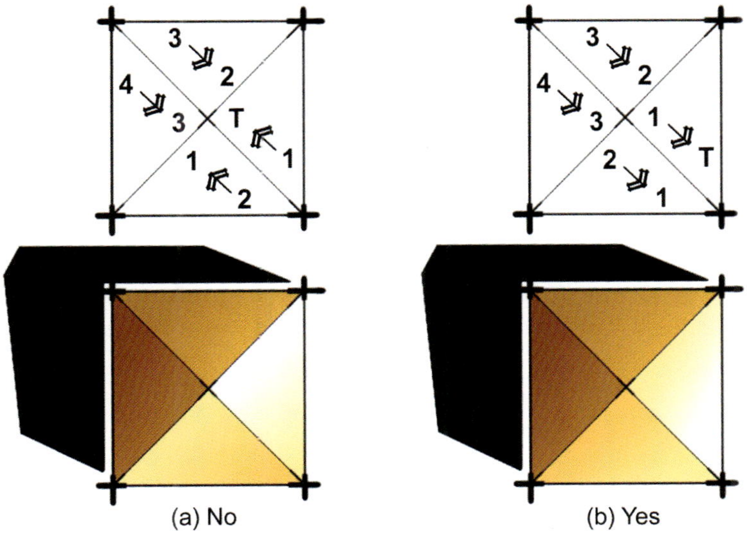

Figure 9-8. (a) Gradients are drawn incorrectly in conflicting directions. (b) All gradients are drawn correctly in the same direction.

When using gradients to shade round surfaces, like trees, you may want your shading to radiate from a darkest point rather than graduating in a linear fashion. Consider, for example, how the shading in Figure 9-9(c) is more suggestive of a spherical form than in (b).

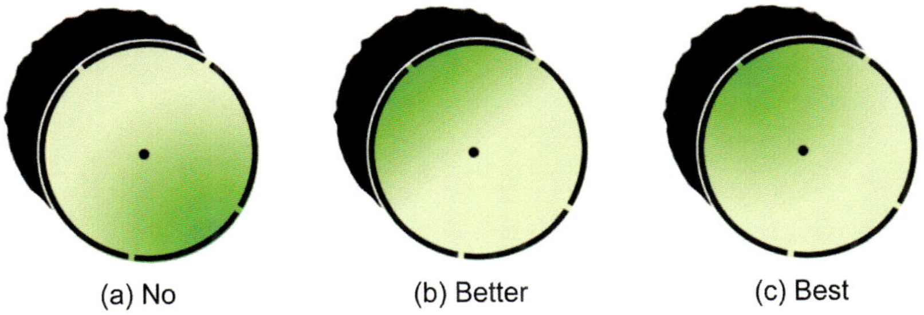

Figure 9-9. (a) Shading does not match shadow. (b) Shading with linear gradient. (c) Shading with radial gradient.

Many graphics applications will allow you to choose a radial rather than a linear gradient; but, the same effect can be accomplished by merely painting with a large, soft brush.

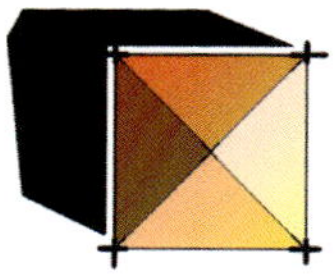

Radiant Gradient

This technique is a derivation of the previous one. Instead of graduating the colors from darker to lighter shades of the same color, though, the gradient adjusts from comparable shades of two unique colors. Consider the illustration in Figure 9-10 where the gradients move from shades of red to shades of yellow.

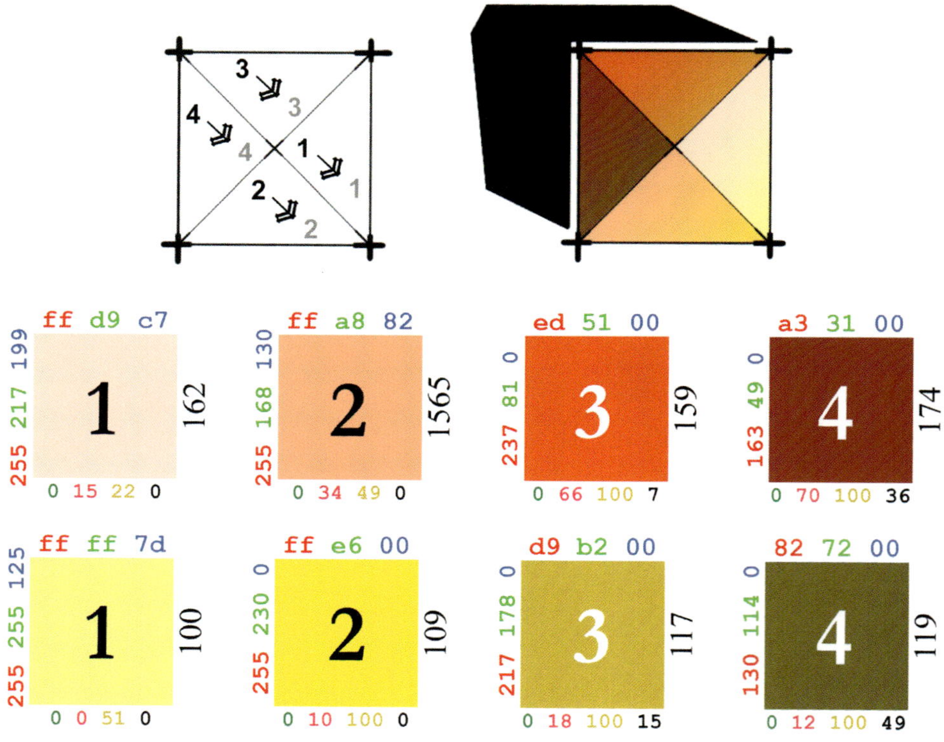

Figure 9-10. This gradient shading evolves from shades of red to shades of yellow.

Figure 9-11 shows more examples of this technique.

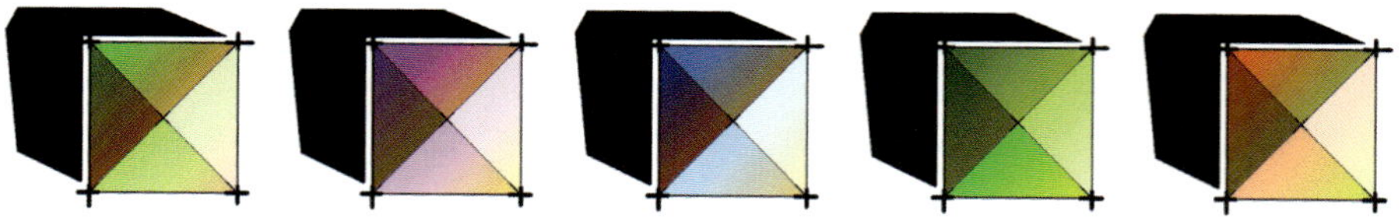

Figure 9-11. (Left to right) Green to red, purple to yellow, blue to orange, green to olive, and red to olive.

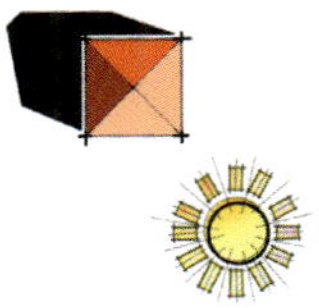

Shadow Match

An important technique is to ensure that your shading and shadows agree. Consider the trees in Figure 9-12. The darkest part of the tree should be adjacent to the shadow, as in (b) and (c). Additionally, the accent marks should be most prominent in the darker sections, as in (c).

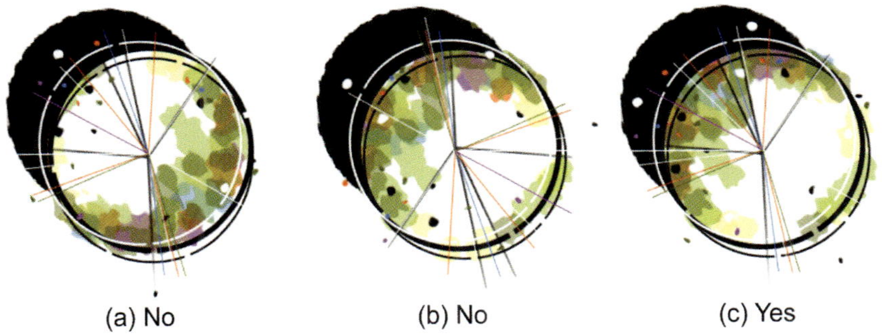

Figure 9-12. (a) It is unrealistic for the lightest part of a tree to be adjacent to a shadow. (b) The shading is appropriate; but, the accent is contradicting. (c) The shading and shadow correlate, and the accents are consistent with the shading.

If the shading does not correlate with the shadows, you will either confuse or mislead your audience. Consider the buildings in Figure 9-13. The shadow and shading are consistent in (a), but the shading contradicts the shadow in (b). Your audience may erroneously presume that this roof is identical to the roof in (c), which pitches downward to the center. Notice that the shadow in (c) mimics a cube, therefore the shadow and the shading are consistent for this peculiar, inverted roof.

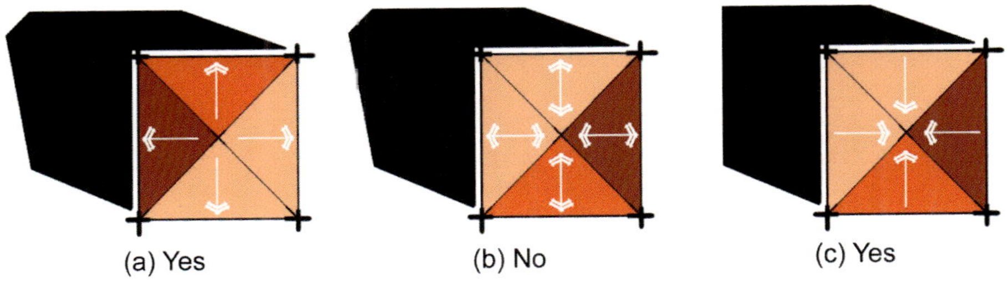

Figure 9-13. (a) Shading and shadow match. (b) Shading contradicts shadow. (c) Shading and shadow match—the roof is inverted!

10 STEP-BY-STEP

In the previous chapters, a number of principles, strategies, and techniques were introduced to help you draw well on the computer. In this chapter, you will see step-by-step examples that utilize these skills to draw specific examples.

First, examples of symbols for functional diagrams are introduced. These examples will acquaint you with some very basic drawing skills. Afterwards, examples of master plan graphics are illustrated. These master plan graphics build upon the fundamental drawing skills introduced with the functional diagram graphics; but, they also demonstrate more sophisticated techniques specific to Adobe Photoshop—including filters and tools for scaling and distorting your drawings.

The examples are not intended to be comprehensive. They are, however, a good sampling of drawings that touch upon all of the techniques discussed previously in the book. If you complete all of the examples, you will almost certainly acquire the confidence and expertise to draw well on the computer.

Most examples should be able to stand alone. That is, you should be able to skip around. You do not need to complete them sequentially. Hopefully, you will be able to find an example that you can use immediately in your own drawings.

Do not presume that each example is the optimal way to draw that symbol. Often, I will use alternative ways to accomplish the same goal in the hopes that you may discover a new way to draw well. Do not be surprised if you can draw the same symbols more quickly or efficiently another way. Do, however, be open to exploring new ways to draw. Though it may not be the most effective way to draw that specific symbol, that same technique may have very practical applications to something else you may want to draw.

All of the drawings were done within Adobe Photoshop. Almost all of the drawings were done on a canvas with 200 or 300 pixels per inch (ppi). Recall that the resolution affects the choices you make regarding your line hierarchy. If you intend to draw using a different resolution, then you should consider changing some of the values used in the drawings proportionally to your new resolution. For example, if you prefer to draw at a resolution of 100 ppi instead of 200 ppi, then you may want to halve the paintbrush diameters. Also, some filters within Photoshop require you to draw in RGB mode. Recognize that if you choose to draw in another mode (e.g., CMYK, indexed), then you may not be able to accomplish all the tasks in the following examples.

I hope you find the following examples helpful.

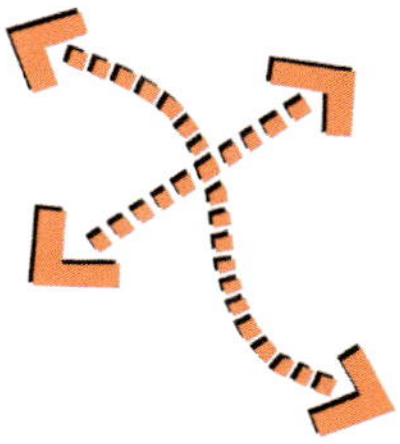

Functional Diagrams | Circulation – Quick

This example illustrates how to quickly draw circulation patterns for a functional diagram. The techniques used in this example include the following:

Straighten Up | Erase | Merge | Label Contrast | Color Palette

This drawing was originally drawn on a canvas with a resolution of 300 pixels per inch. Afterwards, it was scaled down to fit within these pages.

Step 1: Draw the general path of the circulation.

- Draw lines along the path of the circulation.
  - Create a new layer and name it *Circulation Path*.
  - Choose a paintbrush for the Brush Tool and draw the arrow line.
    - `Master Diameter = 30 px`
    - `Hardness = 100%`

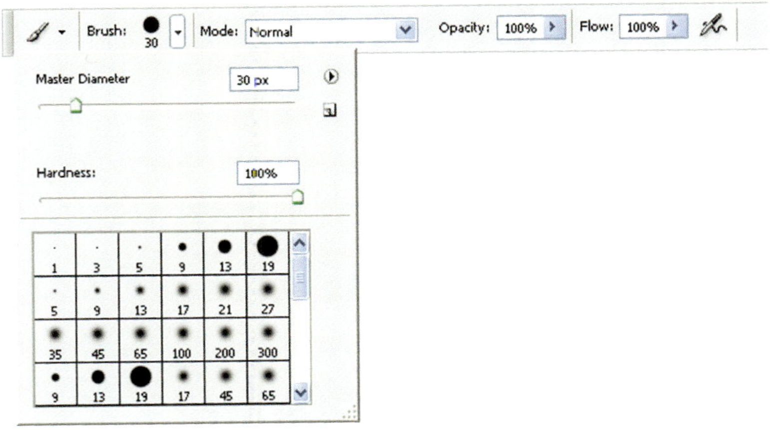

- Draw the arrowheads.
  - Create a new layer and name it *Arrowheads*.
  - Choose a paintbrush for the Brush Tool and draw the arrow line.
    - `Master Diameter = 50 px`
    - `Hardness = 100%`

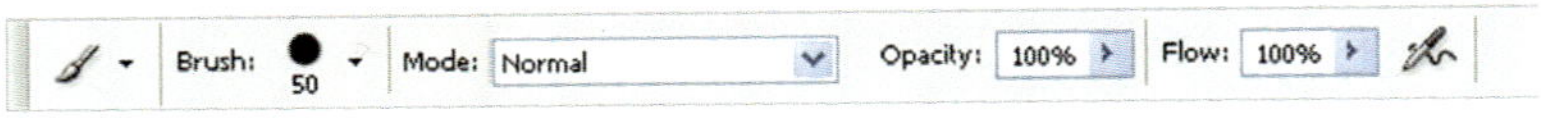

Step 1: Draw the general path of the circulation.

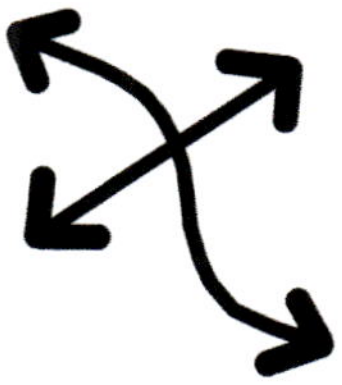

Step 2: Sharpen the arrowheads.

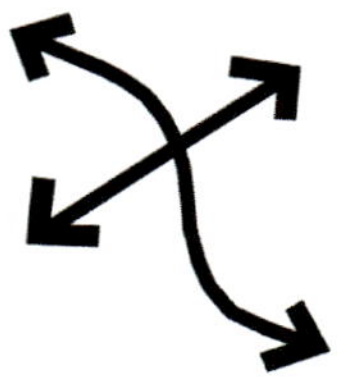

Step 2: Sharpen the arrowheads.

You can sharpen the arrowheads by erasing from your previous brush strokes. By holding down the [Shift] key between mouse clicks, you can create straight strokes.

- Sharpen the arrowheads by erasing the edges from your previous brush strokes.
  - Click on the layer ***Arrowheads*** to choose it.
  - Choose a brush for the Eraser Tool and erase the edges of the arrowheads.
    - `Master Diameter = 30 px`
    - `Hardness = 100%`

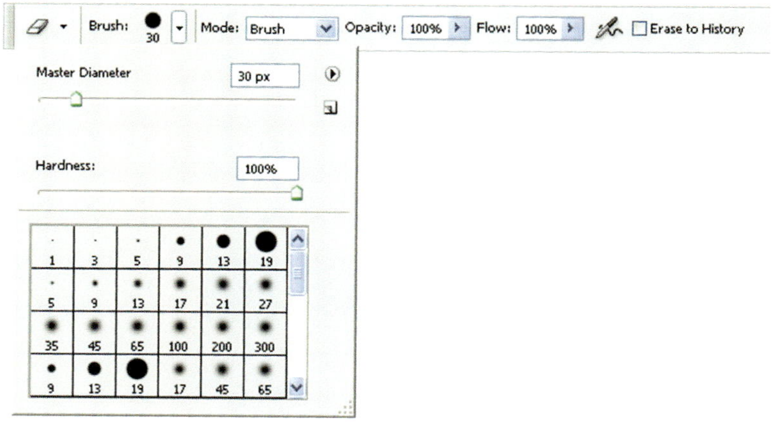

Step 3: Refine the circulation.

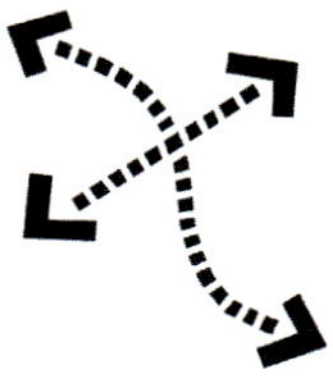

Step 3: Refine the circulation.

In this step, you are going to erase from the circulation path to create a dashed line.

- Erase from the circulation path.
  - Click on the layer ***Circulation Path*** to choose it.
  - Choose a brush for the Eraser Tool and erase along the path line work.
    - `Master Diameter = 15 px`
    - `Hardness = 100%`
      - This eraser brush size is half the diameter of the brush you used to draw the line originally.

Step 4: Add color and depth.

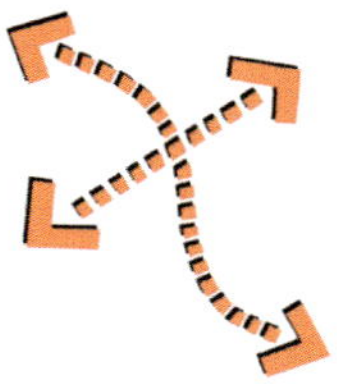

Step 4: Add color and depth.

In this step, you will merge the refined line work, copy it, change its color, and use the original line work as a de facto shadow.

- Merge the refined line work.
  - Click on the layer ***Circulation Path*** to choose it.
  - While holding down the [Ctrl] key, click on the layer ***Arrowheads*** to choose it too.
  - Click on the right mouse button and select "Merge Layers" from the pop-up dialog box.
  - Rename the merged layer ***Circulation***.

- Copy the merged layer.
  - Click on the layer *Circulation* to choose it.
  - You can copy the selected layer by either:
    - Clicking the right mouse button, selecting "Duplicate Layer..." from the pop-up menu, and then clicking [OK] on the Duplicate Layer dialog box.
    - Or, you can simply drag the layer to the "Create a new layer" icon.
- With the Move Tool, shift the layer you just copied.
- Change the color of the duplicated layer.
  - Click on the layer *Circulation copy* to choose it.
  - **Select > All**
  - With the Move Tool, hit the [up arrow] on your keyboard, then hit the [down arrow].
  - Change the foreground color to brick red (`#FF8257`).
  - **Edit > Fill**
  - Click the [OK] button.

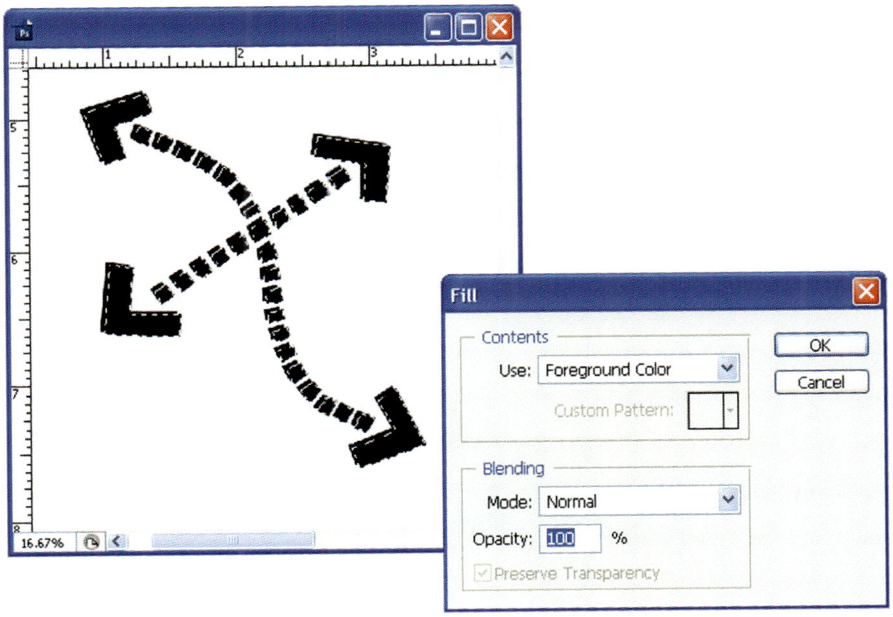

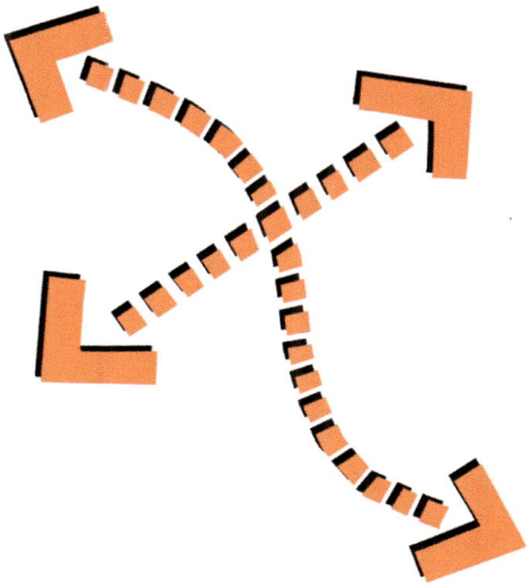

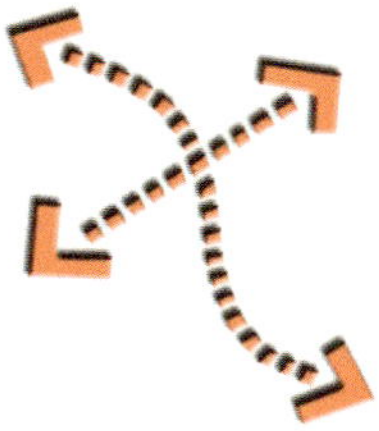

Functional Diagrams | Circulation – Fast

This example illustrates an alternative to quickly draw circulation patterns for a functional diagram. The techniques used in this example include the following:

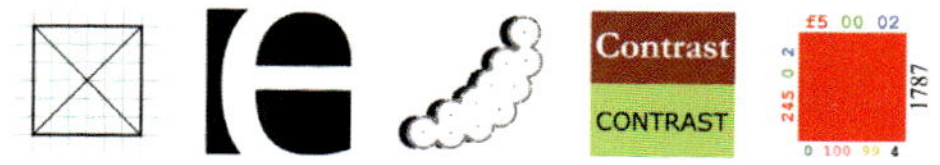

Straighten Up | Erase | Merge | Label Contrast | Color Palette

This drawing was originally drawn on a canvas with a resolution of 300 pixels per inch. Afterwards, it was scaled down to fit within these pages.

Step 1: Draw the general form of the circulation, as before.

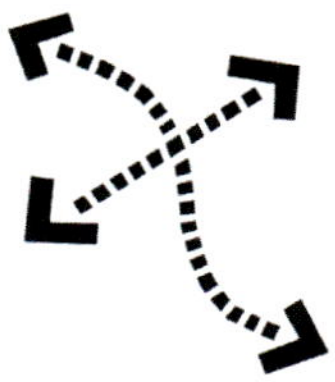

Step 1: Draw the general form of the circulation, as before.

Repeat Steps 1 to 3 from the previous example, Circulation – Quick.

Step 2: Change the color.

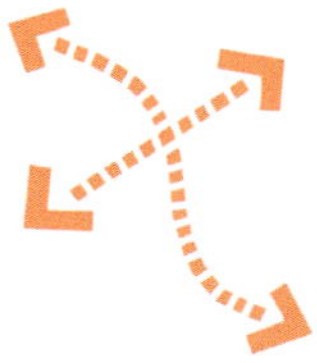

Step 2: Change the color.

- Change the color of the symbol.
  - Click on the layer *Circulation* to choose it.
  - **Select > All**
  - With the Move Tool, hit the [up arrow] on your keyboard, then hit the [down arrow].
  - Change the foreground color to brick red (`#FF8257`).
  - **Edit > Fill**
  - Click the [OK] button.

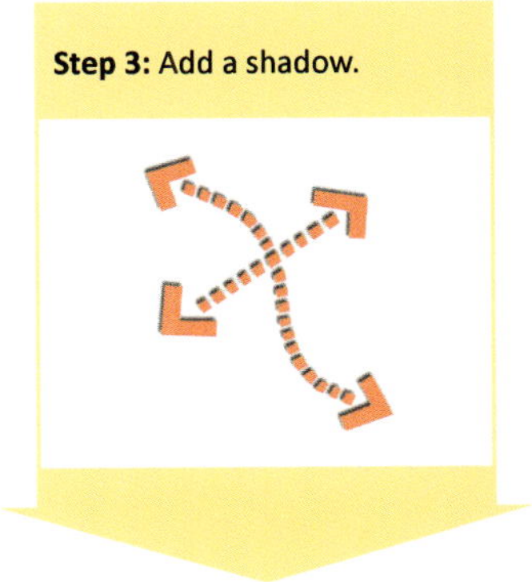

Step 3: Add a shadow.

Photoshop provides a number of filters that you can apply to your drawings. In the next two steps, we will use filters to add a shadow and emboss the edges of the circulation symbol.

- Add a shadow to the symbol.
  - Right-click on the layer *Circulation* and select "Blending Options..." from the pop-up menu.

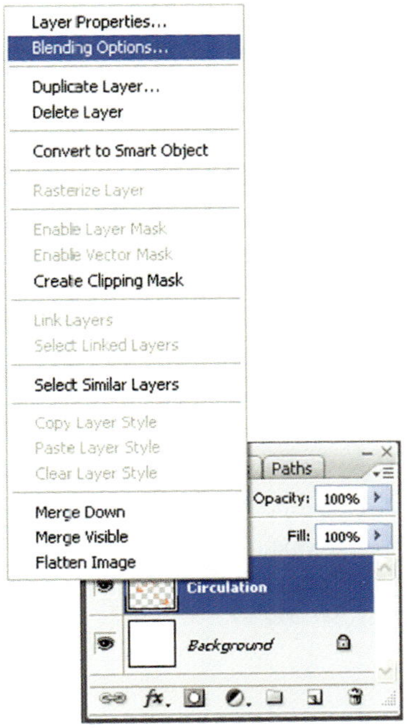

- Click on the "Drop Shadow" tab on the Layer Style dialog box.
  - Drop Shadow Structure:
    - `Blend Mode = Multiply`
    - `Opacity = 75%`
    - `Angle = -60`
    - `Use Global Light = checked`
    - `Distance = 5 px`
    - `Spread = 0%`
    - `Size = 5 px`
- Click the [OK] button.

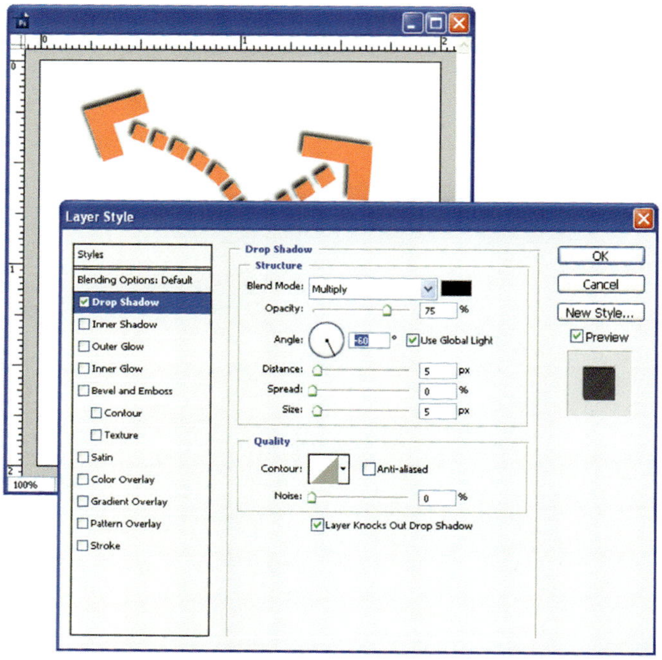

- Emboss the edges of the circulation symbol.
    - Right-click the layer ***Circulation*** and select "Blending Options..." from the pop-up menu.
    - Click on the "Bevel & Emboss" tab on the Layer Style dialog box.
        - Bevel and Emboss Structure: `Size = 5 px`
        - Bevel and Emboss Shading: `Angle = -60`
    - Click the [OK] button.

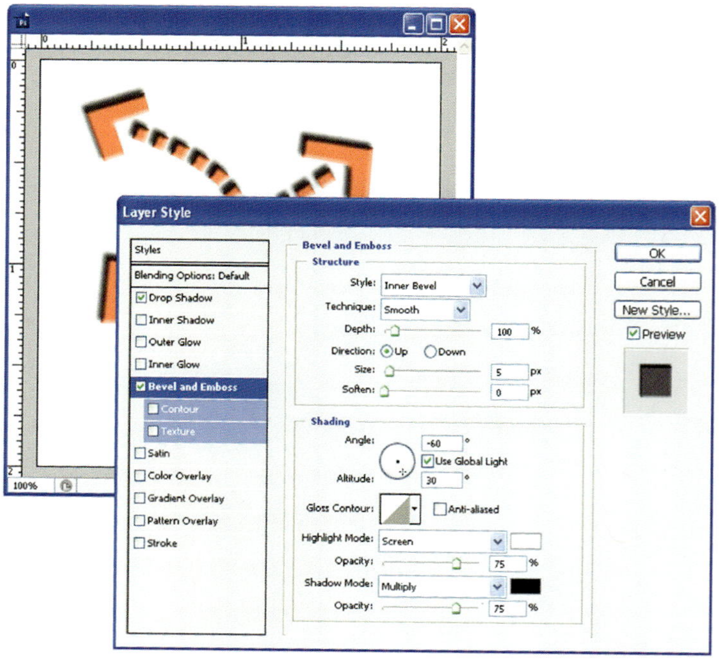

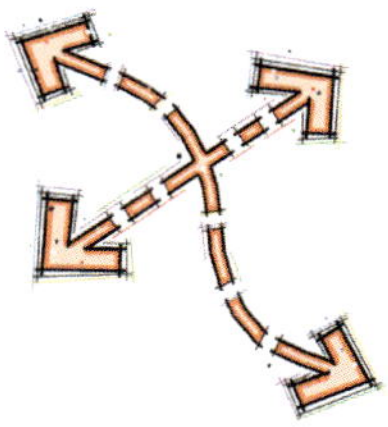

Functional Diagrams | Circulation

This example illustrates a more complete alternative to drawing circulation patterns for a functional diagram. The techniques used in this example include the following:

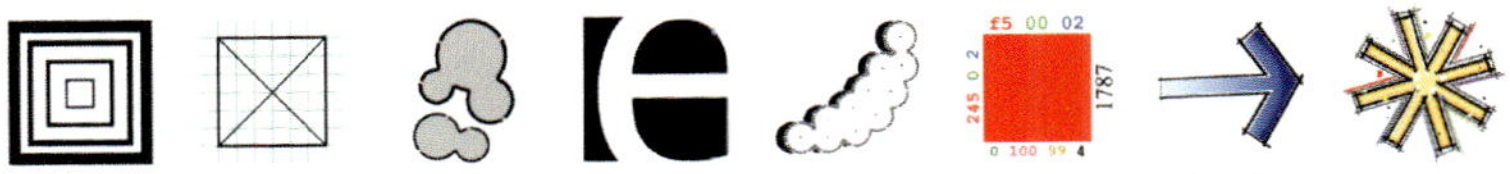

Line Hierarchy | Straighten Up | Best Stroke | Erase | Merge | Color Palette | Light Then Dark | Accent

This drawing was originally drawn on a canvas with a resolution of 300 pixels per inch. Afterwards, it was scaled down to fit within these pages.

Step 1: Draw the general form of the circulation, as before.

Repeat Steps 1 and 2 from the previous example, Circulation – Quick.

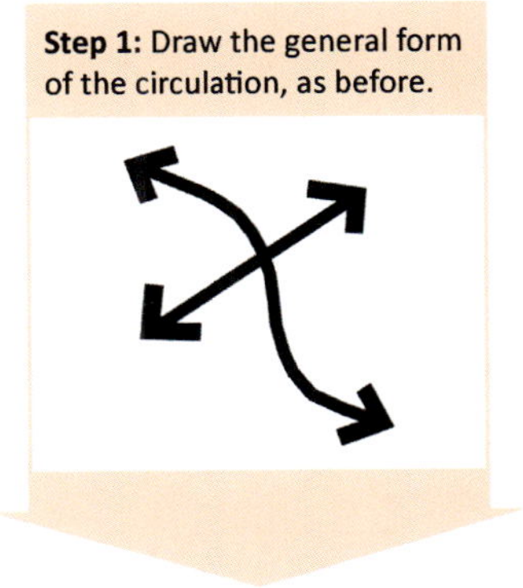

Step 2: Add an outline.

- Merge the circulation path and arrowheads into one layer.
  - Click on the layer *Circulation Path* to choose it.
  - While holding down the [Ctrl] key, click on the layer *Arrowheads* to choose it too.
  - Click on the right mouse button and select "Merge Layers" from the pop-up dialog box.
  - Rename the merged layer *Circulation*.

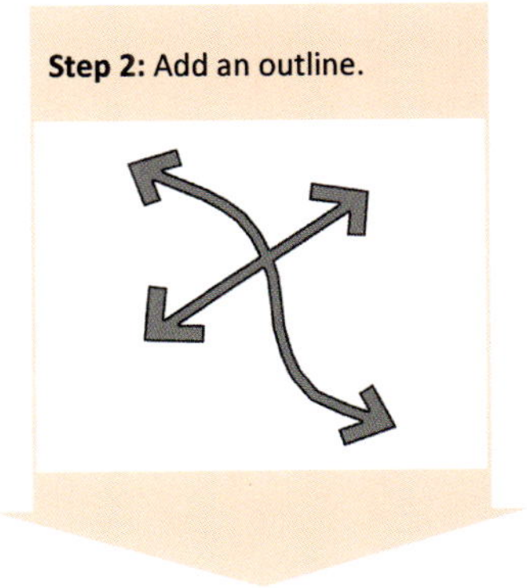

- Draw an outline around the merged layers.
  - Click on the layer ***Circulation*** to choose it.
  - Change the layer `Opacity = 50%`.
  - **Select > All**
  - With the Move Tool, hit the [up arrow] on the keyboard, then hit the [down arrow].
  - Change the foreground color to black (`#000000`).
  - Create a new layer and name it ***Stroke***.
  - **Edit > Stroke**
    - `Width = 5 px`
  - Click the [OK] button.

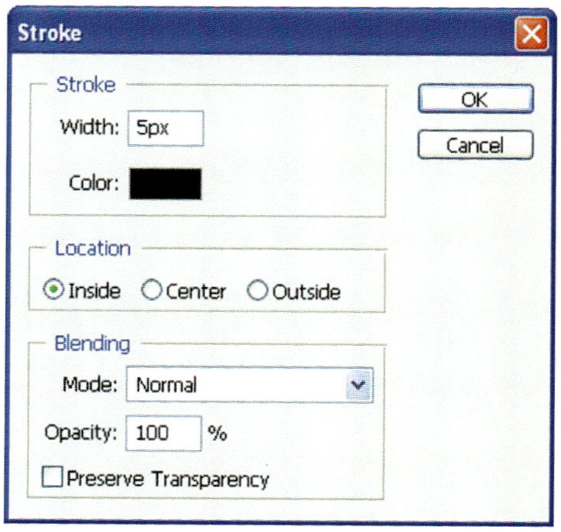

Step 3: Erase the outline from the arrowheads.

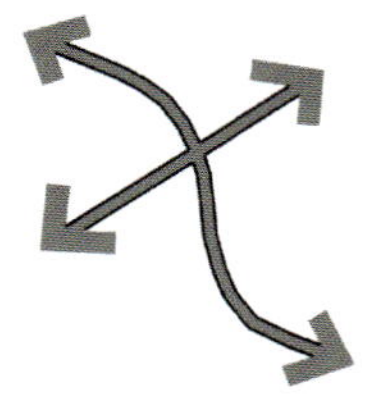

Step 3: Erase the outline from the arrowheads.

- Erase the outline from the arrowheads.
  - Click on the layer ***Stroke*** to choose it.
  - Choose a brush for the Eraser Tool and erase the new stroke from the arrowheads.
    - `Master Diameter = 20 px`
    - `Hardness = 100%`

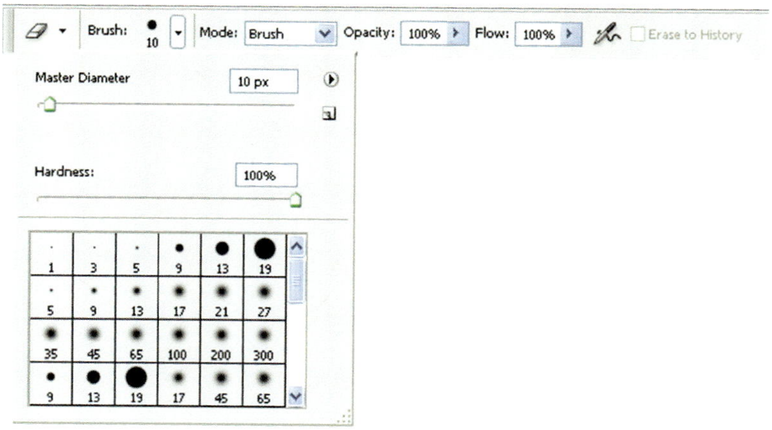

Step 4: Draw an outline for the arrowheads.

- Draw outlines for the arrowheads.
  - Create a new layer and name it *Arrowhead Outlines*.
  - Choose a paintbrush for the Brush Tool and draw outlines over the arrowheads.
    - `Master Diameter = 5 px`
    - `Hardness = 100%`
      - Hold down the [Shift] key between mouse clicks for straight lines.

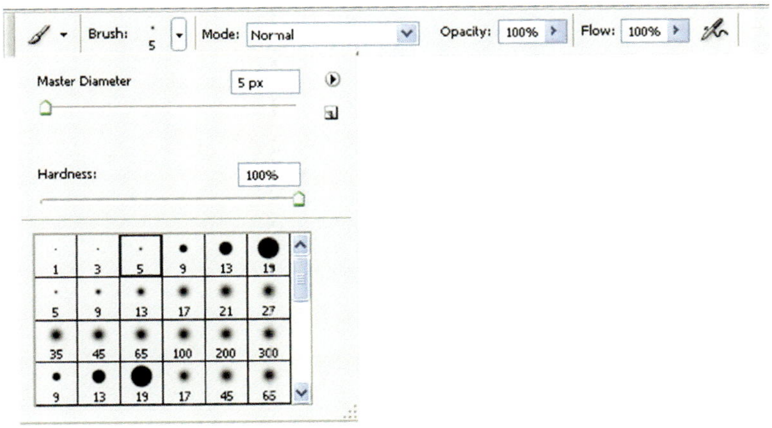

Step 4: Draw an outline for the arrowheads.

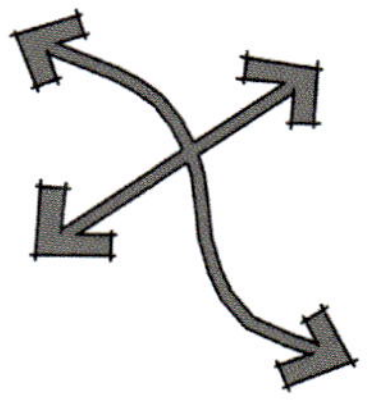

Step 5: Erase from the circulation path.

In the next two steps, you are going to refine the circulation path by erasing from your previous line work. First, you will erase from the basic form of the symbol. Then, you will erase from its outline. You will use two erasers with sizes proportional to each other. This will allow your line work to extend and overlap at intersections.

- Erase from the basic form of the circulation symbol.
  - Click on the layer *Circulation* to choose it.
  - Choose a brush for the Eraser Tool and draw outlines over the arrowheads.
    - `Master Diameter = 30 px`
    - `Hardness = 100%`

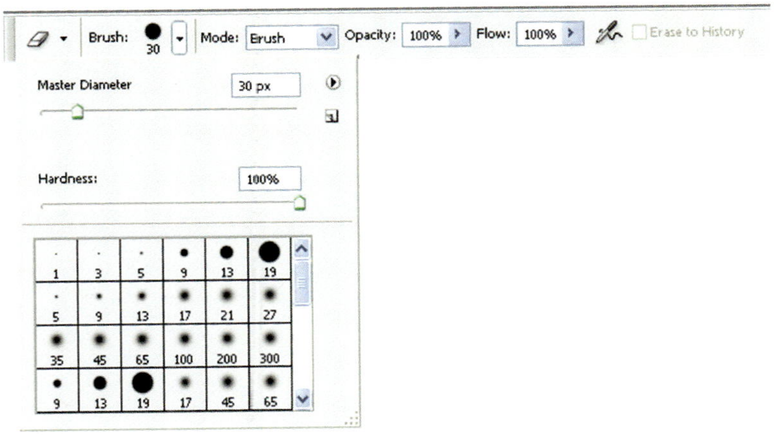

Step 5: Erase from the circulation path.

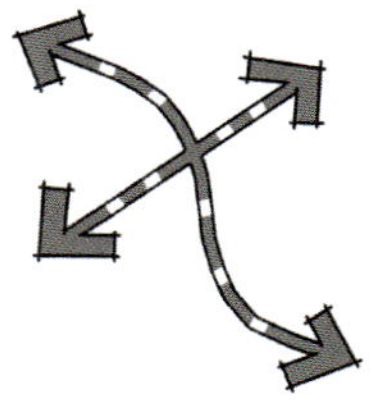

Step 6: Erase from the path outline.

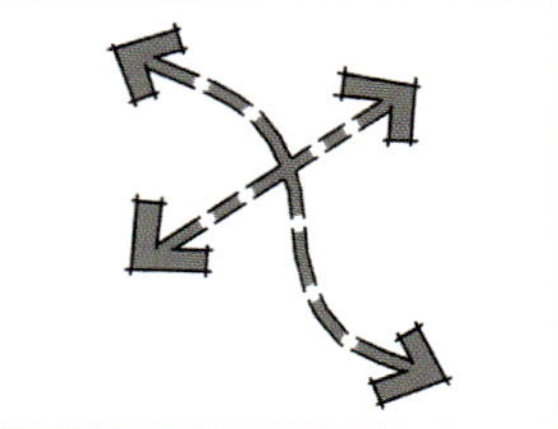

Step 6: Erase from the path outline.

- Erase from the outline of the circulation symbol.
  - Click on the layer *Circulation Outline* to choose it.
  - Choose a brush for the Eraser Tool and draw outlines over the arrowheads.
    - `Master Diameter = 15 px`
    - `Hardness = 100%`

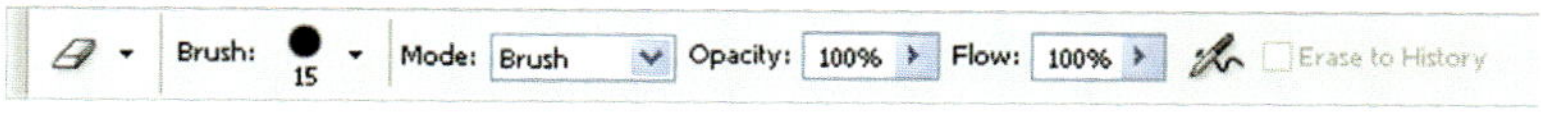

Step 7: Refine the line work.

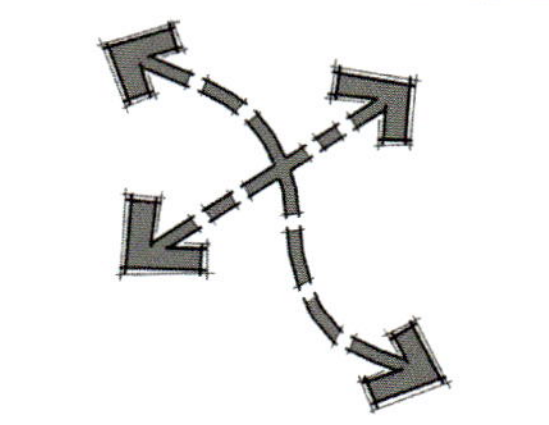

Step 7: Refine the line work.

In this step you are going to add emphasis to the arrowheads by drawing another outline around them using a thinner brush. Using this thinner brush, you will also draw perpendicular lines to the circulation path.

- Enhance the arrowheads.
  - Click on the layer *Arrowhead Outlines* to choose it.
  - Choose a paintbrush for the Brush Tool and draw another outline around the arrowheads.
    - `Master Diameter = 3 px`
    - `Hardness = 100%`

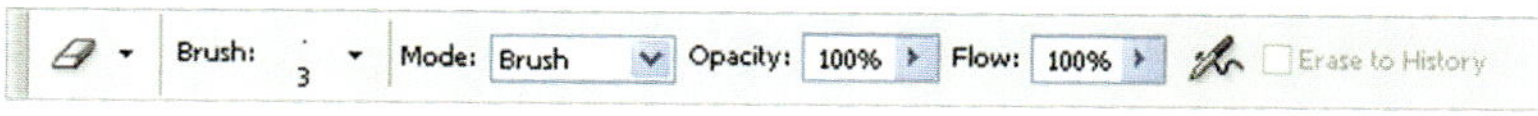

- Refine the circulation path.
  - Click on the layer *Stroke* to choose it.
    - With the same paintbrush, add perpendicular lines to the circulation path to close the outlines where you previously erased.

Step 8: Add color to the symbol.

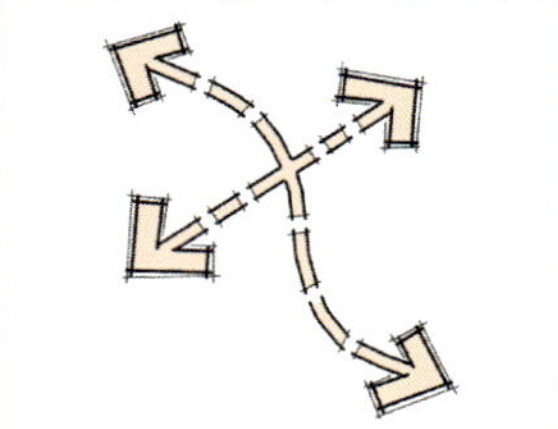

Step 8: Add color to the symbol.

- Change the color of the circulation symbol.
  - Click on the layer *Circulation* to choose it.
  - Change the layer `Opacity = 100%`.
  - **Select > All**
  - With the Move Tool, hit the [up arrow] on your keyboard, then hit the [down arrow].
  - Change the foreground color to light red (`#FFD9C7`).
  - **Edit > Fill**
  - Click the [OK] button.

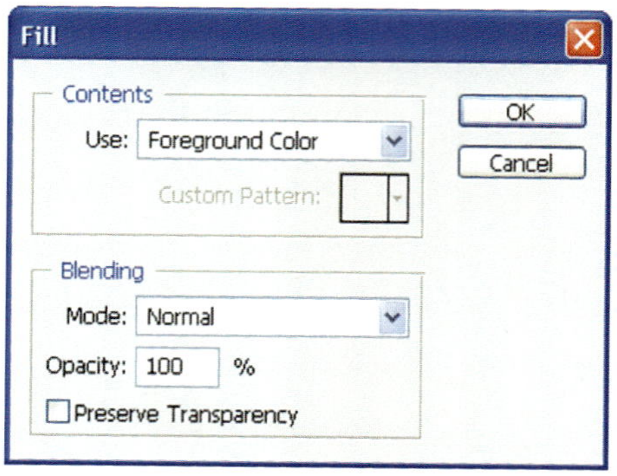

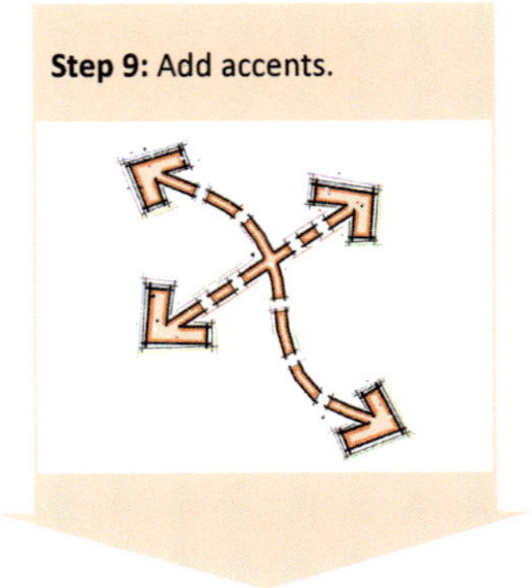

Step 9: Add accents.

- Add accent color to the circulation symbol.
  - Click on the layer *Circulation* to choose it.
  - **Select > All**
  - With the Move Tool, hit the [up arrow] on your keyboard, then hit the [down arrow].
  - Change the foreground color to red (`#FF8257`).
  - **Edit > Stroke**
    - `Width = 10 px`
    - `Location = Inside`
  - Click the [OK] button.

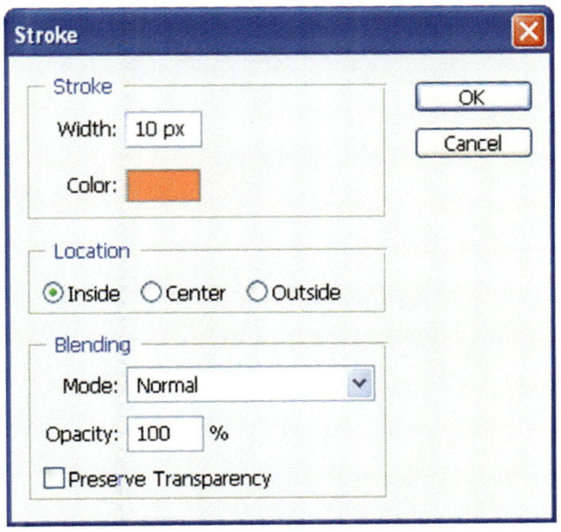

- Add accents to the symbol.
  - Create a new layer and name it *Accents*.
  - Using various brush sizes and colors, add accent brush strokes around the outline.

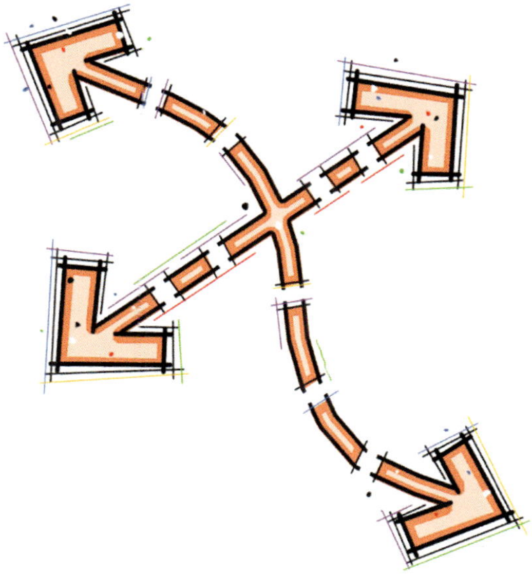

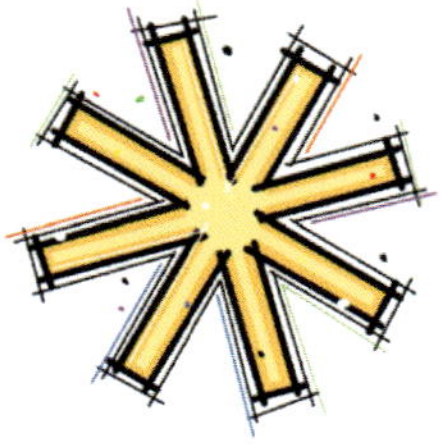

Functional Diagrams | Focal Point

This example illustrates a symbol for a focal point within a functional diagram. You might also use this symbol for entry points, high points, low points, or any other specific location on a diagram. The techniques used in this example include the following:

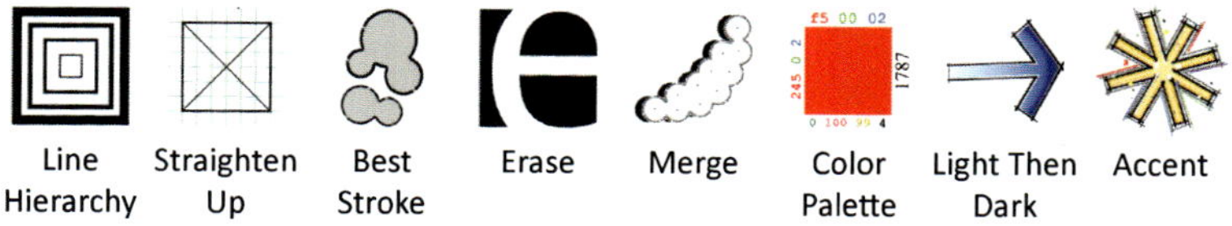

This drawing was originally drawn on a canvas with a resolution of 300 pixels per inch. Afterwards, it was scaled down to fit within these pages.

Step 1: Draw the general form of the symbol.

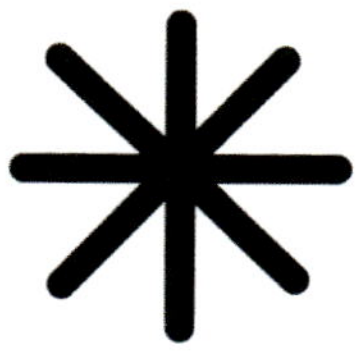

Step 1: Draw the general form of the symbol.

- Draw the general form for the symbol.
  - Create a new layer and name it *Brush 30*.
  - Choose a paintbrush for the Brush Tool and draw the symbol.
    - `Master Diameter = 30 px`
    - `Hardness = 100%`
      - Hold down the [Shift] key between mouse clicks to draw straight lines.

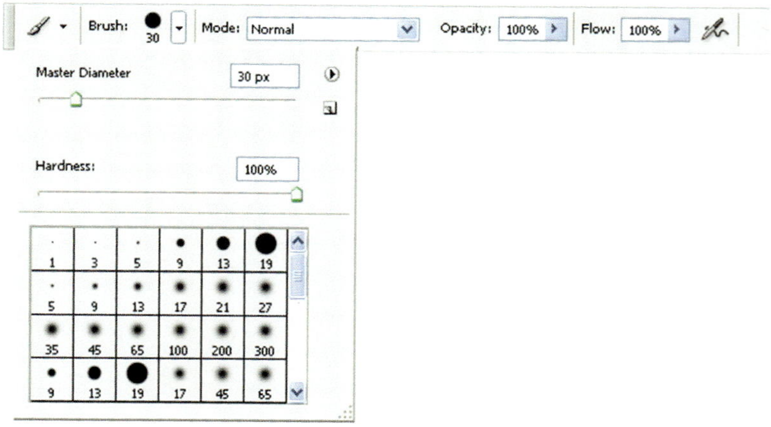

Step 2: Sharpen the symbol.

- Sharpen the symbol by erasing the end of each line segment.
    - Click on the layer *Brush 30* to choose it.
    - Choose a brush for the Eraser Tool and erase the new stroke from the arrowheads.
        - `Master Diameter = 30 px`
        - `Hardness = 100%`

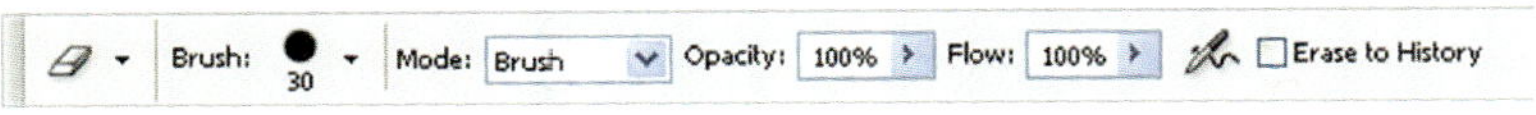

Step 2: Sharpen the symbol.

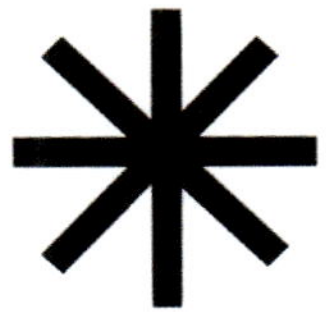

Step 3: Reduce the opacity.

- Reduce the layer opacity so that you will be able to see your work in the following steps.
    - `Opacity = 50%`

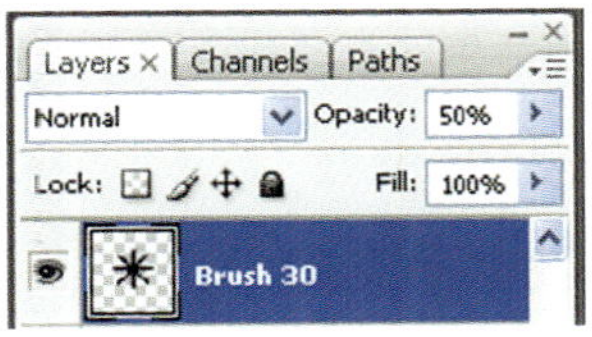

Step 3: Reduce the opacity.

Step 4: Draw an outline.

- Draw an outline for the symbol.
    - Create a new layer and name it *Outline*.
    - Choose a paintbrush for the Brush Tool and draw outlines over the symbol.
        - `Master Diameter = 5 px`
        - `Hardness = 1C0%`

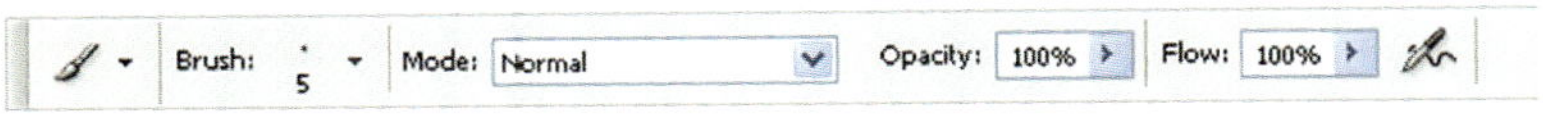

Step 4: Draw an outline.

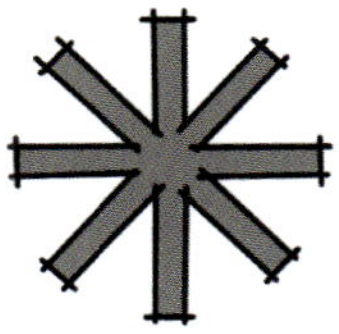

Step 5: Refine the outline.

- Refine the outline by adding more detail.
    - Choose a thinner paintbrush for the Brush Tool and draw another outline around the symbol.
        - `Master Diameter = 3 px`
        - `Hardness = 100%`

Step 5: Refine the outline.

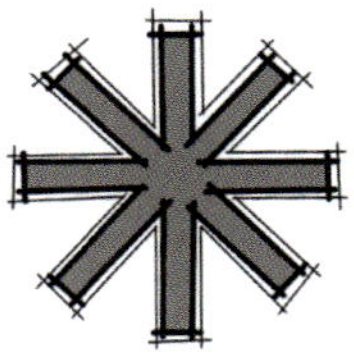

Step 6: Add color to the symbol.

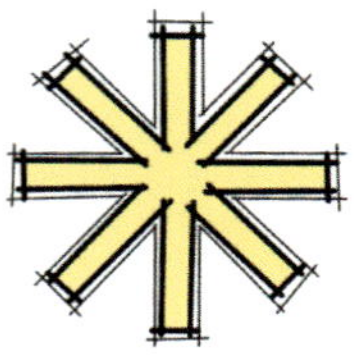

Step 6: Add color to the symbol.

- Change the color of the symbol.
  - Click on the layer *Brush 30* to choose it.
  - Change the layer `Opacity = 100%.`
  - **Select > All**
  - With the Move Tool, hit the [up arrow] on your keyboard, then hit the [down arrow].
  - Change the foreground color to light tan (`#FFE3BC`).
  - **Edit > Fill**
  - Click the [OK] button.

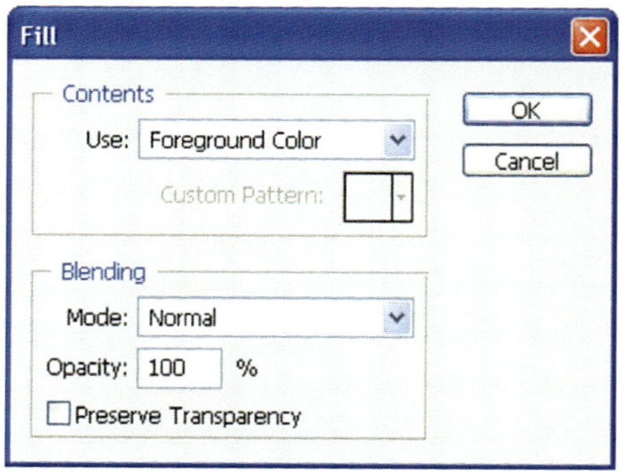

Step 7: Enhance the color of the symbol.

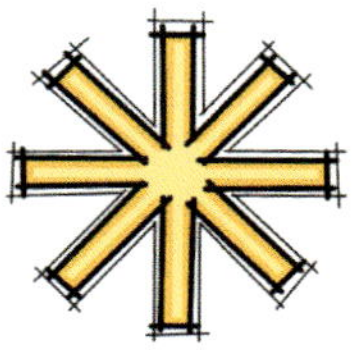

Step 7: Enhance the color of the symbol.

- Add accent color to the symbol.
  - Click on the layer *Brush 30* to choose it.
  - **Select > All**
  - With the Move Tool, hit the [up arrow] on your keyboard, then hit the [down arrow].
  - Change the foreground color to tan (`#FFBA3D`).
  - **Edit > Stroke**
    - `Width = 10 px`
    - `Location = Inside`
  - Click the [OK] button.

Step 8: Rotate the symbol and add accents.

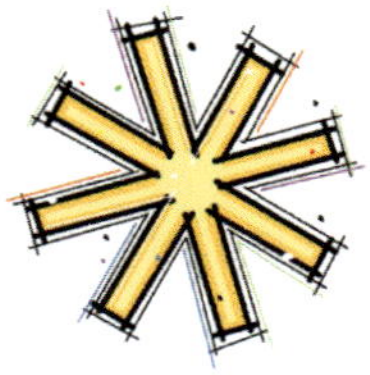

Step 8: Rotate the symbol and add accents.

- Rotate the symbol.
  - Click on the layer *Brush 30* to choose it.
  - **Edit > Transform > Rotate**
    - `Angle = 15 degrees`
  - Hit the [Enter] key.
  - Repeat the above steps for the layer *Outline*.

- Add accents to the symbol.
  - Create a new layer and name it *Accents*.
  - Using various brush sizes and colors, add accent brush strokes and dots to the symbol.

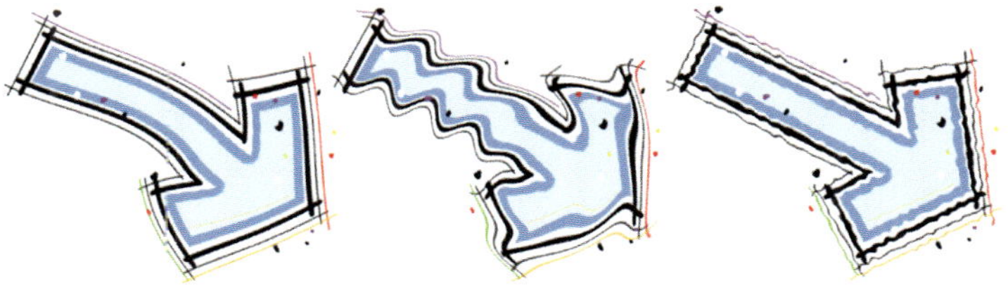

Functional Diagrams | Prevailing Winds

This step-by-step example illustrates how to draw arrow symbols for prevailing winds within a functional diagram. The techniques used in this example include the following:

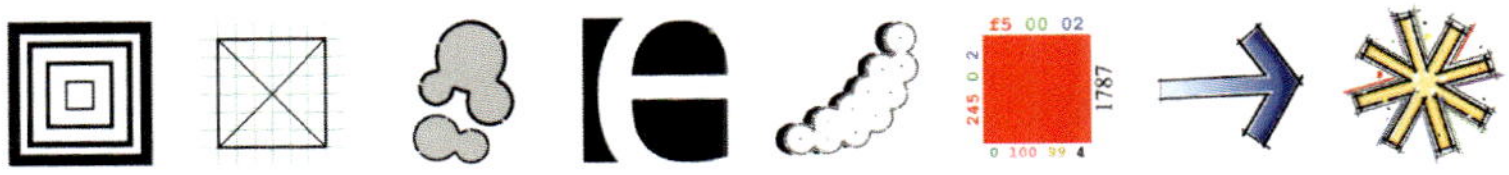

This drawing was originally drawn on a canvas with a resolution of 300 pixels per inch. Afterwards, it was scaled down to fit within these pages.

Step 1: Draw the general form of the symbol.

Step 1: Draw the general form of the symbol.

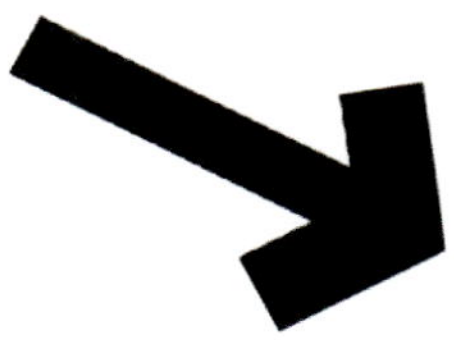

- Draw the arrow line.
  - Create a new layer and name it *Arrow Line*.
  - Choose a paintbrush for the Brush Tool and draw the arrow line.
    - `Master Diameter = 50 px`
    - `Hardness = 100%`
      - Hold down the [Shift] key between mouse clicks for straight lines.

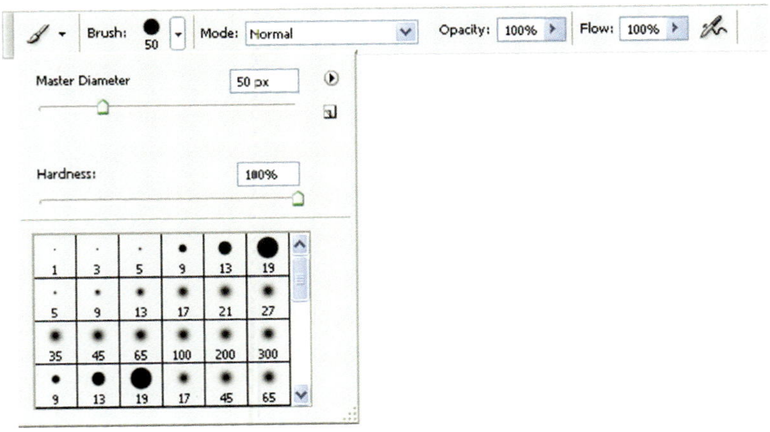

- Draw the arrowhead.
  - Create a new layer and name it *Arrowhead.*
  - Choose a thicker paintbrush for the Brush Tool and draw the arrowhead.
    - `Master Diameter = 75 px`
    - `Hardness = 100%`

- Sharpen the arrow line and arrowhead.
  - Click on the layer *Arrow Line* to choose it.
  - Choose a brush for the Eraser Tool and erase the edges of the arrow line.
    - `Master Diameter = 50 px`
    - `Hardness = 100%`
  - Repeat for the arrowhead.

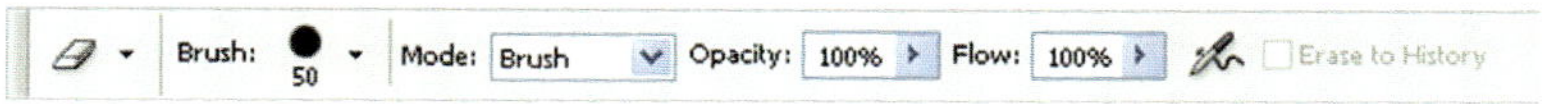

Step 2: Outline the symbol.

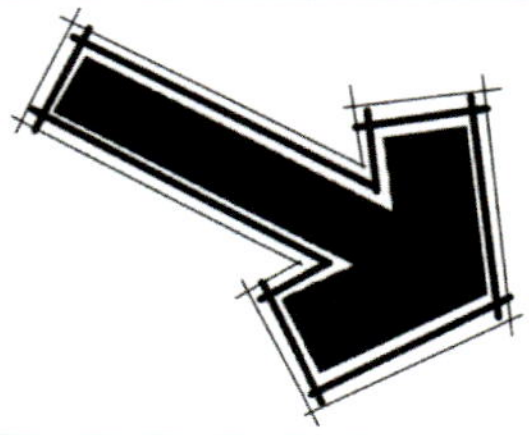

Step 2: Outline the symbol.

- Draw an outline around the symbol.
  - Create a new layer and name it *Outline*.
  - Choose a paintbrush for the Brush Tool and draw a bold outline around the symbol.
    - `Master Diameter = 5 px`
    - `Hardness = 100%`

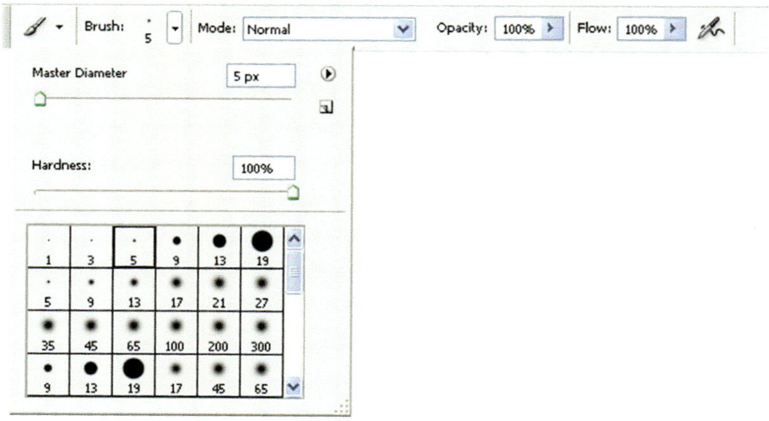

- Draw another outline around the symbol.
  - Choose a thinner paintbrush for the Brush Tool and draw a thin outline around the symbol.
    - `Master Diameter = 3 px`
    - `Hardness = 100%`

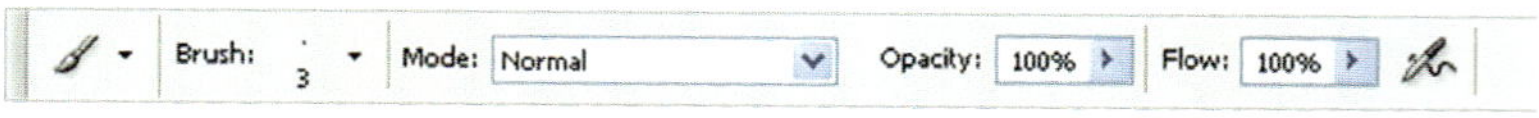

Step 3: Change the color of the symbol.

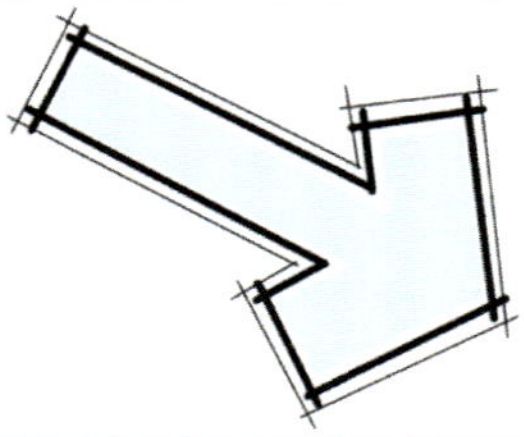

Step 3: Change the color of the symbol.

- Merge the arrow line and arrowhead.
  - Click on the layer *Arrow Line* to choose it.
  - While holding down the [Ctrl] key, click on the layer *Arrowhead* to choose it too.
  - Click on the right mouse button and select "Merge Layers" from the pop-up dialog box.
  - Rename the merged layer *Arrow*.

- Change the color of the symbol.
    - Click on the layer *Arrow* to choose it.
    - **Select > All**
    - With the Move Tool, hit the [up arrow] on your keyboard, then hit the [down arrow].
    - Change the foreground color to light blue (`#DBF5FF`).
    - **Edit > Fill**
    - Click the [OK] button.

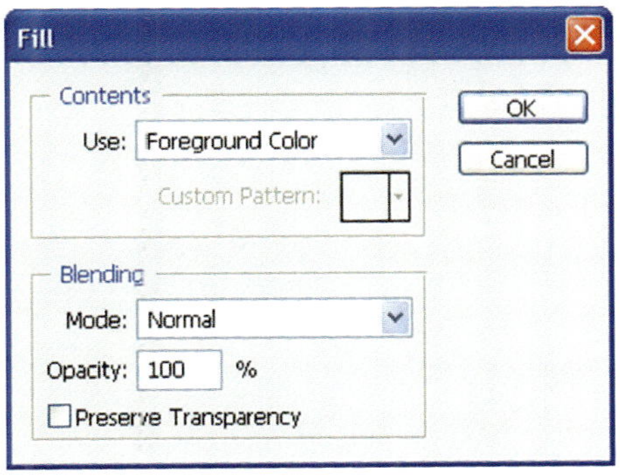

Step 4: Enhance the color and add accents.

Step 4: Enhance the color and add accents.

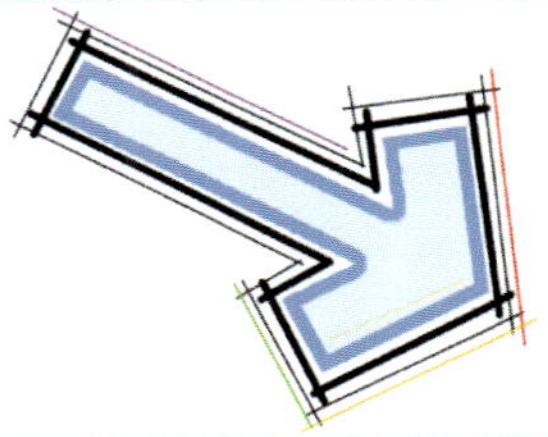

- Add accent color to the symbol.
    - Click on the layer *Arrow* to choose it.
    - **Select > All**
    - With the Move Tool, hit the [up arrow] on your keyboard, then hit the [down arrow].
    - Change the foreground color to light blue (`#5C96FF`).
    - **Edit > Stroke**
        - `Width = 10 px`
        - `Location = Inside`
    - Click the [OK] button.

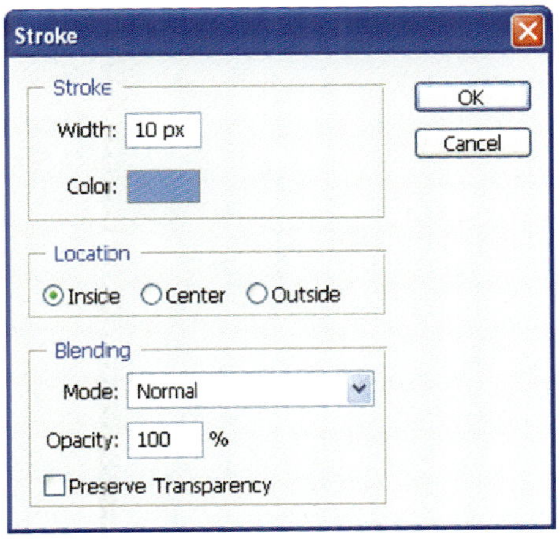

- Add accents to the outline.
    - Click on the layer *Outline* to choose it.
    - Using various brush sizes and colors, add accent brush strokes around the outline.

Step 5: Distort the symbol.

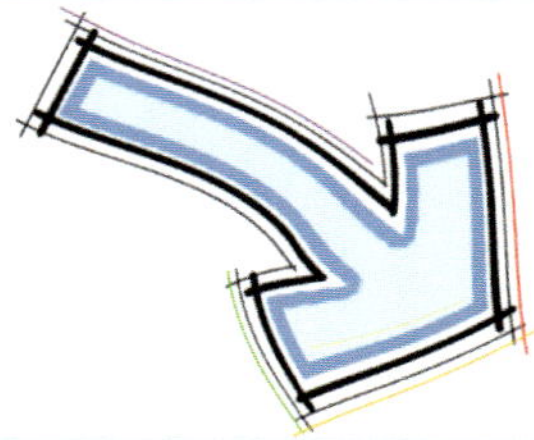

Step 5: Distort the symbol.

- Merge the arrow and its outline.
  - Click on the layer *Arrow* to choose it.
  - While holding down the [Ctrl] key, click on the layer *Outline* to choose it too.
  - Click on the right mouse button and select "Merge Layers" from the pop-up dialog box.
  - Rename the merged layer *Arrow and Outline*.
- Distort the symbol using a filter.
  - Click on the layer *Arrow and Outline* to choose it.
  - **Filter > Distort > Twirl...**
    - `Angle = 30 degrees`
  - Click the [OK] button.

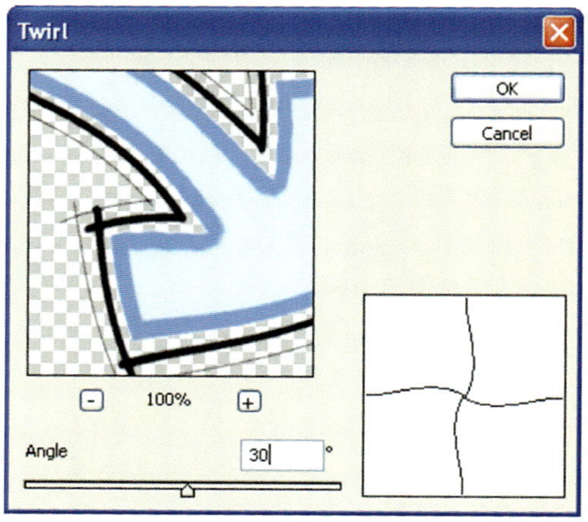

Step 6: Add accents to the symbol.

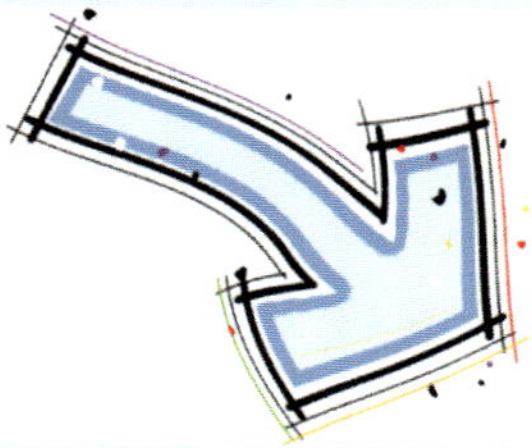

Step 6: Add accents to the symbol.

- Add accents dots to the symbol.
  - Create a new layer and name it *Accents*.
  - Using various brush sizes and colors, add accent brush strokes to they symbol.

Step 5(b): Distort the symbol.

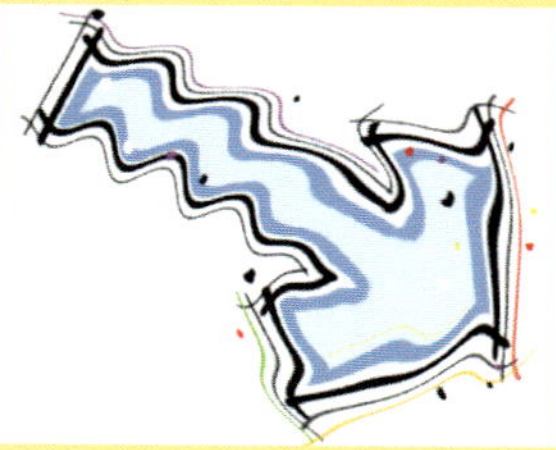

Step 5(b): Distort the symbol.

Rather than distorting the symbol with the Twirl filter, you can use the ZigZag filter to create a more dramatic distortion.

- Distort the symbol using a filter.
  - Click on the layer *Arrow and Outline* to choose it.
  - **Filter > Distort > ZigZag...**
    - `Amount = 10`
    - `Ridges = 5`
    - `Style = Around Center`
  - Click the [OK] button.

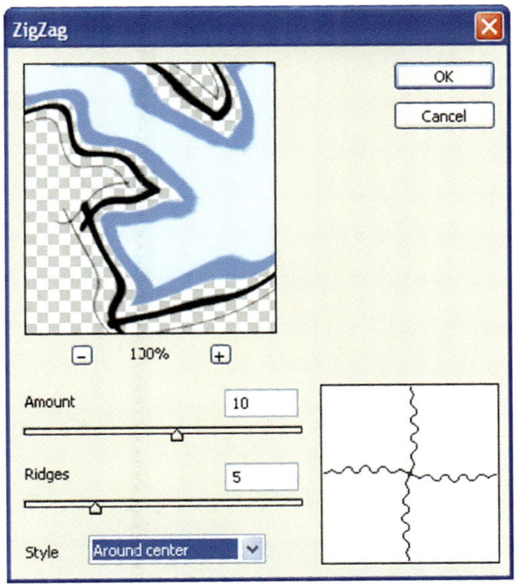

Step 5(c): Distort the symbol.

The Ripple filter is another alternative to using the Twirl or ZigZag filters.

- Distort the symbol using a filter.
  - Click on the layer *Arrow and Outline* to choose it.
  - **Filter > Distort > Ripple...**
    - `Amount = 100%`
    - `Size = Medium`
  - Click the [OK] button.

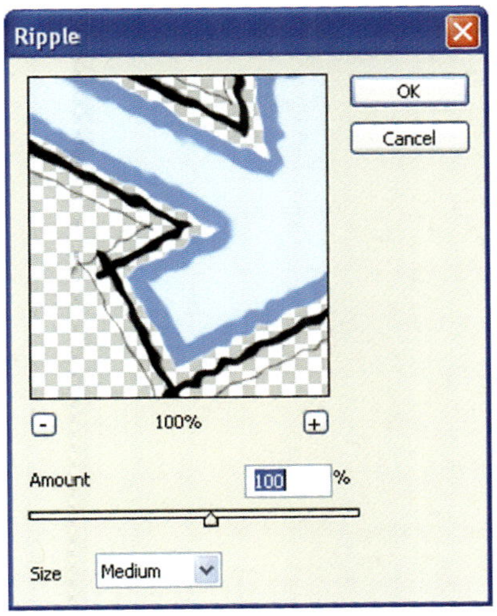

Step 5(c): Distort the symbol.

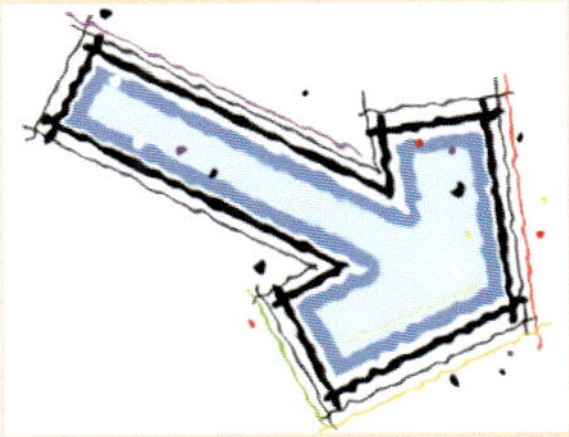

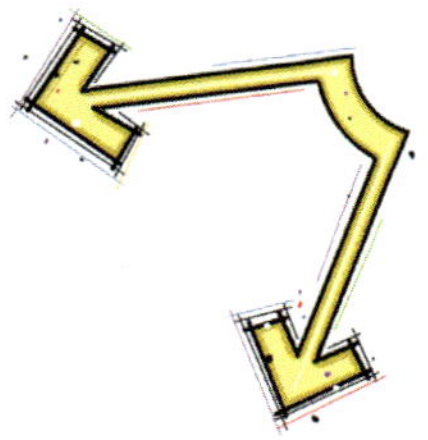

Functional Diagrams | Views

This example illustrates how to draw symbols for views within a functional diagram. The techniques used in this example include the following:

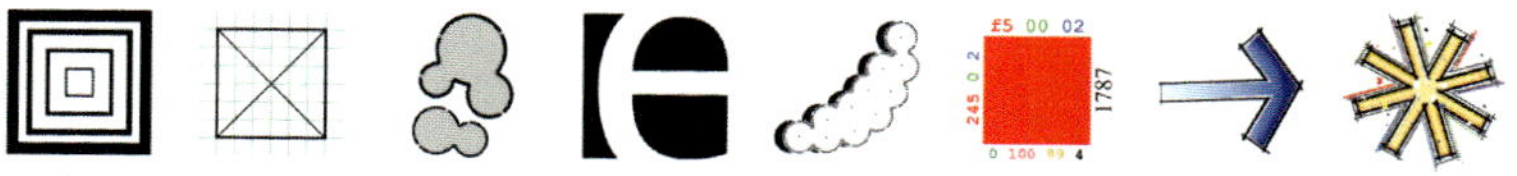

Line Hierarchy | Straighten Up | Best Stroke | Erase | Merge | Color Palette | Light Then Dark | Accent

This drawing was originally drawn on a canvas with a resolution of 300 pixels per inch. Afterwards, it was scaled down to fit within these pages.

Step 1: Draw a circle.

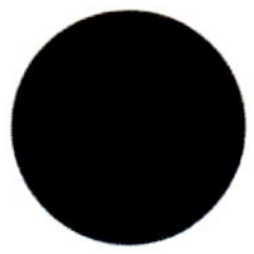

Step 1: Draw a circle.

- Draw a circle.
  - Create a new layer and name it ***Brush 300***.
  - Choose a paintbrush for the Brush Tool and draw your circle.
    - `Master Diameter = 300 px`
    - `Hardness = 100%`
      - To draw the circle, you merely need to touch the canvas with your large, sharp brush.
      - Because you are drawing at 300 pixels per inch (ppi), the diameter of your brush is 1 inch.

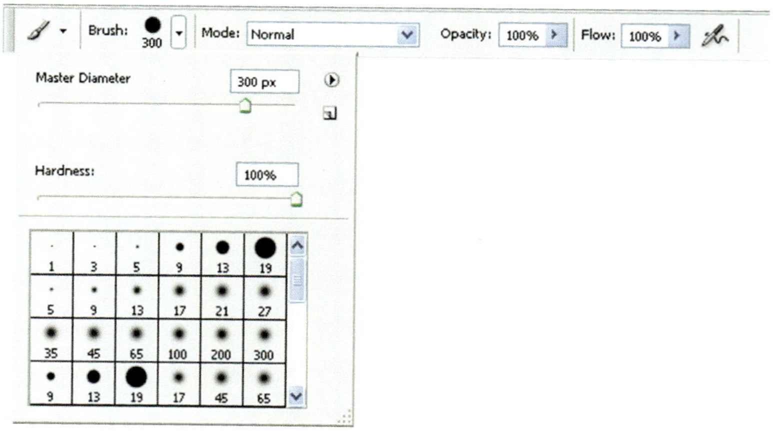

Step 2: Change the opacity.

- Reduce the layer opacity so that you will be able to see your work in the following steps.
  - `Opacity = 50%`

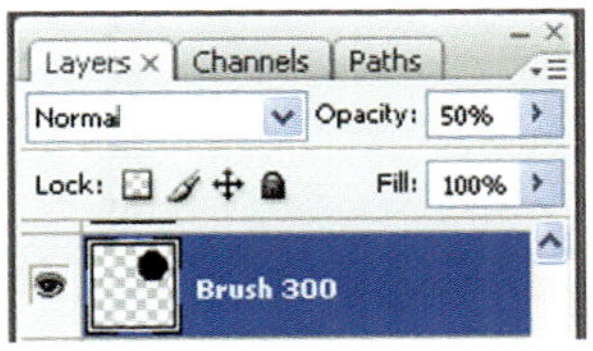

Step 2: Change the opacity.

Step 3: Stroke an outline.

- Create an outline from the circle.
  - Click on the layer *Brush 300* to choose it.
  - **Select > All**
  - With the Move Tool, hit the [up arrow] on your keyboard, then hit the [down arrow].
  - Create a new layer and name it *Stroke 50*.
  - **Edit > Stroke**
    - `Width = 50 px`
    - `Location = Inside`
  - Click the [OK] button.

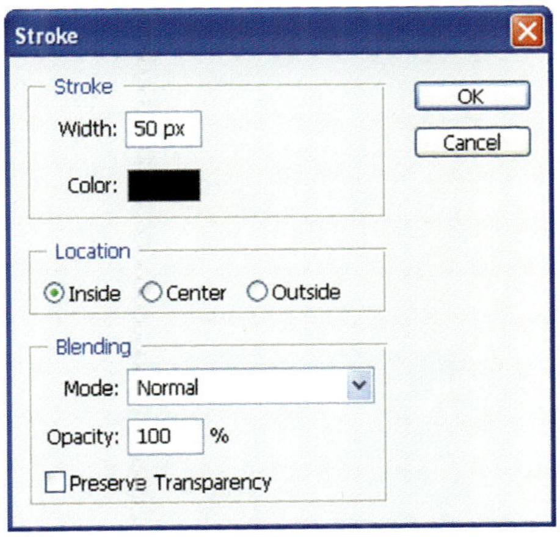

Step 3: Stroke an outline.

Step 4: Draw the view boundaries.

- Draw the boundaries for the views.
  - Create a new layer and name it *View Span*.
  - Choose a paintbrush for the Brush Tool.
    - `Master Diameter = 30 px`
    - `Hardness = 100%`
      - Draw from a point outside the circle to the radius, and then back outside the circle.

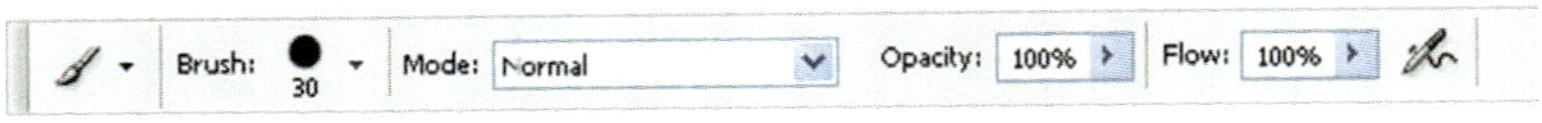

Step 4: Draw the view boundaries.

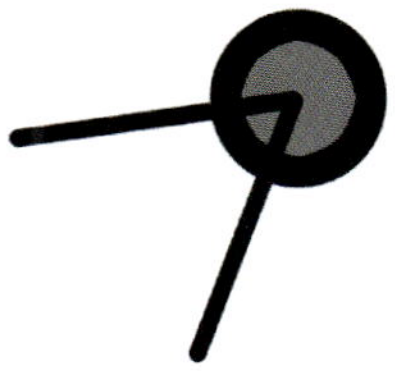

Step 5: Trim the view span.

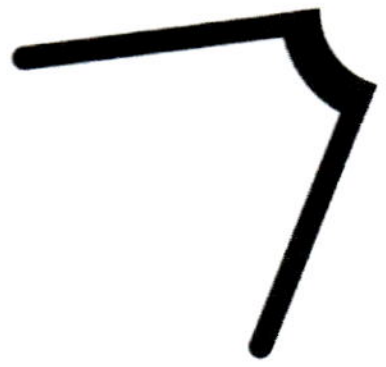

Step 5: Trim the view span.

- Merge the circle outline with the view span line work.
  - Click on the layer ***Stroke 50*** to choose it.
  - While holding down the [Ctrl] key, click on the layer ***View Span*** to choose it too.
  - Click on the right mouse button and select "Merge Layers" from the pop-up dialog box.
  - Rename the merged layer *View Lines*.
- Trim the merged layer.
  - Click on the layer *View Lines* to choose it.
  - Choose a large brush for the Eraser Tool and erase from the radius.
    - `Master Diameter = 200 px`
    - `Hardness = 100%`
  - Afterwards, choose a much smaller brush and erase as required until it is neat.

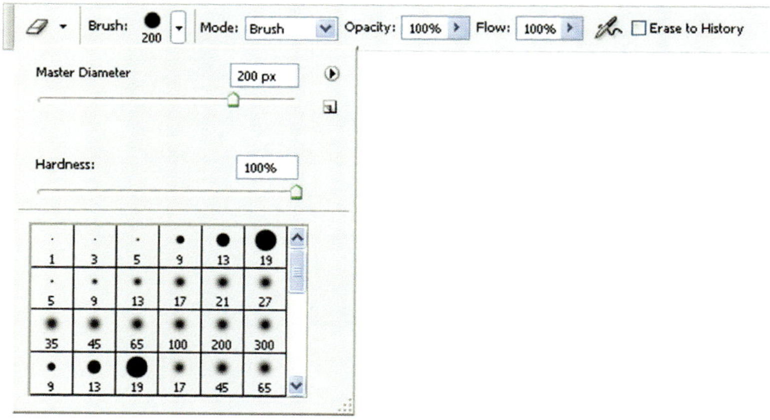

Step 6: Add arrowheads.

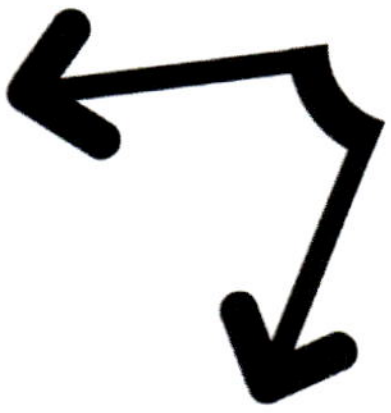

Step 6: Add arrowheads.

- Draw the arrowheads.
  - Create a new layer and name it *Arrowheads.*
  - Choose a thicker paintbrush for the Brush Tool and draw the arrowhead.
    - `Master Diameter = 50 px`
    - `Hardness = 100%`

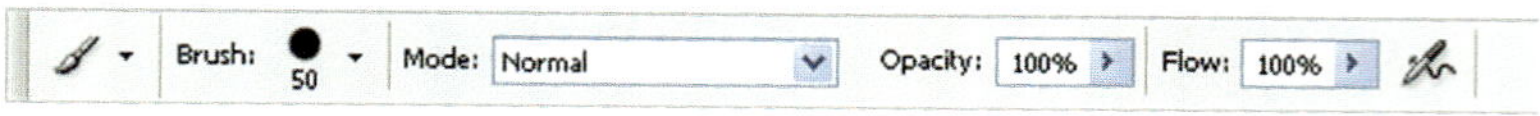

Step 7: Sharpen the arrowheads.

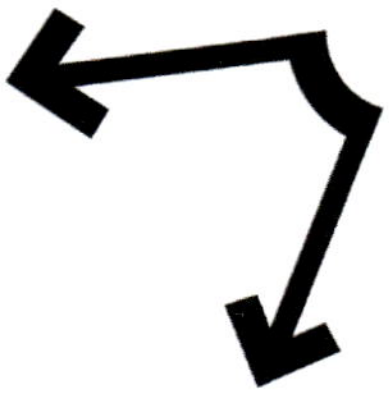

Step 7: Sharpen the arrowheads.

- Refine the arrowheads by erasing the edges of your previous brush strokes.
  - Create a new layer and name it *Arrowheads.*
  - Choose a brush for the Eraser Tool and erase the edges of the arrowheads.
    - `Master Diameter = 15 px`
    - `Hardness = 100%`

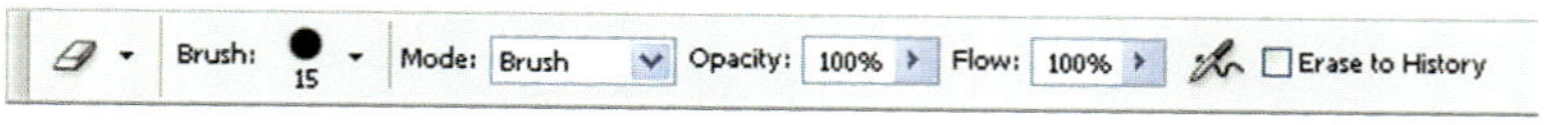

Step 8: Change the opacity.

- Merge the line work with the arrowheads.
  - Click on the layer ***View Lines*** to choose it.
  - While holding down the [Ctrl] key, click on the layer ***Arrowheads*** to choose it too.
  - Click on the right mouse button and select "Merge Layers" from the pop-up dialog box.
  - Rename the merged layer ***Views***.
- Reduce the layer opacity so that you will be able to see your work in the following steps.
  - `Opacity = 50%`

Step 8: Change the opacity.

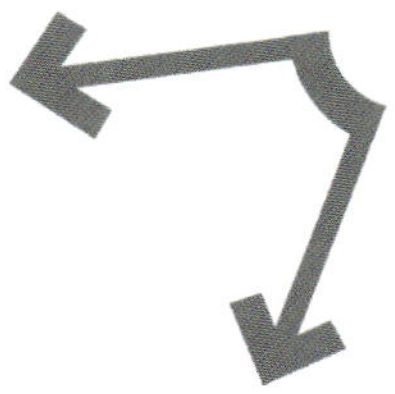

Step 9: Outline the symbol.

- Draw an outline around the merged layers.
  - Click on the layer ***Views*** to choose it.
  - **Select > All**
  - With the Move Tool, hit the [up arrow] on your keyboard, then hit the [down arrow].
  - Change the foreground color to black (`#000000`).
  - Create a new layer and name it ***Outline***.
  - **Edit > Stroke**
    - `Width = 5 px`
    - `Location = Inside`
  - Click the [OK] button.

Step 9: Outline the symbol.

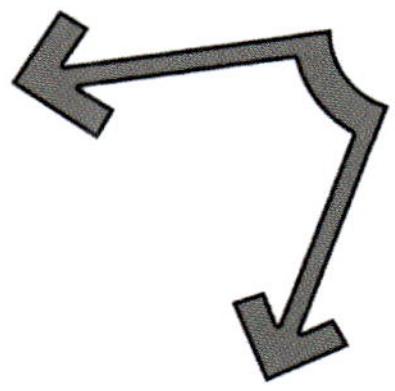

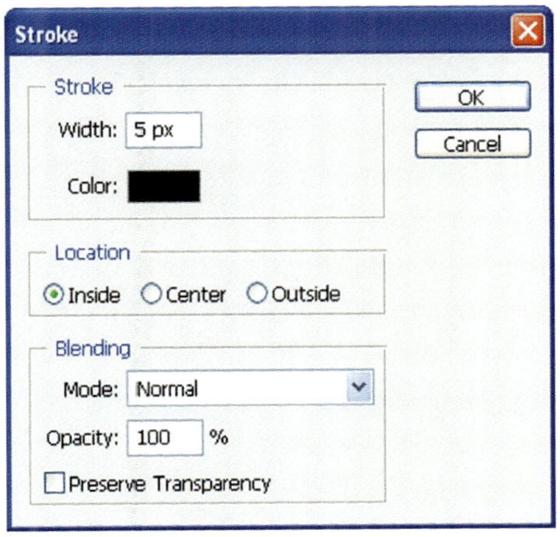

Step 10: Erase arrowhead outlines.

- Erase the line work from the arrowheads.
  - Click on the layer ***Outline*** to choose it.
  - Choose a brush for the Eraser Tool and erase the new stroke from the arrowheads.
    - `Master Diameter = 10 px`
    - `Hardness = 100%`

Step 10: Erase arrowhead outlines.

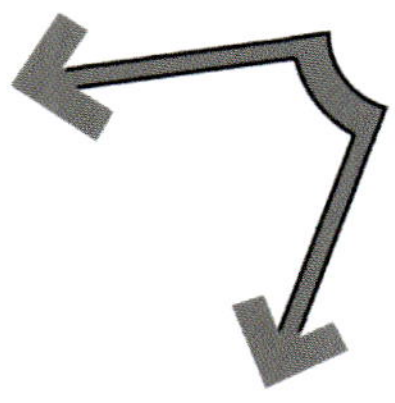

Step 11: Draw new outlines for the arrowheads.

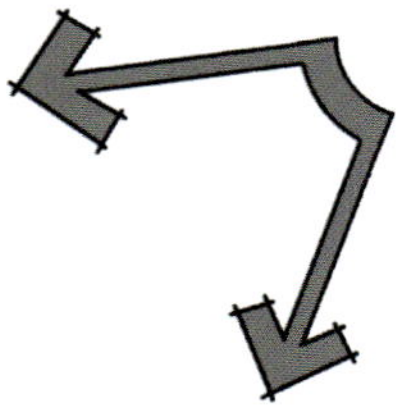

Step 11: Draw new outlines for the arrowheads.

- Draw outlines for the arrowheads.
  - Click on the layer ***Outline*** to choose it.
  - Choose a paintbrush for the Brush Tool and draw new outlines for the arrowheads.
    - `Master Diameter = 5 px`
    - `Hardness = 100%`
      - Hold down the [Shift] key between mouse clicks for straight lines.

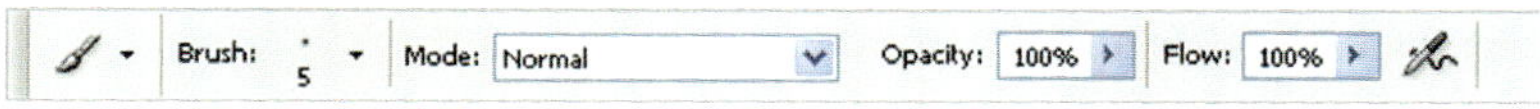

Step 12: Refine arrowheads.

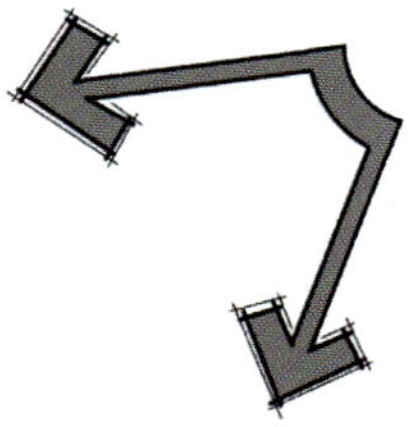

Step 12: Refine arrowheads.

- Refine the arrowhead line work.
  - Choose a thinner paintbrush for the Brush Tool and draw another set of outlines for the arrowheads.
    - `Master Diameter = 3 px`
    - `Hardness = 100%`

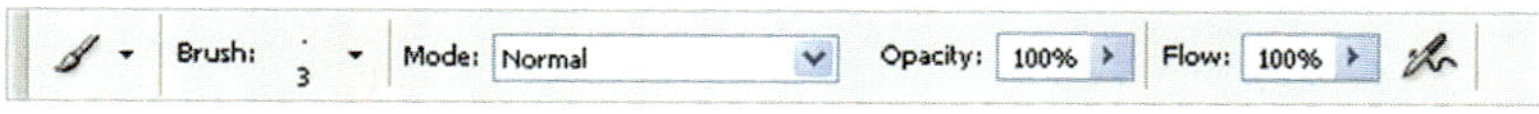

Step 13: Add color.

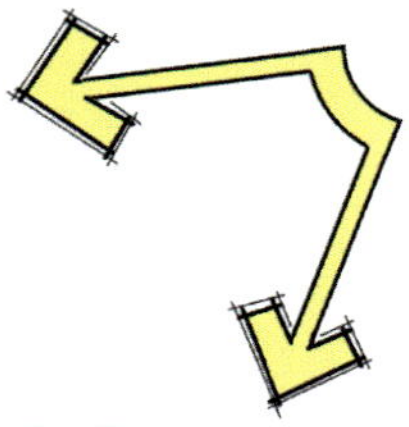

Step 13: Add color.

- Change the base color of the symbol.
  - Click on the layer ***Views*** to choose it.
  - Change the layer `Opacity = 100%`.
  - **Select > All**
  - With the Move Tool, hit the [up arrow] on your keyboard, then hit the [down arrow].
  - Change the foreground color to light yellow (`#FFFF7D`).
  - **Edit > Fill**
  - Click the [OK] button.

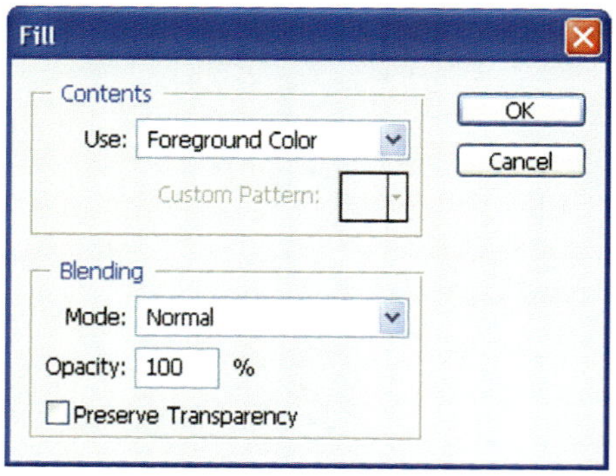

Step 14: Refine the color.

Step 14: Refine the color.

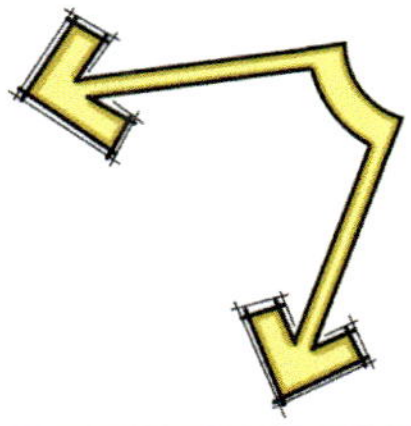

- Add accent color to the symbol.
  - Click on the layer ***Views*** to choose it.
  - **Select > All**
  - With the Move Tool, hit the [up arrow] on your keyboard, then hit the [down arrow].
  - Change the foreground color to a darker yellow (`#D9B200`).
  - **Edit > Stroke**
    - `Width = 10 px`
    - `Location = Inside`
  - Click the [OK] button.

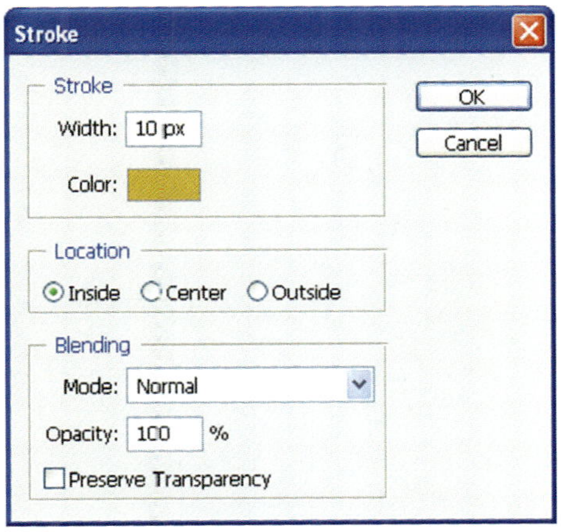

Step 15: Add accents.

Step 15: Add accents.

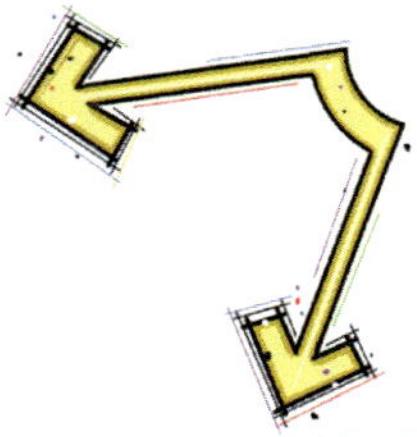

- Add accents to the symbol.
  - Create a new layer and name it ***Accents***.
  - Using various brush sizes and colors, add accent brush strokes and dots to the symbol.

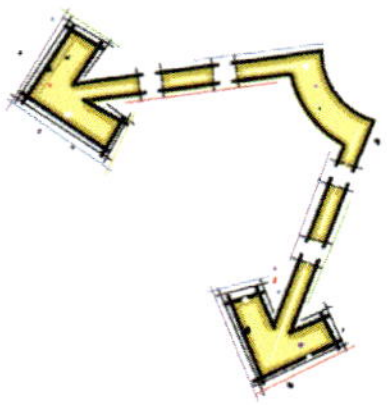

Functional Diagrams | Filtered Views

This example illustrates how to draw symbols for filtered views within a functional diagram. It is a refinement of the previous example, Views. The techniques used in this example include the following:

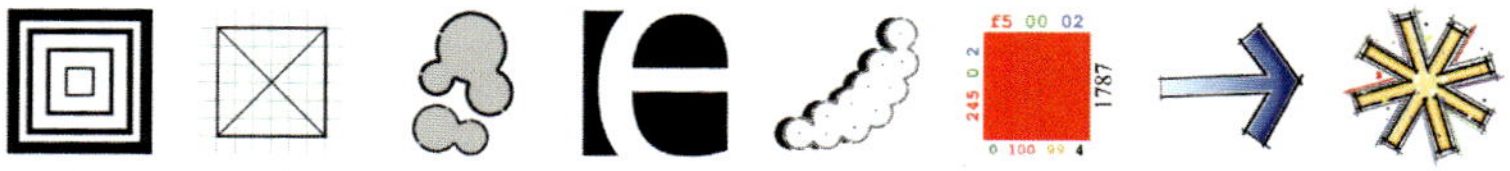

Line Hierarchy | Straighten Up | Best Stroke | Erase | Merge | Color Palette | Light Then Dark | Accent

This drawing was originally drawn on a canvas with a resolution of 300 pixels per inch. Afterwards, it was scaled down to fit within these pages.

Step 1: Draw the basic form, then refine the arrowheads.

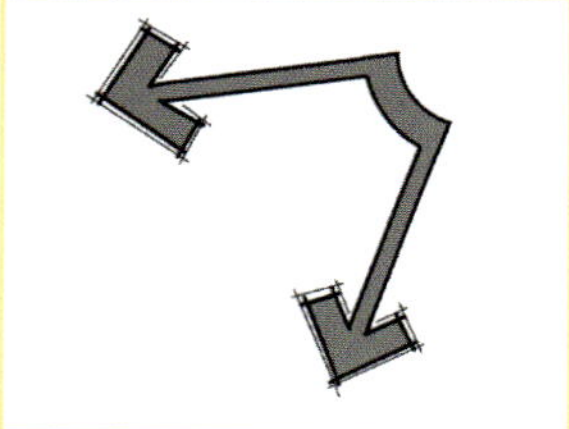

Step 1: Draw the basic form, as before, then refine the arrowheads.

This example builds upon the previous one, so you should repeat Steps 1 to 11 in the previous example before proceeding.

- Refine the arrowhead line work.
    - Click on the layer ***Outline*** to choose it.
    - Choose a thin paintbrush for the Brush Tool and draw another set of outlines around the arrowheads.
        - `Master Diameter = 3 px`
        - `Hardness = 100%`

Step 2: Erase from the view boundaries.

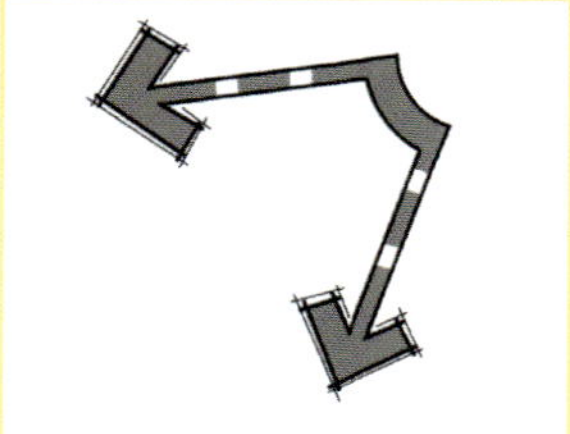

Step 2: Erase from the view boundaries.

In the next two steps, you are going to refine the view boundaries by erasing from your previous line work. First, you will erase from the basic form of the symbol. Then, you will erase from its outline. You will use two erasers with sizes proportional to each other. This will allow your line work to extend and overlap at the intersections.

- Erase from the basic form of the symbol.
    - Choose a brush for the Eraser Tool and erase from the view boundaries.
        - `Master Diameter = 30 px`
        - `Hardness = 100%`
            - Hold down the [Shift] key between mouse clicks to erase in straight lines.

Step 3: Erase from the view boundary outlines.

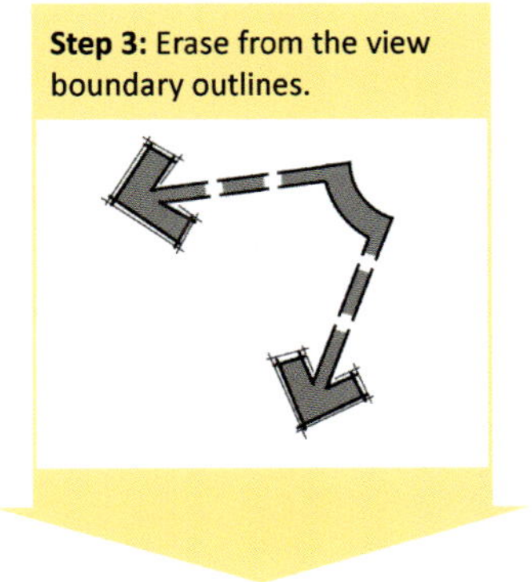

- Erase from the outline of the view boundaries.
  - Choose a brush for the Eraser Tool and erase from the view boundaries.
    - `Master Diameter = 15 px`
    - `Hardness = 100%`

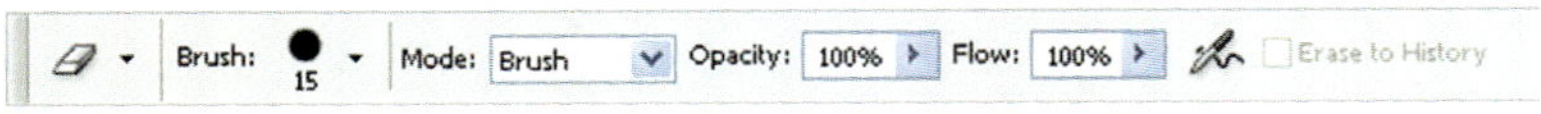

Step 4: Refine the symbol line work.

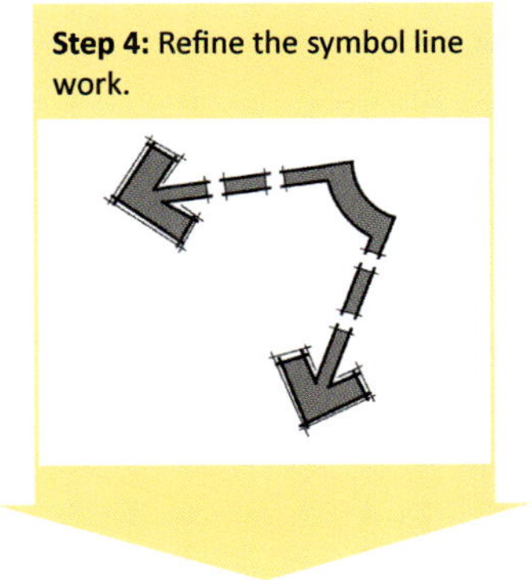

In this step you are going to add emphasis to the arrowheads by drawing another outline around them using a thinner brush. Using the same brush, you will draw perpendicular lines where you erased from the view boundaries.

- Add a thin outline to the arrowheads.
  - Click on the layer ***Arrowheads*** to choose it.
  - Choose a thin paintbrush for the Brush Tool and draw another set of outlines around the arrowheads.
    - `Master Diameter = 3 px`
    - `Hardness = 100%`

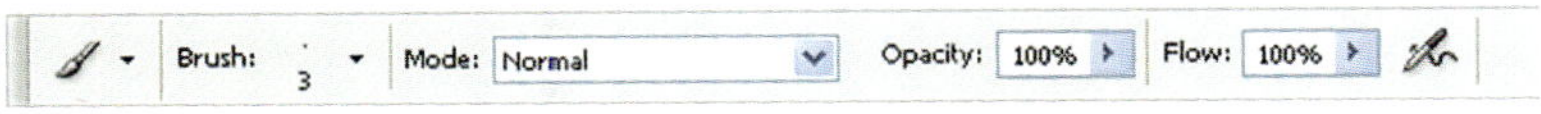

- Draw perpendicular lines where you erased from the view boundaries.
  - Click on the layer ***Outline*** to choose it.
  - With the same paintbrush, add perpendicular lines to the view boundaries to close the outlines where you previously erased.

Step 5: Add color to the symbol.

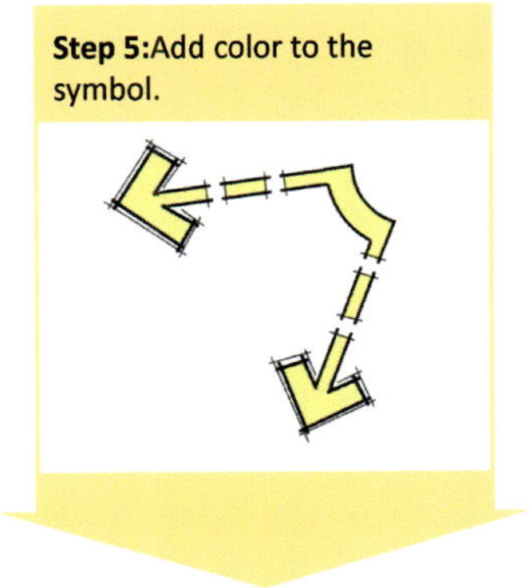

- Change the base color of the symbol.
  - Click on the layer ***Views*** to choose it.
  - Change the layer `Opacity = 100%`.
  - **Select > All**
  - With the Move Tool, hit the [up arrow] on your keyboard, then hit the [down arrow].
  - Change the foreground color to light yellow (`#FFFF7D`).
  - **Edit > Fill**
  - Click the [OK] button.

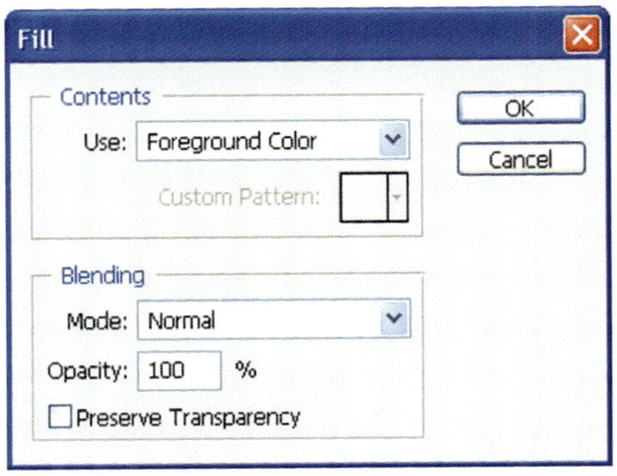

Step 6: Refine the color and add accents.

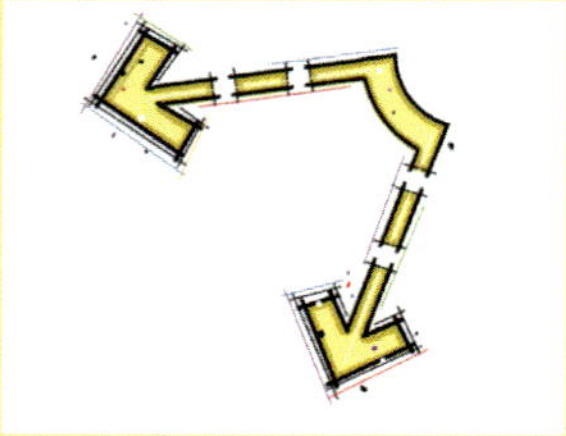

Step 6: Refine the color and add accents.

- Add accent color to the symbol.
  - Click on the layer *Views* to choose it.
  - **Select > All**
  - With the Move Tool, hit the [up arrow] on your keyboard, then hit the [down arrow].
  - Change the foreground color to a darker yellow (`#D9B200`).
  - **Edit > Stroke**
    - `Width = 10 px`
    - `Location = Inside`
  - Click the [OK] button.

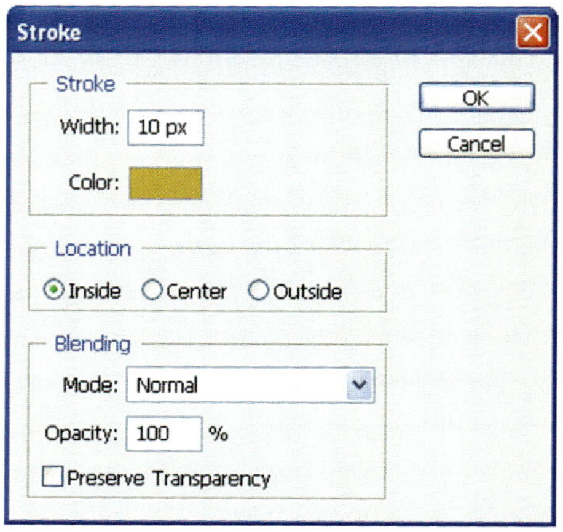

- Add accents to the symbol.
  - Create a new layer and name it *Accents*.
  - Using various brush sizes and colors, add accent brush strokes and dots to the symbol.

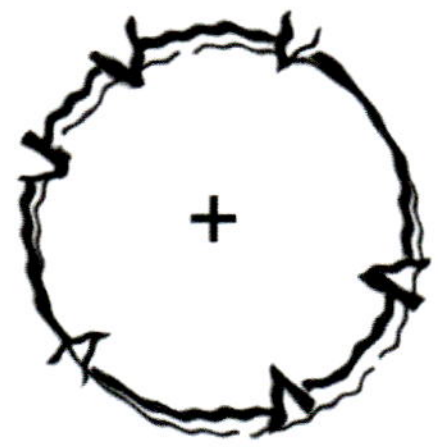

Master Plan Graphics | Deciduous Tree

This example illustrates how to draw a simple, black-and-white symbol for a deciduous tree. The techniques used in this example include the following:

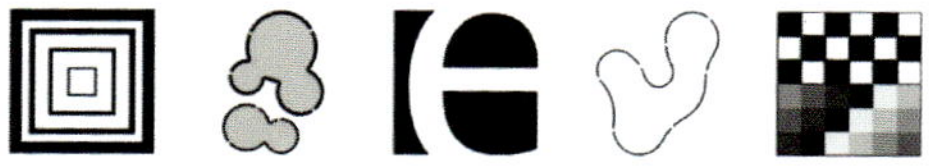

This drawing was originally drawn on a canvas with a resolution of 200 pixels per inch. Afterwards, it was scaled down to fit within these pages.

Step 1: Draw a simple outline of a circle.

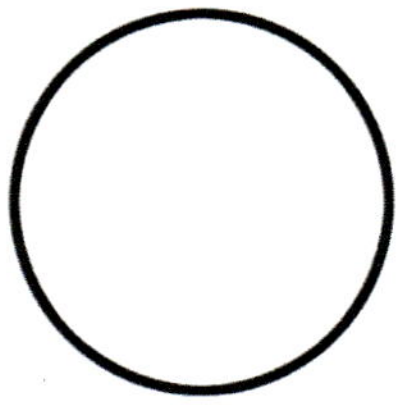

Step 1: Draw a simple outline of a circle.

- Draw the a simple circle.
  - Create a new layer and name it ***Brush 200***.
  - Choose a paintbrush for the Brush Tool and draw a circle by simply touching the brush to the canvas.
    - `Master Diameter = 200 px`
    - `Hardness = 100%`

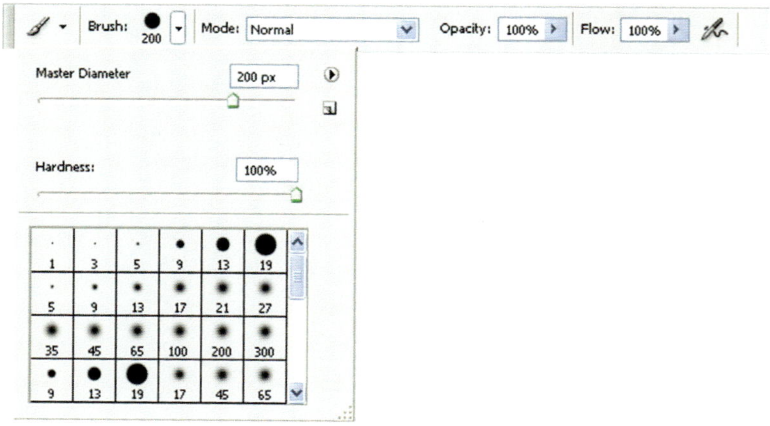

- Reduce the opacity of your fill so that you can see your work in the next steps.
  - `Opacity = 25%`

- Draw a thick outline around the circle.
  - Click on the layer *Brush 200* to choose it.
  - **Select > All**
  - With the Move Tool, hit the [up arrow] on your keyboard, then hit the [down arrow].
  - Create a new layer and name it *Thick Outline*.
  - Change the foreground color to black (`#000000`).
  - **Edit > Stroke...**
    - `Width = 5 px`
    - `Location = Inside`
  - Click the [OK] button.

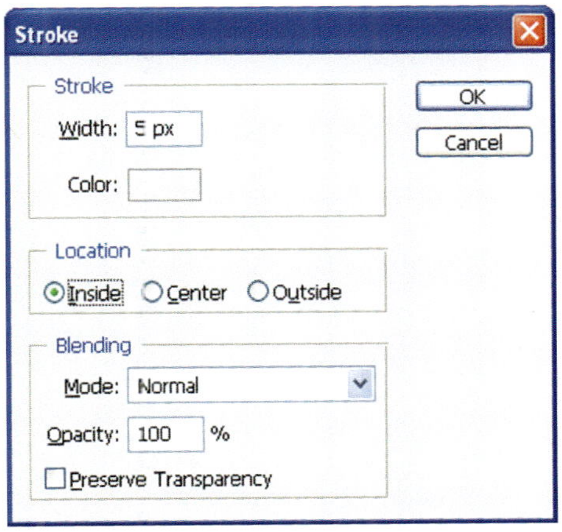

Step 2: Add more detail to the symbol.

Step 2: Add more detail to the symbol.

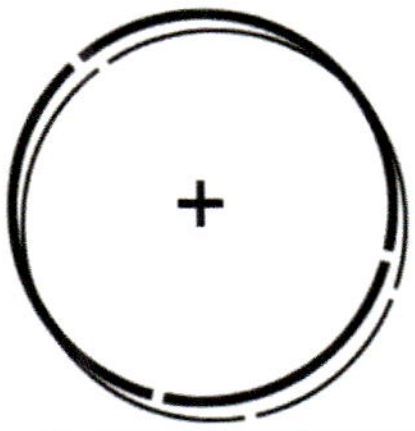

- Draw a thin outline around the circle.
  - Click on the layer *Brush 200* to choose it.
  - **Select > All**
  - With the Move Tool, hit the [up arrow] on your keyboard, then hit the [down arrow].
  - Create a new layer and name it *Thin Outline*.
  - **Edit > Stroke**
    - `Width = 2 px`
    - `Location = Inside`
  - Click the [OK] button.
  - With the Move Tool, shift the outline to the right and down.

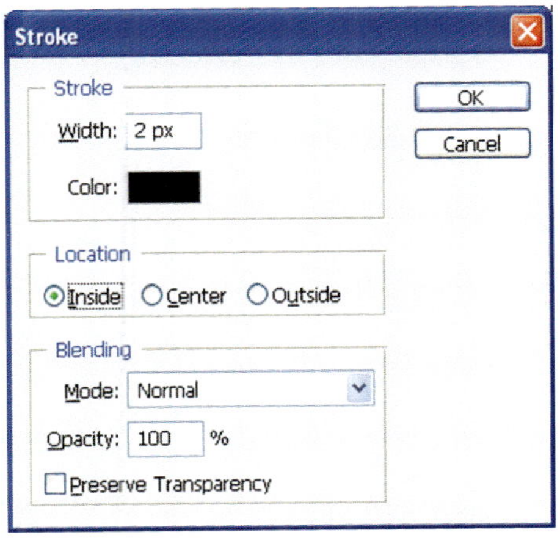

- Anchor the center of the symbol.
  - Select the Horizontal Type Tool and type a '+' over the center of the circle.
    - `Font = Arial`
    - `Size = 18 pt`
  - Rename this layer ***Text +***.
- Erase from the outlines so that there are gaps.
  - Click on the layer ***Thin Outline*** to choose it.
  - Choose a brush for the Eraser Tool and erase from the outlines of they symbol.
    - `Master Diameter = 5 px`
    - `Hardness = 100%`
  - Click on the layer ***Thick Outline*** to choose it, and erase as you did before.

Step 3: Add sharp 'V' strokes.

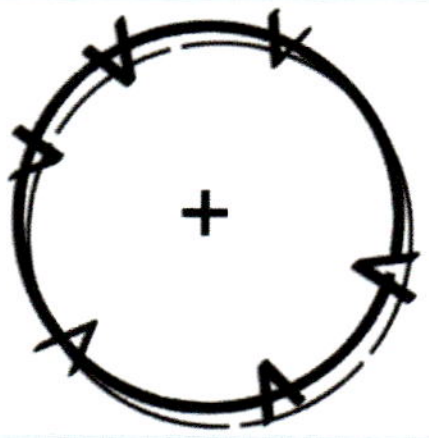

Step 3: Add sharp 'V' strokes.

- Load a new set of paintbrushes.
  - With the Brush Tool, click on the [v] icon by the brush to open the Brush Preset picker.
  - From the Brush Preset Picker, click the [>] icon to open the Brush Preset pop-up and select "Calligraphic Brushes."

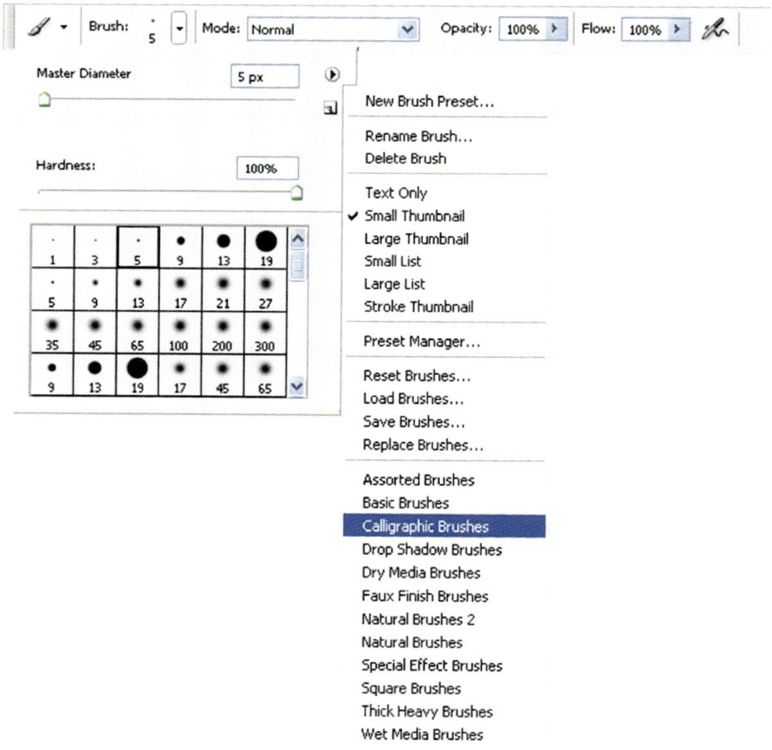

- Draw the 'V' brush strokes.
  - Create a new layer and name it ***V Strokes***.
  - Choose a (calligraphic) paintbrush and draw 'V' strokes around the outside of the symbol.
    - `Master Diameter = 7 px`
    - `Hardness = 100%`

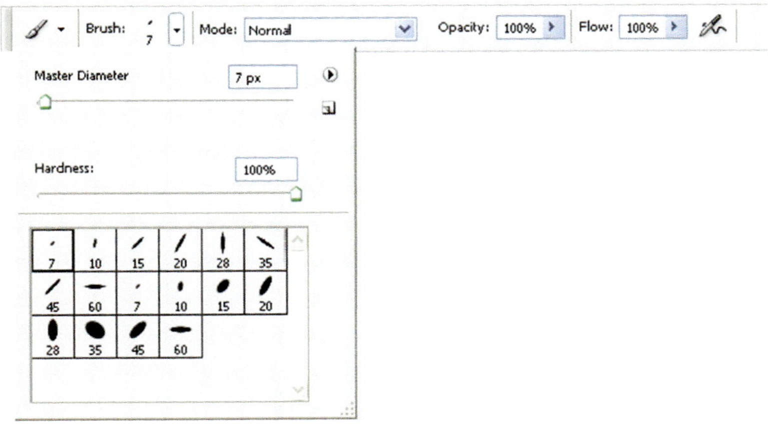

- Reload the default set of paintbrushes.
  - With the Brush Tool, click on the [v] icon by the brush to open the Brush Preset picker.
  - From the Brush Preset Picker, click the [>] icon to open the Brush Preset pop-up and select "Reset Brushes..."

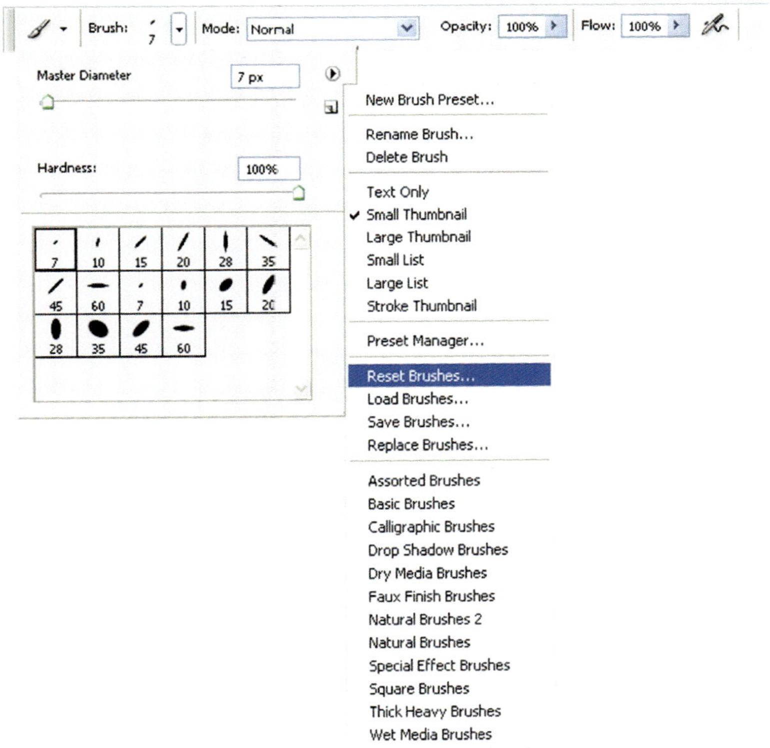

Step 4: Erase from the bold outline.

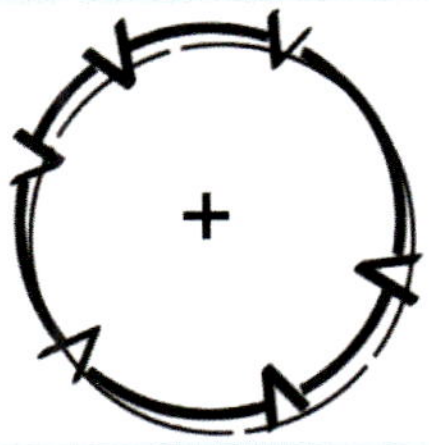

Step 4: Erase from the bold outline.

- Erase from the bold outline where the 'V' strokes intersect.
  - Click on the layer *Thick Outline* to choose it.
  - Choose a brush for the Eraser Tool and erase where the 'V' strokes intersect.
    - `Master Diameter = 19 px`
    - `Hardness = 100%`

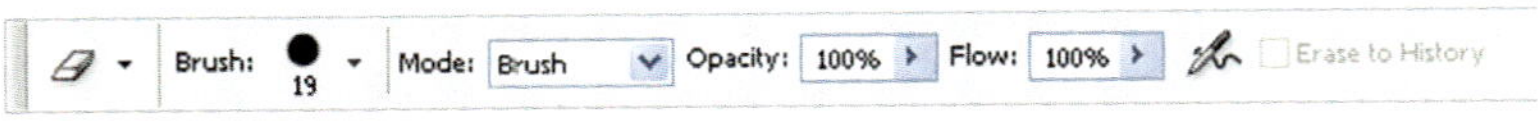

Step 5: Distort the line work.

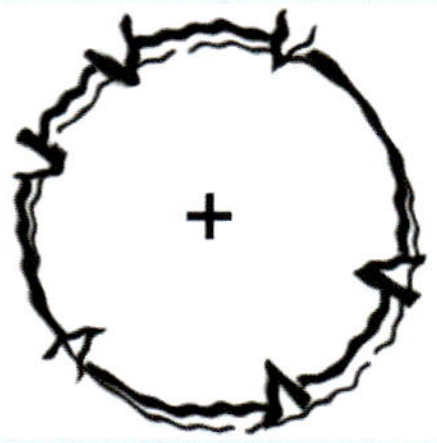

Step 5: Distort the line work.

- Merge the line work into one layer.
  - Click on the layer ***Thick Outline*** to choose it.
  - While holding down the [Ctrl] key, click on the layers ***Thin Outline*** and ***V Strokes*** to choose them too.
  - Click the right mouse button and select "Merge Layers" from the pop-up dialog box.
  - Rename the merged layer ***Line Work***.
- Distort the symbol using a filter.
  - Click on the layer ***Line Work*** to choose it.
  - **Filter > Distort > Ripple...**
    - `Amount = 100%`
    - `Size = Large`
  - Click the [OK] button.

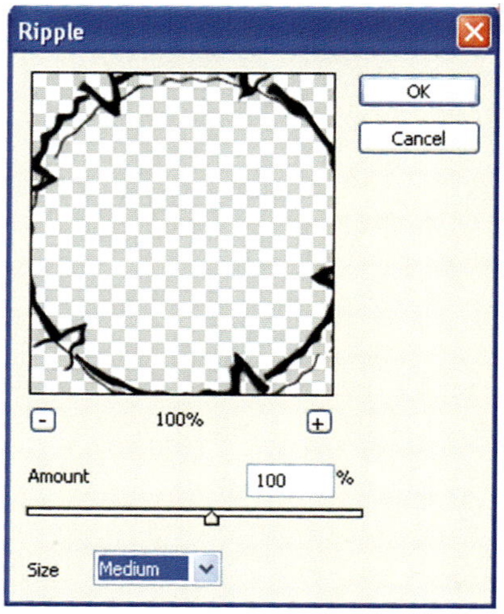

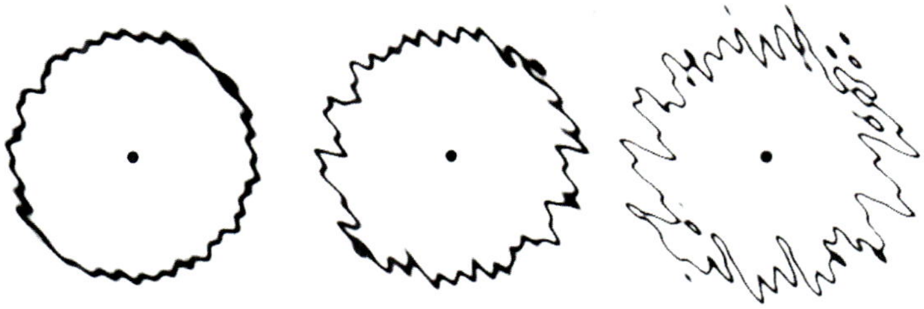

Master Plan Graphics | Trees

This step-by-step example illustrates how to draw simple, black-and-white symbols for a tree. The techniques used in this example include the following:

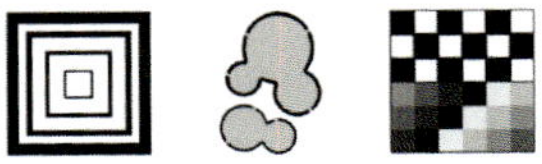

Line Hierarchy | Best Stroke | Black & White

This drawing was originally drawn on a canvas with a resolution of 200 pixels per inch. Afterwards, it was scaled down to fit within these pages.

Step 1: Draw a simple outline of a circle.

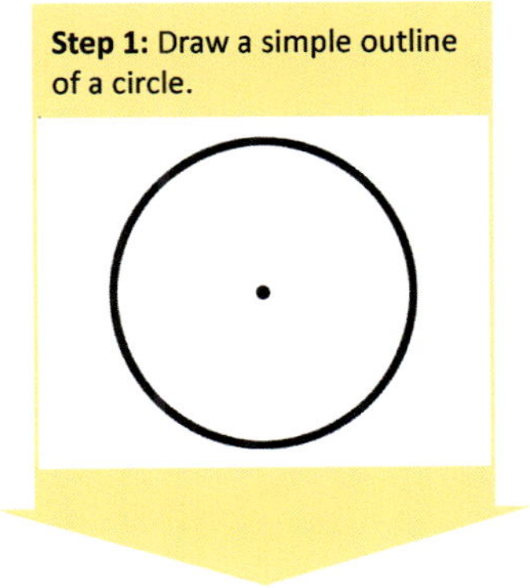

- Draw the a simple circle.
  - Create a new layer and name it ***Brush 200***.
  - Choose a paintbrush for the Brush Tool and draw a circle by simply touching the brush to the canvas.
    - `Master Diameter = 200 px`
    - `Hardness = 100%`

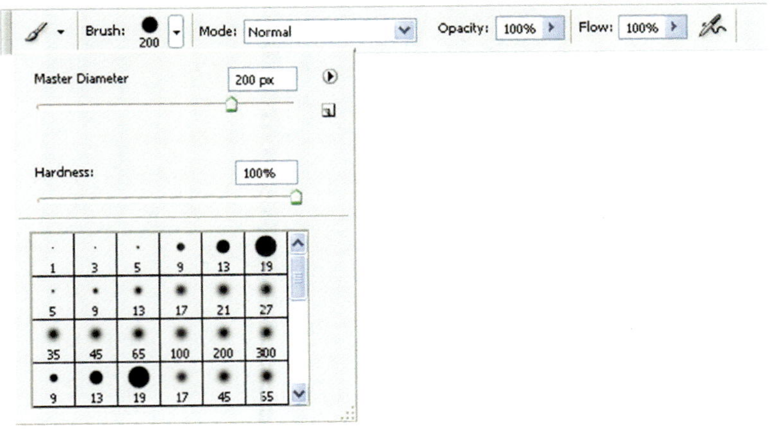

- Reduce the opacity of your fill so that you can see your work in the next steps.
  - `Opacity = 25%`

- Draw a thick outline around the circle.
    - Click on the layer *Brush 200* to choose it.
    - **Select > All**
    - With the Move Tool, hit the [up arrow] on your keyboard, then hit the [down arrow].
    - Create a new layer and name it *Thick Outline*.
    - Change the foreground color to black (`#000000`).
    - **Edit > Stroke...**
        - `Width = 5 px`
        - `Location = Inside`
    - Click the [OK] button.

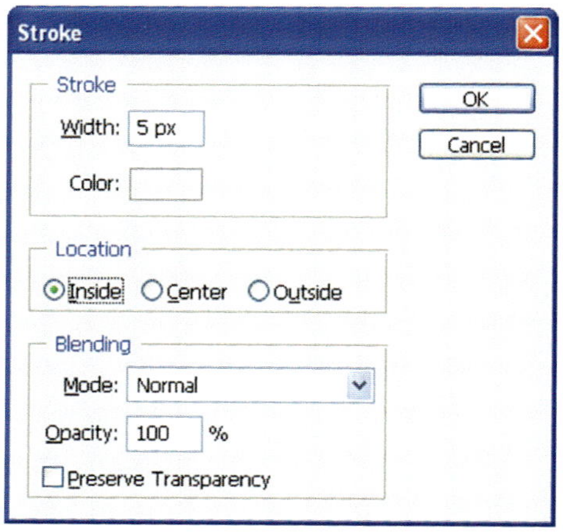

- Anchor the center of the symbol.
    - Select a paintbrush for the Brush Tool and draw a dot in the center of the circle.
        - `Master Diameter = 7 px`
        - `Hardness = 100%`

Step 2: Distort the line work.

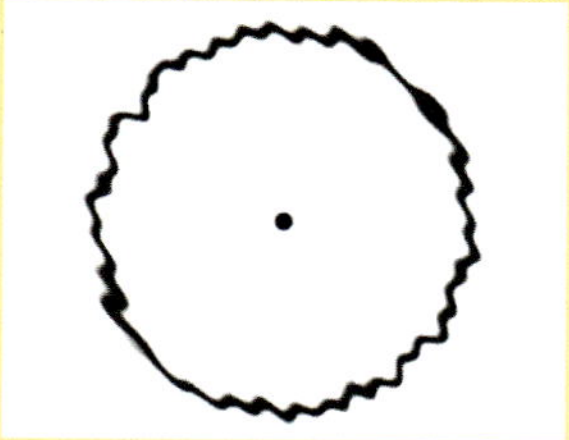

Step 2: Distort the line work.

- Distort the symbol using a filter.
    - Click on the layer *Thick Outline* to choose it.
    - **Filter > Distort > Ripple...**
        - `Amount = 100%`
        - `Size = Large`
    - Click the [OK] button.

Step 2(b): Alternative distortion.

- Distort the symbol using a filter.
    - Click on the layer *Thick Outline* to choose it.
    - **Filter > Distort > Ripple...**
        - `Amount = 200%`
        - `Size = Large`
    - Click the [OK] button.

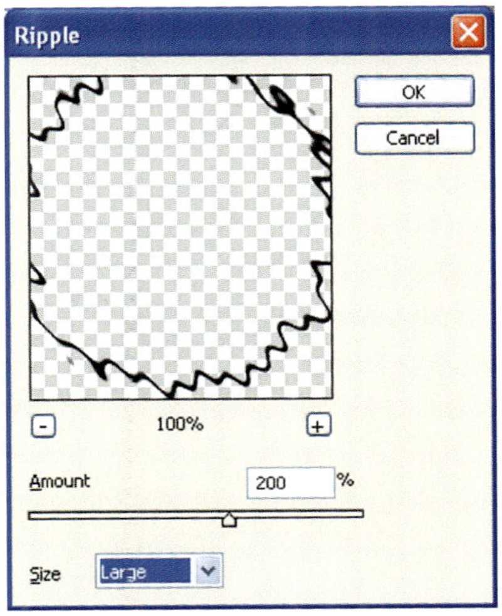

Step 2(b): Alternative distortion.

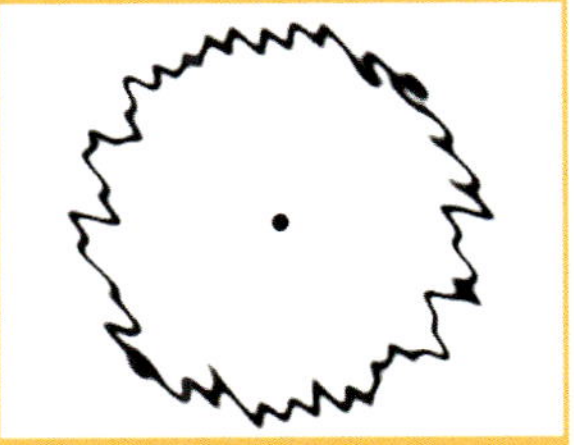

Step 2(c): Alternative distortion.

- Distort the symbol using a filter.
    - Click on the layer *Thick Outline* to choose it.
    - **Filter > Distort > Ripple...**
        - `Amount = 500%`
        - `Size = Large`
    - Click the [OK] button.

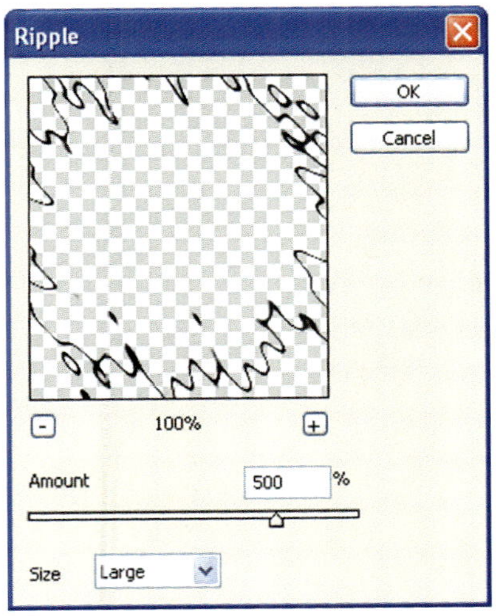

Step 2(c): Alternative distortion.

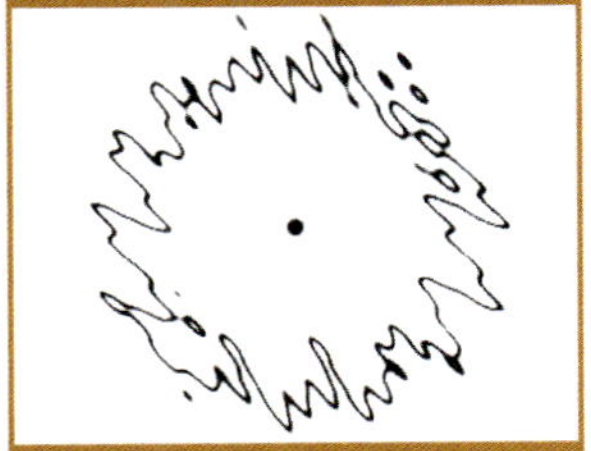

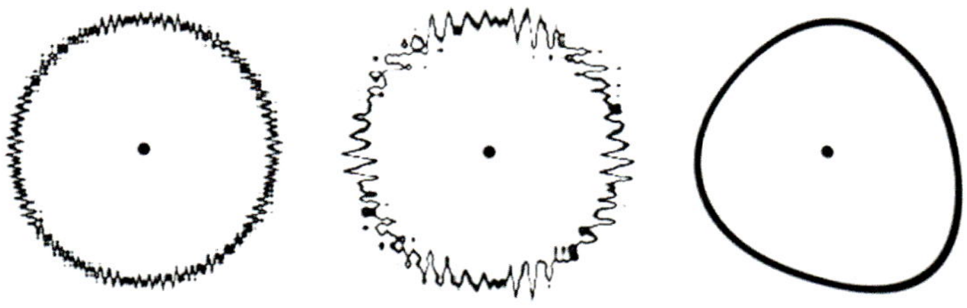

Master Plan Graphics | Trees

This step-by-step example illustrates how to draw simple, black-and-white symbols for a tree. The techniques used in this example include the following:

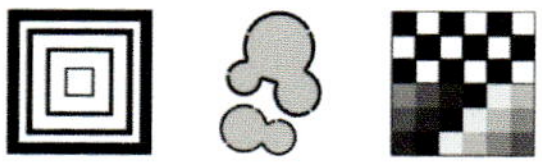

Line Hierarchy | Best Stroke | Black & White

This drawing was originally drawn on a canvas with a resolution of 200 pixels per inch. Afterwards, it was scaled down to fit within these pages.

Step 1: Draw a simple outline of a circle.

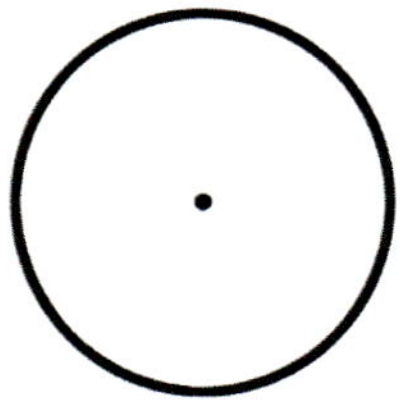

Step 1: Draw a simple outline of a circle.

- Repeat Step 1 from the previous example.

Step 2: Distort the line work.

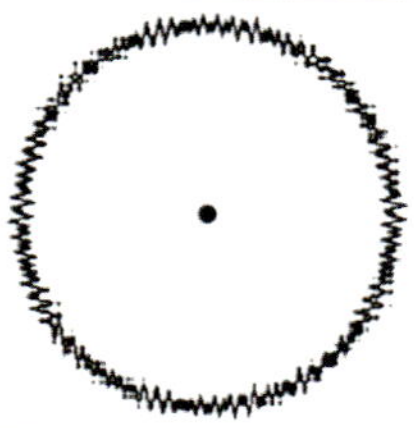

Step 2: Distort the line work.

- Distort the symbol using a filter.
  - Click on the layer *Thick Outline* to choose it.
  - **Filter > Distort > Wave...**
    - `Number of Generators = 3`
    - `Wavelength = 1 to 5`
    - `Amplitude = 1 to 5`
    - `Scale = 100% (Horizontal), 100% (Vertical)`
    - `Type = Sine`
  - Click the [OK] button.

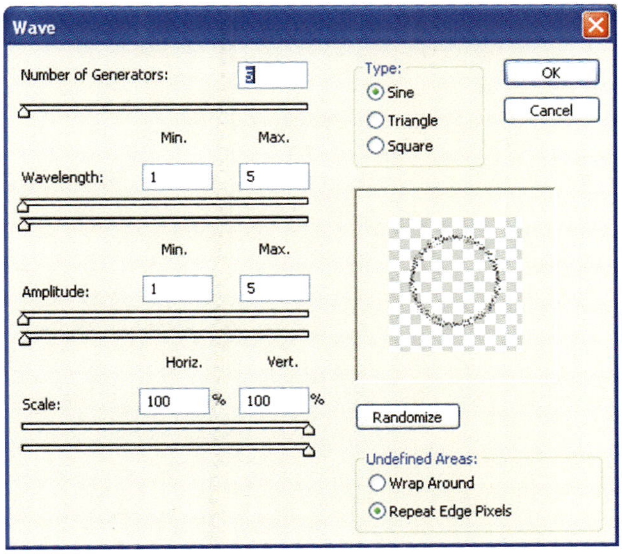

Step 2(b): Alternative distortion.

- Distort the symbol using a filter.
  - Click on the layer *Thick Outline* to choose it.
  - **Filter > Distort > Wave...**
    - `Number of Generators = 5`
    - `Wavelength = 1 to 10`
    - `Amplitude = 1 to 10`
    - `Scale = 100% (Horizontal), 100% (Vertical)`
    - `Type = Sine`
  - Click the [OK] button.

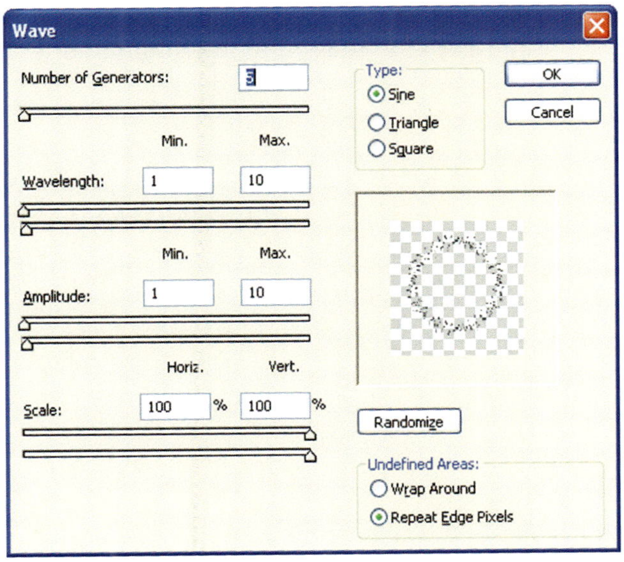

Step 2(b): Alternative distortion.

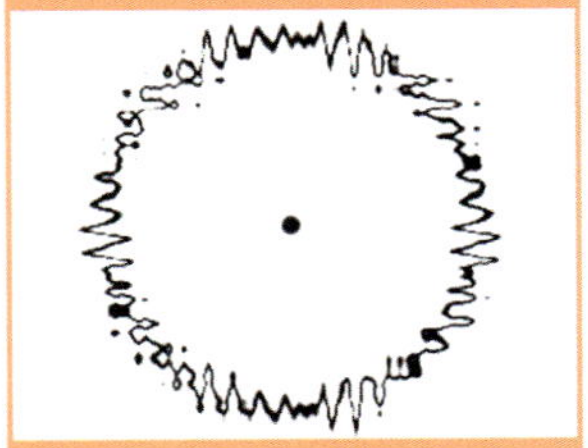

Step 2(c): Alternative distortion.

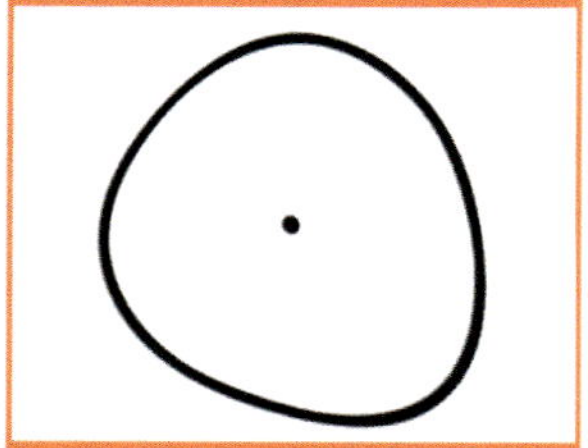

Step 2(c): Alternative distortion.

- Distort the symbol using a filter.
  - Click on the layer ***Thick Outline*** to choose it.
  - **Filter > Distort > Wave...**
    - `Number of Generators = 3`
    - `Wavelength = 100 to 150`
    - `Amplitude = 5 to 5`
    - `Scale = 100% (Horizontal), 100% (Vertical)`
    - `Type = Sine`
  - Click the [OK] button.

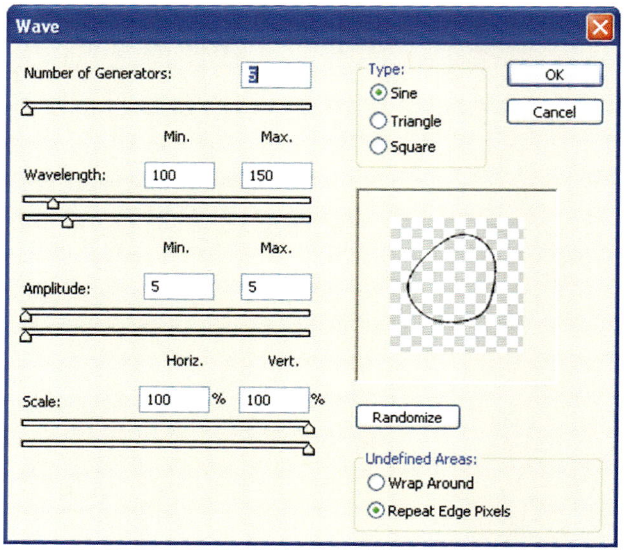

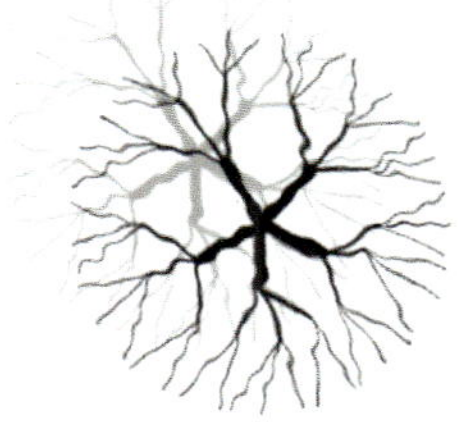

Master Plan Graphics | Deciduous Tree

This example illustrates how to draw a simple, black-and-white symbol for a deciduous tree. The techniques used in this example include the following:

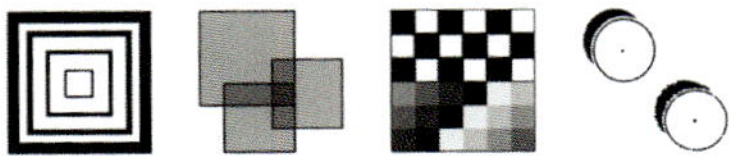

Line Hierarchy | Layer Opacity | Black & White | Dead or Alive

This drawing was originally drawn on a canvas with a resolution of 200 pixels per inch. Afterwards, it was scaled down to fit within these pages.

Step 1: Draw the symbol limits.

- Draw a circle to help visualize the space you want to draw within.
  - Create a new layer and name it ***Brush 200***.
  - Choose a paintbrush for the Brush Tool and draw a circle by simply touching the brush to the canvas.
    - `Master Diameter = 200 px`
    - `Hardness = 100%`
      - Because the diameter is 200 pixels and the resolution is 200 pixels per inch (ppi), the diameter will be equal to 1 inch.

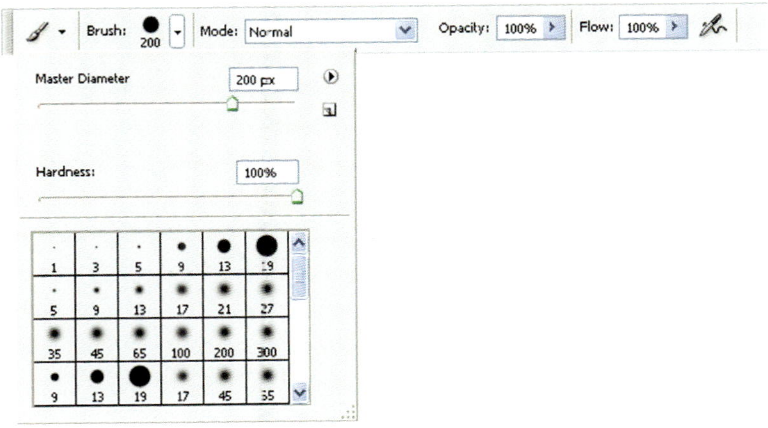

Step 1: Draw the symbol limits.

- Reduce the opacity of your fill so that you can see your work in the next steps.
    - `Opacity = 50%`

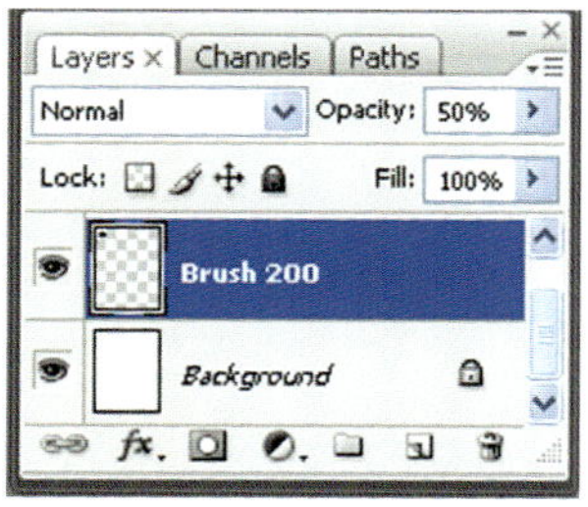

Step 2: Draw the trunk and main branches.

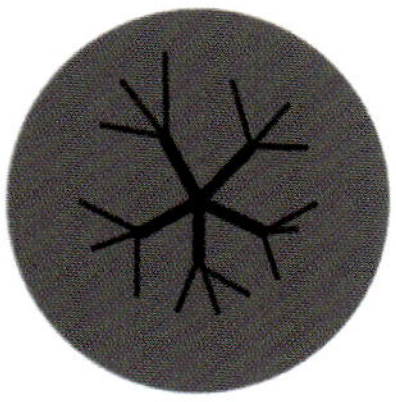

Step 2: Draw the trunk and main branches.

- Draw the trunk.
    - Create a new layer and name it *Branches*.
    - Choose a paintbrush for the Brush Tool and draw lines radiating from the center.
        - `Master Diameter = 5 px`
        - `Hardness = 100%`

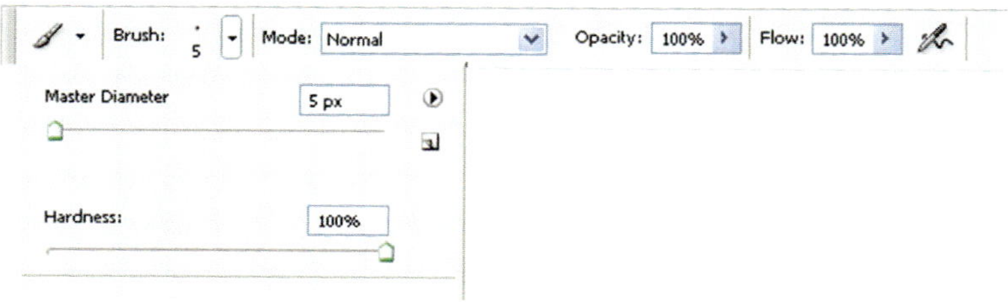

- Draw the main branches.
    - Choose a thinner paintbrush for the Brush Tool and draw three branches radiating from each thicker branch.
        - `Master Diameter = 2 px`
        - `Hardness = 100%`

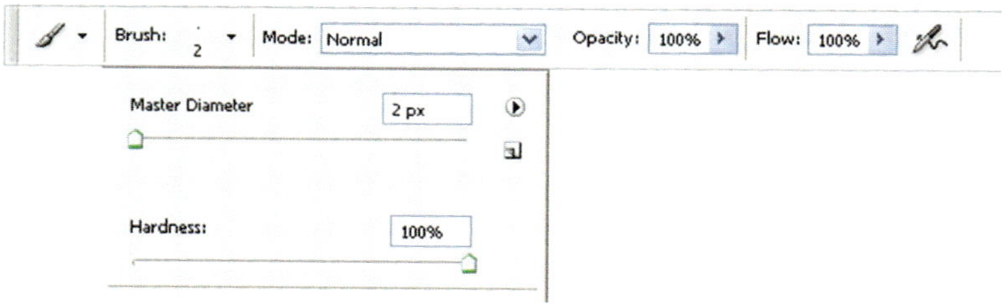

Step 3: Draw additional branches.

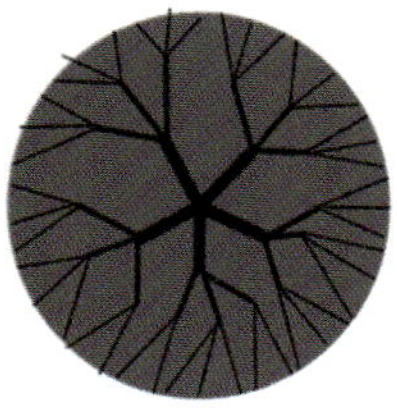

Step 3: Draw additional branches.

- Draw additional branches.
    - Choose a thinner paintbrush for the Brush Tool and draw two or three branches from each of the outer branches.
        - `Master Diameter = 1 px`
        - `Hardness = 100%`
            - Make sure these last branches reach the limits of the circle edge.

Step 4: Distort the symbol.

Step 4: Distort the symbol.

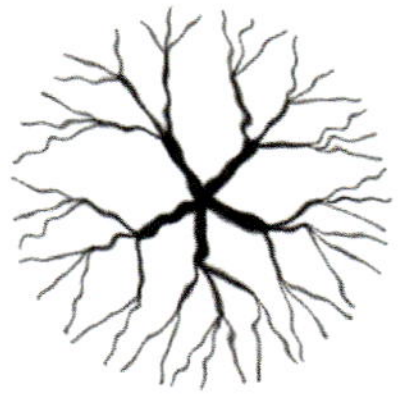

- Distort the branches with a filter.
  - Click on the layer ***Branches*** to choose it.
  - **Filter > Distort > Ripple**
    - `Amount = 100%`
    - `Size = Medium`
  - Click the [OK] button.

Step 5: Add a shadow.

Step 5: Add a shadow.

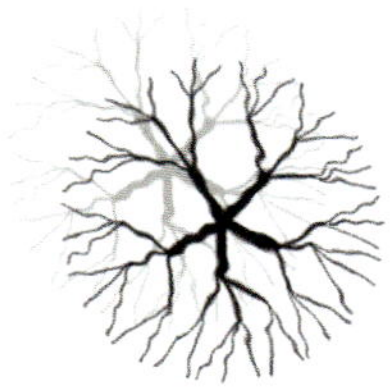

- Use a copy of the symbol to create a shadow.
  - Click on the layer ***Branches*** to choose it.
  - You can copy the selected layer by either:
    - Hitting the right mouse button key, selecting "Duplicate Layer..." from the pop-up menu, and then clicking [OK] on the Duplicate Layer dialog box.
    - Or, you can simply drag the layer to the "Create a new layer" icon.
  - With the Move Tool, shift the copied layer up and to the left.
  - Rename the copied layer ***Shadow***.
  - Change the layer `Opacity = 20%`.

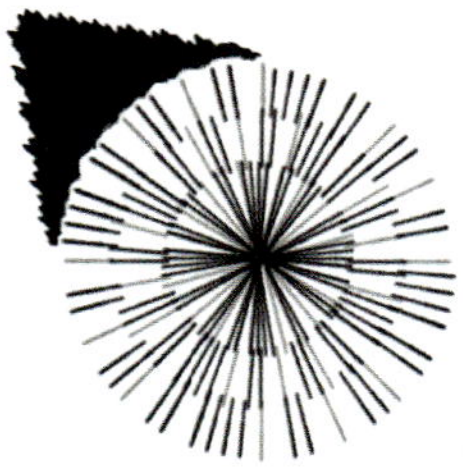

Master Plan Graphics | Coniferous Tree

This example illustrates how to draw a simple, black-and-white symbol for a coniferous tree. The techniques used in this example include the following:

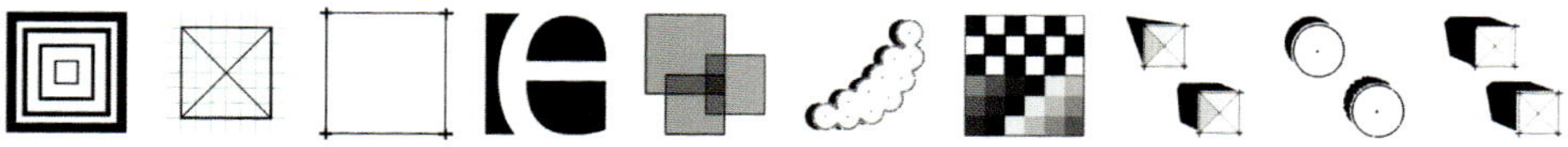

Line Hierarchy | Straighten Up | Hit-Go-Hit | Erase | Layer Opacity | Merge | Black & White | Inform | Dead or Alive | Shadow Gap

This drawing was originally drawn on a canvas with a resolution of 200 pixels per inch. Afterwards, it was scaled down to fit within these pages.

Step 1: Draw the symbol limits.

Step 1: Draw the symbol limits.

- Draw a circle to help visualize the space you want to draw within.
  - Create a new layer and name it ***Brush 200***.
  - Choose a paintbrush for the Brush Tool and draw a circle by simply touching the brush to the canvas.
    - `Master Diameter = 200 px`
    - `Hardness = 100%`
      - Because the diameter is 200 pixels and the resolution is 200 pixels per inch (ppi), the diameter will be equal to 1 inch.

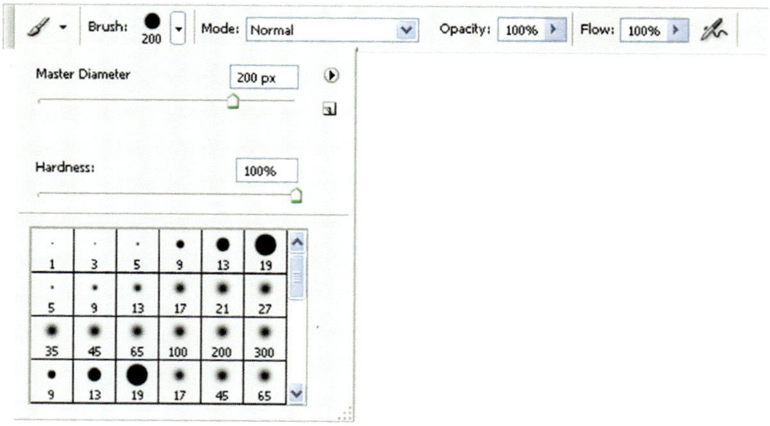

- Reduce the opacity of your fill so that you can see your work in the next steps.
  - `Opacity = 50%`

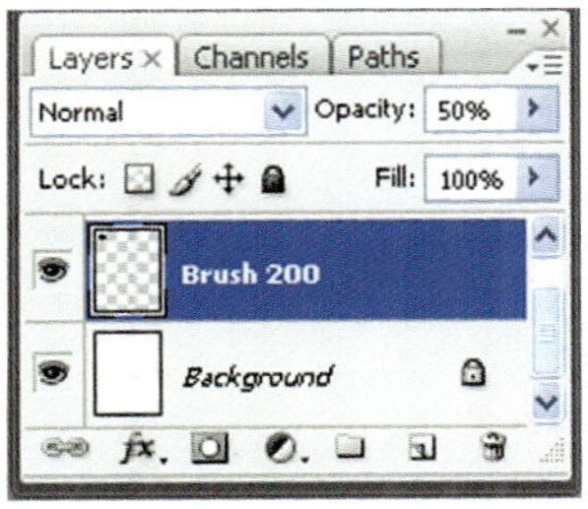

Step 2: Draw the first brush strokes.

Step 2: Draw the first brush strokes.

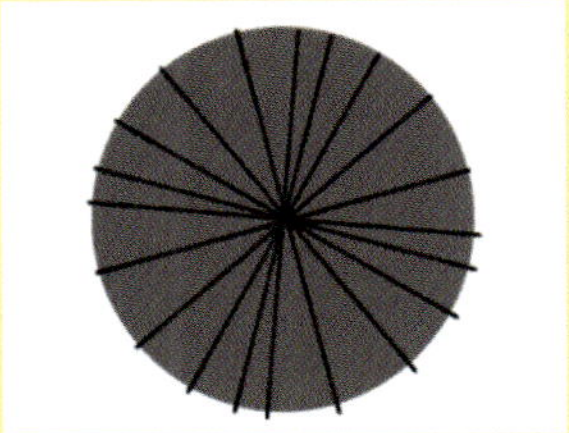

- Draw lines radiating from the center.
  - Create a new layer and name it *Brush 2*.
  - Choose a paintbrush for the Brush Tool and draw lines radiating from the center to the limits of the symbol.
    - `Master Diameter = 2 px`
    - `Hardness = 100%`

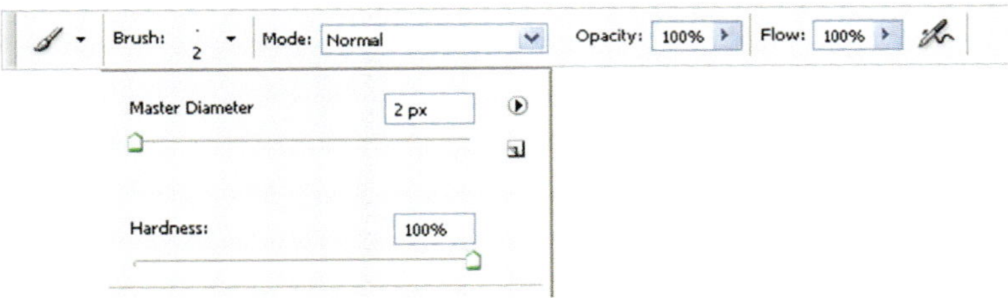

Step 3: Draw additional brush strokes.

Step 3: Draw additional brush strokes.

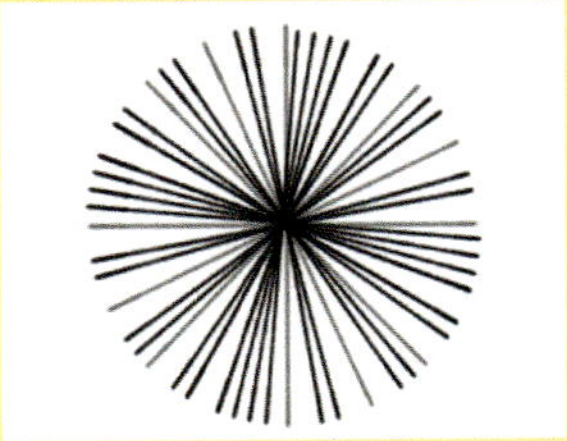

- Draw additional lines as you did before.
  - As before, create new layers named *Brush 2* and draw additional lines.
    - Ordinarily, you want layer names to be distinct from one another; however, you will consolidate these layers into just one layer in just a moment.
  - You may consider changing the layer opacity on one or more layers to give your drawing some more depth and interest.
- Merge all the layers you have drawn lines on.
  - Click on each layer while holding down the [Ctrl] key.
  - Click on the right mouse button and select "Merge Layers..." from the pop-up dialog box.
  - Rename the layer *Brush 2 Merged*.

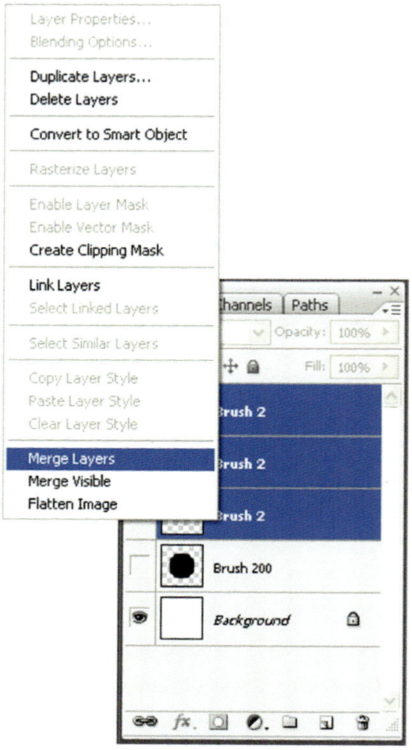

Step 4: Create tiers of branches.

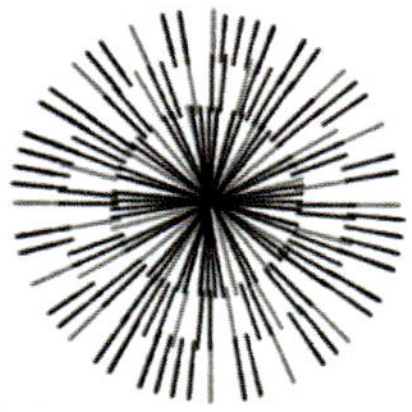

Step 4: Create tiers of branches.

To make tiers of branches, you will copy your original brush strokes and then trim them.

- Make two copies of your merged layer.
  - Click on the layer ***Brush 2 Merged*** to choose it.
  - You can copy the selected layer by either:
    - Hitting the right mouse key, selecting "Duplicate Layer..." from the pop-up menu, and then clicking [OK] on the Duplicate Layer dialog box.
    - Or, you can simply drag the layer to the "Create a new layer" icon.
  - Repeat these steps to make another copy.

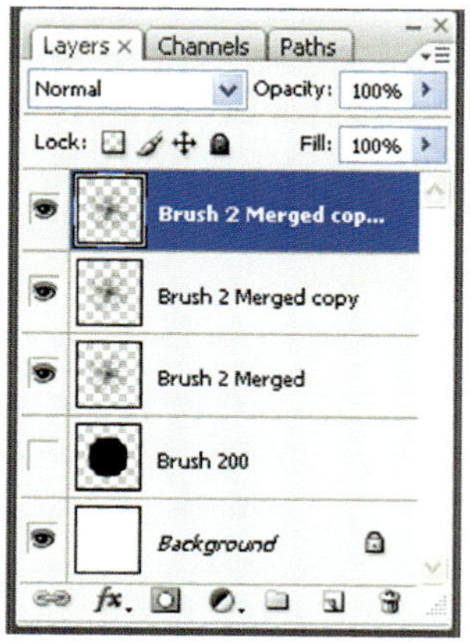

- Rename your copied layers so that you can distinguish between them.
  - Rename the original and two copied layers ***Outside***, ***Middle***, and ***Inside***.

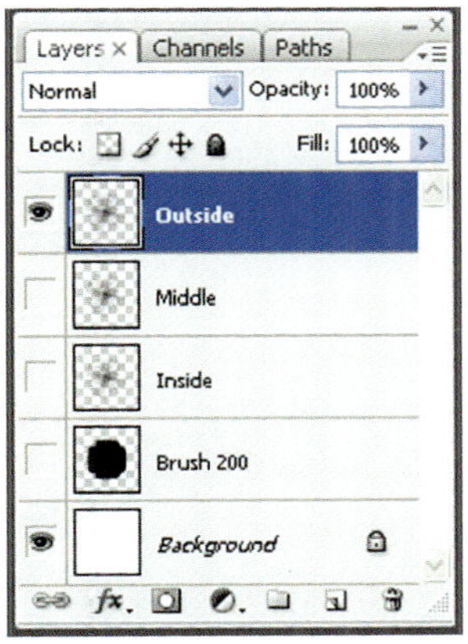

- Trim the outside lines.
  - Turn off the other two layers, ***Middle*** and ***Inside***.
    - For each layer, click on the [eye] on each layer tab so that it disappears and the lines drawn on these layers are no longer visible.
  - Click on the layer ***Brush 200*** to choose it.
  - **Select > All**
  - With the Move Tool, hit the [up arrow] on your keyboard, then hit the [down arrow].
  - **Select > Modify > Contract...**
    - `Contract By = 25 pixels`
  - Click the [OK] button.
  - Click on the layer ***Outside*** to choose it.
  - Hit the [Delete] key to erase the lines within your selection.

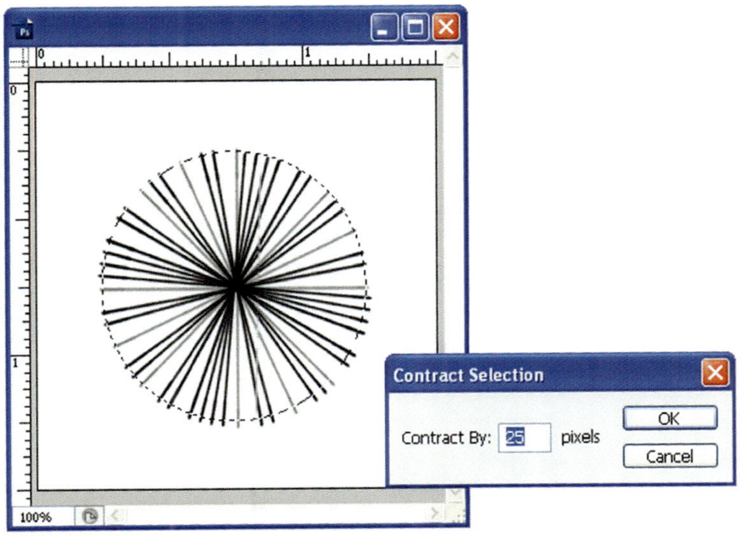

- Trim the outside edges from the middle lines.
  - Click on the space for the [eye] on the layer ***Middle*** so that the eye appears and the lines on this layer are visible again.
  - Turn off the other two layers, ***Outside*** and ***Inside***.
    - For each layer, click on the [eye] so that it disappears and the lines drawn on these layers are no longer visible.
  - Click on the layer ***Brush 200*** to choose it.
  - **Select > All**
  - With the Move Tool, hit the [up arrow] on your keyboard, then hit the [down arrow].
  - **Select > Modify > Contract...**
    - `Contract By = 20 pixels`
  - Click the [OK] button.
  - **Select > Inverse**
  - Click on the layer ***Middle*** to choose it.
  - Hit the [Delete] key to erase the lines within your selection.

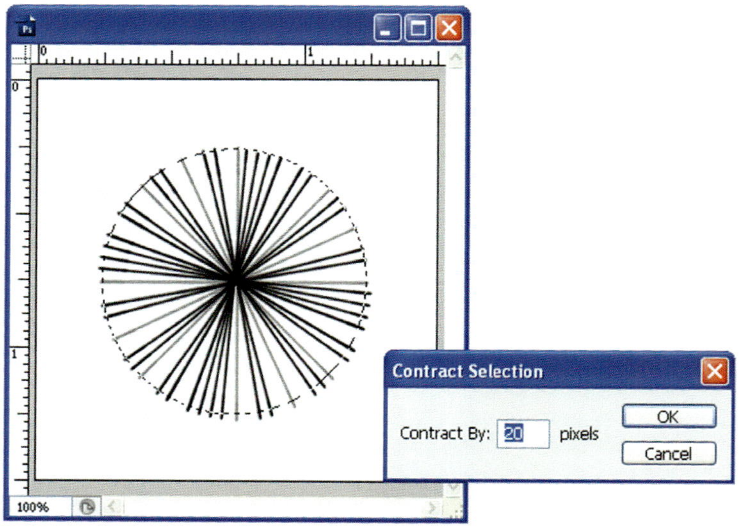

- Trim the inside edges from the middle lines.
  - Click on the layer ***Brush 200*** to choose it.
  - **Select > All**
  - With the Move Tool, hit the [up arrow] on your keyboard, then hit the [down arrow].
  - **Select > Modify > Contract...**
    - `Contract By = 50 pixels`
  - Click the [OK] button.
  - Click on the layer ***Middle*** to choose it.
  - Hit the [Delete] key to erase the lines within your selection.

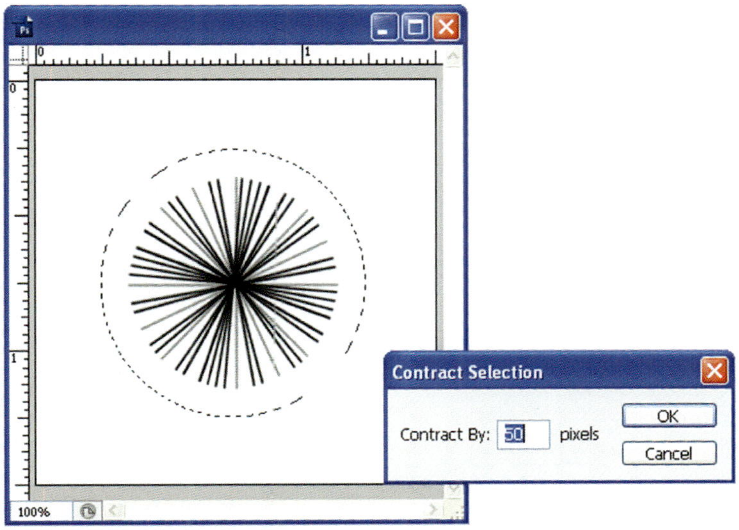

- Rotate the trimmed lines.
  - Click on the layer *Middle* to choose it.
  - **Edit > Transform > Rotate**
    - `Angle = 15 degrees`
  - Hit the [Enter] key.

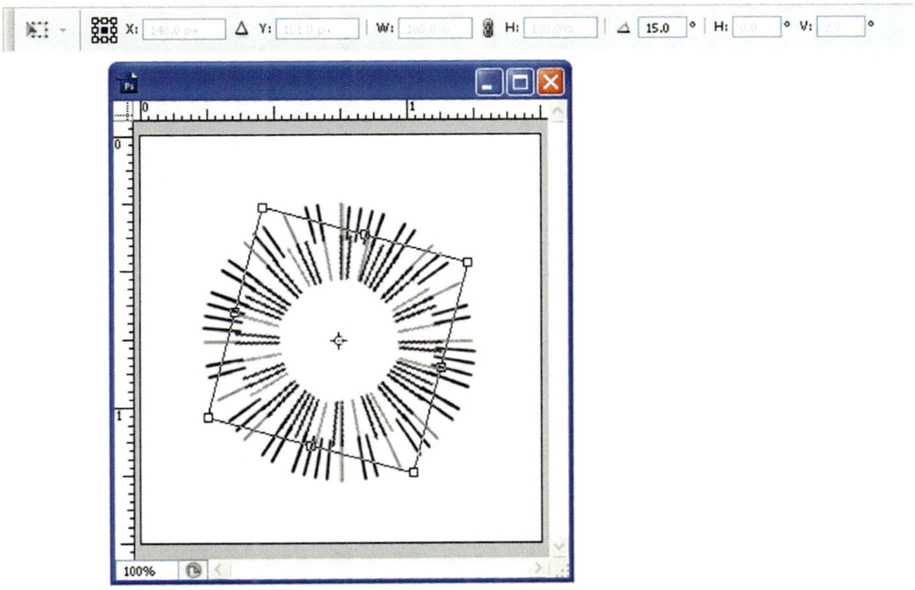

- Trim the inside lines.
  - Click on the space for the [eye] on the layer ***Inside*** so that the eye appears and the lines on this layer are visible again.
  - Turn off the other two layers, *Outside* and *Middle*.
    - For each layer, click on the [eye] so that it disappears and the lines drawn on these layers are no longer visible.

- Trim the inside lines. (continued)
    - Click on the layer ***Brush 200*** to choose it.
    - **Select > All**
    - With the Move Tool, hit the [up arrow] on your keyboard, then hit the [down arrow].
    - **Select > Modify > Contract...**
        - `Contract By = 45 pixels`
    - Click the [OK] button.
    - **Select > Inverse**
    - Click on the layer ***Inside*** to choose it.
    - Hit the [Delete] key to erase the lines within your selection.

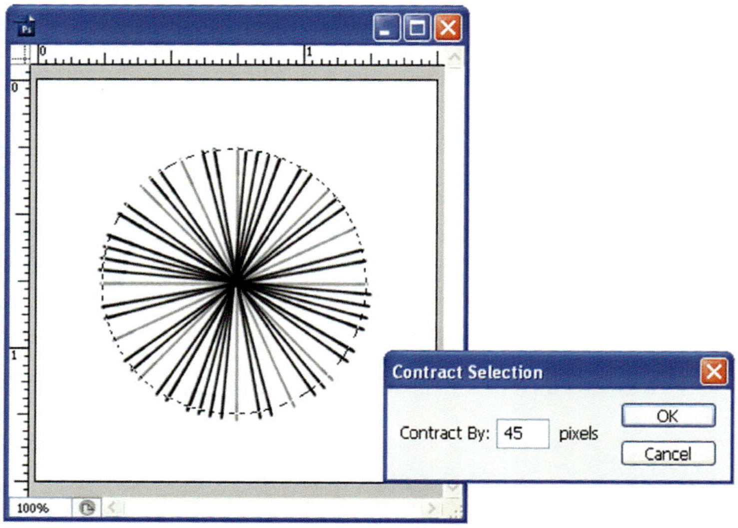

Step 5: Add a shadow.

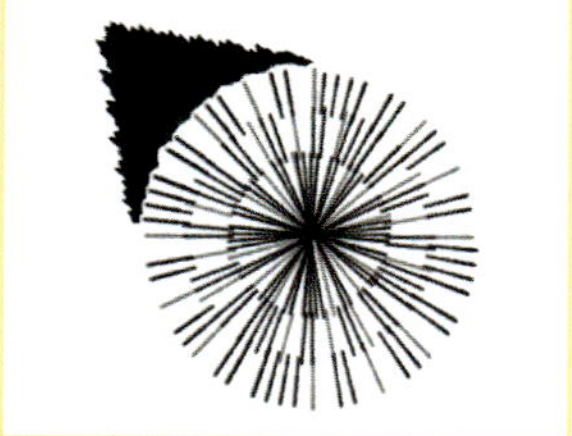

Step 5: Add a shadow.

- Loosely draw a pyramidal shadow.
    - Create a new layer and name it ***Shadow***.
    - Select a paintbrush for the Brush Tool and loosely draw a triangle.
- Trim the shadow.
    - Click on the layer ***Brush 200*** to choose it.
    - **Select > All**
    - With the Move Tool, hit the [up arrow] on your keyboard, then hit the [down arrow].
    - **Select > Modify > Expand...**
        - `Expand By = 5 pixels`
    - Click the [OK] button.
    - Click on the layer ***Shadow*** to choose it.
    - Hit the [Delete] key to erase the shadow within your selection.

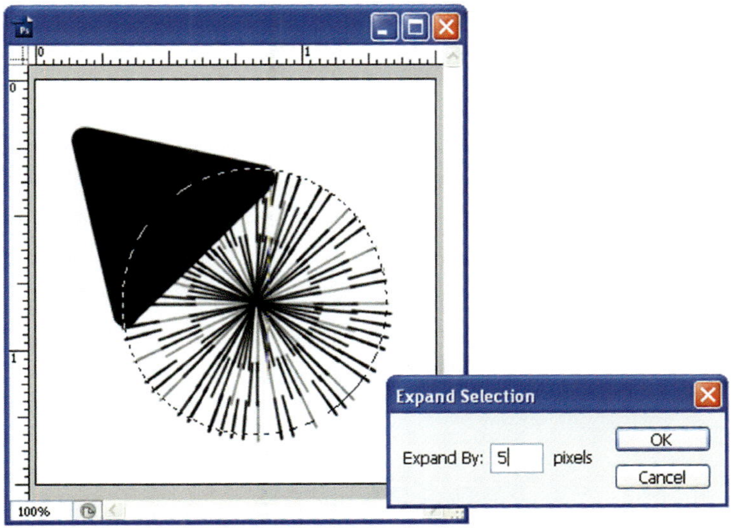

- Distort the shadow using a filter.
  - Click on the layer ***Shadow*** to choose it.
  - **Filter > Distort > Ripple...**
    - `Amount = 100%`
    - `Size = Large`
  - Click the [OK] button.

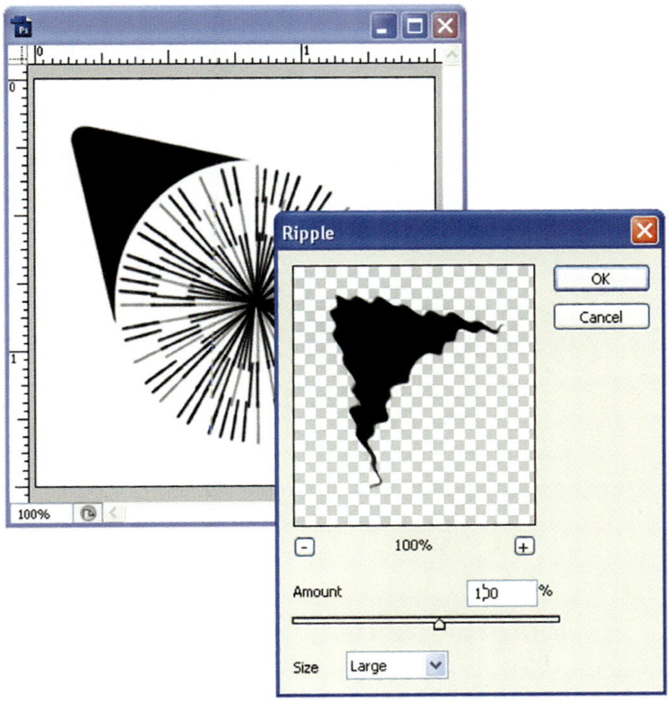

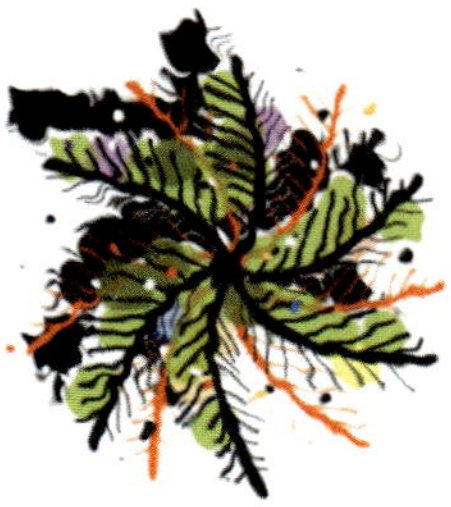

Master Plan Graphics | Palm Tree

This example illustrates how to draw a symbol for a palm tree. The techniques used in this example include the following:

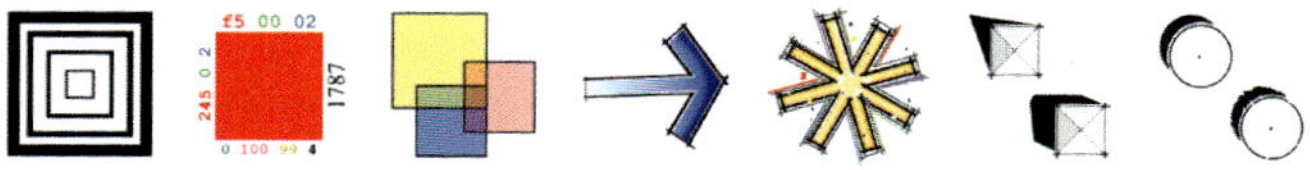

Line Hierarchy | Color Palette | Trans-parency | Light Then Dark | Accent | Inform | Dead or Alive

This drawing was originally drawn on a canvas with a resolution of 200 pixels per inch. Afterwards, it was scaled down to fit within these pages.

Step 1: Draw the symbol limits.

Step 1: Draw the symbol limits.

- Draw a circle to help visualize the space you want to draw within.
  - Create a new layer and name it ***Brush 200***.
  - Choose a paintbrush for the Brush Tool and draw a circle by simply touching the brush to the canvas.
    - `Master Diameter = 200 px`
    - `Hardness = 100%`

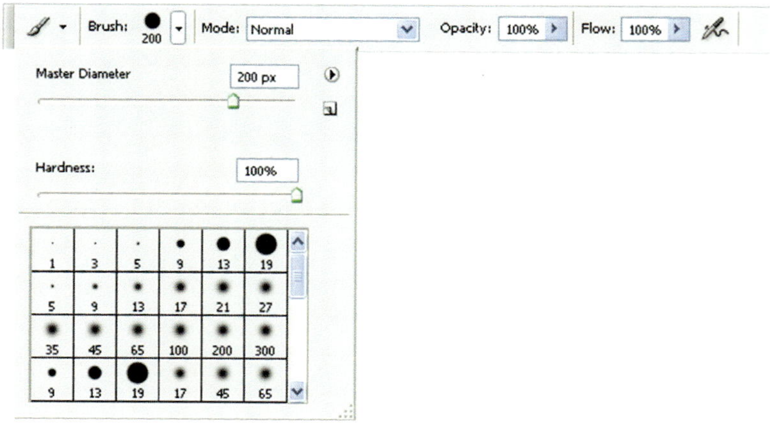

- Reduce the opacity of your fill so that you can see your work in the next steps.
  - `Opacity = 50%`

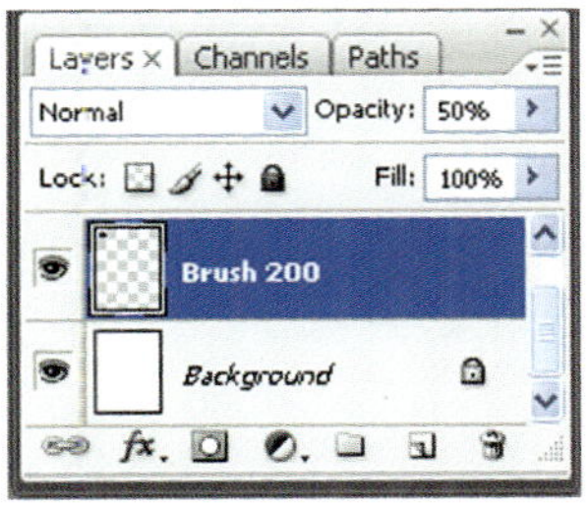

Step 2: Draw thick lines.

- Draw thick lines radiating from the center of the symbol.
  - Create a new layer and name it *Brush 5*.
  - Choose a paintbrush for the Brush Tool and draw brush strokes radiating from the center to the edges of the symbol.
    - `Master Diameter = 5 px`
    - `Hardness = 100%`

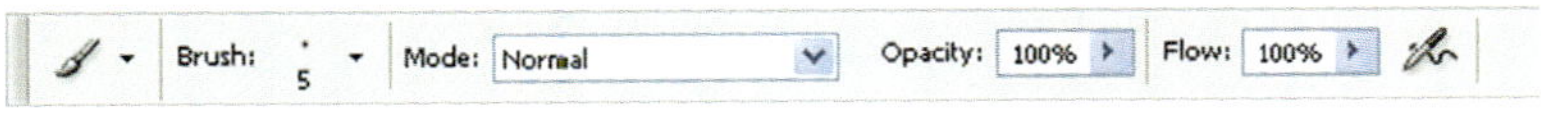

Step 2: Draw thick lines.

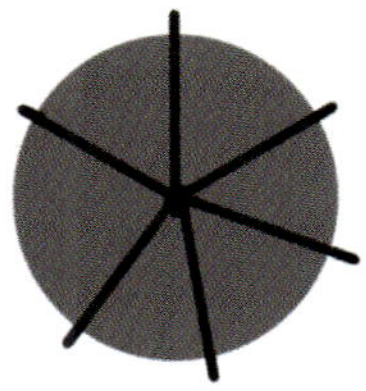

Step 3: Distort the line work.

- Select the area you intend to distort.
  - Click on the layer Brush 5 to choose it.
  - With the Selection Tool, select a square area that is large enough to capture the radiating brush strokes.

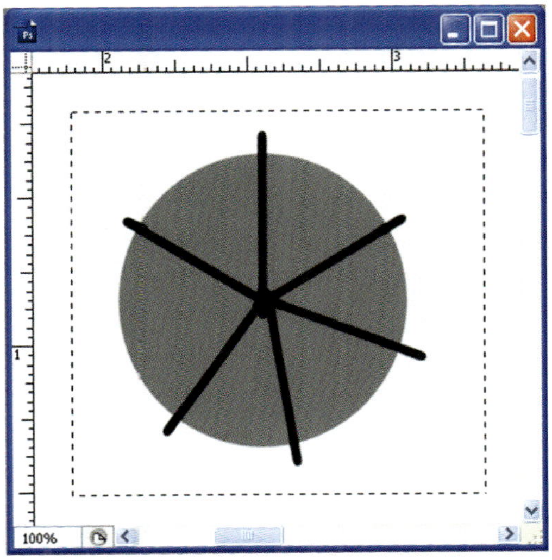

Step 3: Distort the line work.

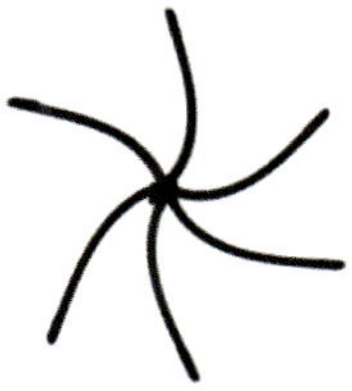

- Distort the line work with a filter.
  - **Filter > Distort > Twirl...**
    - `Angle = 50 degrees`
  - Click on the [OK] button.
  - Rename the layer *Brush 5 Twirl 50d*.

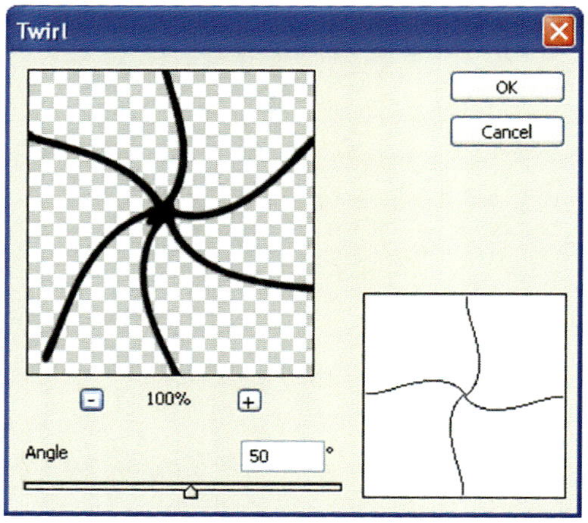

Step 4: Add thick lines.

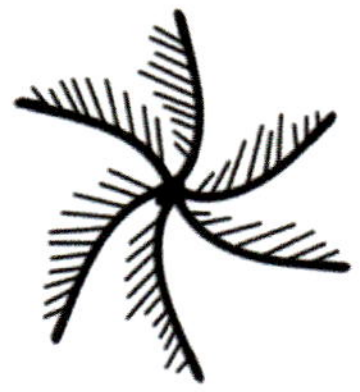

Step 4: Add thick lines.

- Add thick lines to the stems of the fronds.
  - Create a new layer and name it *Brush 3*.
  - Choose a paintbrush for the Brush Tool and draw perpendicular lines to the larger, thicker lines.
    - `Master Diameter = 3 px`
    - `Hardness = 100%`

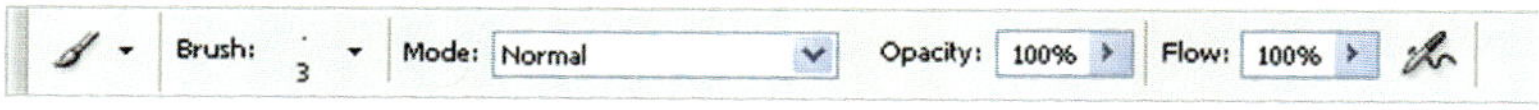

Step 5: Add thin lines.

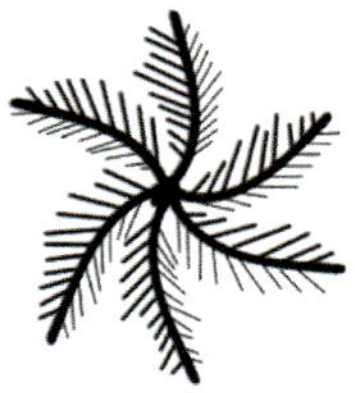

Step 5: Add thin lines.

- Add thin lines to the stems of the fronds.
  - Create a new layer and name it *Brush 1*.
  - Choose a paintbrush for the Brush Tool and draw perpendicular lines to the larger, thicker lines.
    - `Master Diameter = 1 px`
    - `Hardness = 100%`
      - You should consider the source of light (the sun) when deciding whether to draw thick or thin lines on either side of the fronds.

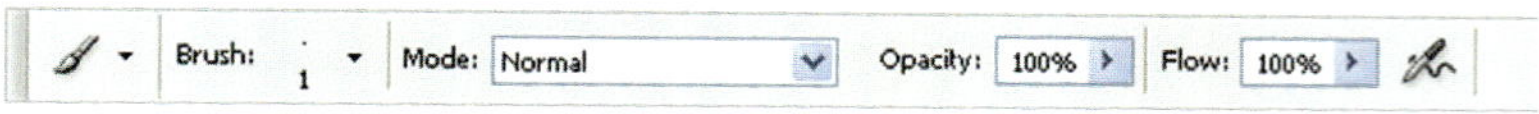

Step 6: Distort the line work.

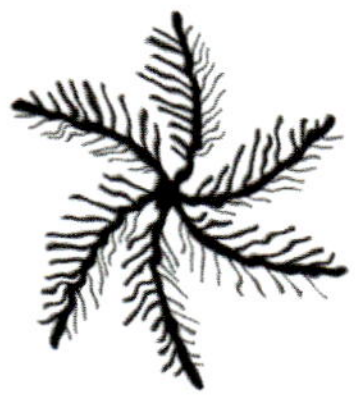

Step 6: Distort the line work.

- Consolidate the layers of your line work.
  - Click on the layer *Brush 5 Twirl 50d* to choose it.
  - While holding down the [Ctrl] key, click the layers *Brush 3* and *Brush 1* to choose them, too.
  - Click on the right mouse button and select "Merge Layers..." from the pop-up dialog box.
  - Rename the merged layer *Fronds*.

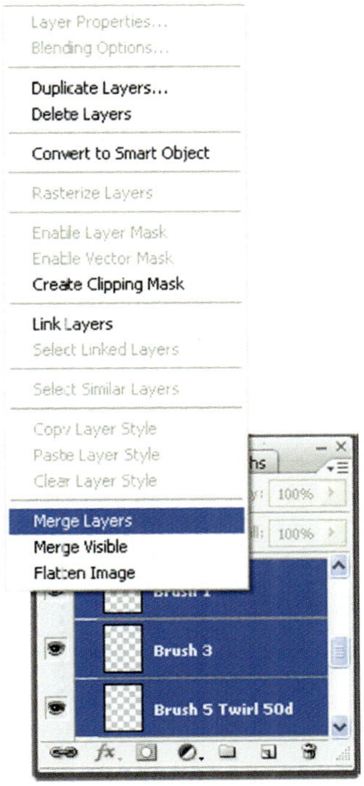

- Distort the line work with a filter.
  - Click on the layer Fronds to choose it.
  - **Filter > Distort > Ripple**
    - `Amount = 100%`
    - `Size = Medium`
  - Click on the [OK] button.

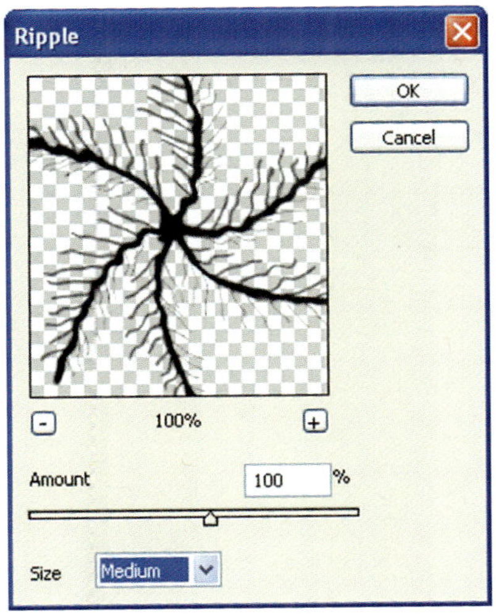

Step 7: Add more fronds.

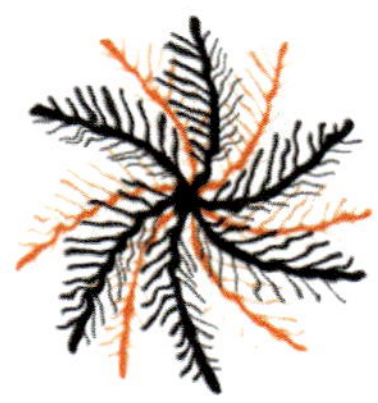

Step 7: Add more fronds.

- Select the current fronds.
    - Click on the layer Fronds to choose it.
    - **Select > All**
    - With the Move Tool, hit the [up arrow] on your keyboard, then hit the [down arrow].
    - **Select > Modify > Contract...**
        - `Contract By = 1 px`
    - Click on the [OK] button.

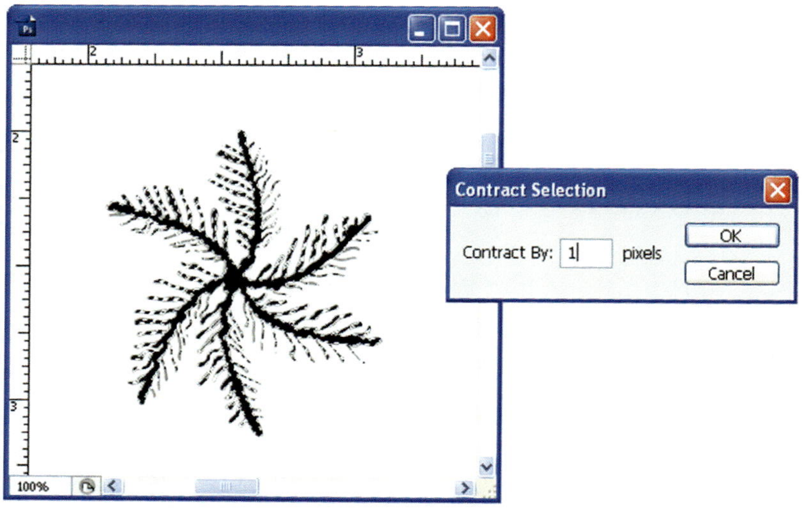

- Create more fronds.
    - Create a new layer and name it *Red Fronds*.
    - Change the foreground color to red (`#ED5100`).
    - **Edit > Fill...**
    - Click the [OK] button.

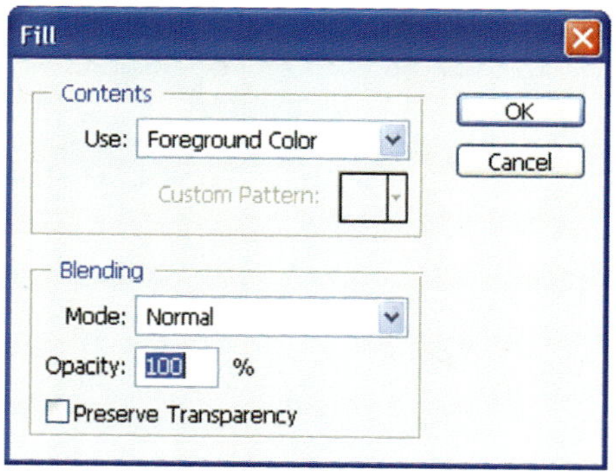

- Rotate the new fronds.
    - **Edit > Transform > Rotate**
        - `Angle = 30 degrees`
    - Click the [OK] button.

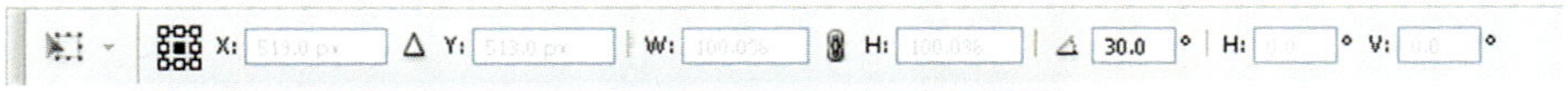

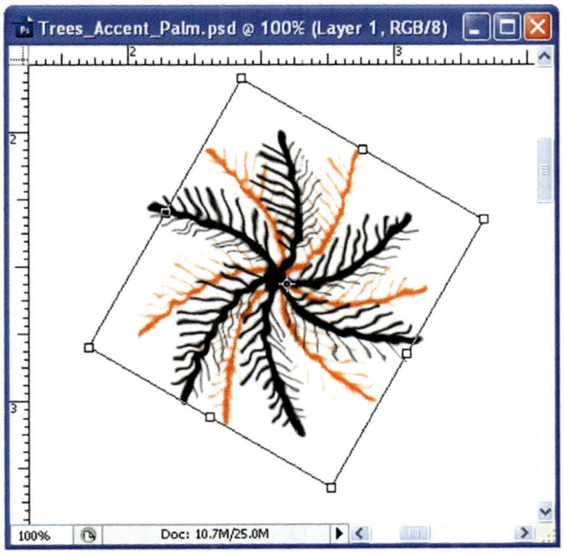

Step 8: Paint the symbol.

Basically, to color the palm you stack somewhat transparent layers of colors on top of one another. You will start with colorful undertones and then add the more dominant greens and olives on top of them. The greens and olives will be less transparent than the foundational colors.

Step 8: Paint the symbol.

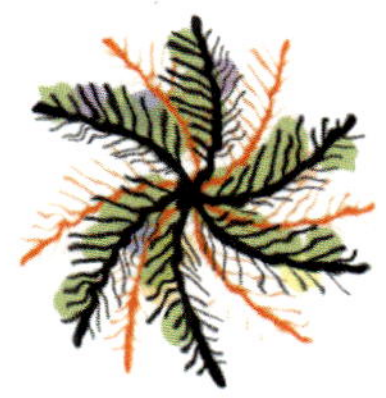

- Paint foundation colors on the drawing.
  - Create a new layer and name it *Brush 25 50%*.
    - This layer name will remind you of the size paintbrush you used, and the layer opacity you will ultimately set.
  - Choose a paintbrush for the Brush Tool and begin painting colors loosely on your drawing.
    - `Master Diameter = 25 px`
    - `Hardness = 100%`
  - Repeat the steps above using various accent colors. Be certain to create a new layer for each color. By separating the colors on unique layers, they will eventually blend together where they overlap.

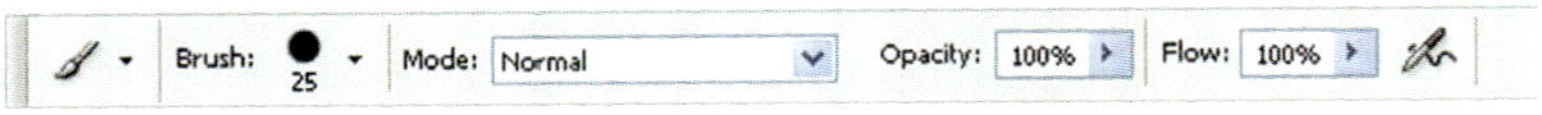

- Blend the colors drawn previously.
  - Reduce the opacity of your fill so that you can see your work in the next steps.
    - `Opacity = 50%`

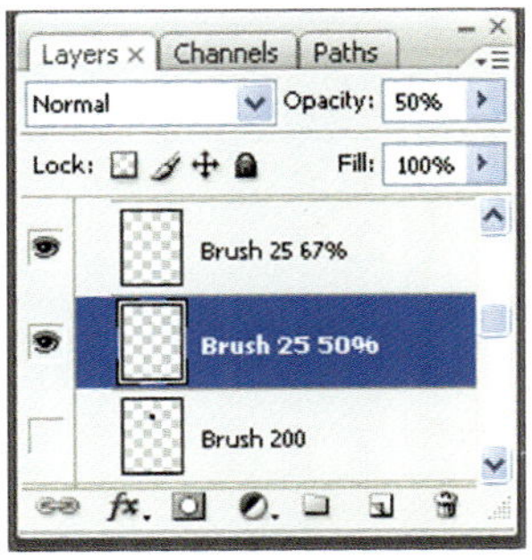

- Paint base colors of green and olive on the drawing.
  - Create a new layer and name it *Brush 25 67%*.
  - Change the foreground color to olive green (#95AB00).
  - Choose a paintbrush for the Brush Tool and paint loosely over the symbol.
  - Repeat the steps above, replacing the foreground color with dark olive (#686B00).
- Blend the colors drawn previously.
  - Reduce the opacity of your fill so that you can see your work in the next steps.
    - `Opacity = 67%`

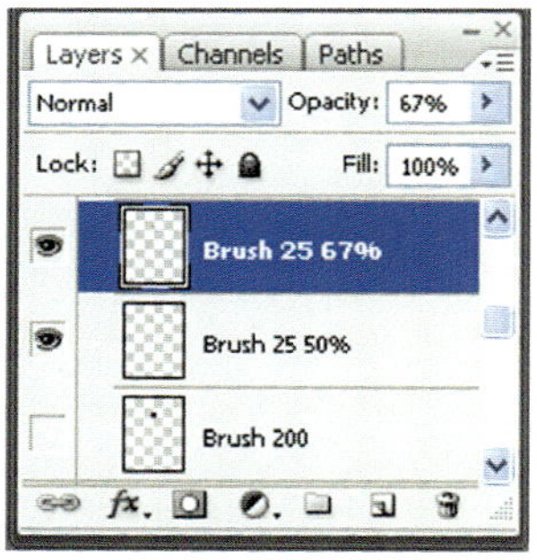

Step 9: Add a shadow.

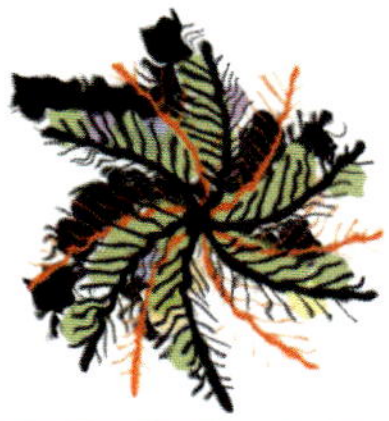

Step 9: Add a shadow.

- Merge the layers that you painted on.
  - While holding down the [Ctrl] key, click on every layer you that you painted on in the previous steps.
  - Click on the right mouse button and select "Merge Layers..." from the pop-up dialog box.
  - Rename the merged layer *Paint*.

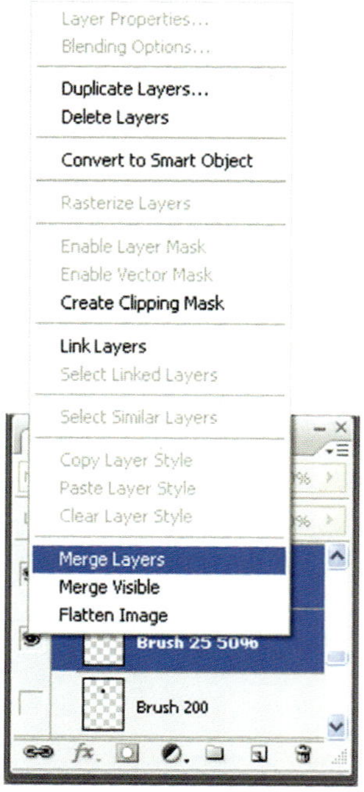

- Distort the merged layer with a filter.
  - **Filter > Distort > Ripple**
    - `Amount = 100%`
    - `Size = Large`
  - Click the [OK] button.

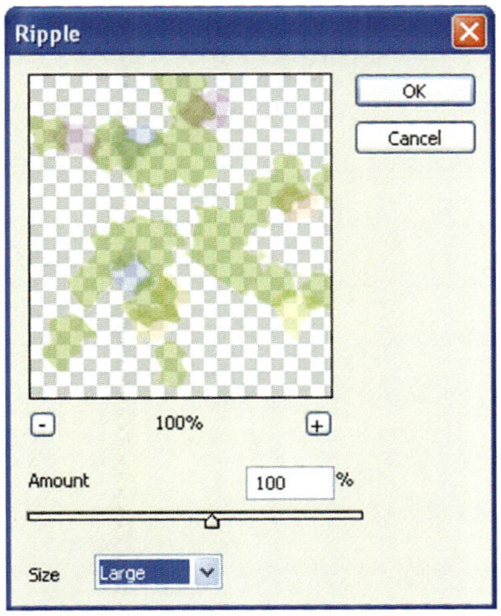

- Create a shadow from your line work and painting.
  - Click on the layer ***Fronds*** to choose it.
  - While holding down the [Ctrl] key, click on the layer ***Paint*** to choose it, too.
  - Drag the selected layers to the "Create a new layer" icon.
  - Your copied layers will now be selected. Click on the right mouse button and select "Merge Layers..." from the pop-up dialog box.
  - Rename the layer ***Shadow***.
- Trim the shadow.
  - Click on the layer ***Fronds*** to choose it.
  - **Select > All**
  - With the Move Tool, hit the [up arrow] on your keyboard, then the [down arrow].
  - Click on the layer ***Shadow*** to choose it.
  - Hit the [Delete] key to erase the selection from the layer.
  - Click on the layer ***Paint*** to choose it.
  - **Select > All**
  - With the Move Tool, hit the [up arrow] on your keyboard, then the [down arrow].
  - Click on the layer ***Shadow*** to choose it.
  - Hit the [Delete] key to erase the selection from the layer.

Step 10: Add accents.

- Add accents to the symbol.
  - Create a new layer and name it ***Accents***.
  - Using various brush sizes and colors, add accent dots and strokes to the symbol.

Step 10: Add accents.

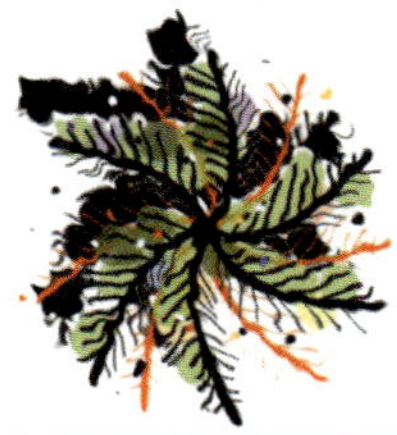

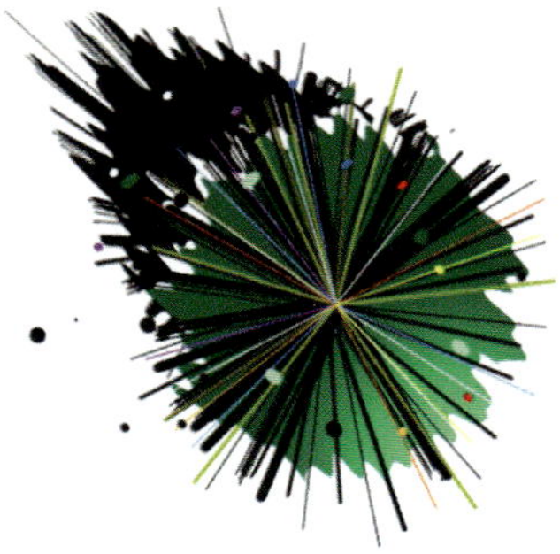

Master Plan Graphics | Coniferous Tree

This example illustrates how to draw a colorful symbol for an evergreen tree. The techniques used in this example include the following:

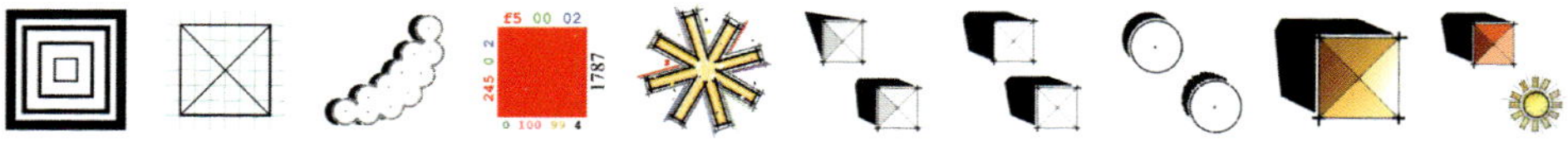

Line Hierarchy | Straighten Up | Merge | Color Palette | Accent | Inform | Shadow Gap | Dead or Alive | Gradient | Shadow Match

This drawing was originally drawn on a canvas with a resolution of 200 pixels per inch. Afterwards, it was scaled down to fit within these pages.

Step 1: Draw a simple, solid circle.

Step 1: Draw a simple, solid circle.

- Draw a circle to help visualize the space you want to draw within.
  - Create a new layer and name it *Brush 200*.
  - Choose a paintbrush for the Brush Tool and draw a circle by simply touching the brush to the canvas.
    - `Master Diameter = 200 px`
    - `Hardness = 100%`

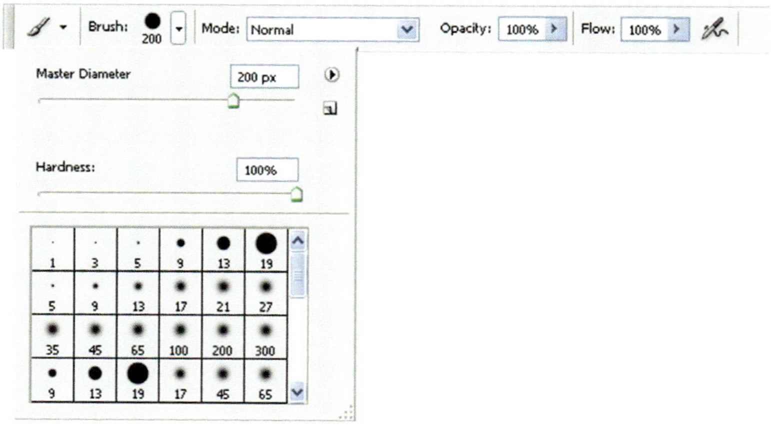

- Reduce the opacity of your new layer so that you can see your work in the next steps.
  - `Opacity = 50%`

Step 2: Paint the first brush strokes.

- Load a new set of paintbrushes.
    - With the Brush Tool, click on the [v] icon by the brush to open the Brush Preset picker.
    - From the Brush Preset Picker, click the [>] icon to open the Brush Preset pop-up and select "Natural Brushes."

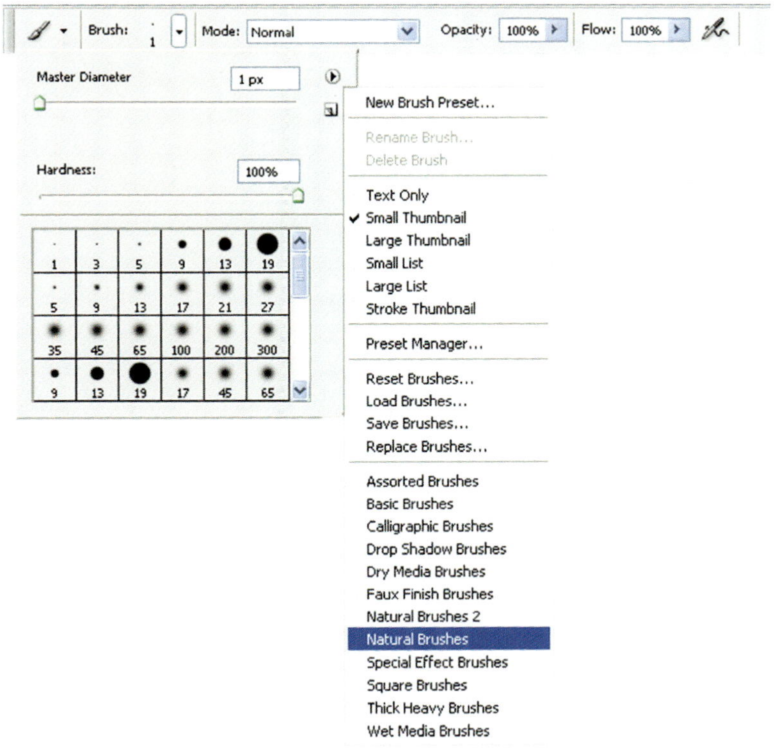

- Draw lines radiating from the center of the symbol.
    - Create a new layer and name it *Needles*.
    - Choose a paintbrush for the Brush Tool and draw lines radiating from the center to the limits of the symbol.
        - `Master Diameter = 12 px`

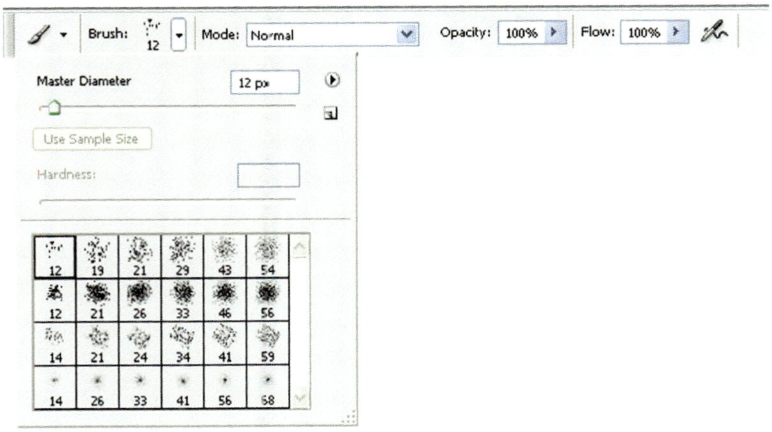

Step 2: Paint the first brush strokes.

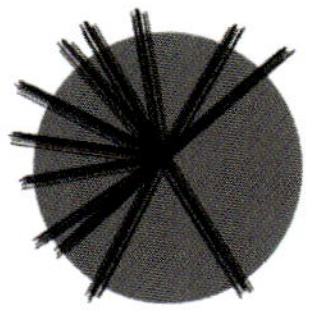

- Reload the default set of paintbrushes.
  - With the Brush Tool, click on the [v] icon by the brush to open the Brush Preset picker.
  - From the Brush Preset Picker, click the [>] icon to open the Brush Preset pop-up and select "Reset Brushes..."

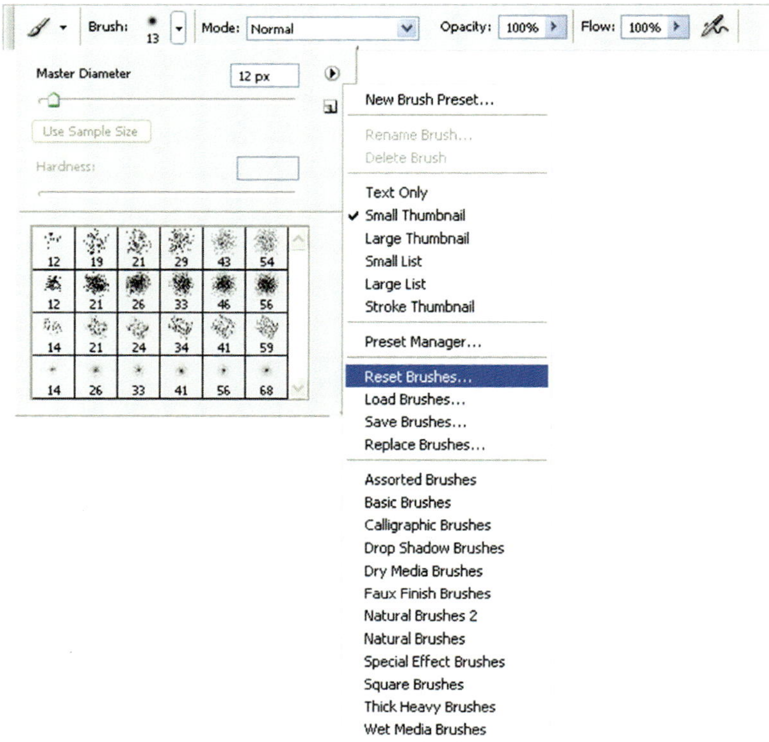

Step 3: Add thinner brush strokes.

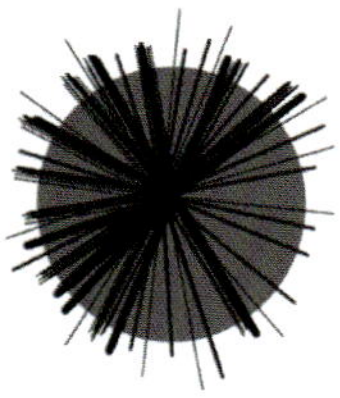

Step 3: Add thinner brush strokes.

- Draw additional brush strokes.
  - Click on the layer ***Needles*** to choose it.
  - Choose a paintbrush for the Brush Tool and draw perpendicular lines to the larger, thicker lines.
    - `Master Diameter = 5 px`
    - `Hardness = 100%`

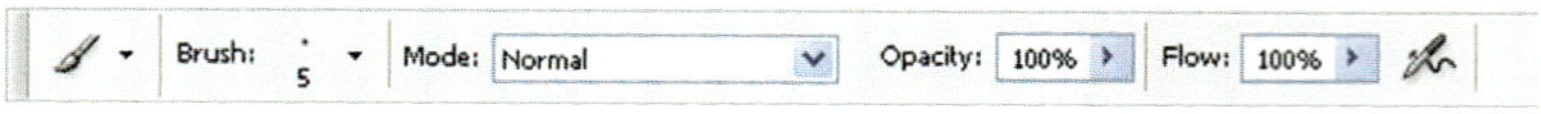

- Draw thinner brush strokes, radiating from the center to the limits of the circle.
  - Choose a paintbrush for the Brush Tool and draw perpendicular lines to the larger, thicker lines.
    - `Master Diameter = 3 px`
    - `Hardness = 100%`

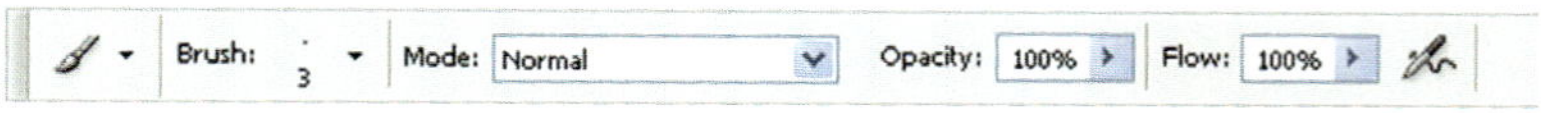

- Draw finer brush strokes, as before.
    - `Master Diameter = 1 px`
    - `Hardness = 100%`

Step 4: Distort the basic circle.

- Distort the basic form of the symbol with a filter.
  - Click on the layer ***Brush 200*** to choose it.
  - **Distort > Filter > Ripple...**
    - `Amount = 100%`
    - `Size = Large`
  - Click the [OK] button.

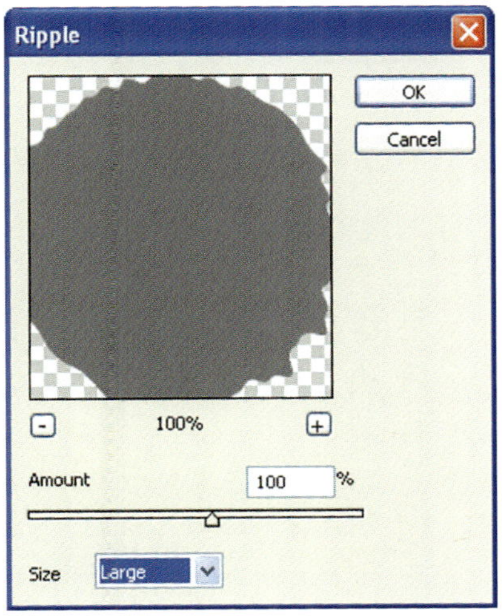

Step 4: Distort the basic circle.

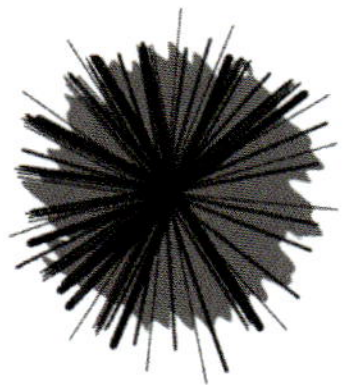

Step 5: Add a shadow.

To create a shadow, you will copy the layers with your line work and the distorted circle, merge them together, and then shift and trim this merged layer.

- Copy the layers with your line work and the distorted circle.
  - Click on the layer ***Brush 200*** to choose it.
  - Holding down the [Ctrl] key, click on the layer ***Needles*** to choose it, too.
  - Drag the layers to the "Create a new layer" icon.
- Merge the copied layers together.
  - Click on the layer ***Brush 200 copy*** to choose it.
  - Holding down the [Ctrl] key, click on the layer ***Needles copy*** to choose it, too.
  - Click on the right mouse button and select "Merge Layers..." from the pop-up dialog box.
  - Rename the layer ***Shadow***.
- Shift the shadow into position.
  - With the Move Tool, shift the shadow up and to the left.
- Trim the shadow.
  - Click on the layer ***Brush 200*** to choose it.
  - **Select > All**
  - With the Move Tool, hit the [up arrow] on your keyboard, then hit the [down arrow].
  - **Select > Modify > Expand...**
    - `Expand By = 5 pixels`
  - Click the [OK] button.
  - Click on the layer ***Shadow*** to choose it.
  - Hit the [Delete] key to erase the shadow from your selection.
  - Click on the layer ***Needles*** to choose it, and repeat the steps above.

Step 5: Add a shadow.

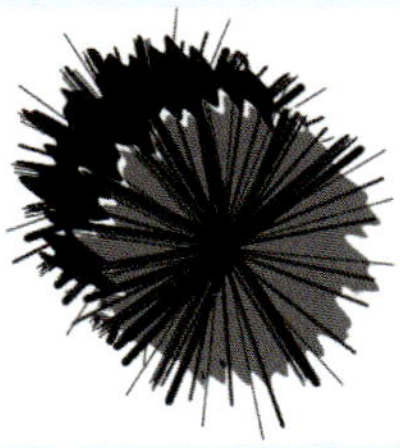

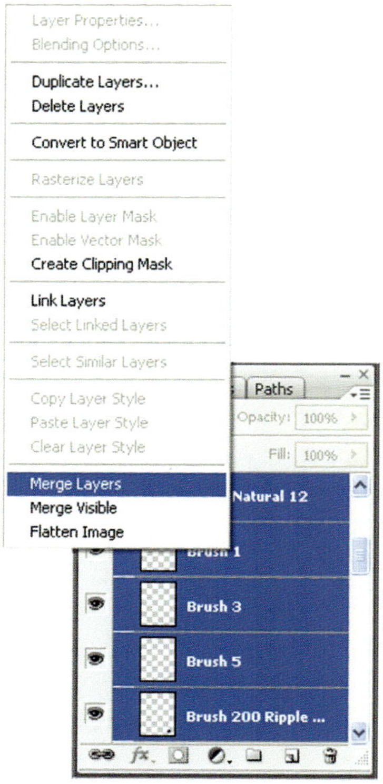

Step 6: Stretch the shadow into a pyramidal form.

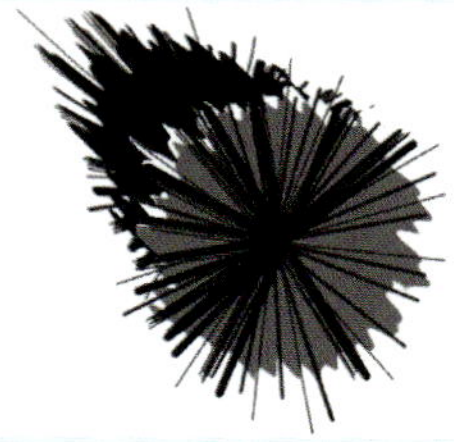

Step 6: Stretch the shadow into a pyramidal form.

- Stretch the shadow.
  - Click on the layer *Shadow* to choose it.
  - **Edit > Transform > Warp**
    - Distort the shadow by dragging the reference points (represented by tiny squares).
  - Click the [OK] button.

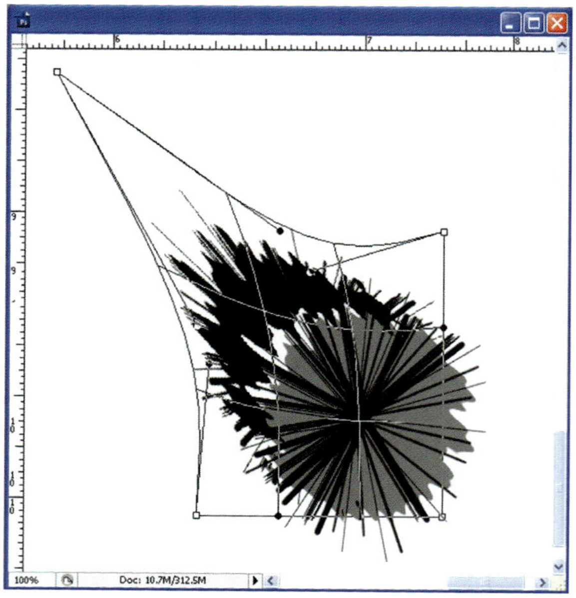

Step 7: Add color to the symbol.

- Paint the tree symbol using a gradient.
  - Change the foreground color to mint green (`#21FF9E`).
  - Change the background color to dark cyan (`#006635`).
  - Click on the layer ***Brush 200*** to choose it.
  - **Select > All**
  - With the Move Tool, hit the [up arrow] on your keyboard, then hit the [down arrow].
  - Create a new layer and name it ***Gradient Fill***.
  - With the Gradient Tool, paint the selected area.
    - `Foreground to Background`
    - `Radial Gradient`
    - `Mode = Normal`
      - Click on the mouse button (and hold it down) near the lower, right portion of your selection, drag the cursor to the upper, left portion, and then release the button.

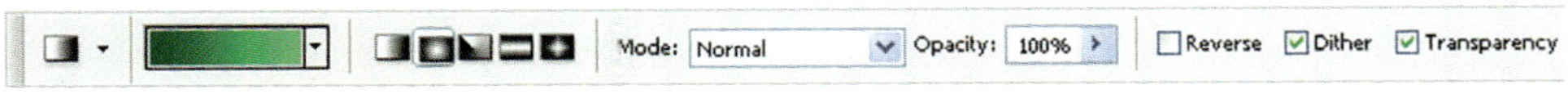

Step 7: Add color to the symbol.

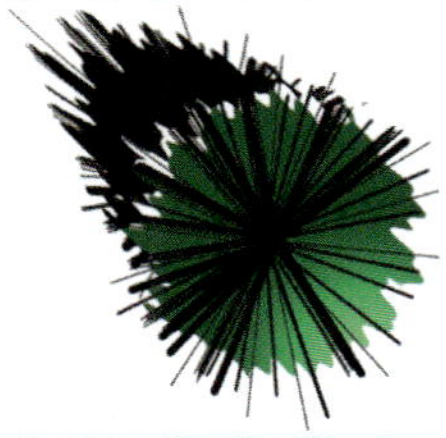

Step 8: Add accents.

- Add accents to the symbol.
  - Create a new layer and name it ***Accents***.
  - Using various brush sizes and colors, add accent dots and strokes to the symbol.

Step 8: Add accents.

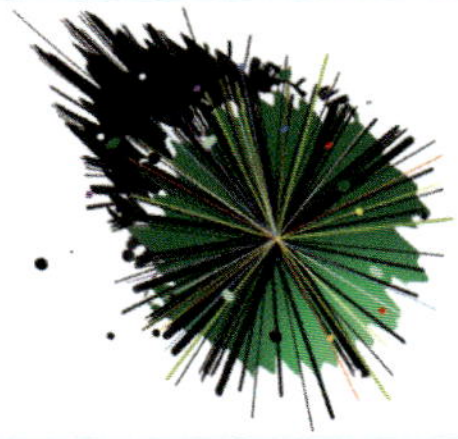

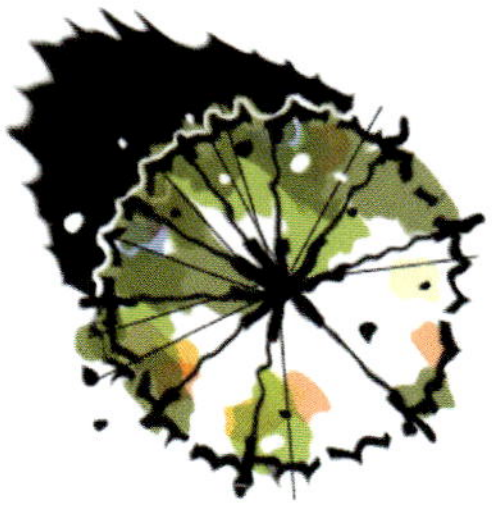

Master Plan Graphics | Coniferous Tree

This example illustrates how to draw a colorful symbol for an evergreen tree. The techniques used in this example include the following:

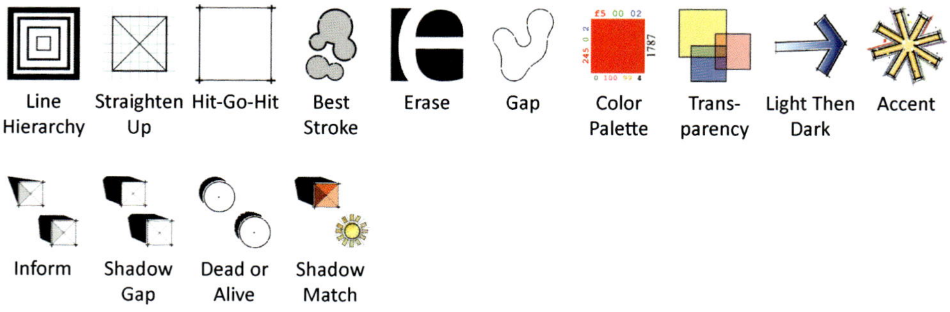

This drawing was originally drawn on a canvas with a resolution of 200 pixels per inch. Afterwards, it was scaled down to fit within these pages.

Step 1: Draw a simple, solid circle.

Step 1: Draw a simple, solid circle.

- Draw the basic form of the tree symbol.
  - Create a new layer and name it ***Brush 200***.
  - Choose a paintbrush for the Brush Tool and draw a circle by simply touching the brush to the canvas.
    - `Master Diameter = 200 px`
    - `Hardness = 100%`

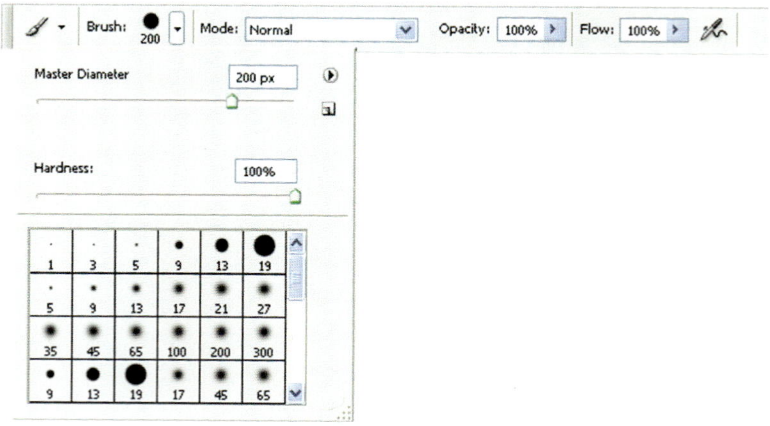

- Reduce the layer opacity so that you can see your work in the next steps.
  - `Opacity = 50%`

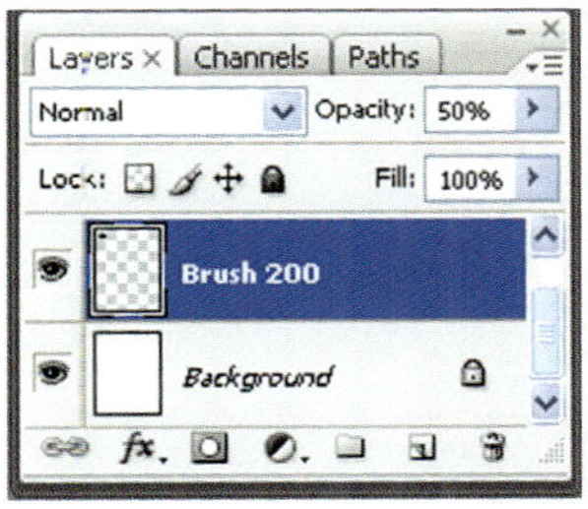

Step 2: Erase from the edges.

Step 2: Erase from the edges.

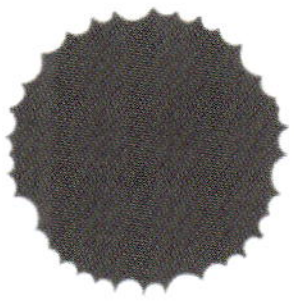

- Erase from the edges of the circle.
  - Click on the layer ***Brush 200*** to choose it.
  - Choose a brush for the Eraser Tool and erase along the edges of the circle.
    - `Master Diameter = 25 px`
    - `Hardness = 100%`
      - Leave some gaps. You will erase with a smaller brush in a moment.

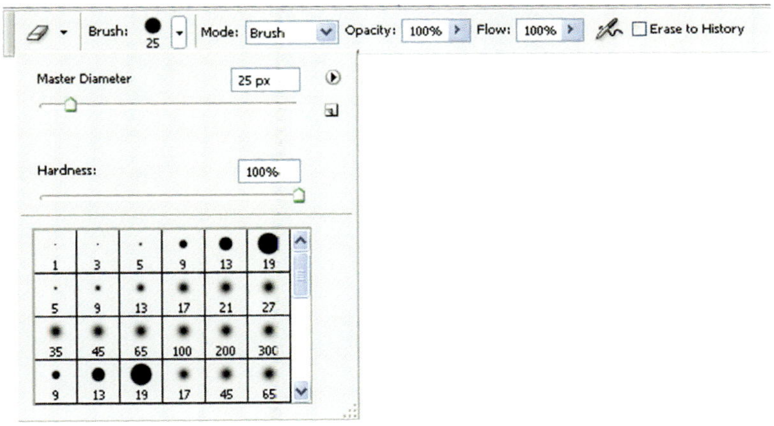

- Erase from the edges of the circle with a smaller brush.
  - Choose a brush for the Eraser Tool and erase along the edges of the circle.
    - `Master Diameter = 15 px`
    - `Hardness = 100%`

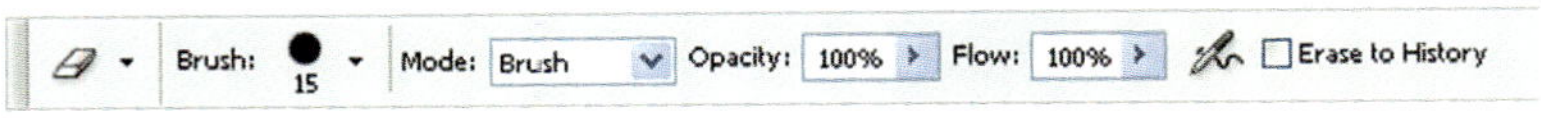

Step 3: Add an outline.

Step 3: Add an outline.

- Draw a thick outline along the perimeter of the symbol.
  - Click on the layer ***Brush 200*** to choose it.
  - **Select > All**
  - With the Move Tool, hit the [up arrow] on your keyboard, then hit the [down arrow].
  - Create a new layer and name it ***Thick Outline***.
  - Change the foreground color to black (`#000000`).
  - **Edit > Stroke**
    - `Width = 5 px, Location = Inside`
  - Click the [OK] button.

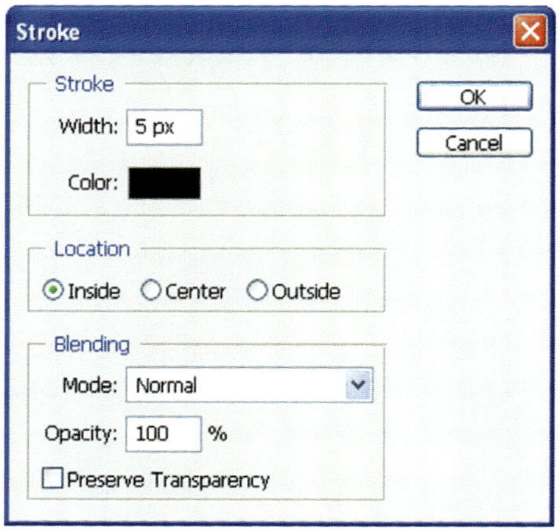

- Erase gaps along the outline.
  - Choose a brush for the Eraser Tool and erase along the outline to create gaps.
    - `Master Diameter = 5 px`
    - `Hardness = 100%`

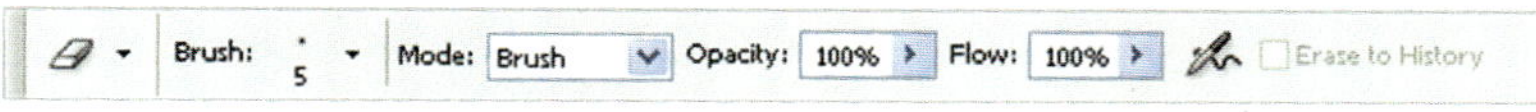

Step 4: Add a shadow.

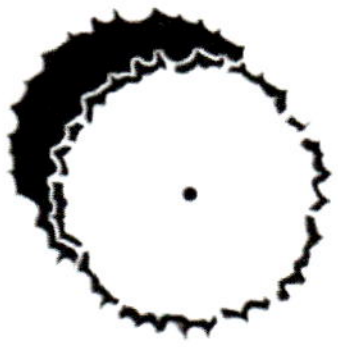

Step 4: Add a shadow.

- Distort the basic form of the tree symbol.
  - Click on the layer *Brush 200* to choose it.
  - **Filter > Distort > Ripple...**
    - `Amount = 100%`
    - `Size = Medium`
  - Click the [OK] button.

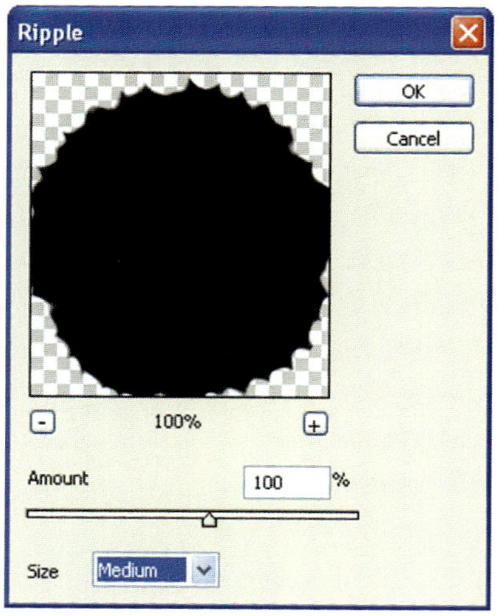

- Distort the outline for the tree symbol.
  - Click on the layer *Thick Outline* to choose it.
  - **Filter > Distort > Ripple...**
    - `Amount = 100%`
    - `Size = Medium`
  - Click the [OK] button.

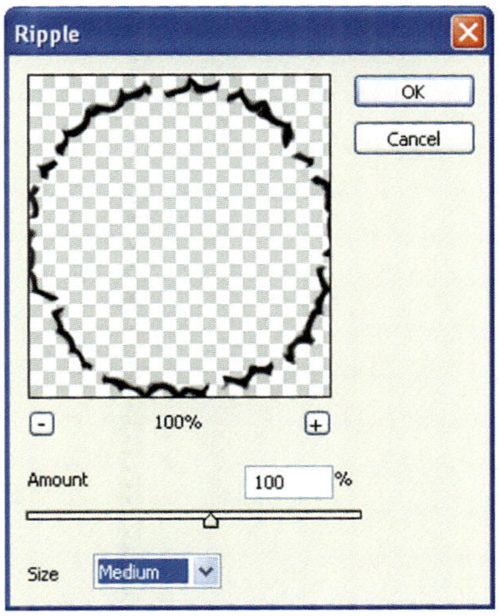

- Copy this layer to create a shadow.
  - Click on the layer ***Brush 200*** to choose it.
  - You can copy the selected layer by either:
    - Hitting the right mouse button, selecting "Duplicate Layer..." from the pop-up menu, and then clicking [OK] on the Duplicate Layer dialog box.
    - Or, you can simply drag the layer up and to the left.
  - With the Move Tool, shift the copied layer up and to the left.
  - Rename the copied layer ***Shadow***.
- Trim the shadow.
  - Click on the layer ***Brush 200*** to choose it.
  - **Select > All**
  - With the Move Tool, hit the [up arrow] on your keyboard, then hit the [down arrow].
  - **Select > Modify > Expand...**
    - `Expand By = 5 pixels`
  - Click the [OK] button.
  - Click on the layer ***Shadow*** to choose it.
  - Hit the [Delete] key to erase the shadow within your selection.
- Anchor the center of the symbol.
  - Click on the layer ***Thick Outline*** to choose it.
  - Choose a paintbrush for the Brush Tool and draw a point in the center of the symbol.
    - `Master Diameter = 9 px`
    - `Hardness = 100%`

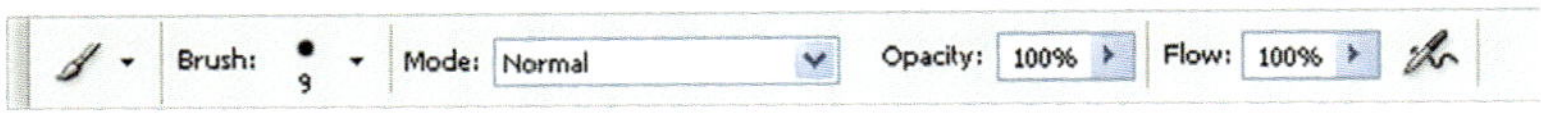

Step 5: Stretch the shadow into a pyramidal form.

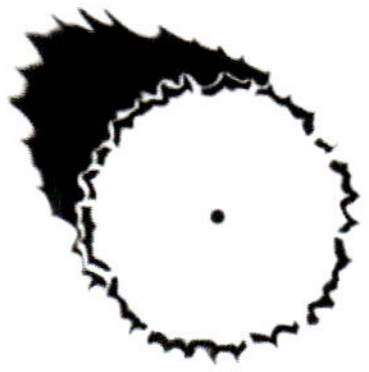

Step 5: Stretch the shadow into a pyramidal form.

- Stretch the shadow into a pyramidal form.
  - Click on the layer ***Shadow*** to choose it.
  - **Edit > Transform > Warp**
    - Distort the shadow by dragging the reference points (represented by squares).
  - Hit the [Enter] key.

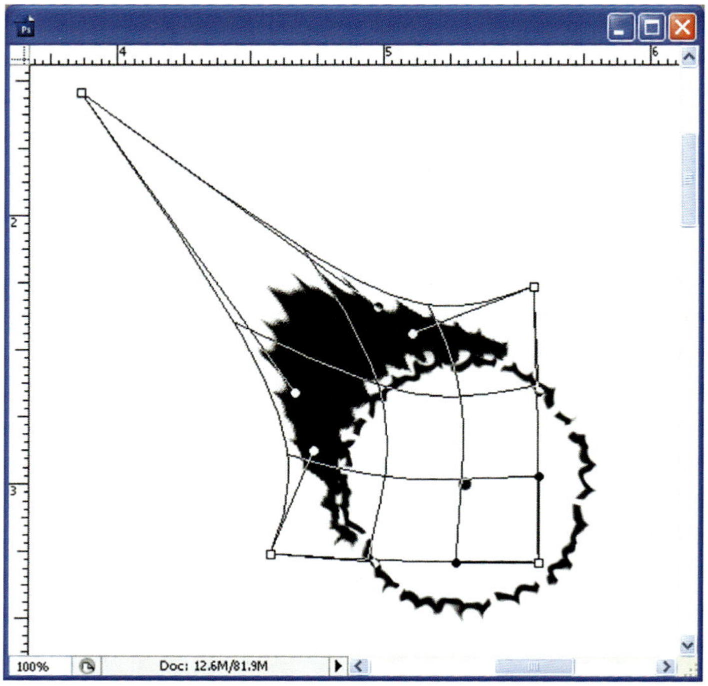

Step 6: Draw thick and thin lines.

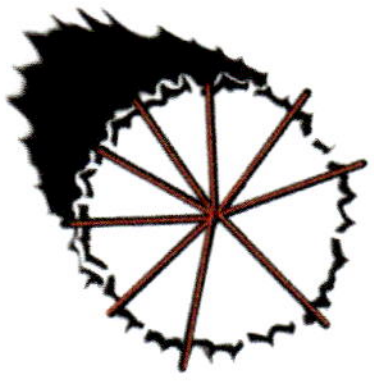

Step 6: Draw thick and thin lines.

- Draw thick lines radiating from the center of the symbol.
  - Create a new layer and name it *Spokes*.
  - Choose a paintbrush for the Brush Tool and draw thick lines radiating from the center..
    - `Master Diameter = 5 px`
    - `Hardness = 100%`

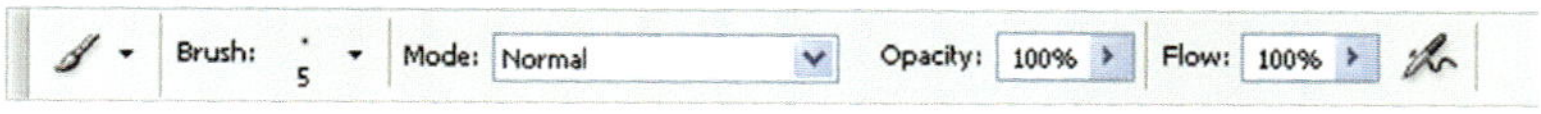

- Prepare to draw thinner lines.
  - Create a new layer and name it *Thin Spokes*.
  - Right-click the tab and select "Blending Options."
  - In the Layer Style dialog box that appears, check the "Color Overlay" checkbox.
    - Accept the default color of red.
  - Click the [OK] button.
- Trace the thick lines you drew previously.
  - Choose a thinner paintbrush for the Brush Tool and trace the larger, thicker lines.
    - `Master Diameter = 3 px`
    - `Hardness = 100%`

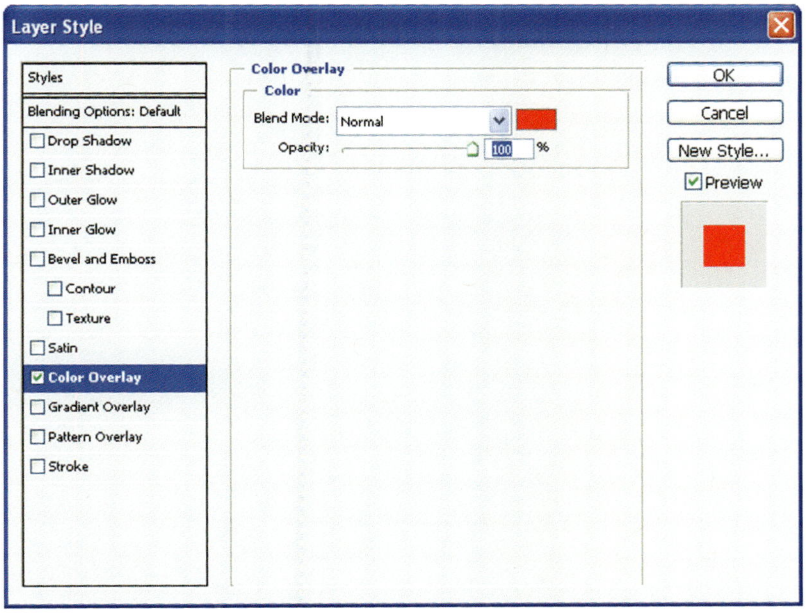

Step 7: Erase from the thick lines.

Step 7: Erase from the thick lines.

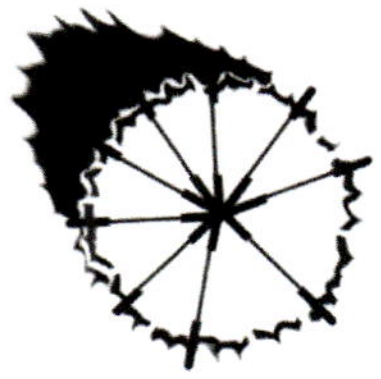

- Erase the center of the thick lines.
  - Choose a brush for the Brush Tool and erase the centers of the thick lines you drew previously.
    - `Master Diameter = 9 px`
    - `Hardness = 100%`

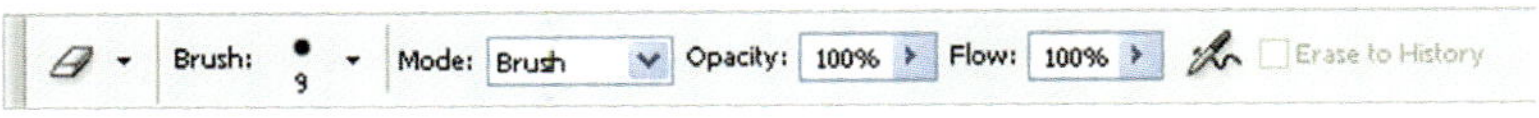

Step 8: Distort the line work.

Step 8: Distort the line work.

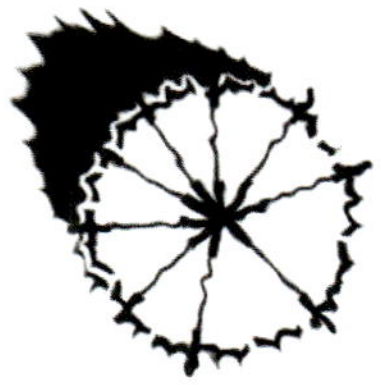

- Turn off the Color Overlay.
  - Click on the layer *Thin Spokes* to choose it.
  - Double-click on the tab within this layer named “Color Overlay.”
  - In the Layer Style dialog box that appears, uncheck the Color Overlay checkbox.
  - Click the [OK] button.
- Merge the layers with the radiating line work.
  - Click on the layer *Spokes* to choose it.
  - Holding down the [Ctrl] key, click the layer *Thin Spokes* to choose it, too.
  - Click on the right mouse button and select “Merge Layers...” from the pop-up dialog box.
  - Rename the layer *Merged Spokes*.

- Distort the radiating line work.
  - Click on the layer *Merged Spokes* to choose it.
  - **Filter > Distort > Ripple**
    - `Amount = 100%`
    - `Size = Medium`
  - Click the [OK] button.

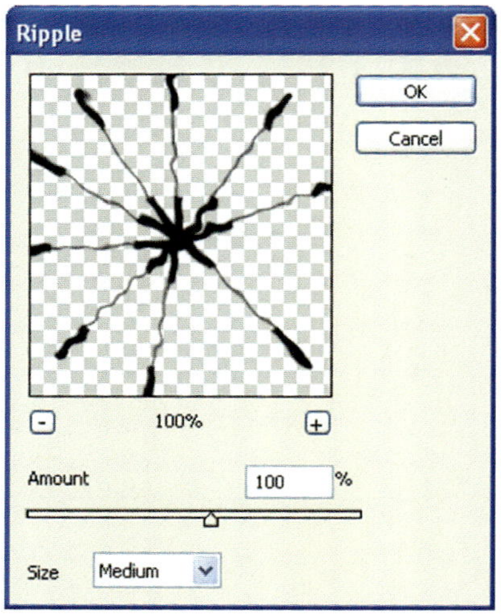

Step 9: Add foundation colors.

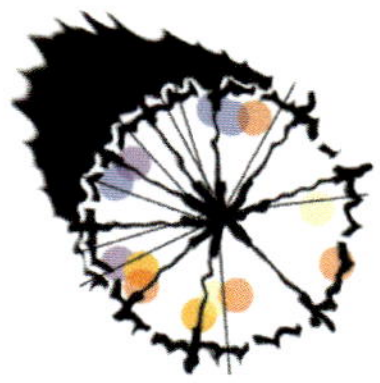

Step 9: Add foundation colors.

- Add color by painting on the drawing.
  - Create a new layer and name it ***Brush 25 50%***.
    - This layer name will remind you of the size paintbrush you used, and the layer opacity you will ultimately set.
  - Choose a paintbrush for the Brush Tool and begin painting colors loosely on the drawing.
    - `Master Diameter = 25 px`
    - `Hardness = 100%`
  - Repeat the steps above using various colors. By separating the colors on unique layers, they will eventually blend together where they overlap.
    - Red (`#FF8257`), Tan (`#FFBA3D`), Blue (`#5C96FF`), Purple (`#DE9CFF`), Yellow (`#FFE600`), Orange (`#FFB300`).

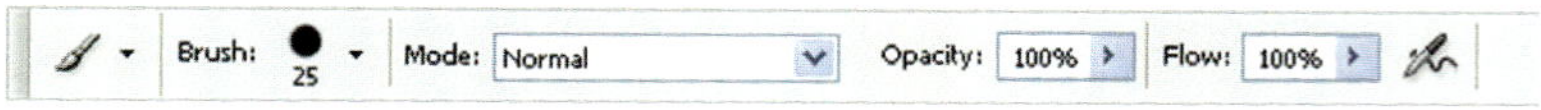

- Blend the colors drawn previously.
  - For each layer that you created in this step, reduce the layer opacity.
    - `Opacity = 50%`

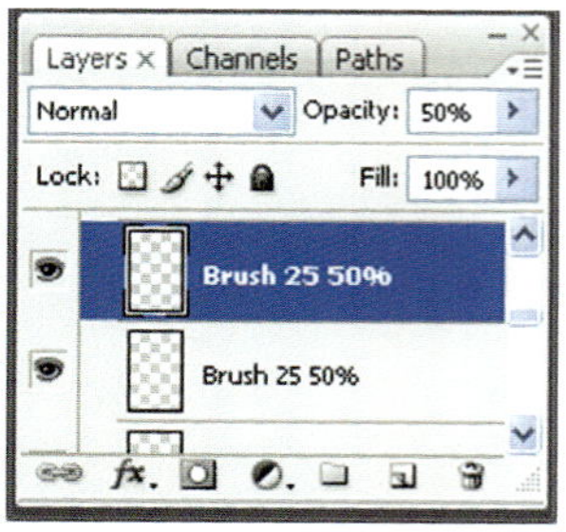

Step 10: Add dominant colors.

Step 10: Add dominant colors.

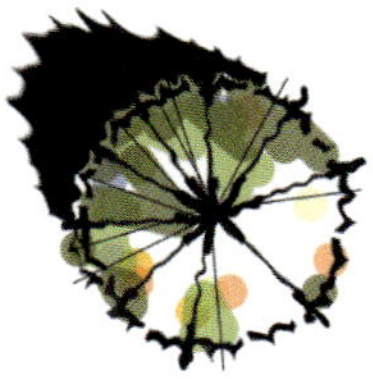

- Add color by painting on the drawing.
    - Create a new layer and name it *Brush 25 67%*.
        - As before, the layer name will remind you about its properties.
        - Change the foreground color to olive green (`#95AB00`).
        - Choose a paintbrush for the Brush Tool and paint the tree symbol primarily where it would appear darkest in the sunlight.
        - Repeat the steps above, replacing the foreground color with dark olive (`#686B00`).

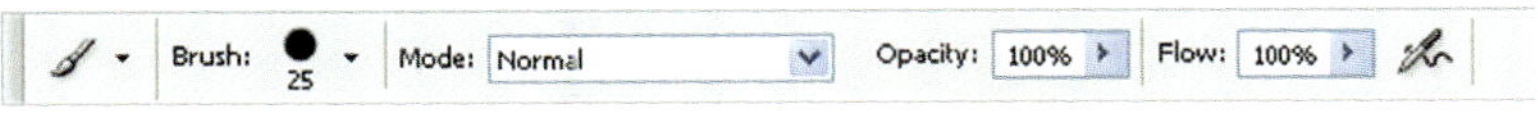

- Blend the colors drawn previously.
    - For each layer that you created in this step, reduce the layer opacity.
        - `Opacity = 67%`

Step 11: Distort the colored brush strokes.

Step 11: Distort the colored brush strokes.

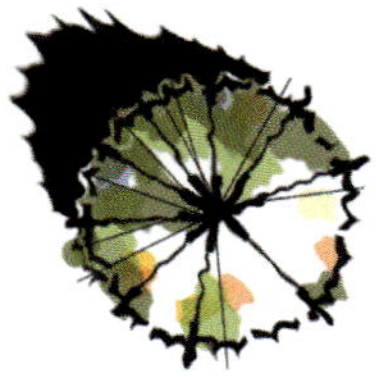

- Merge the layers you just painted.
    - Holding down the [Ctrl] key, click on each layer you just created until you have chosen them all.
    - Click on the right mouse button and select “Merge Layers...” from the pop-up dialog box.
    - Rename the layer *Painted Colors*.
- Distort the colored brush strokes with a filter.
    - Click on the layer Painted Colors to choose it.
    - Filter > Distort > Ripple
    - Amount = 100%, Size = Large
    - Click the [OK] button.

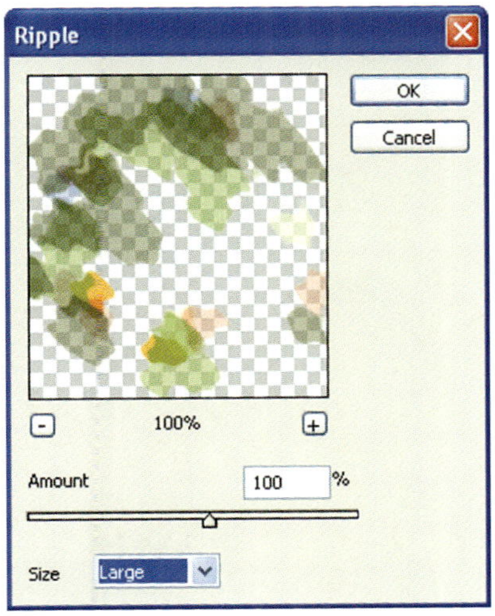

Step 12: Add accents.

Step 12: Add accents.

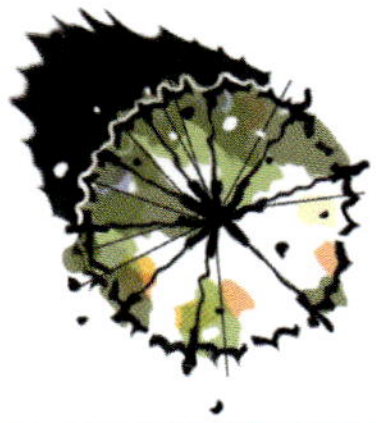

- Add accents to the symbol.
    - Create a new layer and name it *Accents*.
    - Using various brush sizes and colors, add accent dots and strokes to the symbol.

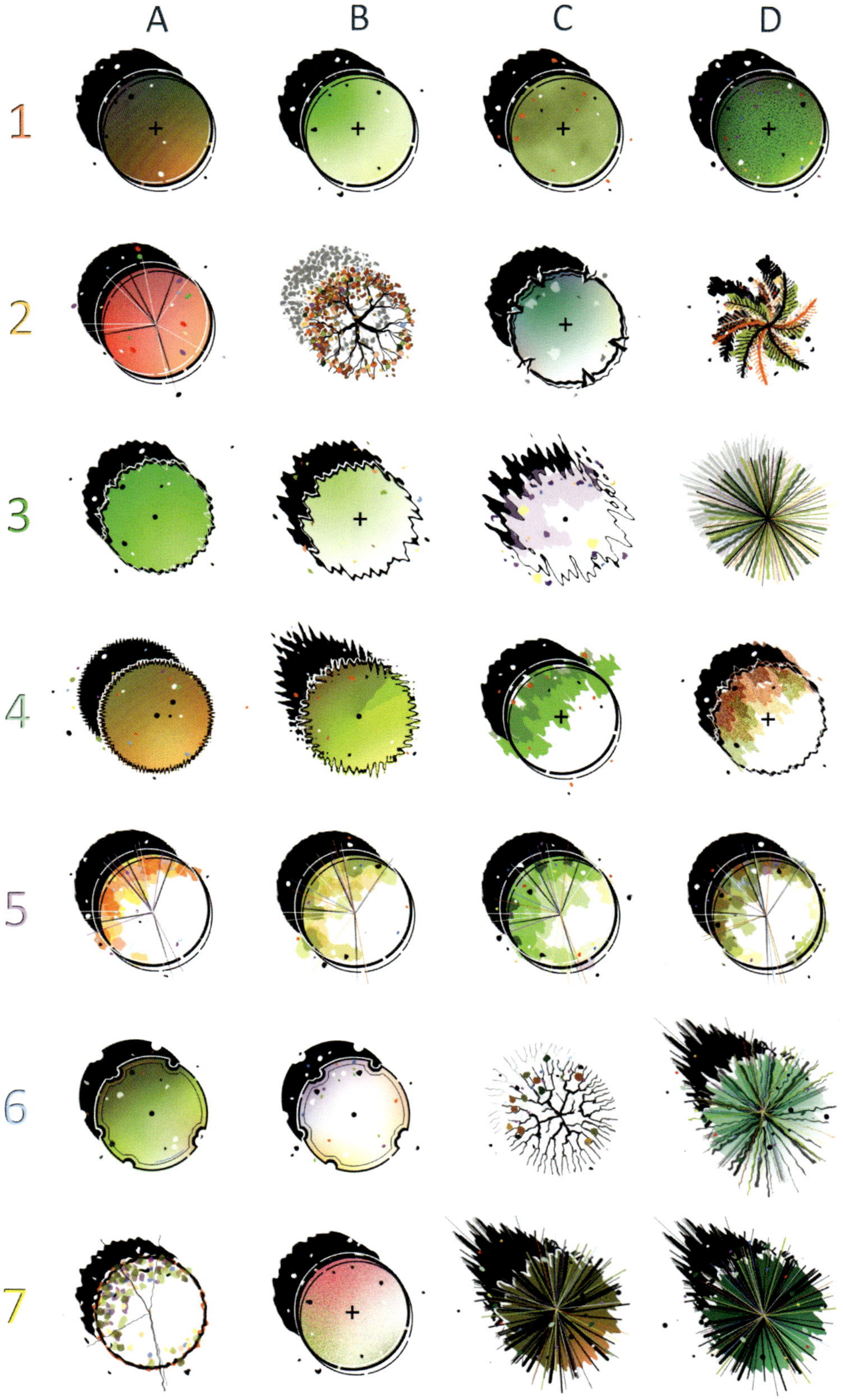

Figure 10-1. This is a sampling of symbols for trees.

Figure 10-2. This table summarizes the techniques used to draw the symbols in Figure 10-1.

	Line Hierarchy	Straighten Up	Hit-Go-Hit	Best Stroke	Erase	Gap	Layer Opacity	Draft Lines	Merge	Color Palette	Blend by Transparency	Soft Glow	Light then Dark	Cloud Color	Noisy Color	Accent	Warm and Cool	Inform with Shadows	Shadow Gap	Dead or Alive	Gradient	Radiant Gradient	Shadow Match
1A	lh			str		gp		dl		cp		sg				ac		is	sg	da		rg	sm
1B	lh			str		gp		dl		cp						ac		is	sg	da	gr		sm
1C	lh			str		gp		dl		cp				cc		ac		is	sg	da			
1D	lh			str		gp		dl		cp		sg			nc	ac		is	sg	da			
2A	lh	su		str		gp		dl		cp						ac		is	sg	da	gr		
2B	lh						lo		m	cp						ac		is		da			sm
2C	lh	su		str	er	gp			m	cp		sg				ac		is	sg	da			sm
2D	lh							dl	m	cp	bt					ac		is		da			
3A	lh			str						cp		sg				ac		is	sg	da	gr		sm
3B	lh			str						cp		sg				ac		is	sg	da			sm
3C	lh			str						cp	bt		ld			ac		is		da			sm
3D	lh	su					lo		m	cp			ld			ac	wc	is		da			sm
4A	lh			str						cp		sg				ac		is	sg	da			
4B	lh			str						cp		sg				ac		is	sg	da		rg	sm
4C	lh			str		gp		dl		cp			ld			ac		is	sg	da			sm
4D	lh			str						cp			ld		nc	ac		is	sg	da			sm
5A	lh	su		str		gp		dl		cp	bt		ld			ac		is	sg	da			sm
5B	lh	su		str		gp		dl		cp	bt		ld			ac		is	sg	da			sm
5C	lh	su		str		gp		dl		cp	bt		ld			ac		is	sg	da			sm
5D	lh	su		str		gp		dl		cp	bt		ld			ac	wc	is	sg	da			sm
6A	lh			str	er	gp			m	cp		sg				ac		is	sg	da	gr		sm
6B	lh			str	er	gp			m	cp		sg				ac	wc	is	sg	da			sm
6C	lh	su					lo		m	cp						ac		is		da			sm
6D	lh	su							m	cp						ac		is	sg	da	gr		sm
7A	lh	su		str		gp				cp						ac		is	sg	da			sm
7B	lh			str		gp		dl		cp		sg				ac	wc	is	sg	da			sm
7C	lh	su	go						m	cp						ac	wc	is	sg	da		rg	sm
7D	lh	su	go						m	cp						ac		is	sg	da	gr		sm

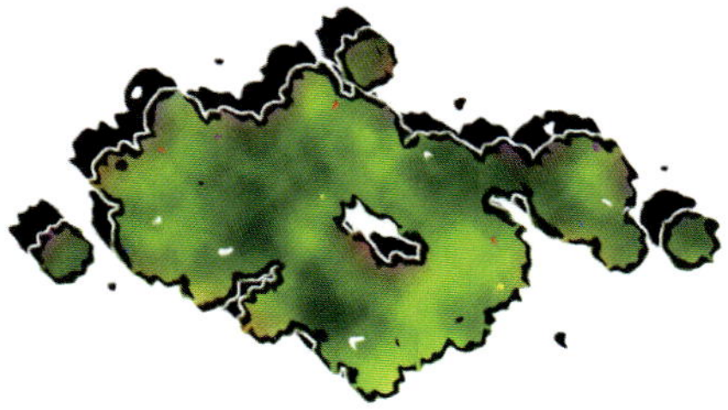

Master Plan Graphics | Tree Mass

This example illustrates how to draw a mass of trees. The techniques used in this example include the following:

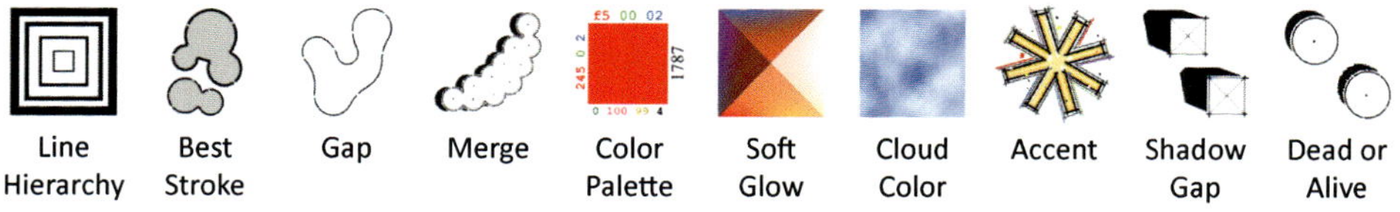

This drawing was originally drawn on a canvas with a resolution of 200 pixels per inch. Afterwards, it was scaled down to fit within these pages.

Step 1: Draw the basic form of the tree mass.

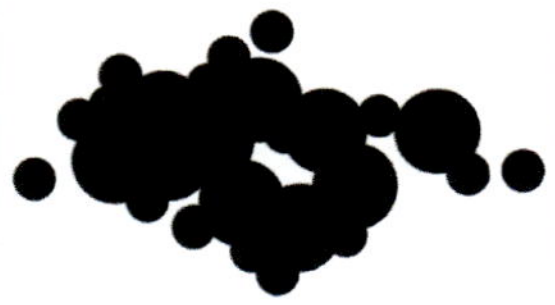

Step 1: Draw the basic form of the tree mass.

- Draw the basic form of the large trees within the tree mass.
  - Create a new layer and name it ***Brush 100-50***.
  - Choose a paintbrush for the Brush Tool and draw a circle by simply touching the brush to the canvas.
    - `Master Diameter = 100 px`
    - `Hardness = 100%`
      - Because the diameter is 100 pixels and the resolution is 200 pixels per inch (ppi), the diameter will be equal to one-half inch.

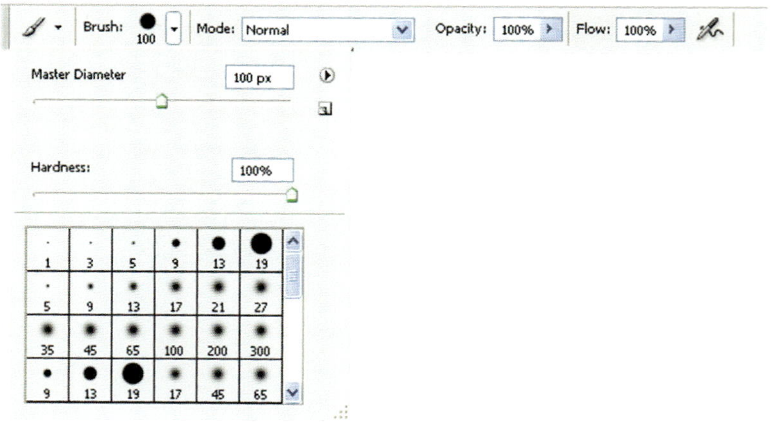

- Draw the basic form of the smaller trees.
  - Click on the layer ***Brush 100-50*** to choose it.
  - Choose a paintbrush for the Brush Tool and draw a circle by simply touching the brush to the canvas.
    - `Master Diameter = 50 px`
    - `Hardness = 100%`
      - Because the diameter is 50 pixels and the resolution is 200 pixels per inch (ppi), the diameter will be equal to one-quarter inch.

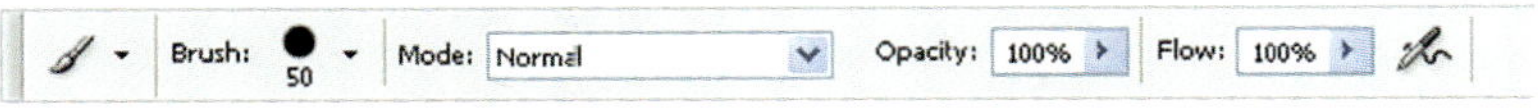

Step 2: Add an outline around the tree mass.

- Reduce the opacity of your fill so that you can see your work in the next steps.
  - `Opacity = 50%`

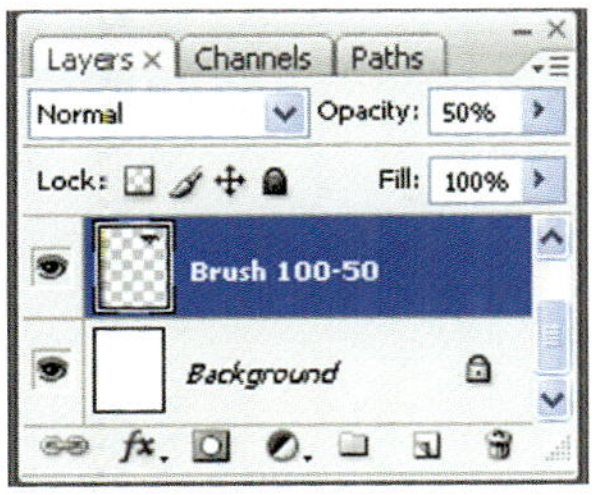

- Draw an outline around the tree mass.
  - Click on the layer ***Brush 100-50*** to choose it.
  - **Select > All**
  - With the Move Tool, hit the [up arrow] on your keyboard, then hit the [down arrow].
  - Change the foreground color to black (`#000000`).
  - Create a new layer and name it ***Outline***.
  - **Edit > Stroke**
    - `Width = 5px`
    - `Location = Inside`
  - Click the [OK] button.

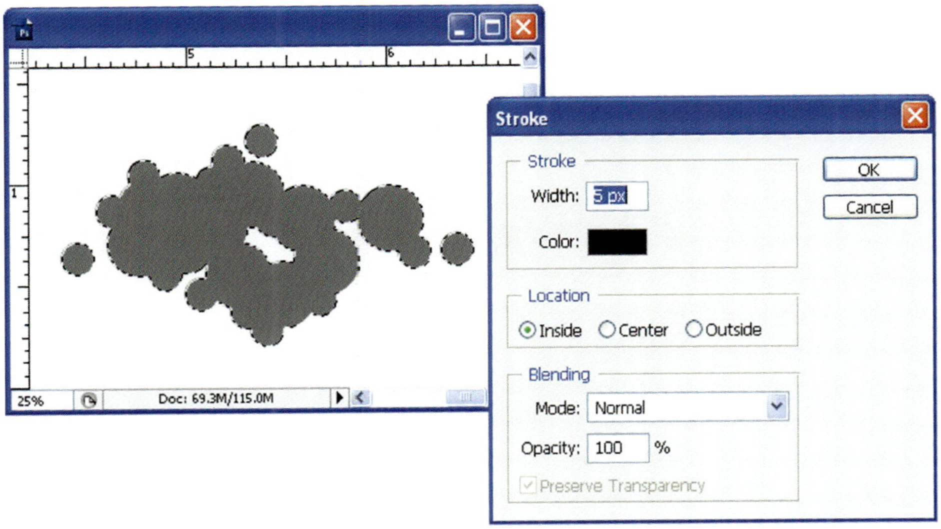

Step 2: Add an outline around the tree mass.

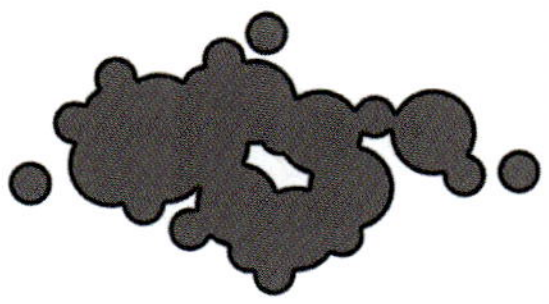

Step 3: Erase gaps from the outline.

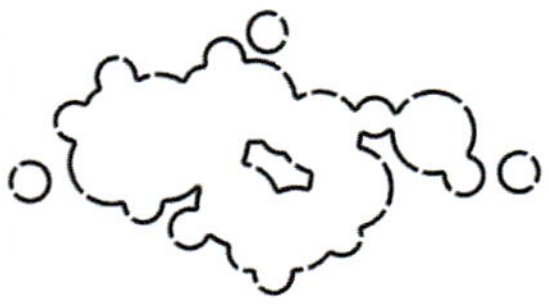

Step 3: Erase gaps from the outline.

- Erase from the outlines so that there are gaps.
    - Click on the layer ***Outline*** to choose it.
    - Chose a brush for the Eraser Tool and erase from the outlines of the symbol.
        - `Master Diameter = 5 px`
        - `Hardness = 100%`

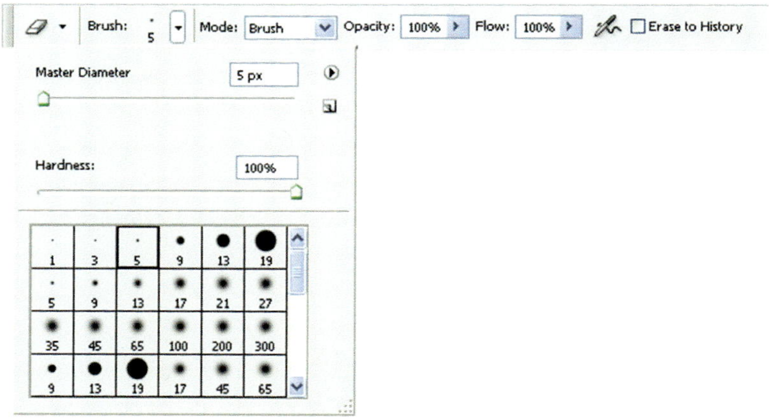

Step 4: Distort the line work.

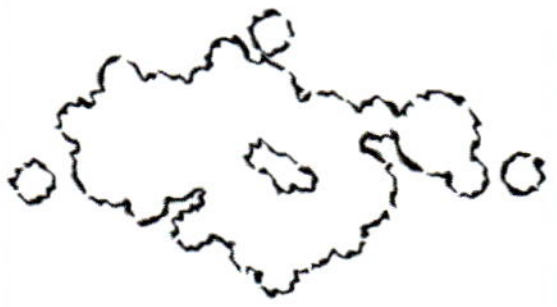

Step 4: Distort the line work.

- Distort the line work with a filter.
    - Click on the layer ***Outline*** to choose it.
    - **Distort > Filter > Ripple...**
        - `Amount = 200%`
        - `Size = Medium`
    - Click the [OK] button.

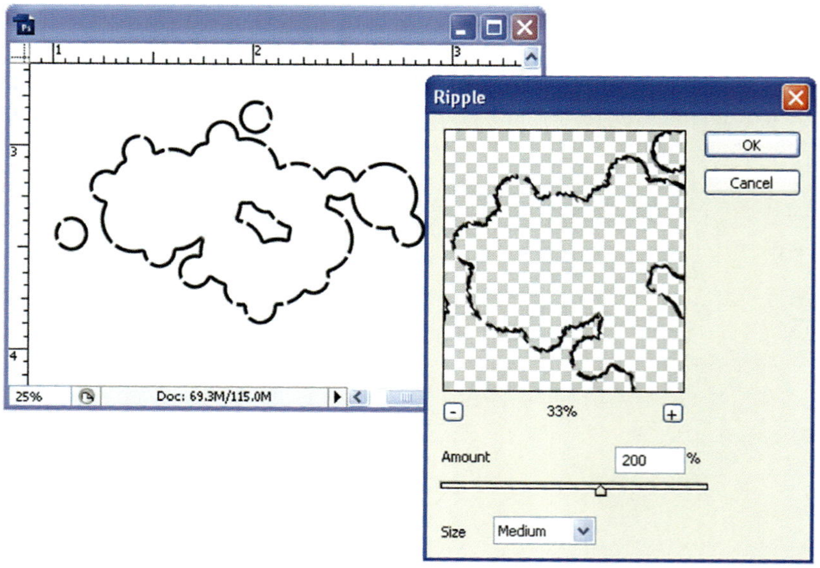

Step 5: Add shadows.

Step 5: Add shadows.

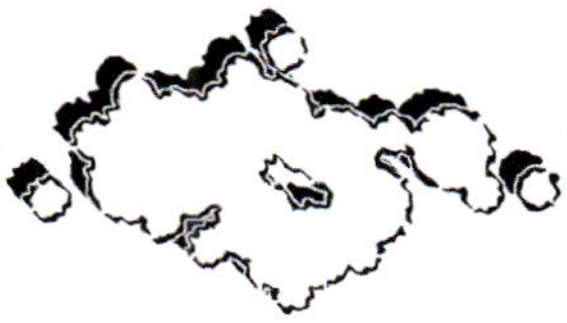

- Distort the basic form of the trees, just as you distorted the line work.
  - Click on the layer ***Outline*** to choose it.
  - **Distort > Filter > Ripple...**
    - `Amount = 200%`
    - `Size = Medium`
  - Click the [OK] button.
- Copy the basic form of the tree mass to create a shadow.
  - Click on the layer ***Brush 100-50*** to choose it.
  - You can copy the selected layer by either:
    - Hitting the right mouse key, selecting "Duplicate Layer..." from the pop-up menu, and then clicking [OK] on the Duplicate Layer dialog box.
    - Or, you can simply drag the layer to the "Create a new layer" icon.
  - With the Move Tool, shift the copied layer up and to the left.
  - Rename the copied layer ***Shadow***.
- Trim the shadow.
  - Click on the layer ***Brush 100-50*** to choose it.
  - **Select > All**
  - With the Move Tool, hit the [up arrow] on your keyboard, then hit the [down arrow].
  - **Select > Modify > Expand...**
    - `Expand By = 5 pixels`
  - Click the [OK] button.
  - Click on the layer ***Shadow*** to choose it.
  - Hit the [Delete] key to erase the shadow within the selection.

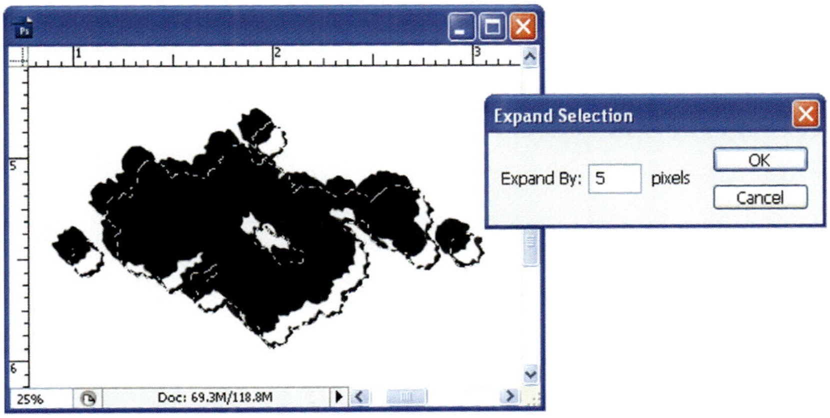

Step 6: Add color to the tree mass.

Step 6: Add color to the tree mass.

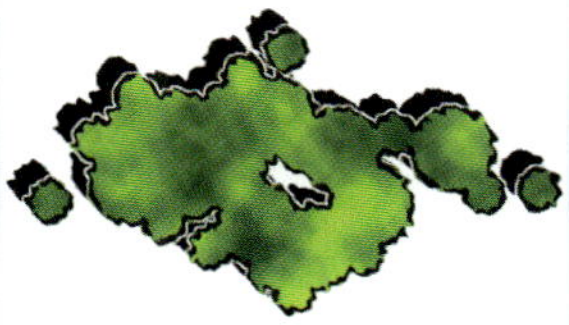

- Add color to the tree mass.
  - Change the foreground color to light olive (`#CCFF26`).
  - Change the background color to dark green (`#0D4000`).
  - Click on the layer ***Brush 100-50*** to choose it.
  - **Select > All**
  - With the Move Tool, hit the [up arrow] on the keyboard, then hit the [down arrow].
  - **Filter > Render > Clouds**

Step 7: Add a soft color glow along the edges.

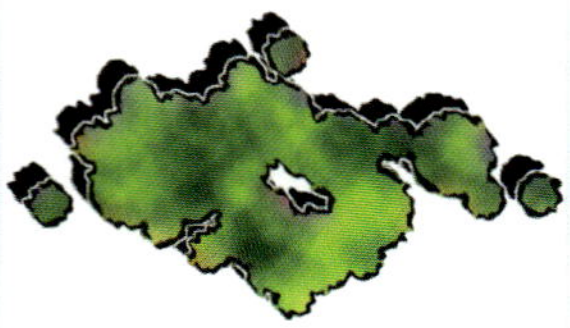

Step 7: Add a soft color glow along the edges.

- Select the area you want to paint within.
  - Click on the layer ***Brush 100-50*** to choose it.
  - **Select > All**
  - With the Move Tool, hit the [up arrow] on your keyboard, then hit the [down arrow].
- Paint soft, subtle colors along the edge of the selection.
  - Create a new layer and name it *Soft Glow*.
  - Choose a paintbrush for the Brush Tool and touch the edges of the selection with various accent colors.
    - `Master Diameter = 100 px`
    - `Hardness = 0%`

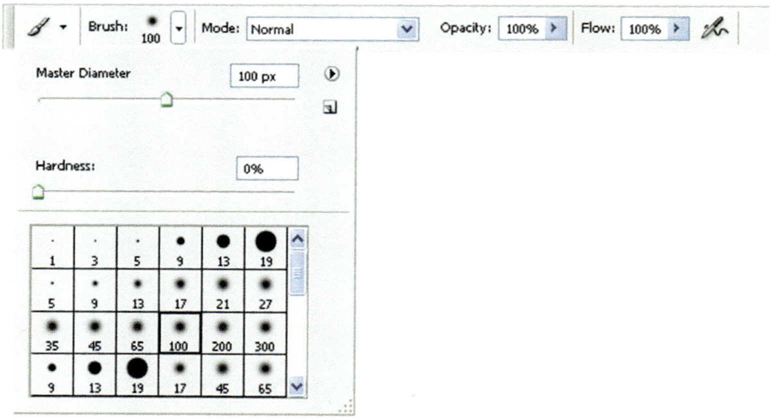

Step 8: Add accents.

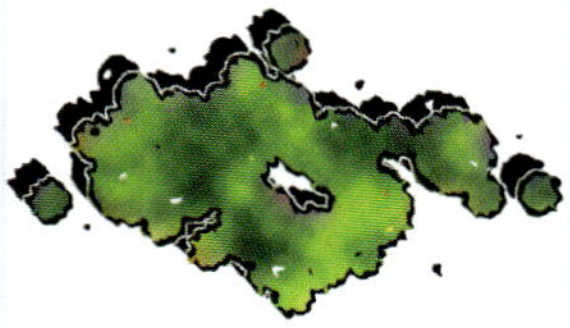

Step 8: Add accents.

- Add accents to the symbol.
  - Create a new layer and name it *Accents*.
  - Using various brush sizes and colors, add accent dots and strokes to the symbol.

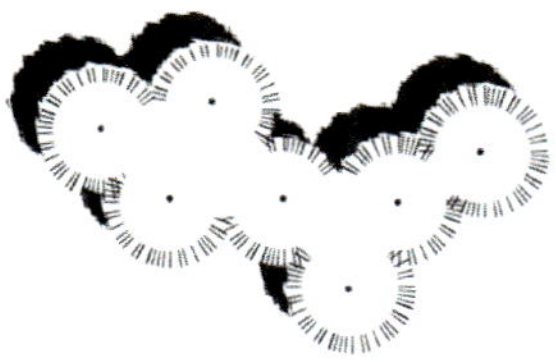

Master Plan Graphics | Shrubs

This example illustrates how to draw a simple, black-and-white grouping of shrubs. The techniques used in this example include the following:

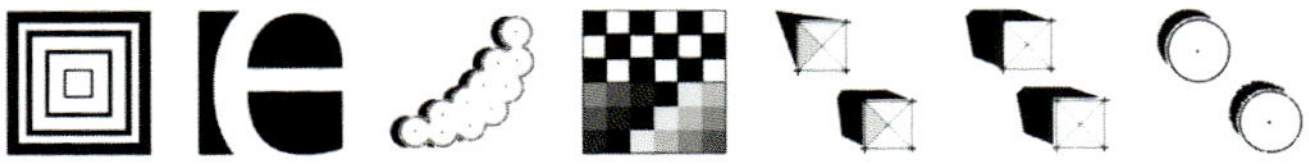

This drawing was originally drawn on a canvas with a resolution of 200 pixels per inch. Afterwards, it was scaled down to fit within these pages.

Step 1: Paste a grouping of symbols.

Step 1: Paste a grouping of symbols.

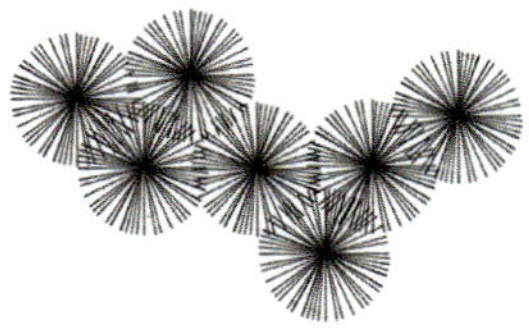

In this example, you begin by pasting a previously drawn tree symbol within your drawing. Then you will scale it to a more appropriate size, copy it repeatedly, and then refine your new grouping until it resembles a shrub mass.

- Copy the symbol from another drawing.
  - Open the drawing with your tree symbol.
  - Click the layer with the symbol you want to recycle to choose it.
  - **Select > All**
  - **Edit > Copy**
    - This will copy the selected layer onto your clipboard.
  - Close your drawing without saving changes.
    - **File > Close**
    - Click the [No] button.
  - **File > New**
    - Specify dimensions large enough for your drawing. For this example, 4" x 2" is probably suitable.
    - Specify a resolution of 200 pixels per inch (ppi).
  - Click the [OK] button.
- Paste the symbol within your drawing.
  - **Edit > Paste**
  - Rename this pasted layer *Shrub*.

- Scale your symbol to a more appropriate size.
    - **Edit > Transform > Scale**
        - `Width = 33%`
        - `Height = 33%`
    - Hit the [Enter] key to commit your changes.

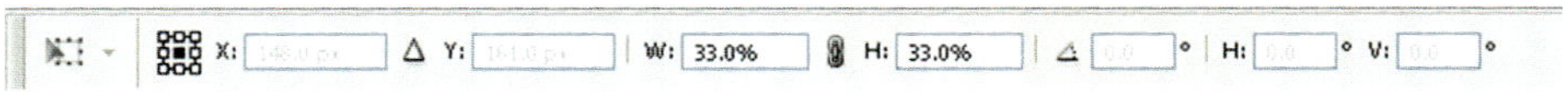

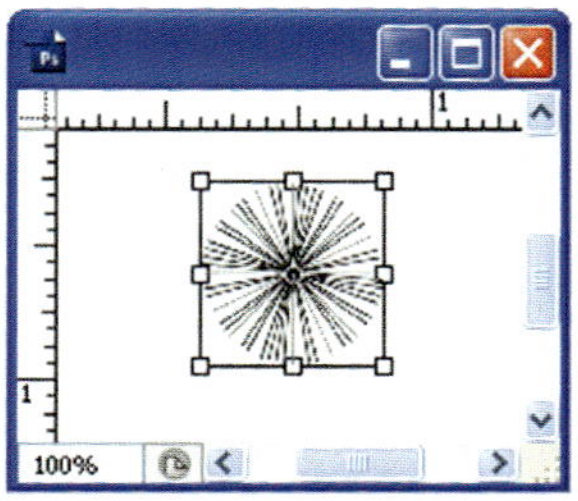

- Make copies of your symbol and paste them into a grouping of symbols.
    - Click on the layer ***Shrub*** to choose it.
    - **Select > All**
    - **Edit > Copy**
    - Paste the symbol into a grouping.
        - **Edit > Paste**
        - With the Move Tool, shift the symbol to a suitable location.
        - Repeat this step until you have a grouping of symbols.
- Consolidate these pasted layers into one composite layer.
    - While holding down the [Ctrl] key, click on each layer that was created when you pasted the symbols into the drawing.
    - Click the right mouse button and select "Merge Layers..." from the pop-up dialog box.
    - Rename the consolidated layer ***Shrubs***.

Step 2: Erase from the center of the symbols.

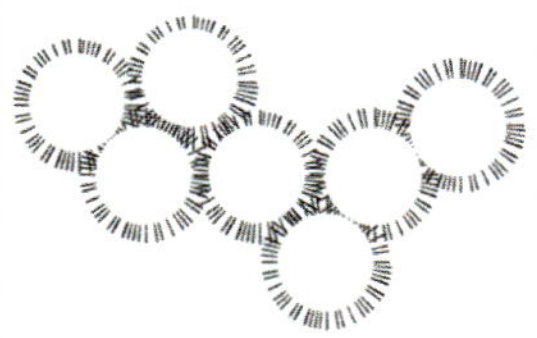

Step 2: Erase from the center of the symbols.

- Erase from the center of the symbols.
    - Click on the layer ***Shrubs*** to choose it.
    - Choose a brush for the Eraser Tool and erase the center of each shrub symbol within your grouping.
        - `Master Diameter = 50 px`
        - `Hardness = 100%`

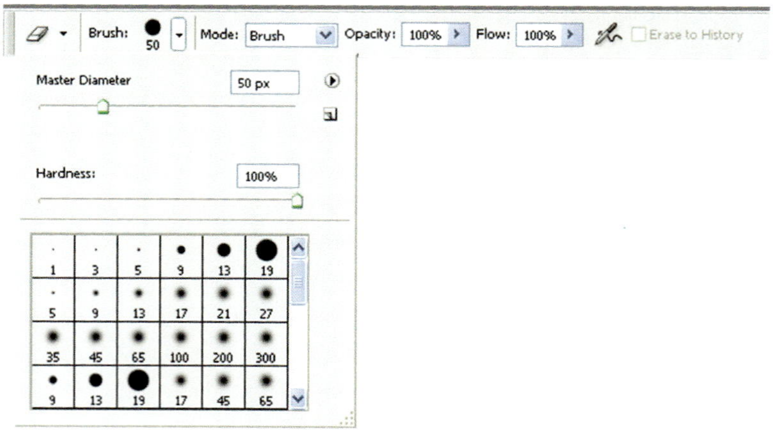

Step 3: Erase from the interior of the grouping.

- Continue erasing from the grouping of symbols.
  - Choose a smaller brush for the Eraser Tool and continue erasing the interior of the shrub grouping until only an outline of dashed lines remains.
    - `Master Diameter = 25 px`
    - `Hardness = 100%`

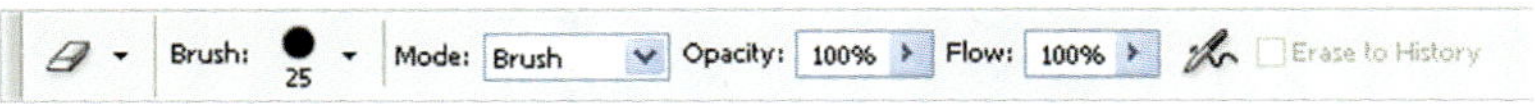

Step 3: Erase from the interior of the grouping.

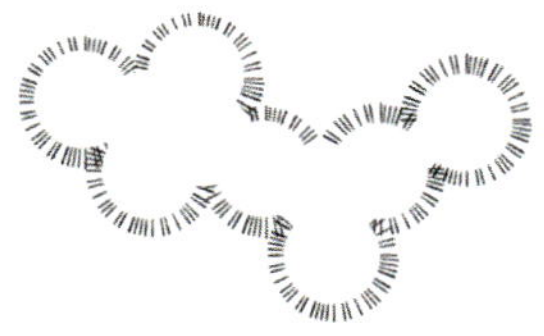

Step 4: Add shadows.

- Anchor the centers of the shrubs.
  - Choose a paintbrush for the Brush Tool and paint a dot in the center of each shrub.
    - `Master Diameter = 5 px`
    - `Hardness = 100%`

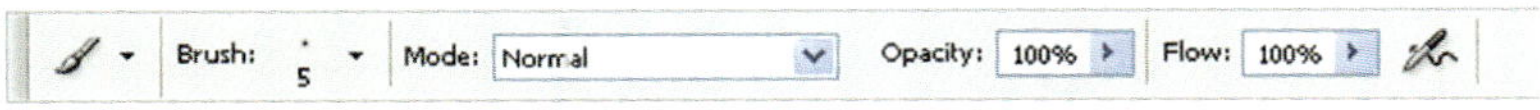

- Paint over the grouping of shrubs.
  - Create a new layer and name it ***Brush 67***.
  - Choose a paintbrush for the Brush Tool and paint over every shrub in the grouping.
    - `Master Diameter = 67 px`
    - `Hardness = 100%`
  - Reduce the layer `Opacity = 50%` so that you can see your work in the following steps.

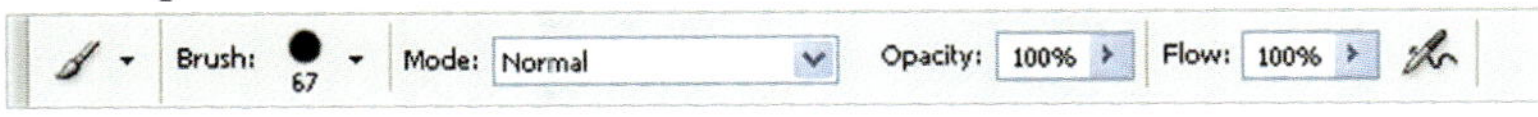

- Copy this new layer to make the shadows from.
  - Click on the layer ***Brush 67*** to choose it.
  - You can copy the selected layer by either:
    - Hitting the right mouse key, selecting "Duplicate Layer..." from the pop-up menu, and then clicking [OK] on the Duplicate Layer dialog box.
    - Or, you can simply drag the layer to the "Create a new layer" icon.
  - With the Move Tool, shift the copied layer up and to the left.
  - Rename the copied layer ***Shadow***.
- Trim the shadows.
  - Click on the layer ***Brush 67*** to choose it.
  - **Select > All**
  - With the Move Tool, hit the [up arrow] on your keyboard, then hit the [down arrow].
  - **Select > Modify > Expand...**
    - `Expand By = 3 pixels`
  - Click on the layer ***Shadow*** to choose it.
  - Hit the [Delete] key to erase the shadow within your selection.

Step 4: Add shadows.

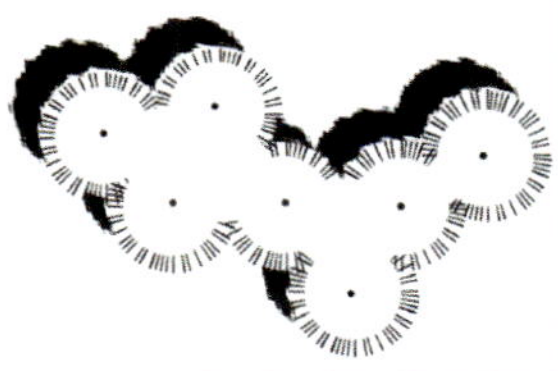

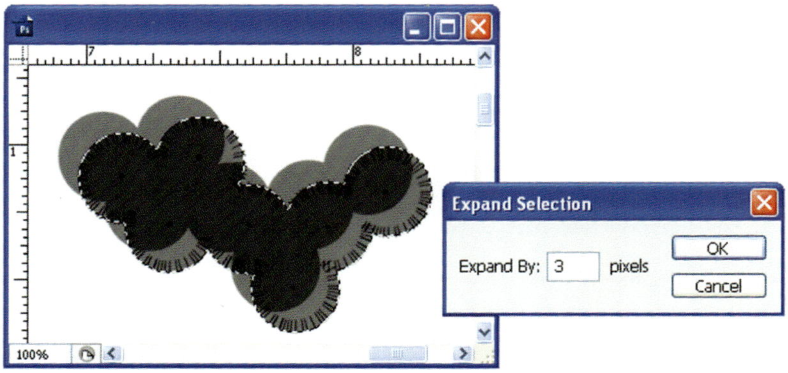

- Distort the shadow of the trees with a filter.
  - Turn off the layer ***Brush 67*** by clicking on the [eye] icon so that it disappears and the layer is no longer visible.
  - Click on the layer ***Shadow*** to choose it.
  - **Filter > Distort > Ripple...**
    - `Amount = 100%`
    - `Size = Small`
  - Click the [OK] button.

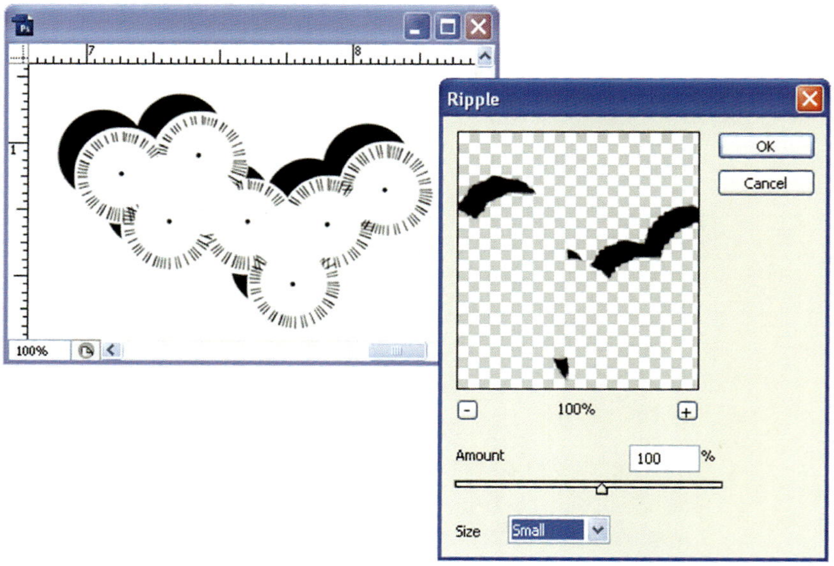

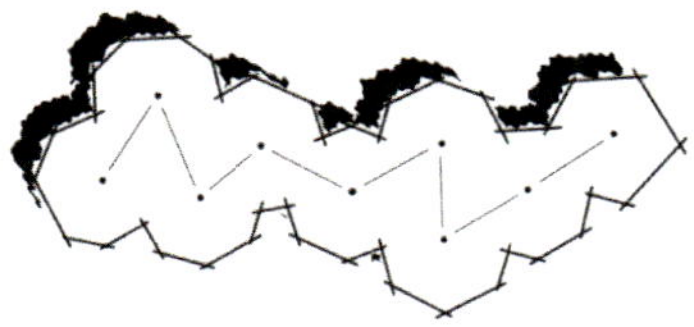

Master Plan Graphics | Shrubs

This example illustrates how to draw a simple, black-and-white grouping of shrubs. The techniques used in this example include the following:

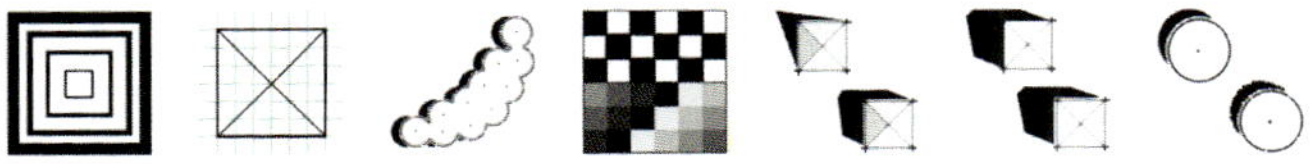

This drawing was originally drawn on a canvas with a resolution of 200 pixels per inch. Afterwards, it was scaled down to fit within these pages.

Step 1: Begin with the basic grouping.

- Paint a basic grouping of shrubs.
  - Create a new layer and name it *Brush 67*.
  - Choose a paintbrush for the Brush Tool and paint a grouping of shrubs.
  - `Master Diameter = 67 px`
  - `Hardness = 100%`

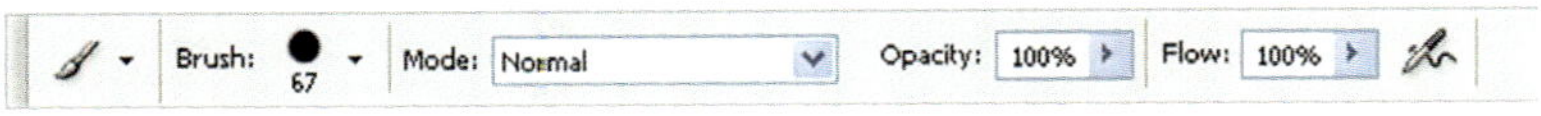

- Reduce the opacity of your fill so that you can see your work in the next steps.
  - `Opacity = 50%`

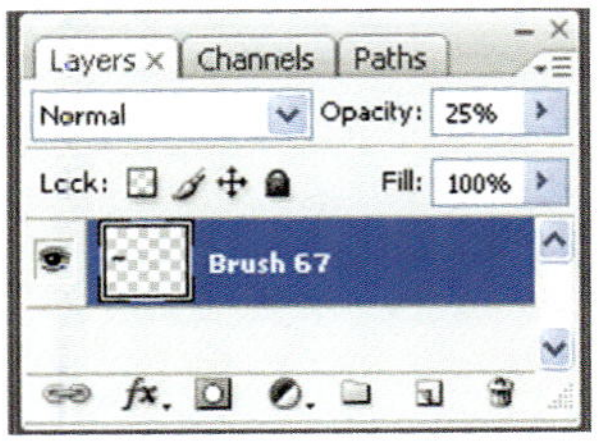

- Anchor the centers of the shrubs.
  - Choose a paintbrush for the Brush Tool and paint a dot in the center of each shrub.
    - `Master Diameter = 5 px`
    - `Hardness = 100%`

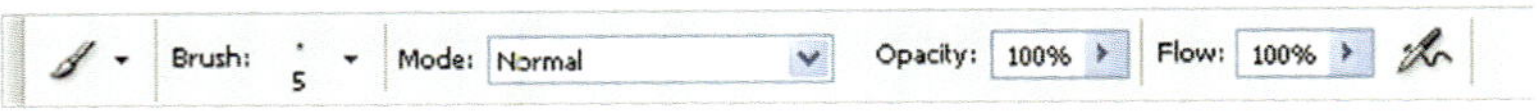

Step 1: Begin with the basic grouping.

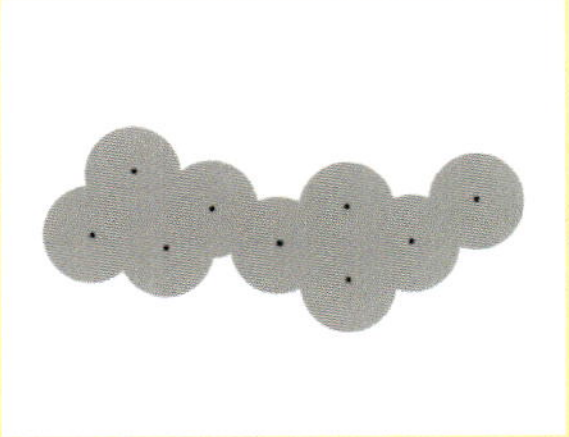

Step 2: Add a thick outline to the grouping.

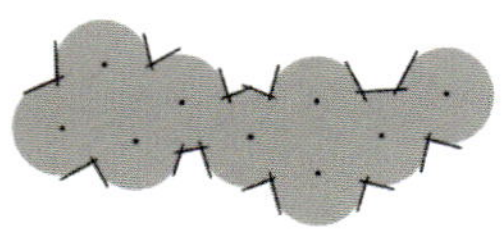

Step 2: Add a thick outline to the grouping.

- Begin to loosely outline the grouping of shrubs.
  - Create a new layer and name it ***Outline***.
  - Choose a paintbrush for the Brush Tool and draw lines where shrubs intersect.
    - `Master Diameter = 3 px`
    - `Hardness = 100%`
      - You begin by drawing where shrubs intersect because this will help communicate the spacing more explicitly.
      - You should allow lines to overlap to ensure that the angles seem sharp.

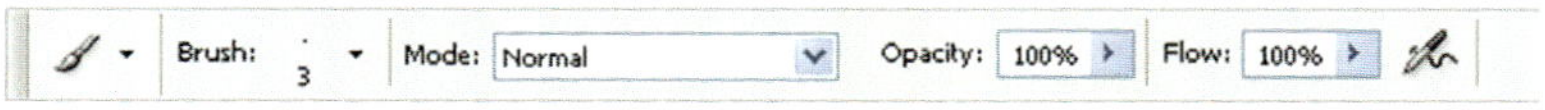

Step 3: Add detail to the outline.

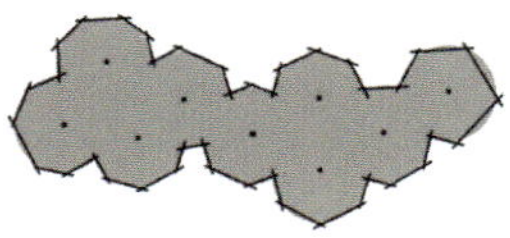

Step 3: Add detail to the outline.

- Continue outlining the grouping of shrubs, as before.

Step 4: Add shadows.

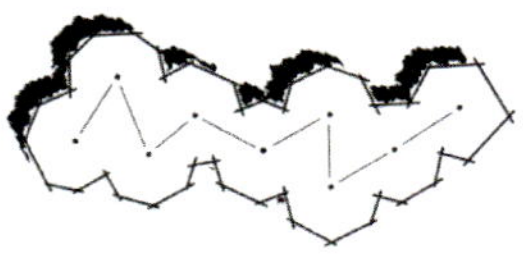

Step 4: Add shadows.

- Copy the layer with the basic form of the trees.
  - Click on the layer ***Brush 67*** to choose it.
  - You can copy the selected layer by either:
    - Hitting the right mouse key, selecting "Duplicate Layer..." from the pop-up menu, and then clicking [OK] on the Duplicate Layer dialog box.
    - Or, you can simply drag the layer to the "Create a new layer" icon.
  - With the Move Tool, shift the copied layer up and to the left.
  - Rename the copied layer ***Shadow***.
- Trim the shadows.
  - Click on the layer ***Brush 67*** to choose it.
  - **Select > All**
  - With the Move Tool, hit the [up arrow] on your keyboard, then hit the [down arrow].
  - **Select > Modify > Expand...**
    - `Expand By = 3 pixels`
  - Click the [OK] button.
  - Click on the layer ***Shadow*** to choose it.
  - Hit the [Delete] key to erase the shadow within your selection.

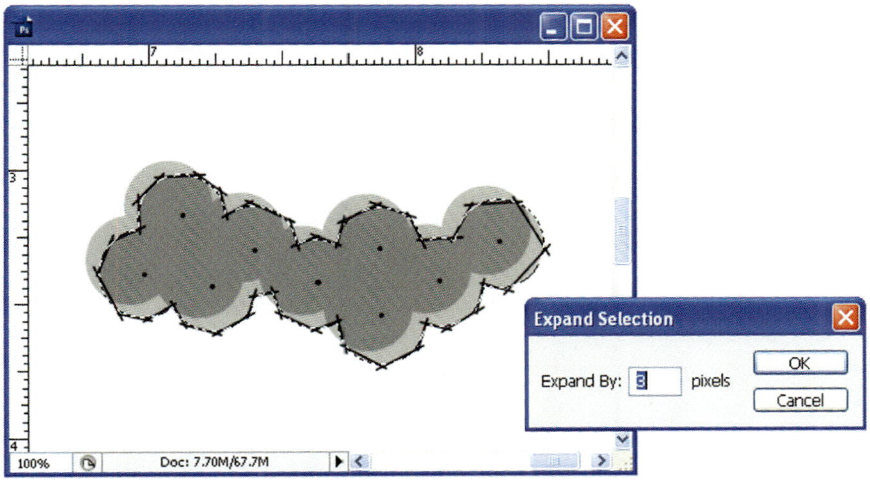

- Distort the shadow of the trees with a filter.
  - Turn off the layer ***Brush 67*** by clicking on the [eye] icon so that it disappears and the layer is no longer visible.
  - Click on the layer ***Shadow*** to choose it.
  - **Filter > Distort > Ripple...**
    - `Amount = 200%`
    - `Size = Small`
  - Click the [OK] button.

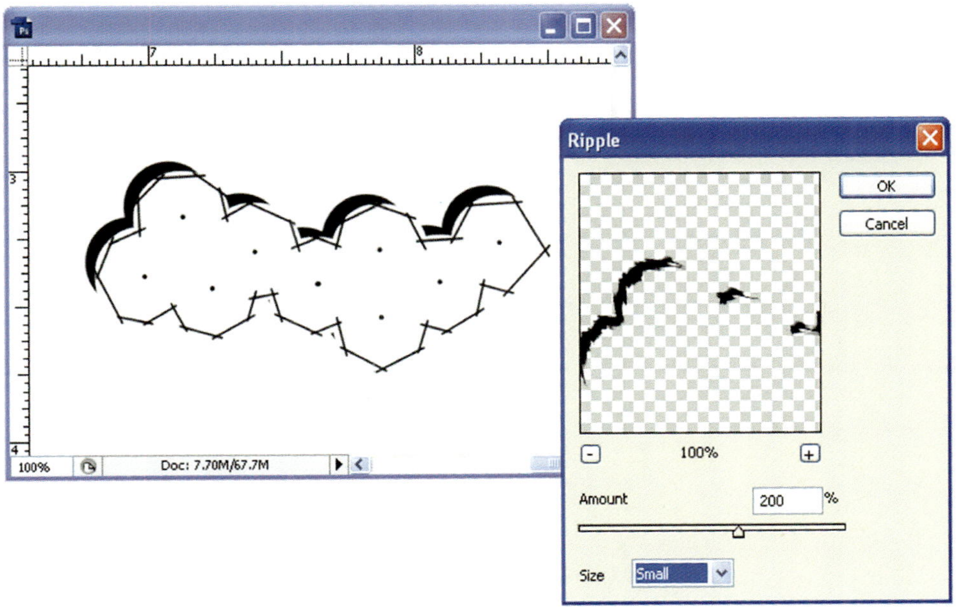

- Accentuate the spacing between the individual shrubs.
  - Create a new layer and name it ***Spacing***.
  - Choose a paintbrush for the Brush Tool and draw lines from center point to center point.
    - `Master Diameter = 1 px, Hardness = 100%`
  - Hold down the [Shift] key between clicks to make straight lines.
  - Choose a large brush for the Eraser Tool and erase along the previously drawn line by clicking on each center point.
    - `Master Diameter = 19 px, Hardness = 100%`

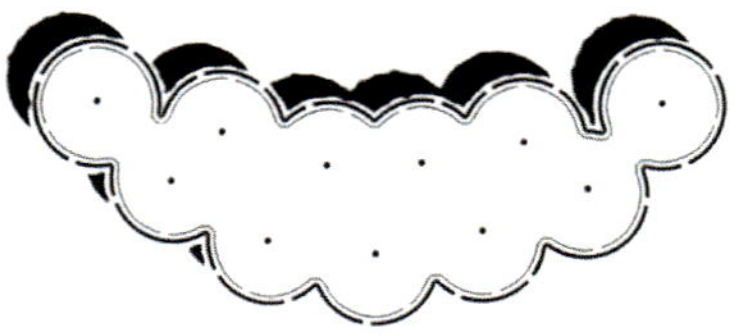

Master Plan Graphics | Shrubs

This example illustrates how to draw a simple, black-and-white grouping of shrubs. The techniques used in this example include the following:

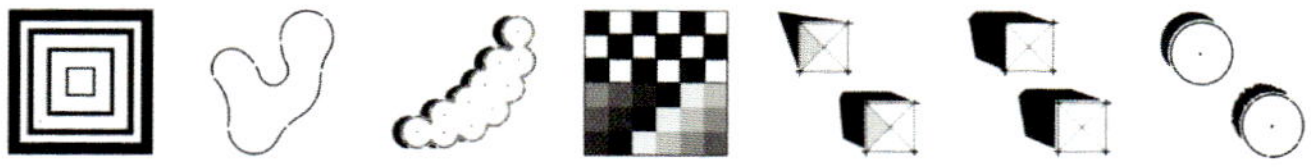

This drawing was originally drawn on a canvas with a resolution of 200 pixels per inch. Afterwards, it was scaled down to fit within these pages.

Step 1: Begin with the basic grouping.

Step 1: Begin with the basic grouping.

- Paint a basic grouping of shrubs.
  - Create a new layer and name it *Brush 67*.
  - Choose a paintbrush for the Brush Tool and paint each shrub in the grouping.
    - `Master Diameter = 67 px`
    - `Hardness = 100%`

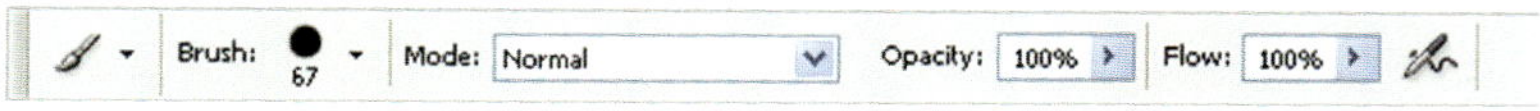

- Reduce the opacity of your fill so that you can see your work in the next steps.
  - `Opacity = 50%`

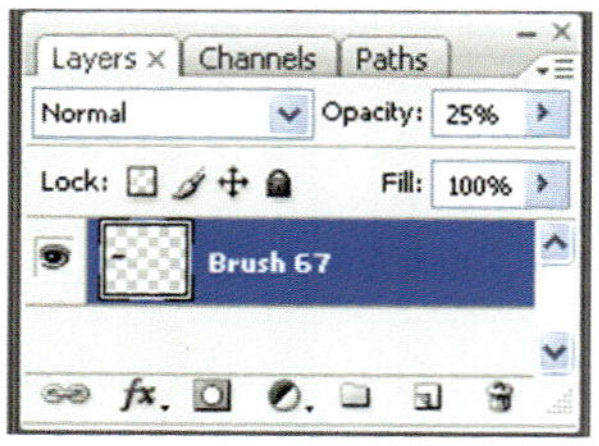

Step 2: Add a thick outline to the grouping.

- Anchor the centers of the shrubs.
  - Choose a paintbrush for the Brush Tool and paint a dot in the center of each shrub.
    - `Master Diameter = 5 px`
    - `Hardness = 100%`

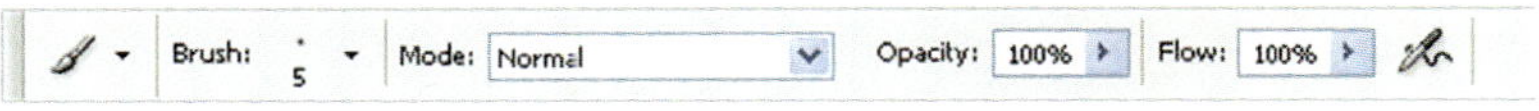

Step 2: Add a thick outline to the grouping.

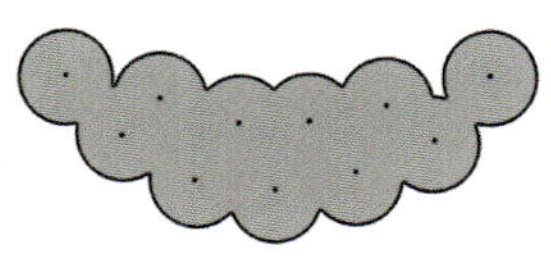

- Draw an outline around the shrubs.
  - Click on the layer ***Brush 67*** to choose it.
  - **Select > All**
  - With the Move Tool, hit the [up arrow] on your keyboard, then hit the [down arrow].
  - Change the foreground color to black (`#000000`).
  - Create a new layer and name it ***Outline***.
  - **Edit > Stroke**
    - `Width = 3px`
    - `Location = Inside`
  - Click the [OK] button.

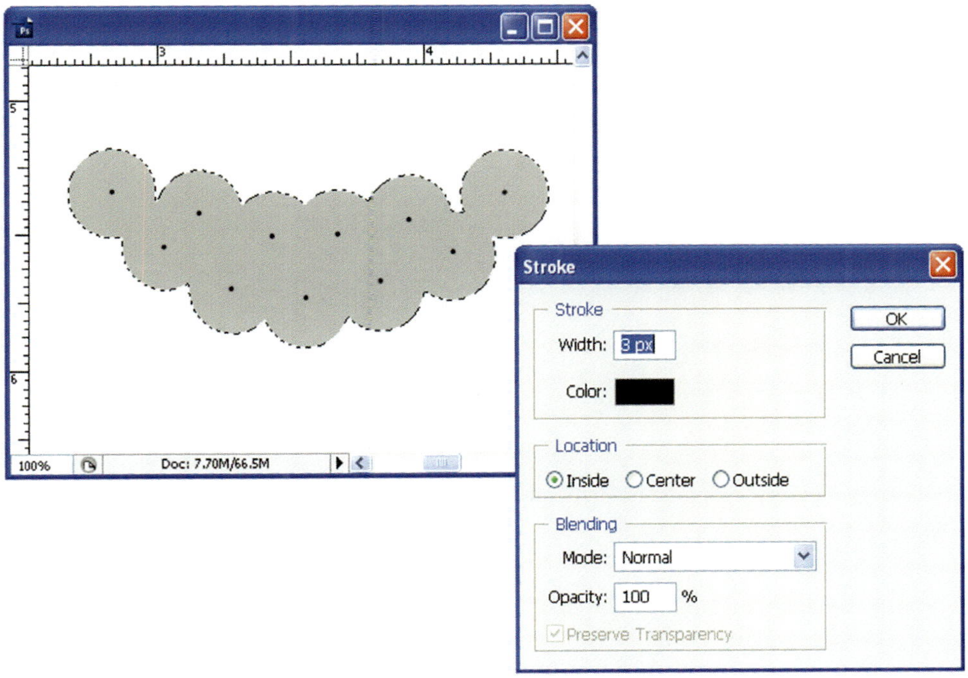

Step 3: Add detail to the outline.

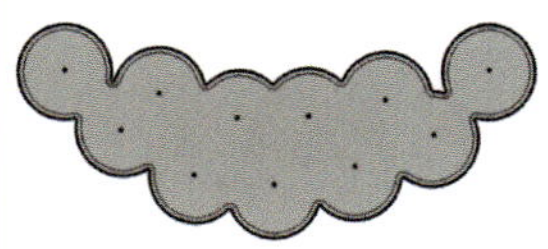

Step 3: Add detail to the outline.

- Select an area to draw an interior line.
  - Click on the layer ***Brush 67*** to choose it.
  - **Select > All**
  - With the Move Tool, hit the [up arrow], then hit the [down arrow].
  - **Select > Modify > Contract...**
    - `Expand By = 6 pixels`
  - Click the [OK] button.

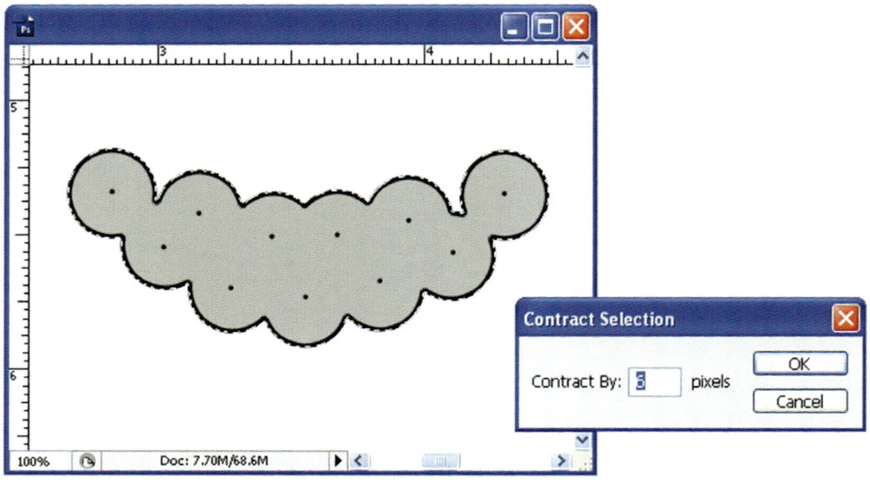

- Draw an interior line.
  - Create a new layer and name it ***Interior Line***.
  - **Edit > Stroke**
    - `Width = 1 px`
    - `Location = Inside`
  - Click the [OK] button.

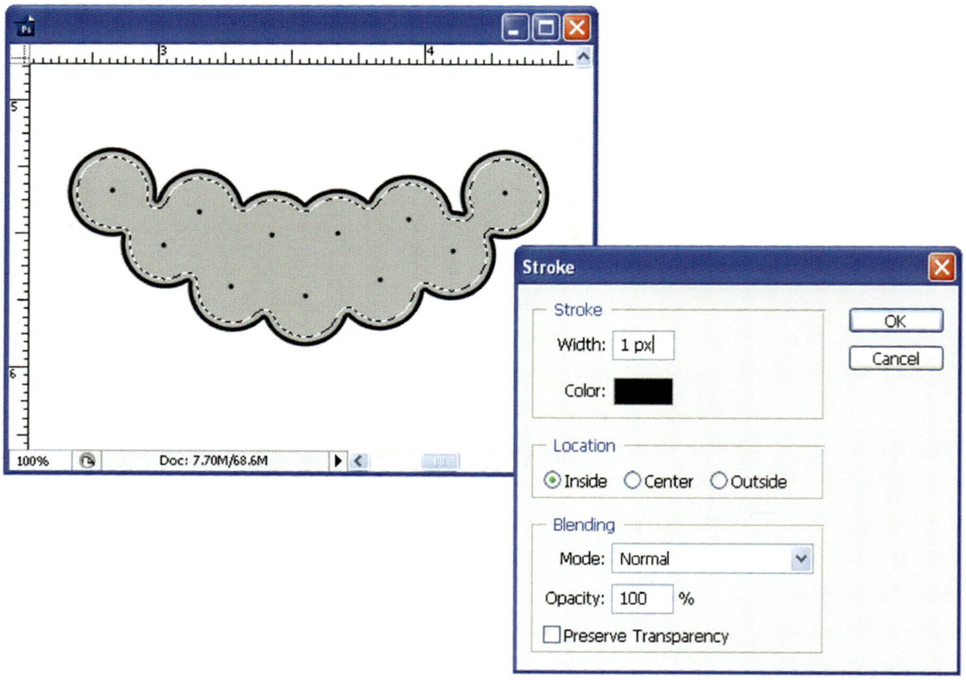

Step 4: Add shadows.

- Erase from the outlines so there are gaps.
  - Click on the layer ***Outline*** to choose it.
  - Choose a brush for the Eraser Tool and erase from the outlines of the symbol.
    - `Master Diameter = 5 px, Hardness = 100%`
  - Repeat the above steps for the layer ***Interior Line***.

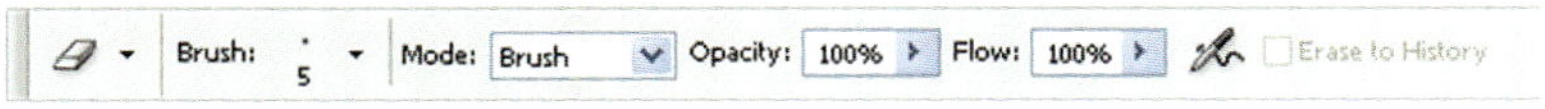

- Copy the layer with the basic form of the trees.
  - Click on the layer ***Brush 67*** to choose it.
  - You can copy the selected layer by either:
    - Hitting the right mouse key, selecting "Duplicate Layer..." from the pop-up menu, and then clicking [OK] on the Duplicate Layer dialog box.
    - Or, you can simply drag the layer to the "Create a new layer" icon.
  - With the Move Tool, shift the copied layer up and to the left.
  - Rename the copied layer ***Shadow***.
- Trim the shadows.
  - Click on the layer ***Brush 67*** to choose it.
  - **Select > All**
  - With the Move Tool, hit the [up arrow] on your keyboard, then hit the [down arrow].
  - **Select > Modify > Expand...**
    - `Expand By = 3 pixels`
  - Click the [OK] button.
  - Click on the layer ***Shadow*** to choose it.
  - Hit the [Delete] key to erase the shadow within your selection.
- Distort the shadow of the trees with a filter.
  - Click on the layer ***Shadow*** to choose it.
  - **Filter > Distort > Ripple...**
    - `Amount = 100%, Size = Small`
  - Click the [OK] button.

Step 4: Add shadows.

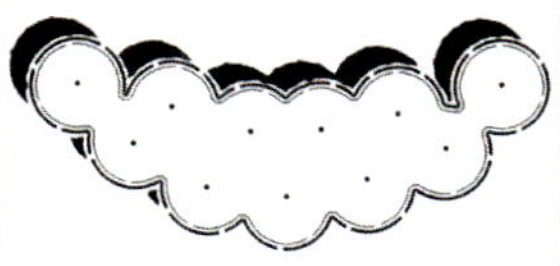

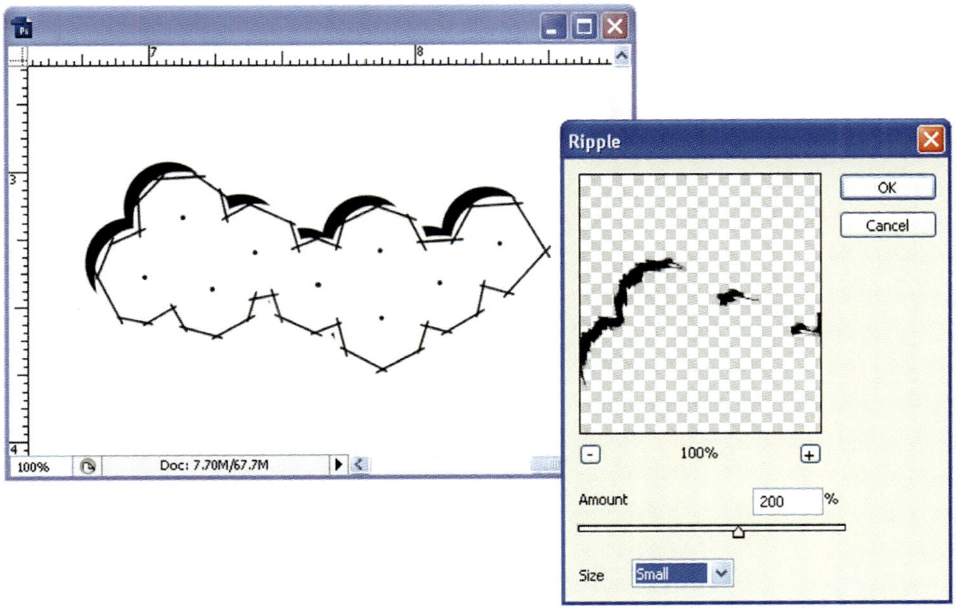

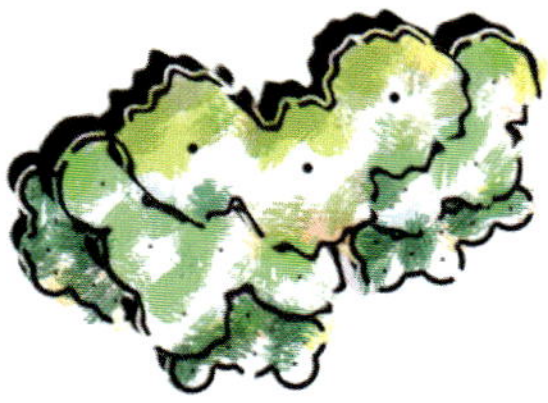

Master Plan Graphics | Shrubs

This example illustrates how to draw a grouping of shrubs. The techniques used in this example include the following:

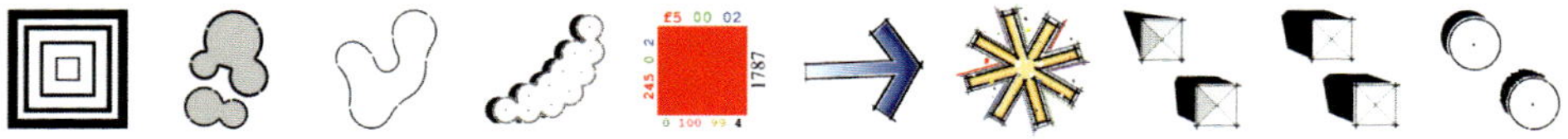

This drawing was originally drawn on a canvas with a resolution of 200 pixels per inch. Afterwards, it was scaled down to fit within these pages.

Step 1: Draw the basic form of each grouping.

Step 1: Draw the basic form of each grouping.

- Draw the largest shrubs.
  - Create a new layer and name it ***Brush 75***.
  - Choose a paintbrush for the Brush Tool and paint each shrub in the grouping.
    - `Master Diameter = 75 px`
    - `Hardness = 100%`

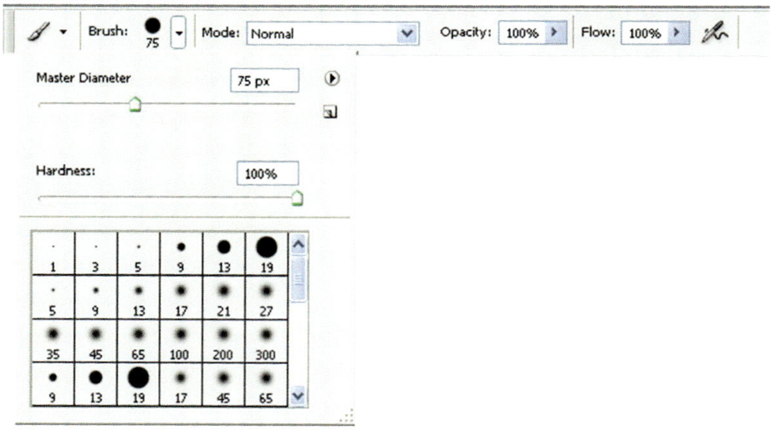

- Draw the medium shrubs.
  - Create a new layer and name it ***Brush 50***.
  - Choose a paintbrush for the Brush Tool and paint each shrub in the grouping.
    - `Master Diameter = 50 px`
    - `Hardness = 100%`

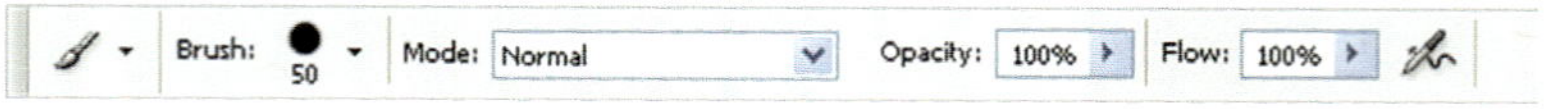

- Draw the smallest shrubs.
  - Create a new layer and name it ***Brush 25***.
  - Choose a paintbrush for the Brush Tool and paint each shrub in the grouping.
    - `Master Diameter = 25 px`
    - `Hardness = 100%`

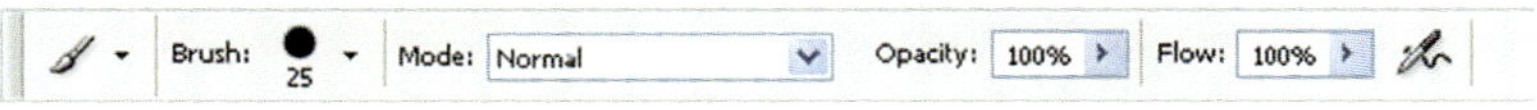

- Change the layer opacity so that you can see your work in the following steps.
  - Click on the layer ***Brush 75*** to choose it.
    - Change the layer `Opacity = 25%`.
  - Click on the layer ***Brush 50*** to choose it.
    - Change the layer `Opacity = 50%`.
  - Click on the layer ***Brush 25*** to choose it.
    - Change the layer `Opacity = 75%`.

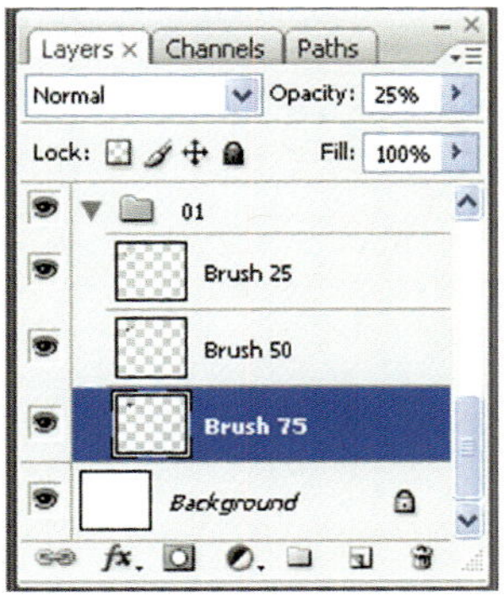

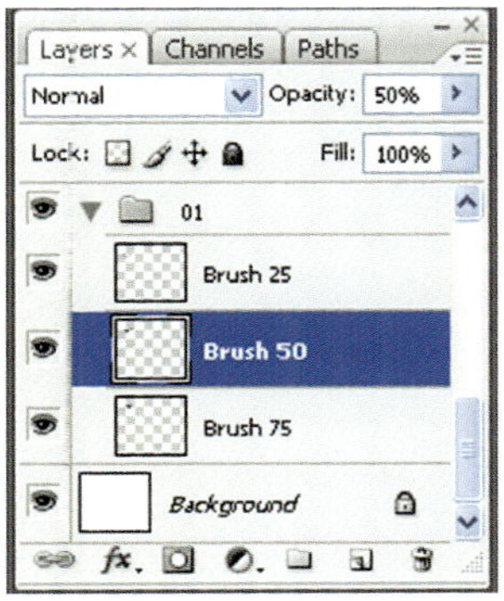

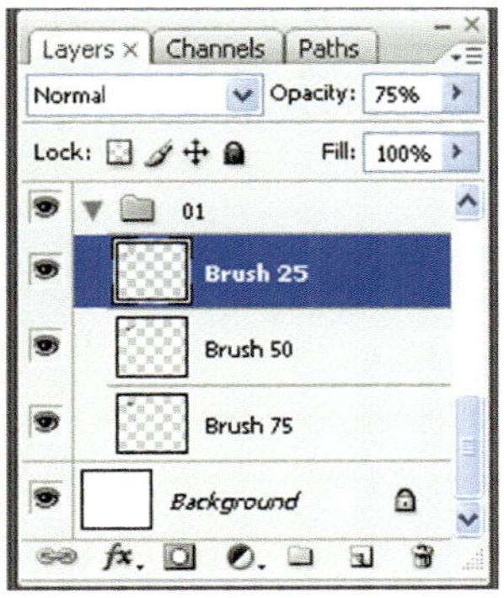

Step 2: Add outlines to the groupings of shrubs.

- Outline the largest shrubs.
  - Click on the layer ***Brush 75*** to choose it.
  - **Select > All**
  - With the Move Tool, hit the [up arrow] on your keyboard, then hit the [down arrow].
  - Create a new layer and name it ***Brush 75 Stroke 3***.
  - **Edit > Stroke...**
    - `Width = 3 px`
    - `Location = Inside`
  - Click the [OK] button.
- Outline the medium shrubs.
  - Click on the layer ***Brush 50*** to choose it.
  - **Select > All**
  - With the Move Tool, hit the [up arrow] on your keyboard, then hit the [down arrow].
  - Create a new layer and name it ***Brush 50 Stroke 3***.
  - **Edit > Stroke...**
    - `Width = 3 px`
    - `Location = Inside`
  - Click the [OK] button.

Step 2: Add outlines to the groupings of shrubs.

- Outline the smallest shrubs.
  - Click on the layer ***Brush 25*** to choose it.
  - **Select > All**
  - With the Move Tool, hit the [up arrow] on your keyboard, then hit the [down arrow].
  - Create a new layer and name it ***Brush 25 Stroke 3***.
  - **Edit > Stroke...**
    - `Width = 3 px`
    - `Location = Inside`
  - Click the [OK] button.

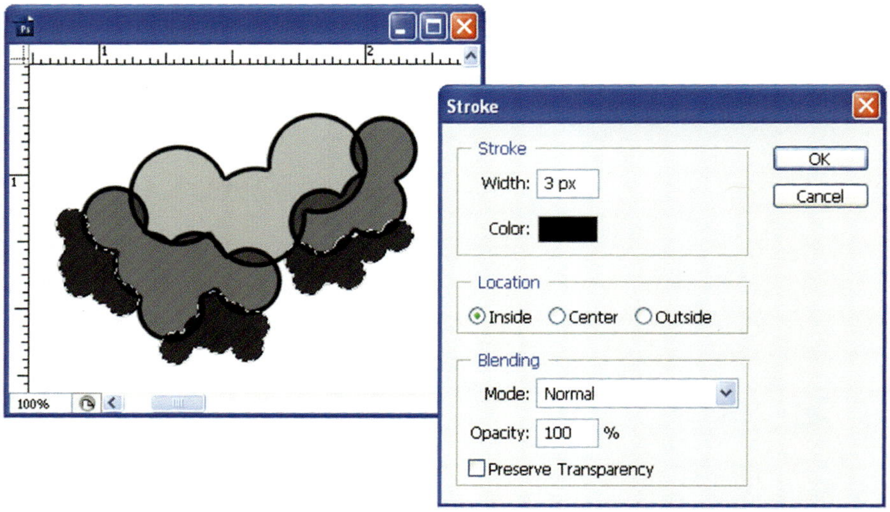

- Erase from the outlines so that there are gaps.
  - Click on the layer ***Brush 75 Stroke 3*** to choose it.
  - Choose a brush for the Eraser Tool and erase along the outlines to create gaps.
    - `Master Diameter = 5 px`
    - `Hardness = 100%`
  - Repeat the above steps for layers ***Brush 50 Stroke 3*** and ***Brush 25 Stroke 3***.

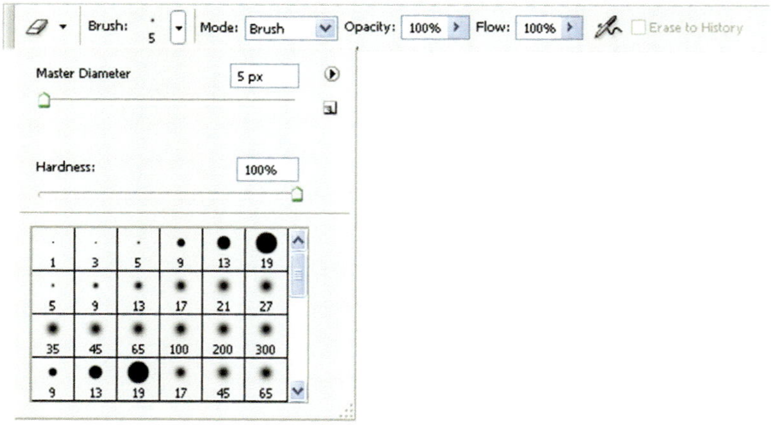

Step 3: Add shadows.

Step 3: Add shadows.

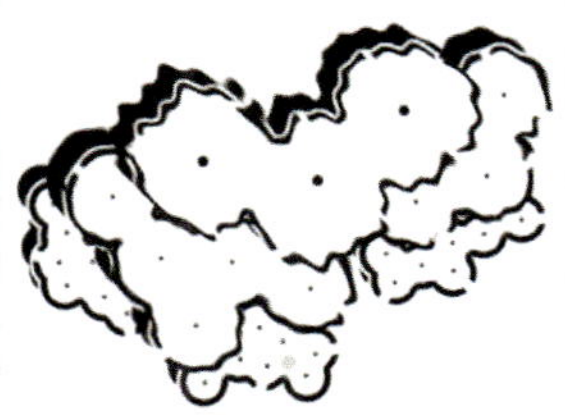

Prior to adding shadows, you will first need to distort the line work and basic form of your shrub groupings. This will allow you to trim your shadows later during this step.

- Distort the line work for the largest shrubs.
  - Click on the layer ***Brush 75 Stroke 3*** to choose it.
  - **Filter > Distort > Ripple...**
    - `Amount = 100%`
    - `Size = Large`
  - Click the [OK] button.

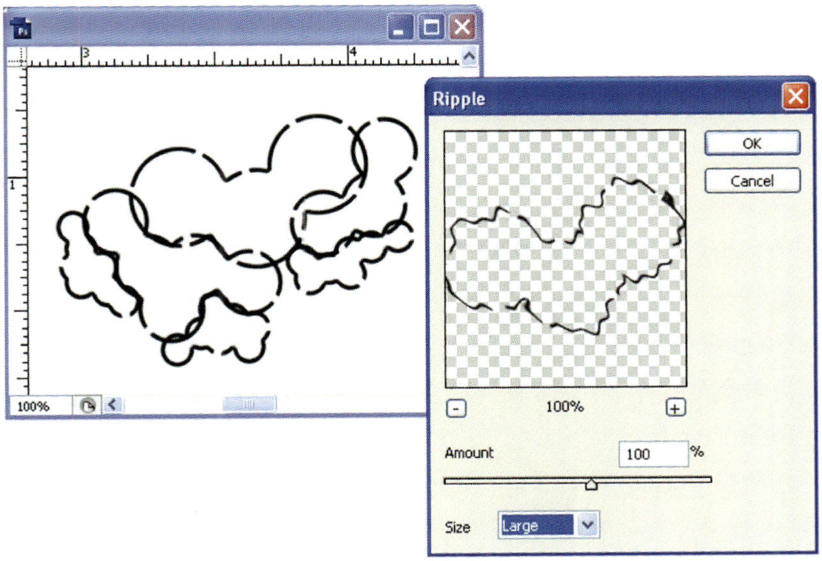

- Distort the basic form for the largest shrubs.
  - Click on the layer ***Brush 75*** to choose it.
  - **Filter > Distort > Ripple...**
    - `Amount = 100%, Size = Large`
  - Click the [OK] button.

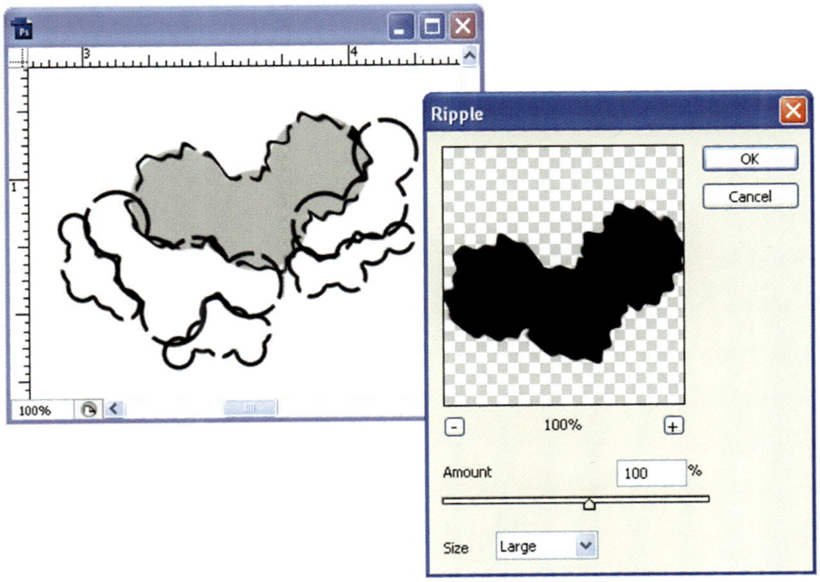

- Copy the layer you just distorted.
  - Click on the layer ***Brush 75*** to choose it.
  - Drag the selected layer to the "Create a new layer" icon.
  - With the Move Tool, shift the copied layer up and to the left.
  - Rename the copied layer ***Shadow 75***.
- Trim the shadow.
  - Click on the layer ***Brush 75*** to choose it.
  - **Select > All**
  - With the Move Tool, hit the [up arrow] on your keyboard, then hit the [down arrow].
  - **Select > Modify > Expand...**
    - `Expand By = 3 pixels`
  - Click the [OK] button.
  - Click on the layer ***Shadow 75*** to choose it.
  - Hit the [Delete] key to erase the shadow within your selection.

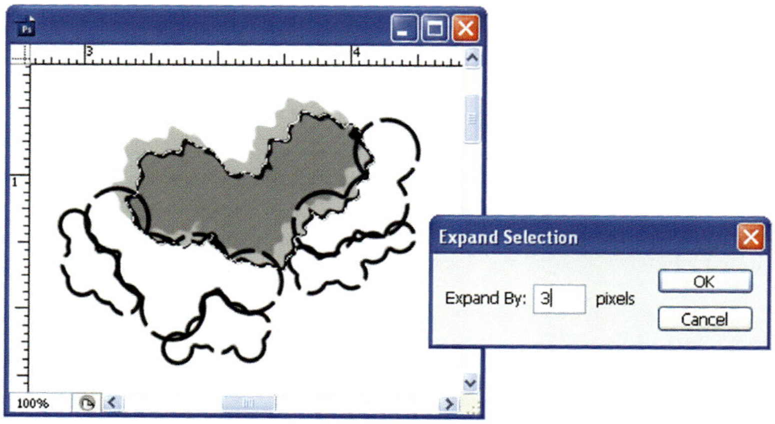

- Distort the line work for the medium shrubs.
  - Click on the layer ***Brush 50 Stroke 3*** to choose it.
  - **Filter > Distort > Ripple...**
    - `Amount = 100%, Size = Large`
  - Click the [OK] button.

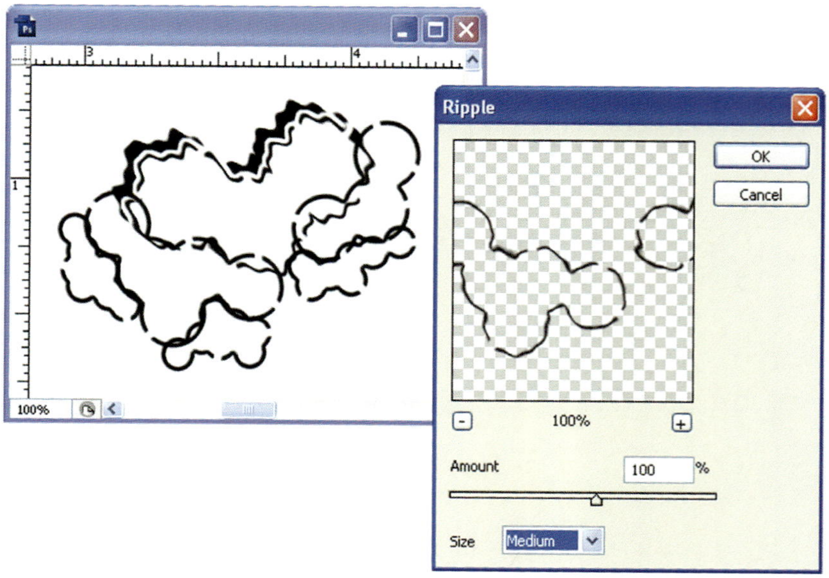

- Distort the basic form of the medium shrubs.
    - Click on the layer ***Brush 50*** to choose it.
    - **Filter > Distort > Ripple...**
        - `Amount = 100%, Size = Large`
    - Click the [OK] button.

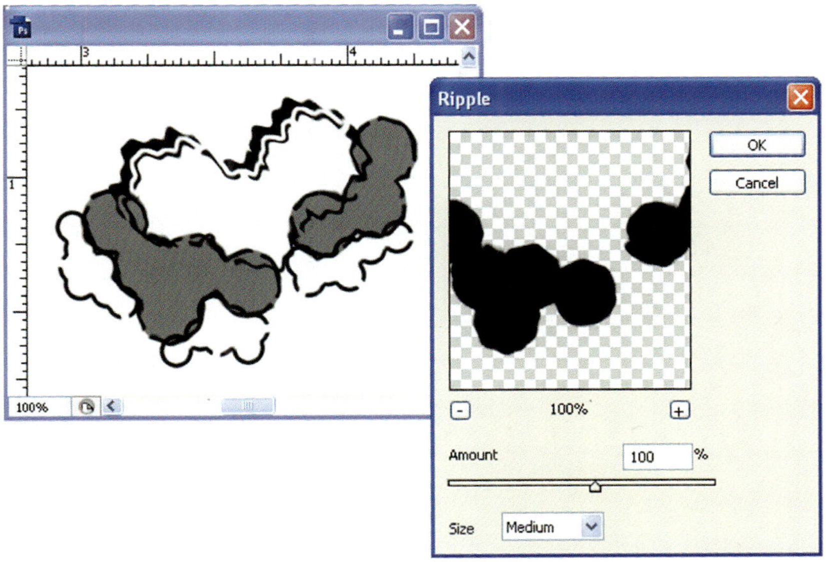

- Copy the layer you just distorted.
    - Click on the layer ***Brush 50*** to choose it.
    - Drag the selected layer to the "Create a new layer" icon.
    - With the Move Tool, shift the copied layer up and to the left.
    - Rename the copied layer ***Shadow 50***.
- Trim the shadow.
    - Click on the layer ***Brush 50*** to choose it.
    - **Select > All**
    - With the Move Tool, hit the [up arrow] on your keyboard, then hit the [down arrow].
    - **Select > Modify > Expand...**
        - `Expand By = 3 pixels`
    - Click the [OK] button.
    - Click on the layer ***Shadow 50*** to choose it.
    - Hit the [Delete] key to erase the shadow within your selection.

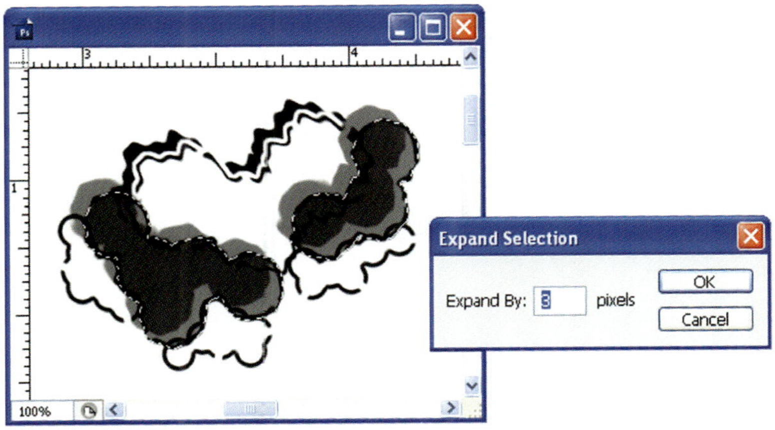

- Trim the shadow, again. Some of it is obscured by the largest shrubs.
    - Click on the layer ***Brush 75*** to choose it.
    - **Select > All**
    - With the Move Tool, hit the [up arrow] on your keyboard, then hit the [down arrow].
    - Click on the layer ***Shadow 50*** to choose it.
    - Hit the [Delete] key to erase the shadow within your selection.

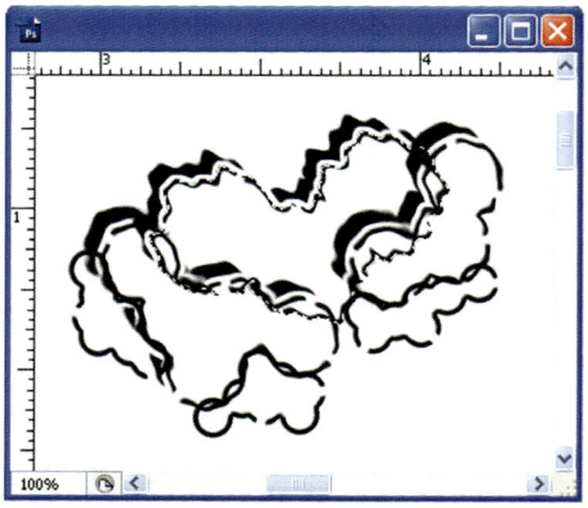

- Copy the layer with the basic form of the smallest shrubs.
    - Click on the layer ***Brush 25*** to choose it.
    - Drag the selected layer to the "Create a new layer" icon.
    - With the Move Tool, shift the copied layer up and to the left.
    - Rename the copied layer ***Shadow 25***.
- Trim the shadow.
    - Click on the layer ***Brush 25*** to choose it.
    - **Select > All**
    - With the Move Tool, hit the [up arrow] on your keyboard, then hit the [down arrow].
    - **Select > Modify > Expand...**
        - `Expand By = 3 pixels`
    - Click the [OK] button.
    - Click on the layer ***Shadow 25*** to choose it.
    - Hit the [Delete] key to erase the shadow within your selection.

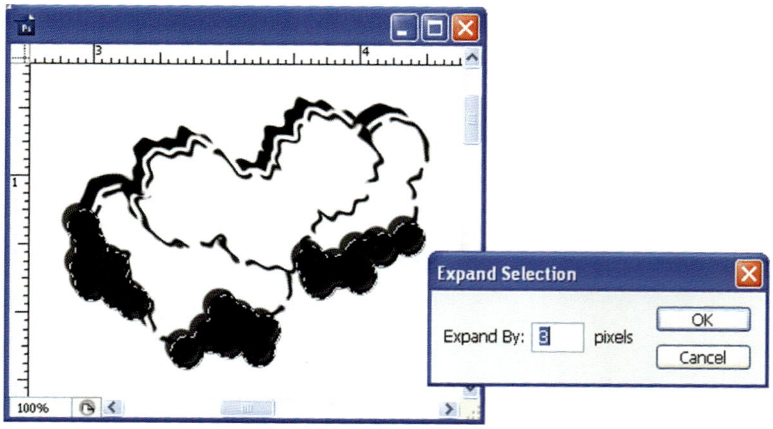

- Trim the shadow, again. Some of it is obscured by the medium shrubs.
  - Click on the layer ***Brush 50*** to choose it.
  - **Select > All**
  - With the Move Tool, hit the [up arrow] on your keyboard, then hit the [down arrow].
  - Click on the layer ***Shadow 25*** to choose it.
  - Hit the [Delete] key to erase the shadow within your selection.

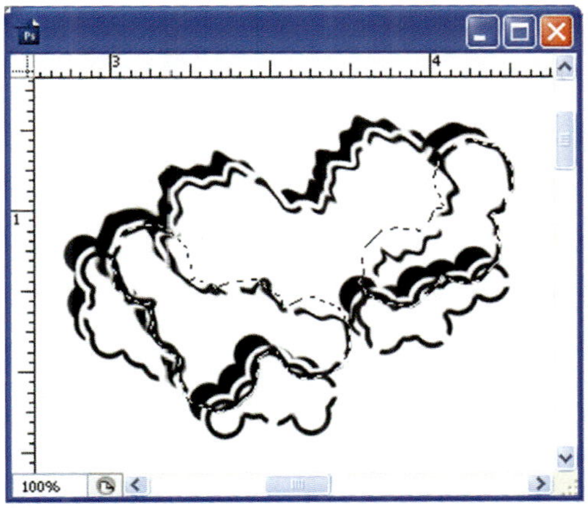

- Trim the shadow, again. Some of it is obscured by the largest shrubs.
  - Click on the layer ***Brush 75*** to choose it.
  - **Select > All**
  - With the Move Tool, hit the [up arrow] on your keyboard, then hit the [down arrow].
  - Click on the layer ***Shadow 25*** to choose it.
  - Hit the [Delete] key to erase the shadow within your selection.

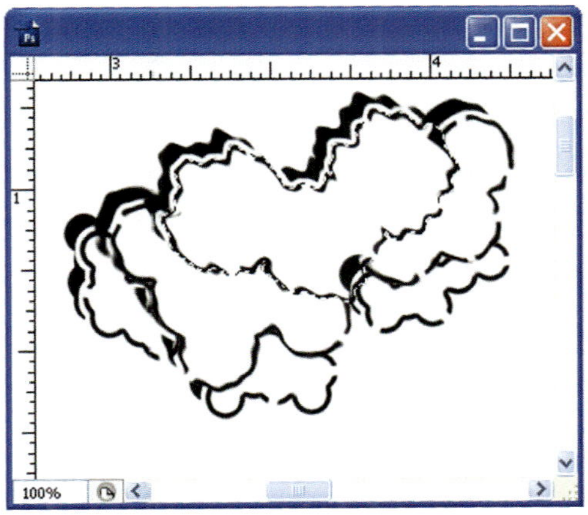

- Anchor the centers of the large shrubs.
  - Create a new layer and name it ***Centers***.
  - Choose a paintbrush for the Brush Tool and paint a dot in the center of each large shrub.
    - `Master Diameter = 5 px`
    - `Hardness = 100%`

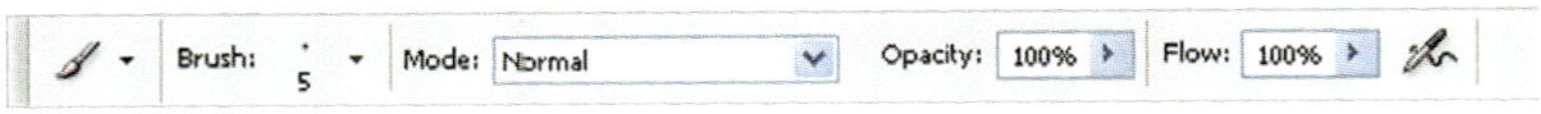

- Anchor the centers of the medium and small shrubs.
  - Choose a paintbrush for the Brush Tool and paint a dot in the center of each large shrub.
    - `Master Diameter = 3 px`
    - `Hardness = 100%`

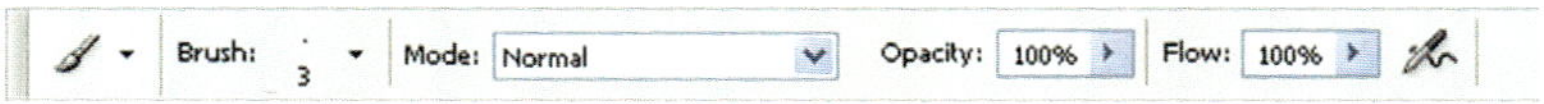

Step 4: Paint the foundation colors.

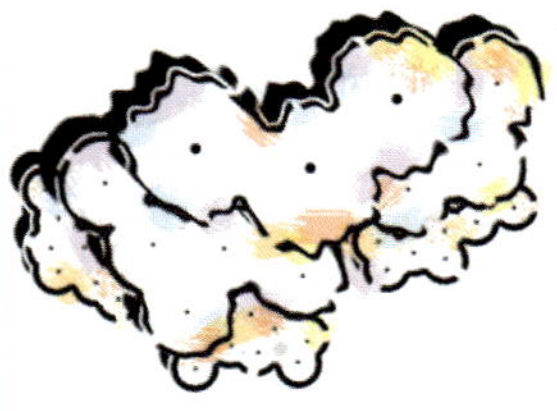

Step 4: Paint the foundation colors.

- Load a new set of paintbrushes.
  - With the Brush Tool, click on the [v] icon by the brush to open the Brush Preset picker.
  - From the Brush Preset Picker, click the [>] icon to open the Brush Preset pop-up and select "Natural Brushes."

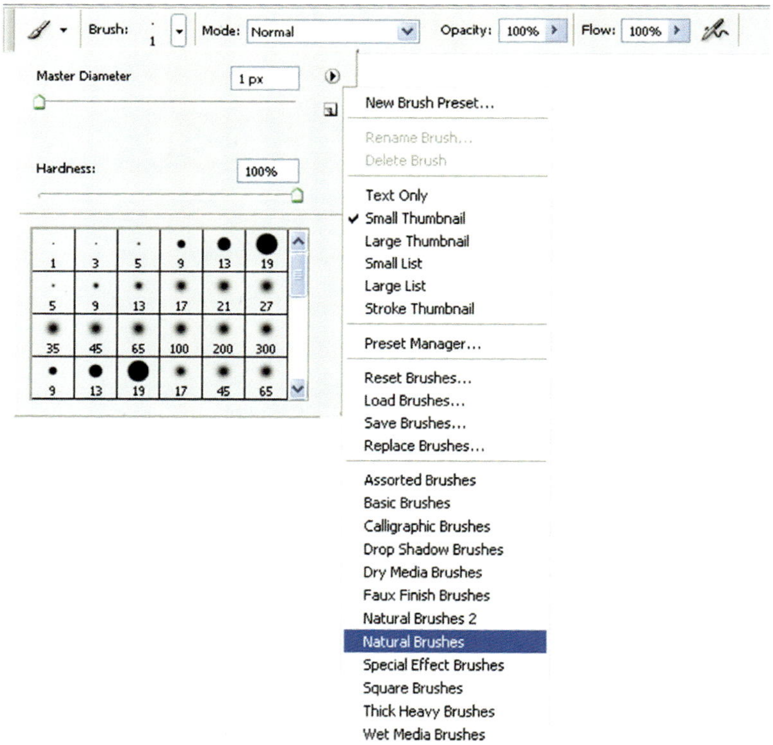

- Paint the shrubs.
  - Create a new layer and name it ***Nat B 19 50%***.
  - Change the foreground color to blue, red, purple, yellow, or orange.
  - Choose a paintbrush for the Brush Tool and paint.
    - `Master Diameter = 19 px`
      - If you are using a dark color, then paint where the sunlight is darkest.
      - If you are using a light color, then paint where the sunlight is brightest.
      - This is not the time to paint with greens (or whatever the dominant color your shrubs should be).
  - Repeat the above steps until your symbol has a good foundation of colorful brush strokes. Each color should be on its own layer.

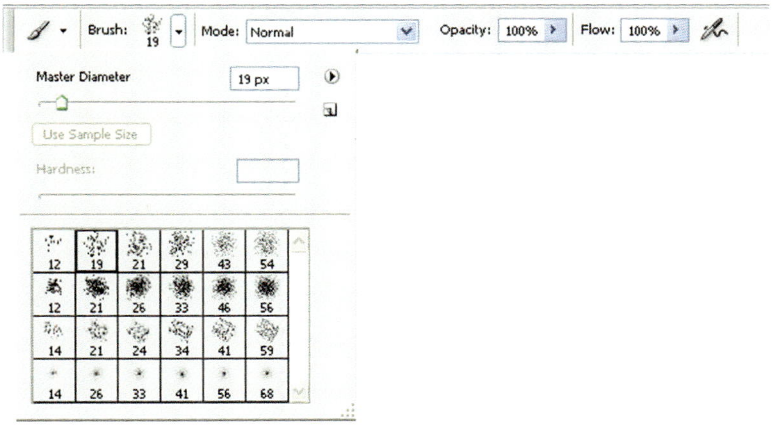

- Change the layer opacity for each of the layers you painted in the previous step.
  - Click on the layer ***Nat B 19 50%*** to choose it.
    - Change the layer `Opacity = 50%`.

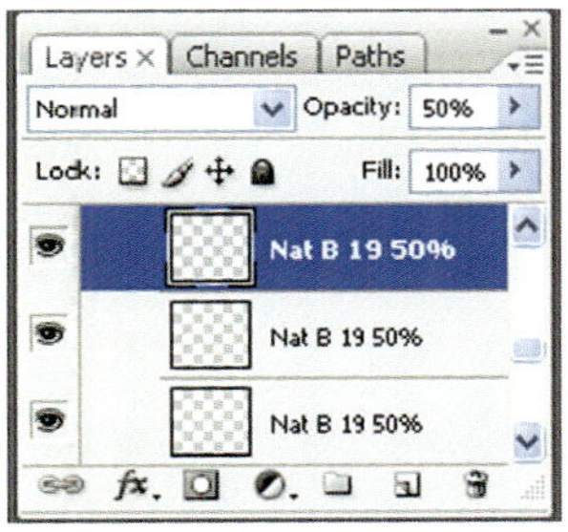

Step 5: Paint the dominant colors.

- Paint the dominant colors for the shrubs.
  - Create a new layer and name it ***Nat B 19 67%***.
  - Change the foreground color to a shade of green.
  - Choose a paintbrush for the Brush Tool and paint where it is darkest in the sunlight.
    - `Master Diameter = 19 px`
  - Repeat the above steps for each grouping of shrubs. Create a new layer for each color you use.
- Change the layer opacity for each of the layers you painted in the previous step.
  - Click on the layer ***Nat B 19 67%*** to choose it.
    - Change the layer `Opacity = 67%`.

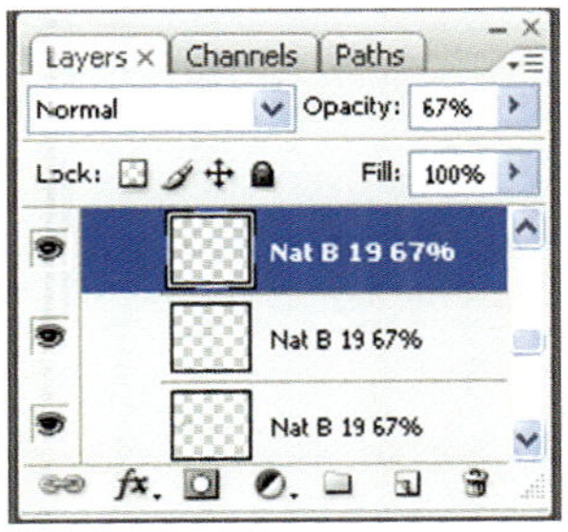

Step 5: Paint the dominant colors.

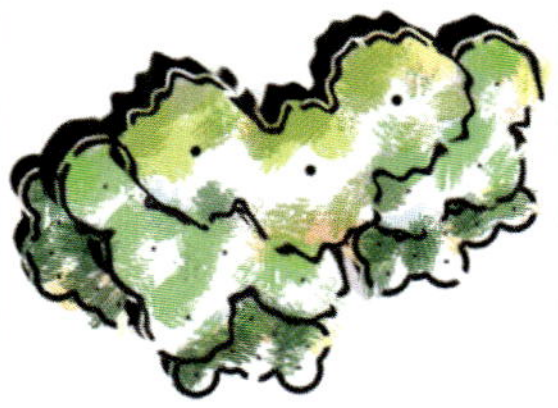

Figure 10-3. These are alternative renderings of the previous example.

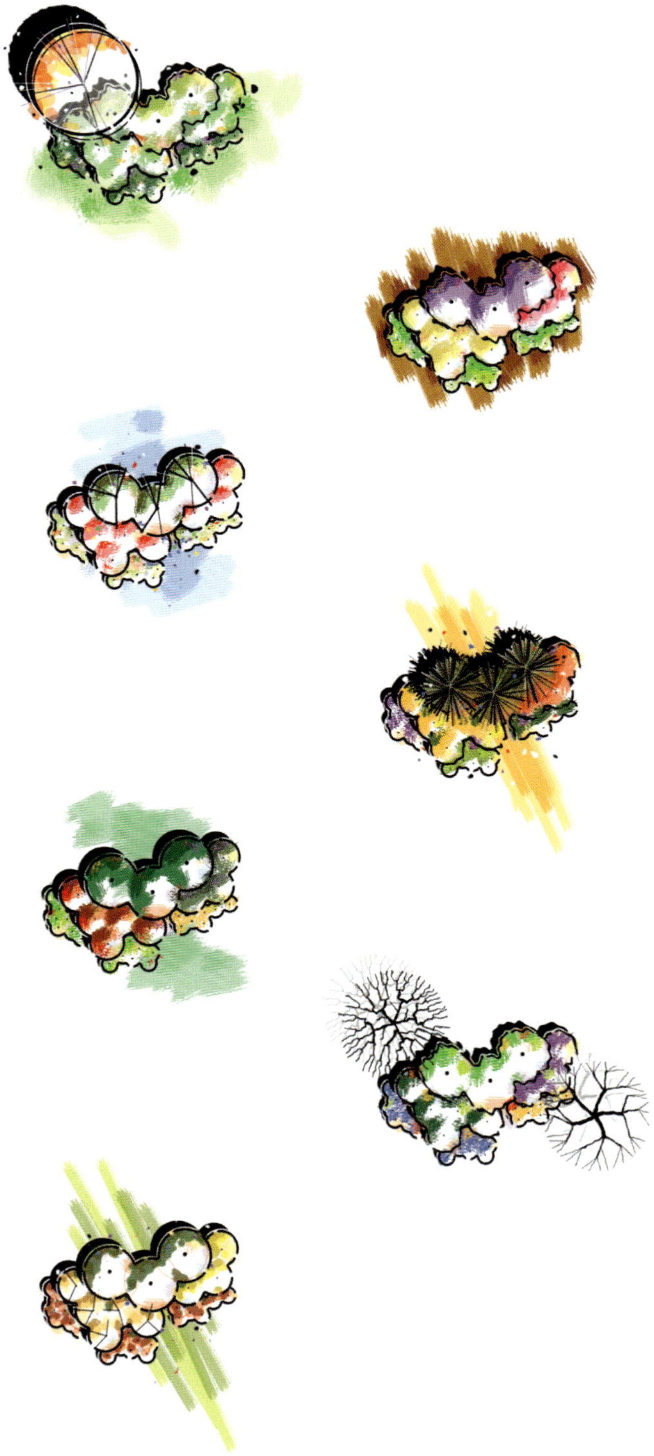

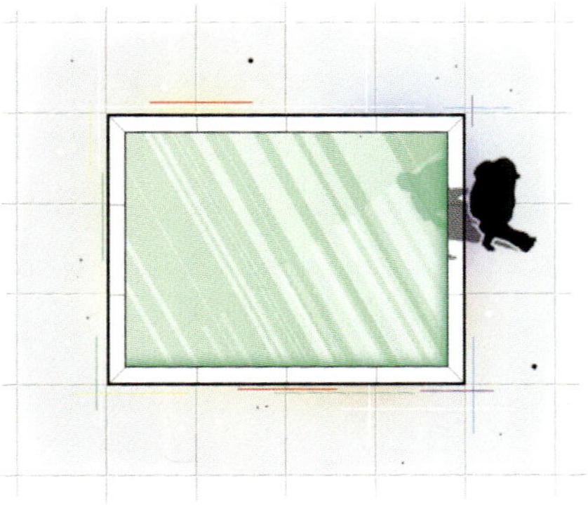

Master Plan Graphics | Reflecting Pool

In this exercise you will draw a simple, elegant reflecting pool. The intent is to create a water surface that mimics glass. The techniques used in this example include the following:

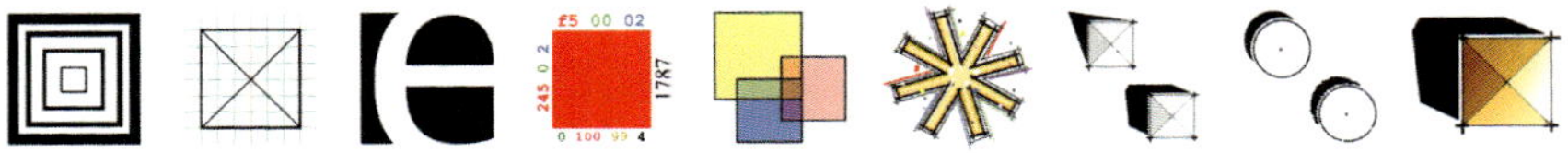

This drawing was originally drawn on a canvas with a resolution of 200 pixels per inch. Afterwards, it was scaled down to fit within these pages.

Step 1: Draw the basic form of the pool.

- Draw the basic shape of the pool.
  - Create a new layer and name it *Pool*.
  - Set the foreground color to black (`#000000`).
  - With the Rectangular Marquee Tool, select a triangle within the canvas.
  - **Edit > Fill**
  - Click the [OK] button.
- Reduce the opacity of your fill so that you can see your work in the next steps.
  - `Opacity = 25%`

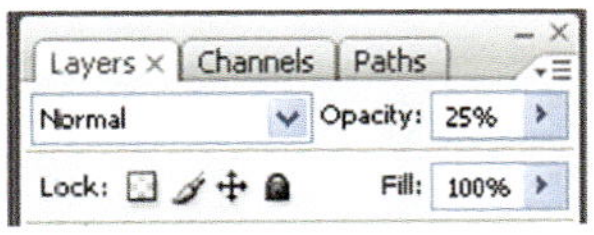

- Draw a thick outline around the pool.
  - Click on the layer *Pool* to choose it.
  - **Select > All**
  - With the Move Tool, hit the [up arrow] on your keyboard, then hit the [down arrow].
  - Create a new layer and name it *Outline*.
  - **Edit > Stroke**
    - `Width = 5 px`
    - `Location = Inside`
  - Click the [OK] button.

Step 1: Draw the basic form of the pool.

- Draw a thinner outline around the pool.
  - **Select > Modify > Contract...**
    - `Contract By = 20 pixels`
  - Click the [OK] button.
  - **Edit > Stroke...**
    - `Width = 2 px`
    - `Location = Inside`
  - Click the [OK] button.

Step 2: Paint the water.

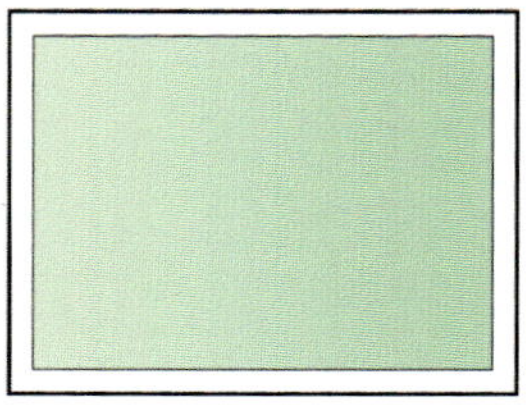

Step 2: Paint the water.

- Paint the water with a gradient.
  - Turn off the layer ***Pool*** by clicking on the [eye] icon on the layer tab so that it disappears and the layer is no longer visible.
  - Click on the layer ***Outline*** to choose it.
  - With the Magic Wand Tool, select the inside of the pool by clicking in the center.
    - `Tolerance = 1`
    - `Contiguous = checked`
  - Change the foreground color to cyan (`#91FFBA`).
  - Change the background color to white (`#FFFFFF`).
  - Create a new layer and name it ***Gradient Fill***.
    - `Foreground to Background`
    - `Linear Gradient`
    - `Mode = Normal`
  - Click the mouse button (and hold it down) near the right side of the selection, drag the cursor to the left side of the selection, and then release the mouse button.

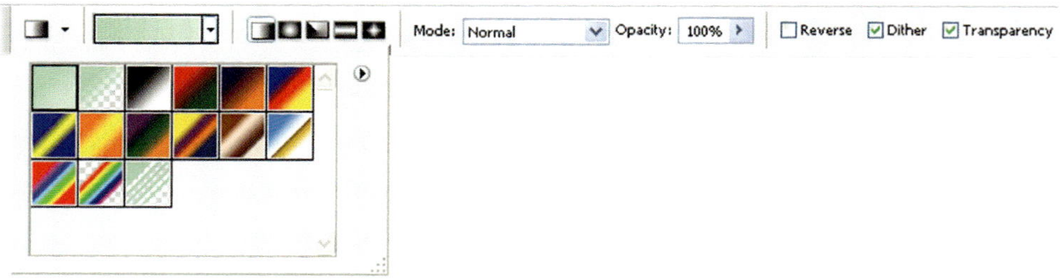

Step 3: Draw reflections on the water surface.

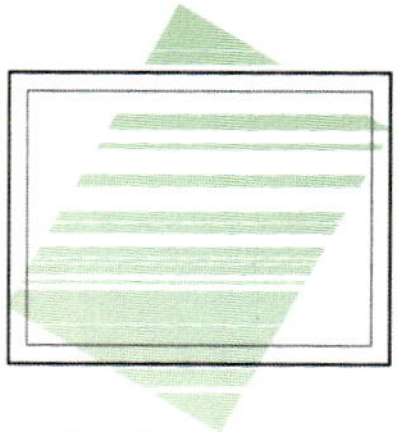

Step 3: Draw reflections on the water surface.

- Choose the surface of the water and rotate it.
  - Click on the layer ***Gradient Fill*** to choose it.
  - **Edit > Transform > Rotate**
    - `Angle = -60 degrees`
  - Hit the [Enter] key to commit the rotation.

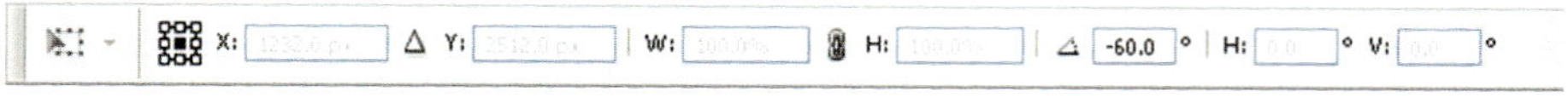

- Draw linear reflections on the water surface by painting on the gradient fill.
  - **Select > All**
  - With the Move Tool, hit the [up arrow] on your keyboard, then hit the [down arrow].
  - Create a new layer and name it ***Stripes***.
  - Change the foreground color to white (`#FFFFFF`).
  - Choose sharp paintbrushes of various sizes with the Brush Tool and paint stripes within the selection.
    - `Master Diameter = varies`
    - `Hardness = 100%`

Step 4: Refine the reflections.

Step 4: Refine the reflections.

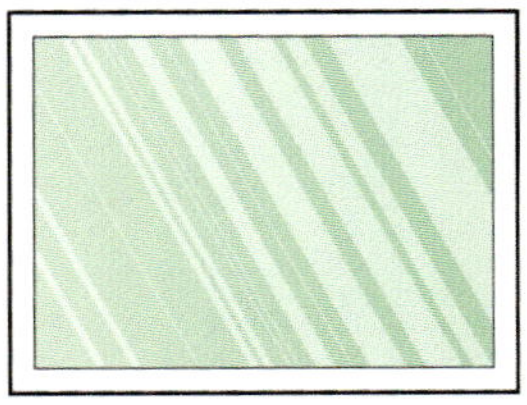

- Make the stripes fainter.
  - Click on the layer ***Gradient Fill*** to choose it.
  - Reduce the layer `Opacity = 50%`.

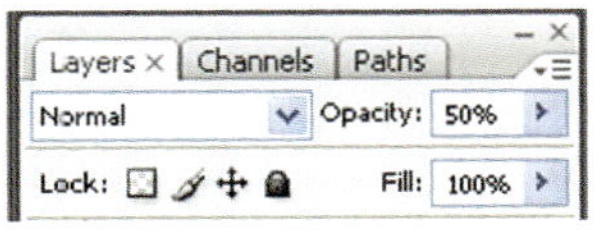

- Rotate the reflections and gradient fill back.
  - Click on the layer ***Gradient Fill*** to choose it.
  - **Edit > Transform > Rotate**
    - `Angle = 60 degrees`
  - Hit the [Enter] key to commit the rotation.
  - Repeat the above steps for the layer Stripes.

Step 5: Add more reflections.

Step 5: Add more reflections.

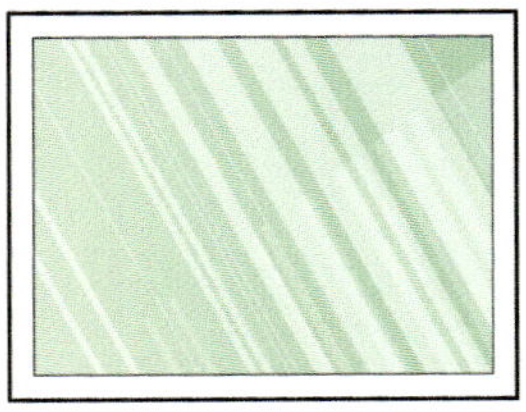

- Add more reflections by copying the original ones and trimming to fit.
  - Click on the layer ***Stripes*** to choose it.
  - Drag the layer to the "Create a new layer" icon.
  - Click on the layer ***Stripes copy*** to choose it.
  - **Edit > Transform > Rotate**
    - `Angle = 90 degrees`
  - Click the [OK] button.
  - With the Move Tool, shift the rotated stripes to your preference.
  - Click on the layer ***Gradient Fill*** to choose it.
  - With the Move Tool, hit the [up arrow] on your keyboard, then hit the [down arrow].
  - **Select > Inverse**
  - Click on the layer ***Stripes copy*** to choose it.
  - Hit the [Delete] key to erase the stripes that are outside the pool.

Step 6: Add accents and details.

Step 6: Add accents and details.

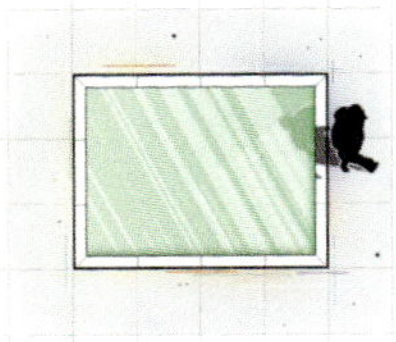

- Add accents and details to the drawing.
  - Create a new layer and name it Accents.
  - Using various brush sizes and colors, add accents and details to the drawing.
  - Consider pasting people and site amenities like chairs to give the drawing scale.

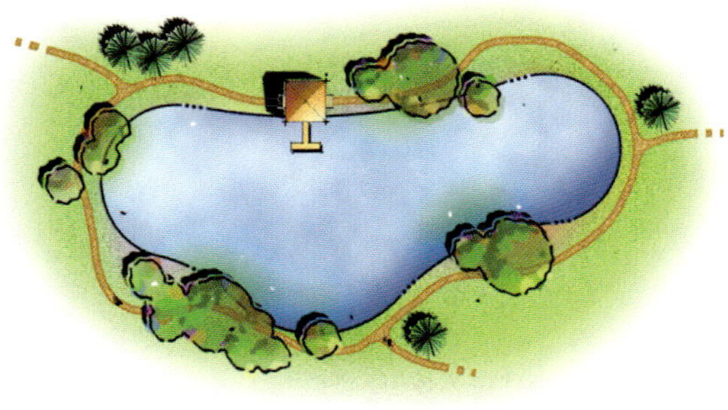

Master Plan Graphics | Lagoons, Lakes, and Ponds

In this exercise you will draw a simple lagoon, lake, or pond. The intent is to create a water surface that mimics glass. The techniques used in this example include the following:

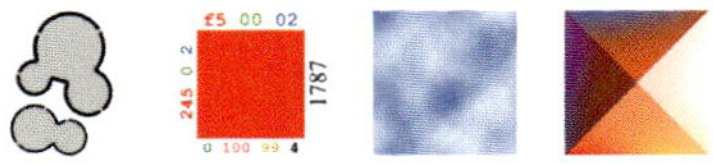

Best Stroke | Color Palette | Cloud Color | Soft Glow

This drawing was originally drawn on a canvas with a resolution of 200 pixels per inch. Afterwards, it was scaled down to fit within these pages.

Step 1: Draw the basic form of the lagoon.

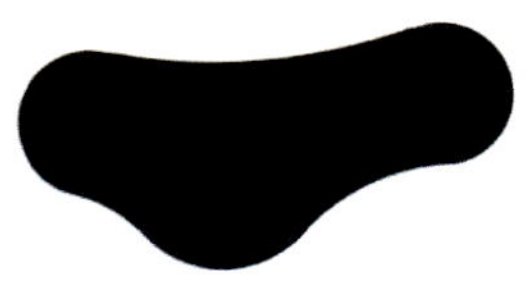

Step 1: Draw the basic form of the lagoon.

Water is often the most important component in a drawing. Draw it well, and it can make your drawing standout whether you add more detail or not. Draw it poorly, and it will not matter how good the rest of your drawing is.

Fortunately, drawing attractive lagoons, lakes, or ponds is neither difficult nor time-consuming. It is so easy, in fact, that many times after I have demonstrated how to do it, previously impressed people were thoroughly disappointed afterwards. They were absolutely certain that it required more effort.

- Draw the basic form of the lagoon.
    - Create a new layer and name it ***Lagoon Form***.
    - Select a sharp paintbrush for the Brush Tool and draw the basic form of the lagoon.
        - `Hardness = 100%`
    - To make sharper, cleaner lagoon edges, use the Eraser Tool to refine your form.

Step 2: Draw an outline around the lagoon.

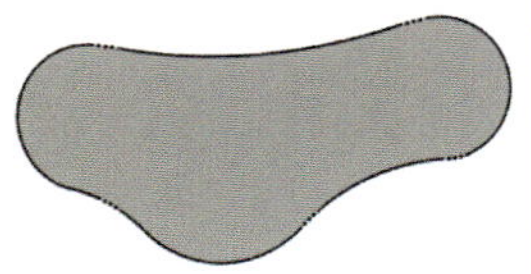

Step 2: Draw an outline around the lagoon.

- Change the layer opacity so that you can see your work going forward.
    - Click on the layer ***Lagoon Form*** to choose it.
        - Change the layer `Opacity = 25%`.

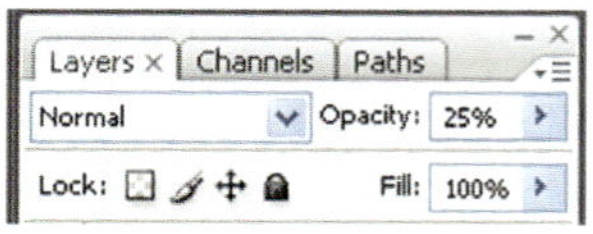

- Draw an outline around the lagoon.
    - Click on the layer ***Lagoon Form*** to choose it.
    - **Select > All**
    - With the Move Tool, hit the [up arrow] on your keyboard, then hit the [down arrow].
    - Create a new layer and name it ***Outline***.
    - **Edit > Stroke**
        - `Width = 3 px`
        - `Location = Inside`
    - Click the [OK] button.

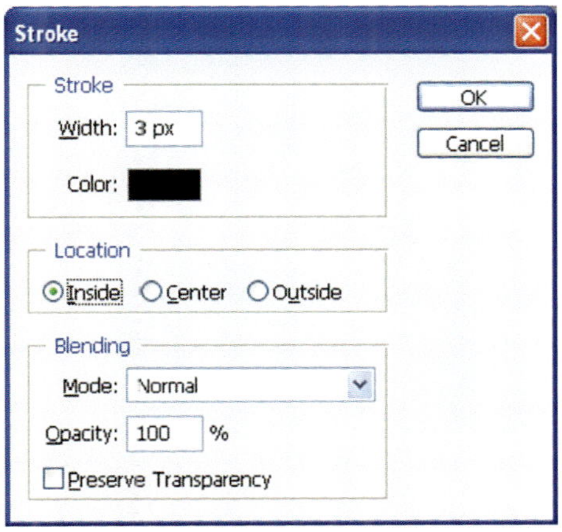

- Erase from the outline.
    - Click on the layer ***Outline*** to choose it.
    - Choose a brush for the Eraser Tool and erase gaps from the outline.
- Draw dots within these gaps.
    - Select a paintbrush for the Brush Tool and add three dots to your outline where you erased.
        - `Master Diameter = 5 px`
        - `Hardness = 100%`
            - Lagoons can be denoted by long dashed lines interrupted by three dots.

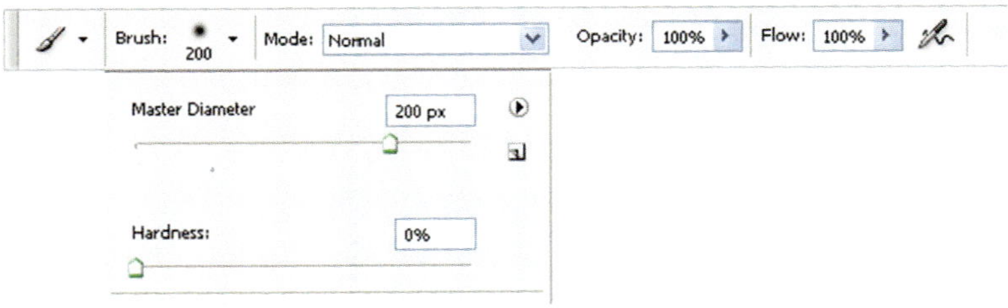

Step 3: Paint the water.

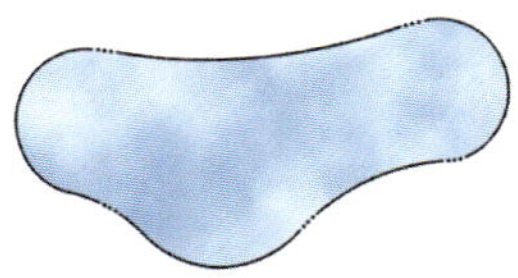

Step 3: Paint the water.

- Choose the colors and select the area to paint.
    - Change the foreground color to light blue (`#96CCFF`).
    - Change the background color to white (`#FFFFFF`).
    - Click on the layer ***Lagoon Form*** to choose it.
    - **Select > All**
    - With the Move Tool, hit the [up arrow] on your keyboard, then hit the [down arrow].
    - Create a new layer and name it ***Lagoon Color***.

- Paint the lagoon.
  - **Filter > Render > Clouds**
    - Be certain that the layer ***Lagoon Outline*** is above the layer ***Lagoon Color***. Otherwise, you won't be able to see the outline around the lagoon.

Step 4: Shade the lagoon edge.

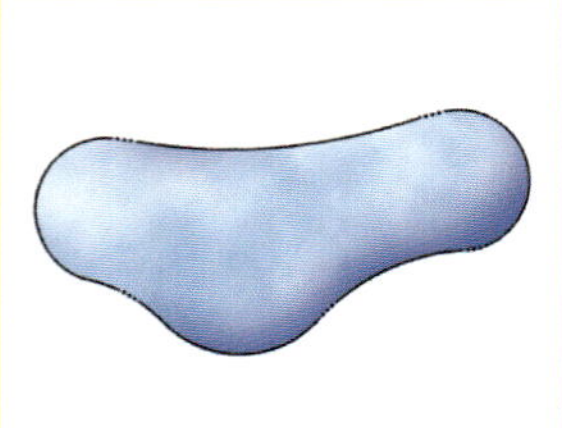

Step 4: Shade the lagoon edge.

- Shade the edge of the lagoon.
  - Change the foreground color to a darker shade of blue (`#5C96FF`).
  - Click on the layer ***Lagoon Color*** to choose it.
  - **Select > All**
  - With the Move Tool, hit the [up arrow] on your keyboard, then hit the [down arrow].
  - Choose a paintbrush for the Brush Tool and paint along the edge of the lagoon. Consider the orientation of the sun when choosing where the lagoon will be darkest.
    - `Master Diameter = 200 px`
    - `Hardness = 0%`

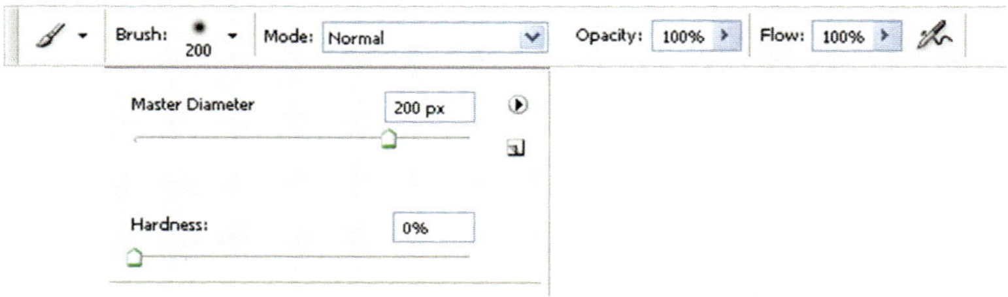

Step 5: Add more detail.

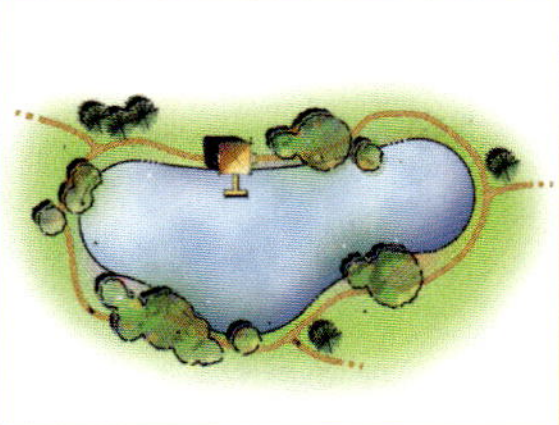

Step 5: Add more detail.

By adding paths, trees, and buildings to your drawing, the scale of the lagoon is more obvious. Notice that the trees at the top of the lagoon reflect off the water somewhat, and that a green glow has been added where the vegetation meets the lagoon edge. Subtle accents like these can add life to your drawings.

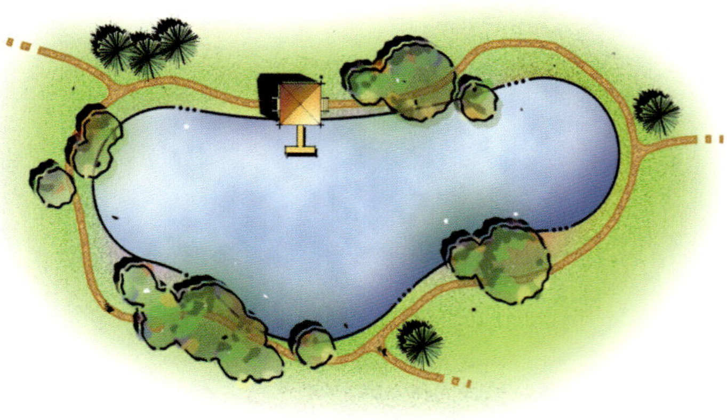

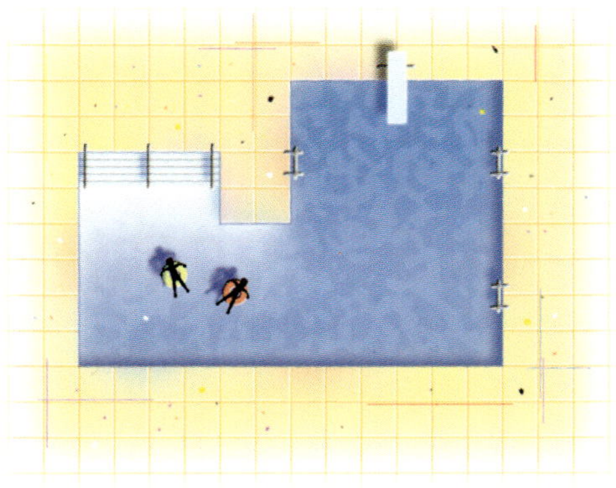

Master Plan Graphics | Swimming Pool

In this exercise you will draw a swimming pool. The techniques used in this example include the following:

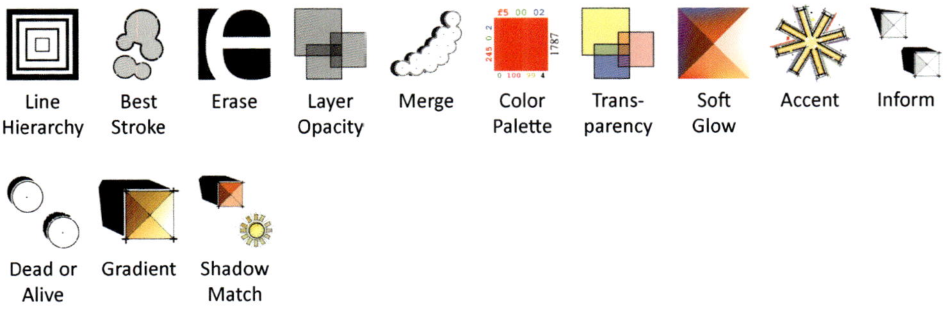

This drawing was originally drawn on a canvas with a resolution of 200 pixels per inch. Afterwards, it was scaled down to fit within these pages.

Step 1: Begin with a black line drawing.

- Begin by drawing a simple, black line drawing of the pool.
  - Choose a paintbrush for the Brush Tool.
    - `Master Diameter = 5 px`
    - `Hardness = 100%`

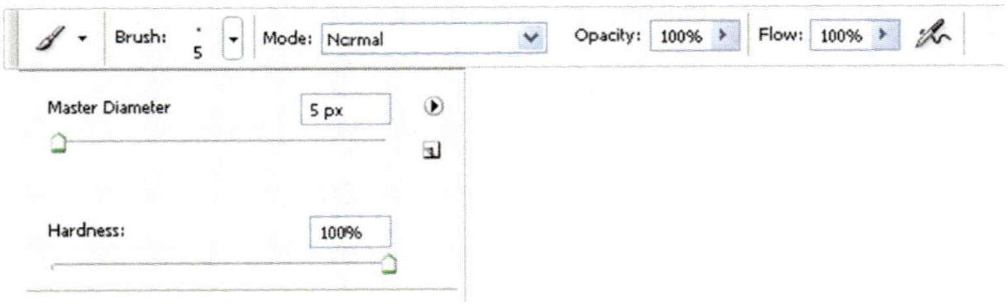

- Create layers for each of the elements you are about to draw.
  - Create a new layer and name it *Pool*.
  - Create a new layer and name it *Diving Board*.
  - Create a new layer and name it *Rails*.
  - Create a new layer and name it *Steps*.
  - Create a new layer and name it *Pool Outline*.

Step 1: Begin with a black line drawing.

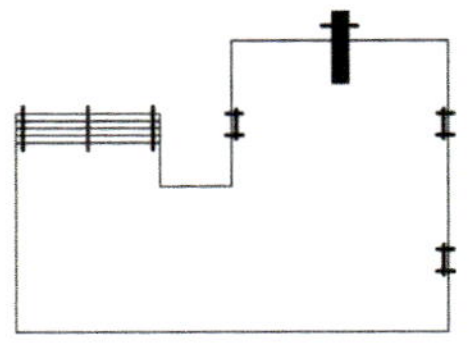

- Create some guidelines to facilitate drawing the swimming pool.
  - **View > New Guide...**
    - `Orientation = Vertical`
    - `Position = 0.25 inches`
  - Click the [OK] button.
  - Repeat the above steps to create the following guides:
    - `Vertical: 1.0, 1.375, and 2.5 inches`
    - `Horizontal: 0.25, 1.0, and 1.75 inches`
- Draw the swimming pool.
  - Using the guides, draw the elements of the pool within the appropriate layers.
  - Draw straight lines by holding down the [Shift] key between mouse clicks.

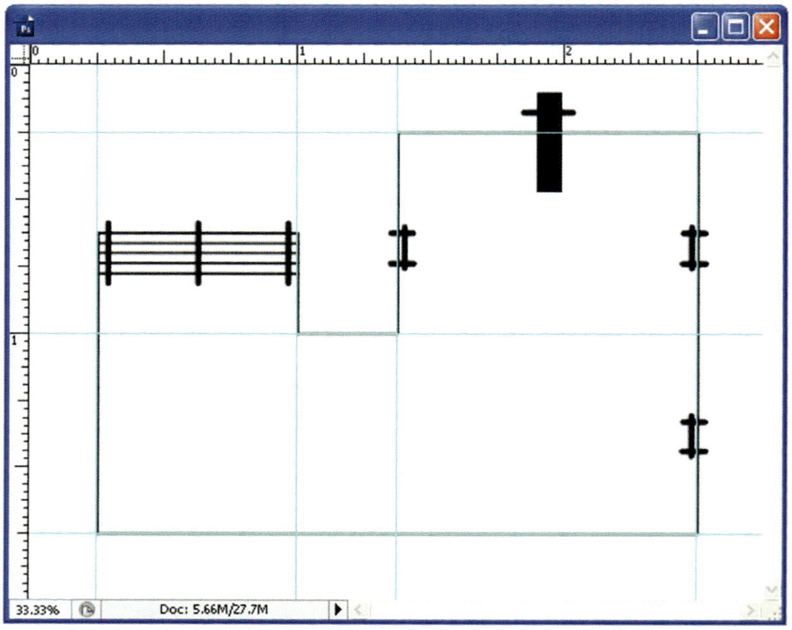

Step 2: Paint the water in the deep end of the pool.

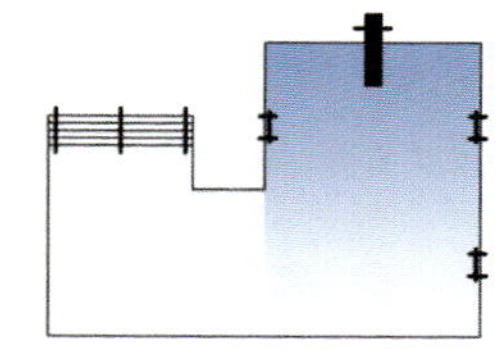

Step 2: Paint the water in the deep end of the pool.

- Paint the water in the deep end of the swimming pool.
  - Change the foreground color to blue (`#5C96FF`).
  - With the Rectangular Marquee Tool, use the guides to select the deep end of the pool.
  - Create a new layer and name it ***Gradient Fill***.
  - With the Gradient Tool, paint the selected area.
    - `Foreground to Transparent`
    - `Linear Gradient`
    - `Mode = Normal`
      - Click the left mouse button (and hold it down) near the top of the selection, drag the cursor to the bottom of the selection, and then release the mouse button.

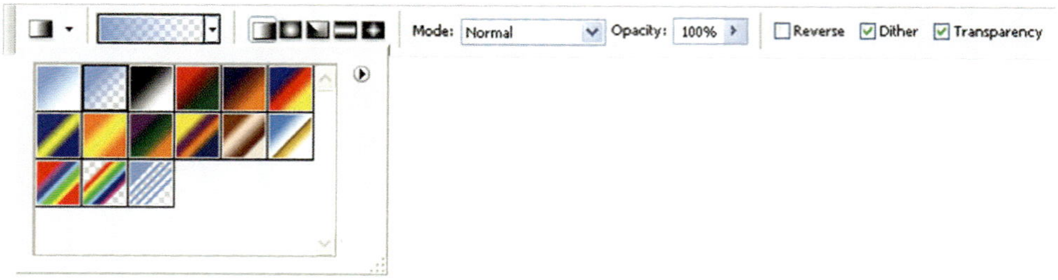

Step 3: Paint the shallow water.

- Paint the water in the shallow end of the swimming pool.
  - Turn off the layer ***Gradient Fill*** by clicking on the [eye] icon on the layer tab so that it disappears and the layer is no longer visible.
  - With the Rectangular Marquee Tool, use the guidelines to select the shallow end of the pool.
  - Create a new layer and name it ***Gradient Fill Shallow***.
  - With the Gradient Tool, paint the selected area as you did before.

Step 3: Paint the shallow water.

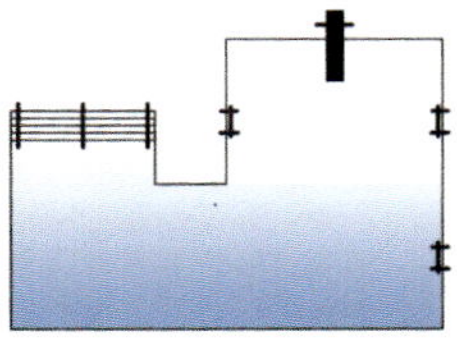

Step 4: Merge the gradient layers.

- Consolidate the two water gradients into one layer.
  - Turn on the layer ***Gradient Fill*** by clicking on the empty space for the [eye] icon so that it reappears and the layer is visible.
  - Click on the layer ***Gradient Fill*** to choose it.
  - While holding down the [Ctrl] key, click on the layer ***Gradient Fill Shallow*** to choose it, too.
  - Right-click either layer and select "Merge Layers..." from the pop-up dialog box.
  - Rename this layer ***Merged Gradients***.

Step 4: Merge the gradient layers.

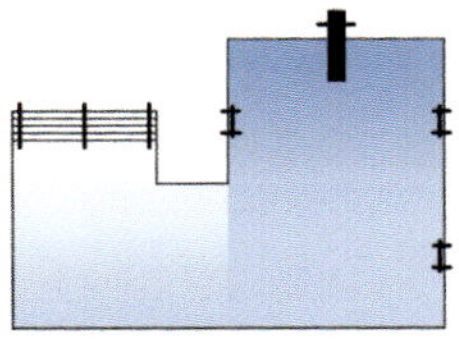

Step 5: Refine the water color gradients.

- Refine the water color by blending where the two gradients meet.
  - Click on the layer ***Merged Gradients*** to choose it.
  - Choose a soft brush for the Smudge Tool and blend the gradients together by clicking where the gradients meet, holding down the mouse button, and dragging the cursor back and forth over the area.
    - `Master Diameter = 13 px`
    - `Hardness = 0%`
    - `Strength = 50%`

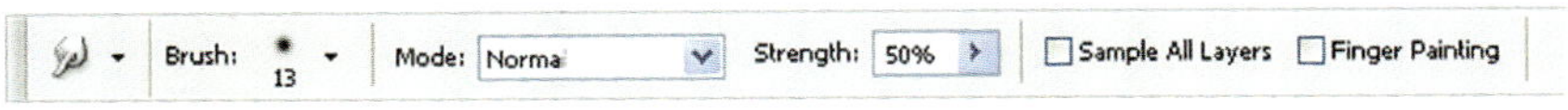

- Soften the edges of the pool.
  - With the Rectangular Marquee Tool, use the guides to select the area within the pool.
  - **Filter > Blur > Gaussian Blur...**
    - `Radius = 10 px`
  - Click the [OK] button.

Step 5: Refine the water color gradients.

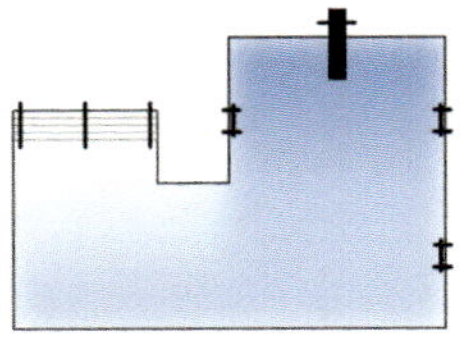

Step 6: Add shadows.

- Add a shadow to the pool edge.
  - With the Rectangular Marquee Tool, use the guides to select the area within the pool.
  - Change the foreground color to dark blue (`#1A6EFF`).
  - Create a new layer and name it ***Pool Shadow***.
  - Choose a soft paintbrush for the Brush Tool and paint along the pool edge.
  - `Master Diameter = 19 px, Hardness = 0%`

Step 6: Add Shadows.

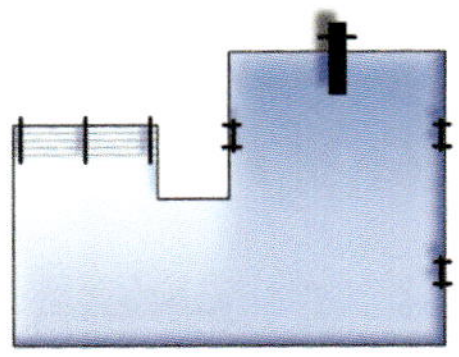

- Add shadows to the diving board, steps, and rails.
  - Choose a small, soft paintbrush for the Brush Tool and draw shadows for the diving board, steps, and rails.
    - `Master Diameter = 9 px`
    - `Hardness = 0%`

Step 7: Add a water texture.

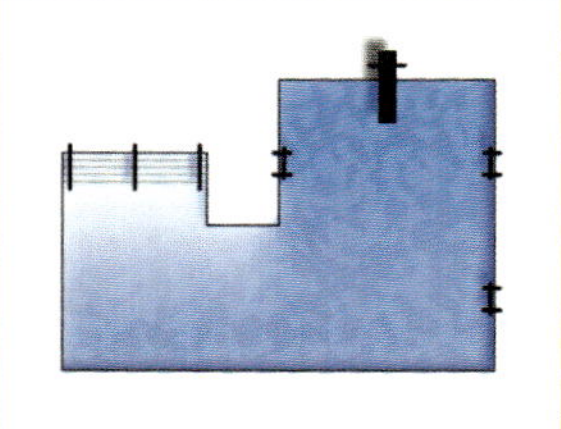

Step 7: Add a water texture.

- Add a water texture using a filter.
  - Click on the layer ***Merged Gradient*** to choose it.
  - **Filter > Distort > Ocean Ripple...**
    - `Ripple Size = 9`
    - `Ripple Magnitude = 9`
  - Click the [OK] button.

Step 8: Add accents and details.

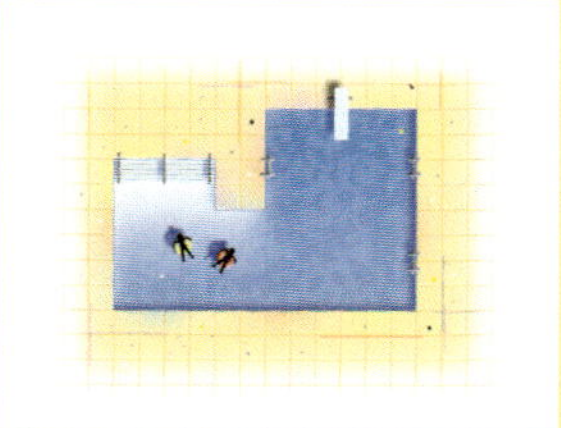

Step 8: Add accents and details.

- Give the diving board a three-dimensional appearance.
  - Click on the layer ***Diving Board*** to choose it.
  - Right-click the layer tab and select "Blending Options..."
  - In the Layer Style dialog box that appears, check the "Outer Glow" checkbox.
    - `Opacity = 75%`
    - `Noise = 0%`
    - `Spread = 0%`
    - `Size = 12 px`

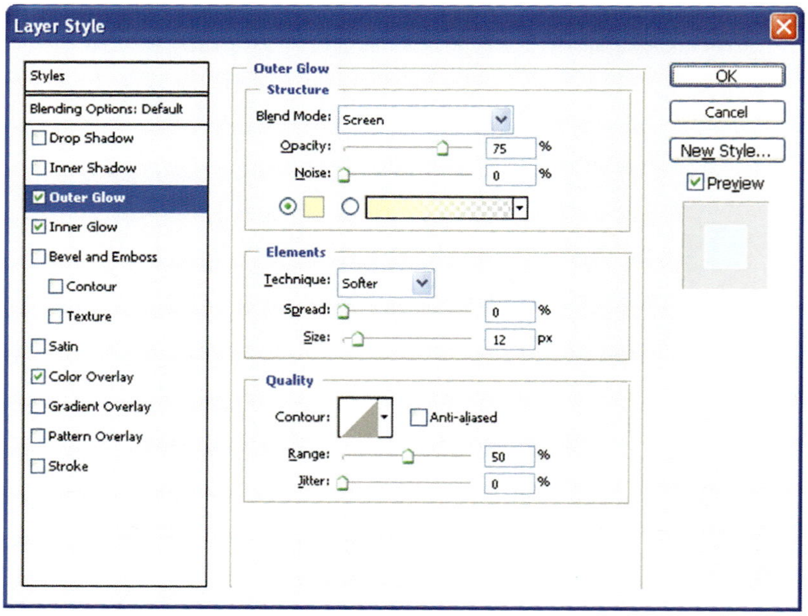

  - While the Layer Style dialog box is still open, check the "Inner Glow" checkbox.
    - `Opacity = 75%`
    - `Noise = 0%`
    - `Spread = 0%`
    - `Size = 12 px`

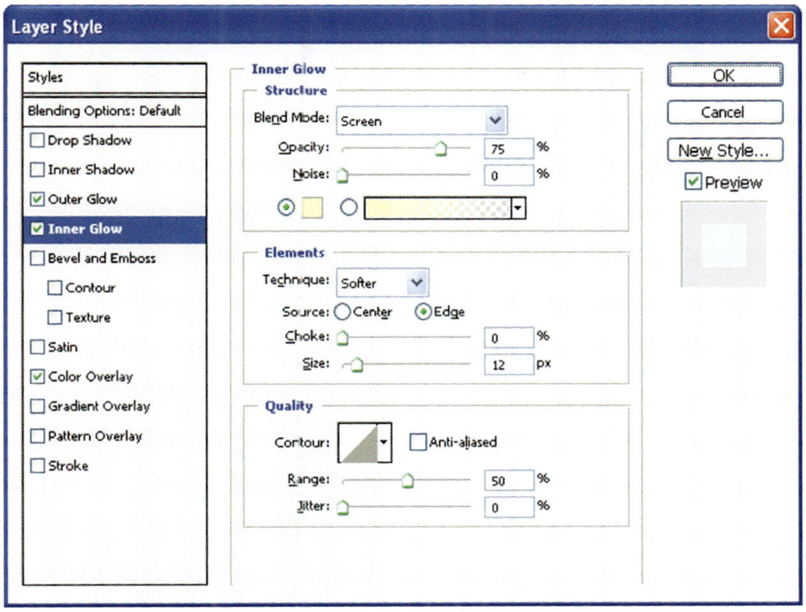

- While the Layer Style dialog box is still open, check the "Color Overlay" checkbox.
  - Change the default color from red to light blue.
    - Click on the red box to the right of the Blend Mode drop-down list.
    - Change the color to light blue (`#DBF5FF`).
    - Click the [OK] button.
  - Click the [OK] button to submit the changes to the outer glow, inner glow, and color overlay.

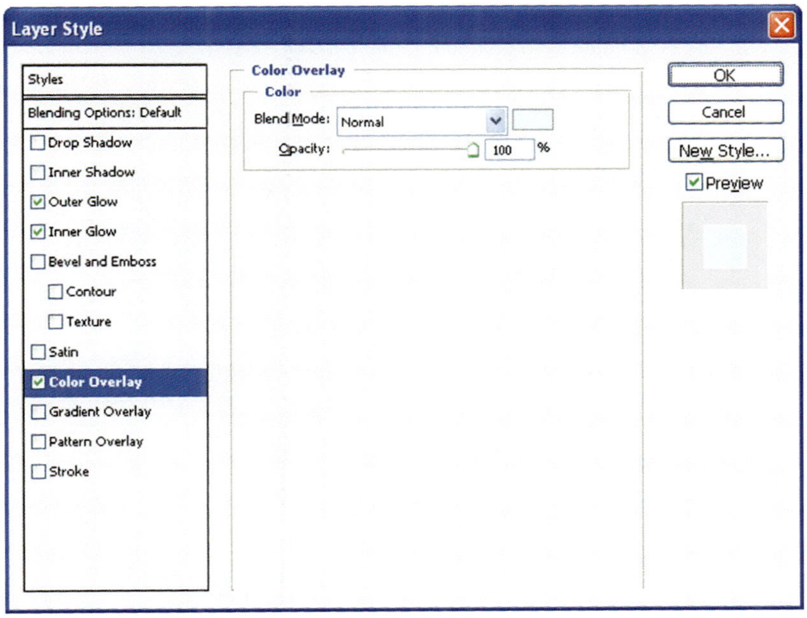

- Give the rails and steps a three-dimensional appearance.
  - Repeat the above steps for the rails and steps.
  - Use the same color blue for the steps; but, use gray (`#BDBDBD`) for the rails.

- Add accents to the drawing.
  - Create a new layer and name it ***Accents***.
  - Using various brush sizes and colors, add accents and details to the drawing.
  - Adding people to your drawing will help give your drawing scale.
    - My preference is to draw people abstractly. Since this drawing is intended to illustrate a pool design, you do not want the people to be the focus of your drawing.

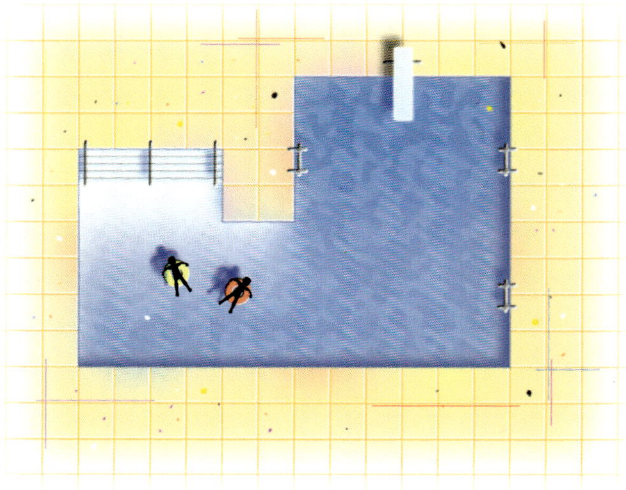

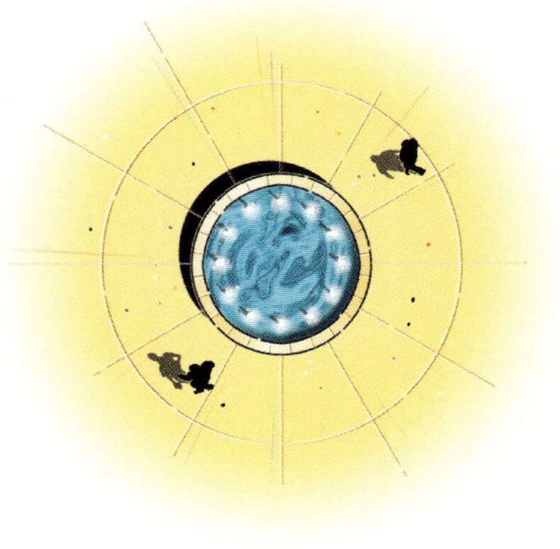

Master Plan Graphics | Fountain

In this exercise you will draw a fountain. The techniques used in this example include the following:

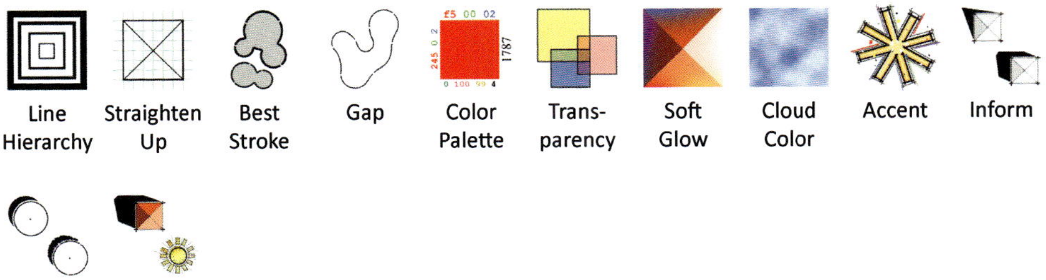

This drawing was originally drawn on a canvas with a resolution of 200 pixels per inch. Afterwards, it was scaled down to fit within these pages.

Step 1: Draw the simple circle.

- Draw the basic form of the fountain, a simple circle.
  - Create a new layer and name it ***Brush 300***.
  - Choose a paintbrush for the Brush Tool and draw a circle by simply touching the brush to the canvas.
    - `Master Diameter = 300 px`
    - `Hardness = 100%`
      - Because the diameter is 300 pixels and the resolution is 200 pixels per inch (ppi), the diameter will be 1.5 inches.

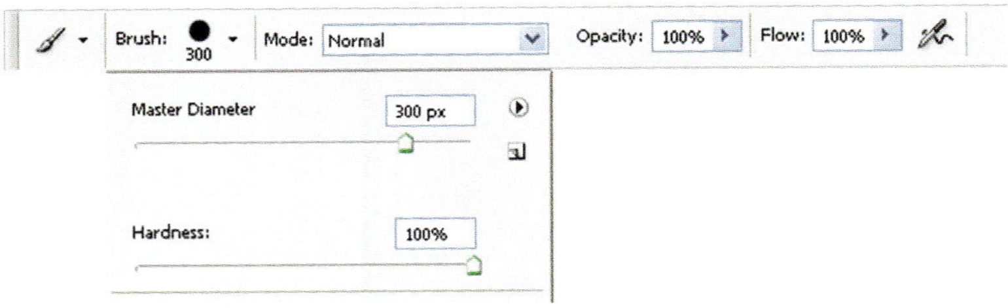

- Change the layer opacity so that you can see your work going forward.
  - Click on the layer ***Brush 300*** to choose it.
    - Change the layer `Opacity = 50%`.

Step 1: Draw a simple circle.

Step 2: Draw a thick outline.

Step 2: Draw a thick outline.

In this step you will draw an outline around the circle. Later you will use this outline to draw a de facto seating bench along the edge of the fountain.

- Draw an outline around the circle.
  - Click on the layer ***Brush 300*** to choose it.
  - **Select > All**
  - With the Move Tool, hit the [up arrow] on your keyboard, then hit the [down arrow].
  - Create a new layer and name it ***Bench***.
  - **Edit > Stroke**
    - `Width = 20 px`
    - `Location = Inside`
  - Click the [OK] button.

Step 3: Create a cloud texture.

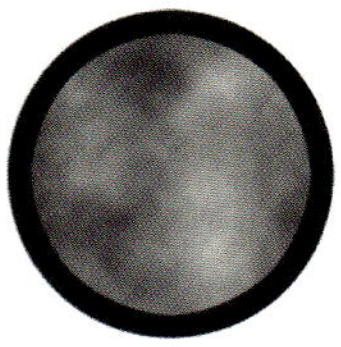

Step 3: Create a cloud texture.

- Create a cloud texture on the water surface.
  - Change back the layer `Opacity = 100%`.
  - Ensure that the foreground and background colors are the default values of black (`#000000`) and white (`#FFFFFF`).
  - Click on the layer ***Brush 300*** to choose it.
  - **Select > All**
  - With the Move Tool, hit the [up arrow] on your keyboard, then the [down arrow].
  - **Filter > Render > Clouds**

Step 4: Soften the water texture.

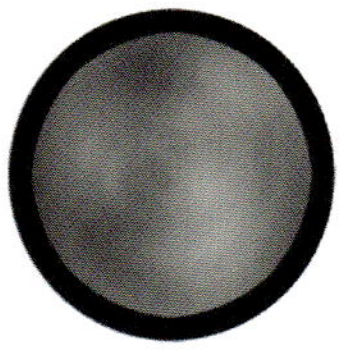

Step 4: Soften the water texture.

- Soften the water (cloud) texture by using a blur filter.
  - **Filter > Blur > Radial Blur...**
    - `Amount = 50`
    - `Blur Method = Spin`
    - `Quality = Good (or Best)`
  - Click the [OK] button.

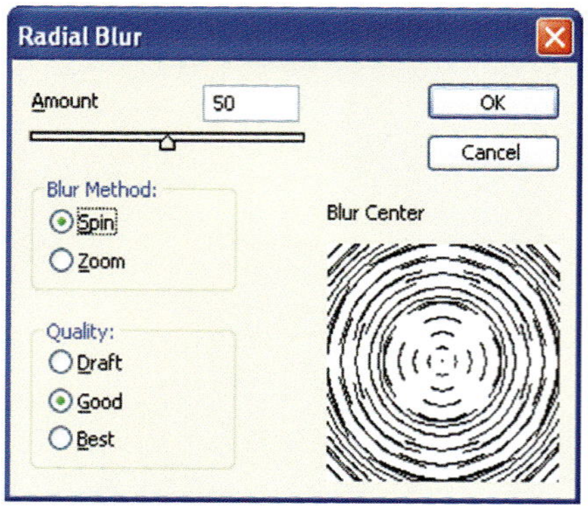

Step 5: Refine the water texture.

- Refine the water texture by applying a filter.
  - **Filter > Sketch > Bas Relief...**
    - `Detail = 10`
    - `Smoothness = 5`
    - `Light = Bottom Right`
  - Click the [OK] button.

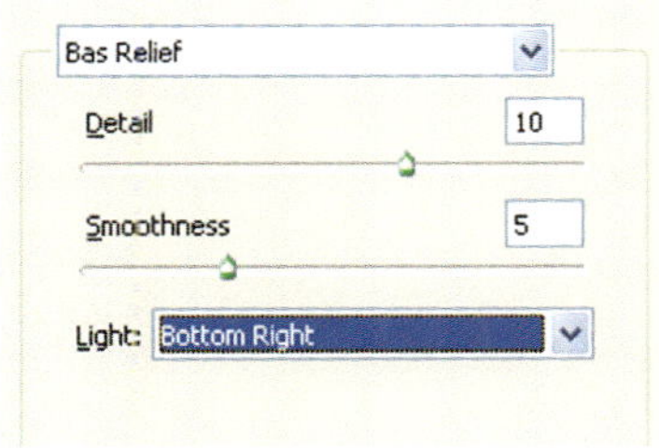

Step 5: Refine the water texture.

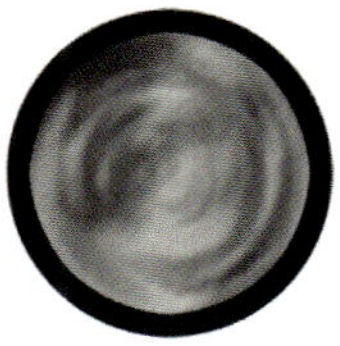

Step 6: Filter the water texture.

- Filter the water texture to give it a shiny, wet appearance.
  - **Filter > Sketch > Chrome...**
    - `Detail = 4`
    - `Smoothness = 7`
  - Click the [OK] button.

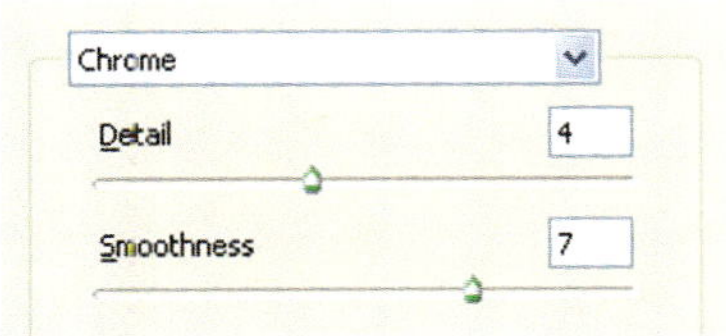

Step 6: Filter the water texture.

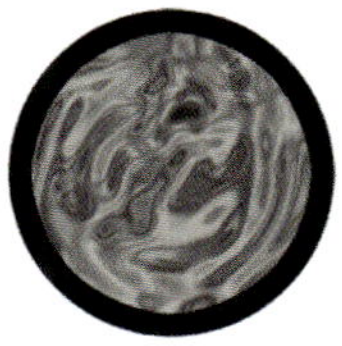

Step 7: Add color to the water.

- Add color to the water by adjusting the color channels of the image.
  - **Image > Adjustments > Channel Mixer...**
    - Adjust the red channel settings (`Output Channel = Red`).
      - `Red = 100%`
      - `Green = 0%`
      - `Blue = -100%`
      - `Constant = 0%`

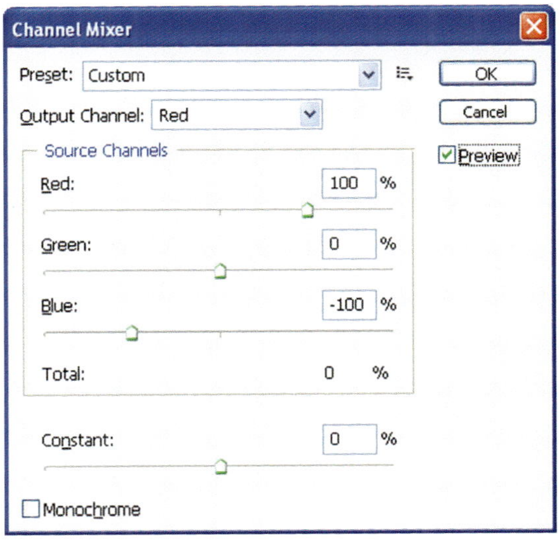

Step 7: Add color to the water.

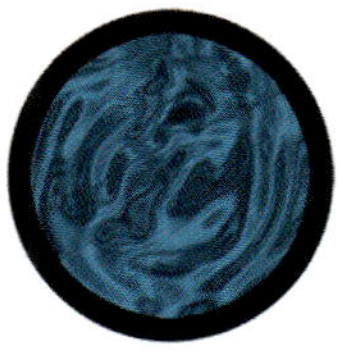

- While still within the Channel Mixer dialog box:
  - Adjust the green channel settings (`Output Channel = Green`).
    - `Red = 0%`
    - `Green = 100%`
    - `Blue = -20%`
    - `Constant = 0%`

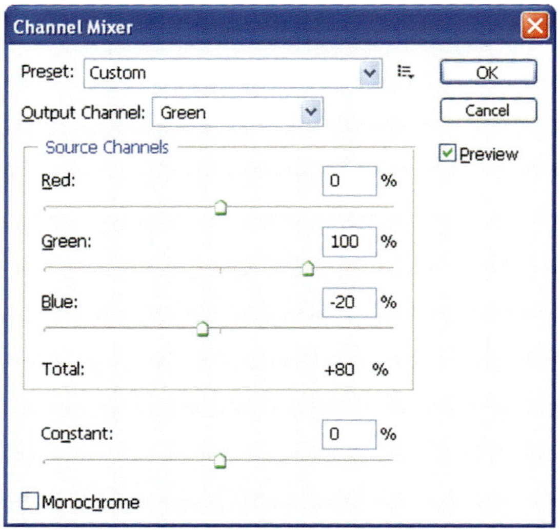

- While still within the Channel Mixer dialog box:
  - Adjust the blue channel settings (`Output Channel = Blue`).
    - `Red = 0%`
    - `Green = 0%`
    - `Blue = 100%`
    - `Constant = 0%`
  - Click the [OK] button.

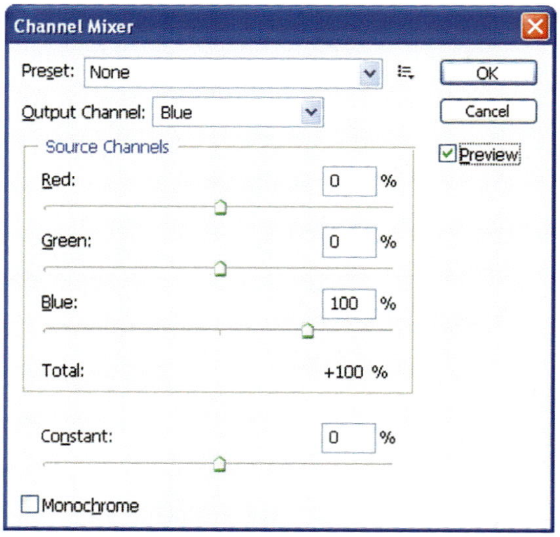

Step 8: Refine the water color.

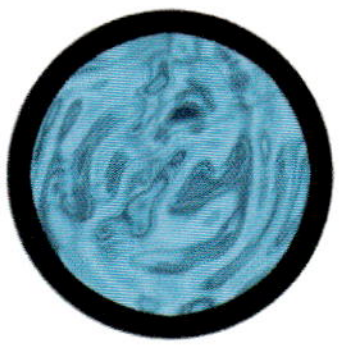

Step 8: Refine the water color.

- Refine the water color by allowing more of the white background to show through.
  - Click on the layer ***Brush 300*** to choose it.
    - Change the layer `Opacity = 50%`.

Step 9: Add shadows and a bench around the fountain.

- Draw an outline around the fountain bench.
  - Click on the layer *Bench* to choose it.
  - **Select > All**
  - With the Move Tool, hit the [up arrow] on your keyboard, then hit the [down arrow].
  - Turn off the layer *Bench* by clicking the [eye] icon so that it disappears and the layer is no longer visible.
  - Change the foreground color to white (`#FFFFFF`).
  - **Edit > Fill**
  - Click the [OK] button.
  - Create a new layer and name it *Bench Outline*.
  - **Edit > Stroke...**
    - `Width = 2 px`
    - `Location = Inside`
  - Click the [OK] button.

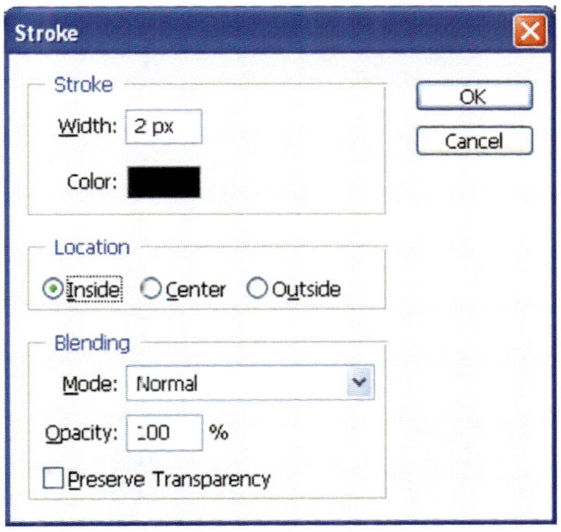

- Add a shadow to the fountain.
  - Click on the layer *Brush 300* to choose it.
  - **Select > All**
  - With the Move Tool, hit the [up arrow] on your keyboard, then hit the [down arrow].
  - Create a new layer and name it *Fountain Shadow*.
  - Change the foreground color to black (`#000000`).
  - **Edit > Fill**
  - Click the [OK] button.
  - With the Move Tool, shift the shadow up and to the left.
- Trim the shadow.
  - Click on the layer *Brush 300* to choose it.
  - **Select > All**
  - With the Move Tool, hit the [up arrow] on your keyboard, then hit the [down arrow].
  - **Select > Modify > Expand**
    - `Expand By = 3 pixels`
  - Click the [OK] button.
  - Click on the layer *Fountain Shadow* to choose it.
  - Hit the [Delete] key to erase the shadow within the selection.

Step 9: Add shadows and a bench around the fountain.

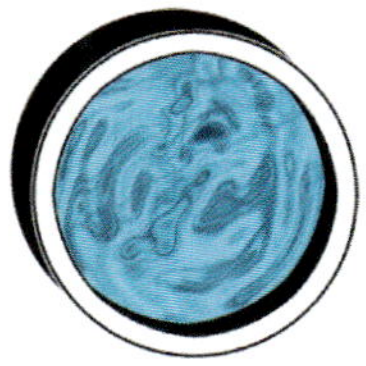

- Add a shadow to the inside of the fountain pool.
  - Click on the layer ***Fountain Bench*** to choose it.
  - **Select > All**
  - With the Move Tool, hit the [up arrow] on your keyboard, then hit the [down arrow].
  - Create a new layer and name it ***Pool Shadow***.
  - **Edit > Fill**
  - Click the [OK] button.
  - With the Move Tool, shift the shadow up and to the left.
- Trim the shadow.
  - With the Polygonal Lasso Tool, select the parts of the shadow that are outside the pool of water.
  - Hit the [Delete] key to erase the shadow within the selection.

Step 10: Refine the shadow in the water.

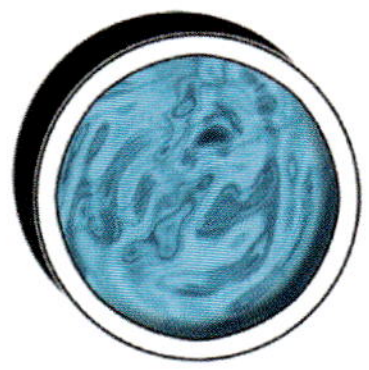

Step 10: Refine the shadow in the water.

- Refine the shadow in the water by changing its color.
  - Click on the layer ***Pool Shadow*** to choose it.
  - Right-click the layer tab and select "Blending Options..."
  - In the Layer Style dialog box that appears, check the "Color Overlay" checkbox.
  - Change the default color from red to blue.
    - Click on the red color box to the right of the Blend Mode drop-down list.
    - With the Eyedropper Tool, select the darkest color of blue within the water.
    - Click the [OK] button.
  - Click the [OK] button for the Layer Style dialog box.

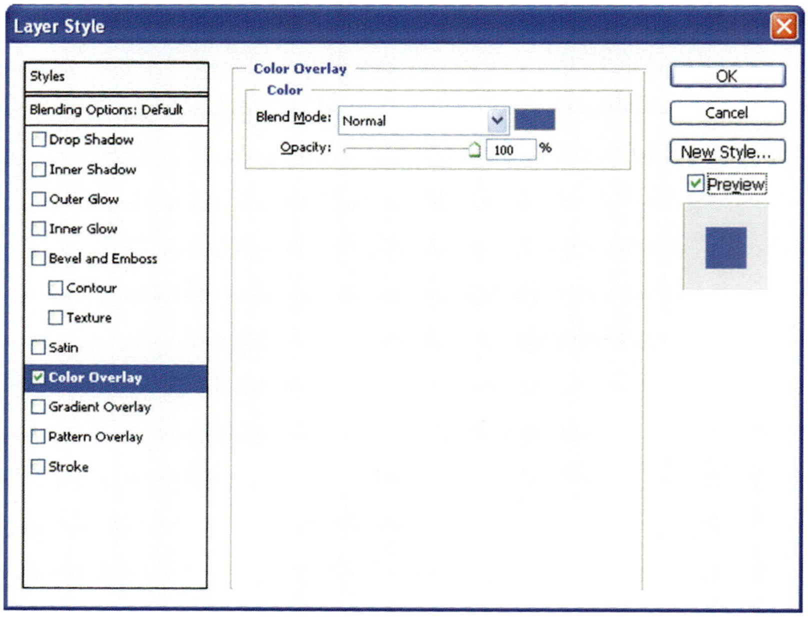

Step 11: Add pavement scoring.

Step 11: Add pavement scoring.

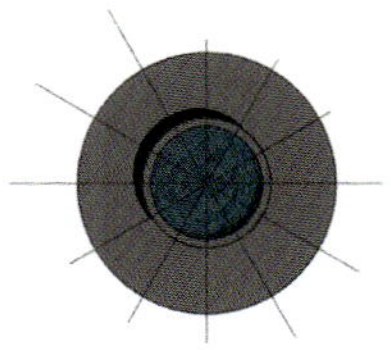

- Draw the pavement scoring pattern.
  - Create a new layer and name it *Scoring*.
  - Choose a paintbrush for the Brush Tool and draw a radiating pavement pattern.
    - `Master Diameter = 2 px`
    - `Hardness = 100%`

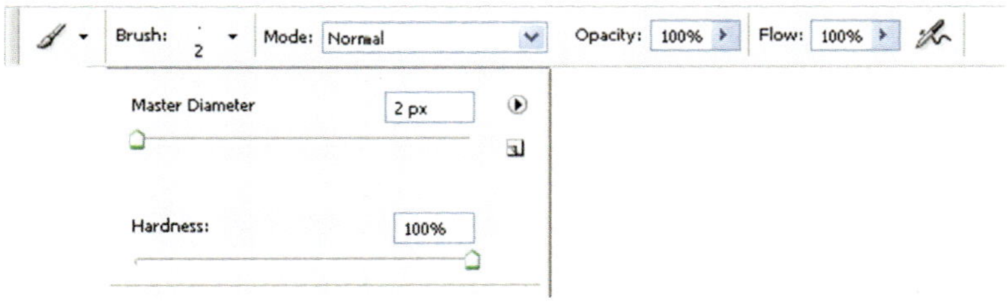

- Draw a circular scoring pattern around the fountain.
  - Create a new layer and name it *Brush 600*.
  - Choose a paintbrush for the Brush Tool and simply touch the canvas directly over the center point of the fountain.
    - `Master Diameter = 600 px`
    - `Hardness = 100%`
  - Reduce the layer `Opacity = 50%`.
  - **Select > All**
  - With the Move Tool, hit the [up arrow] on your keyboard, then hit the [down arrow].
  - Click on the layer *Scoring* to choose it.
  - **Edit > Stroke...**
    - `Width = 2 px`
    - `Location = Inside`
  - Click the [OK] button.

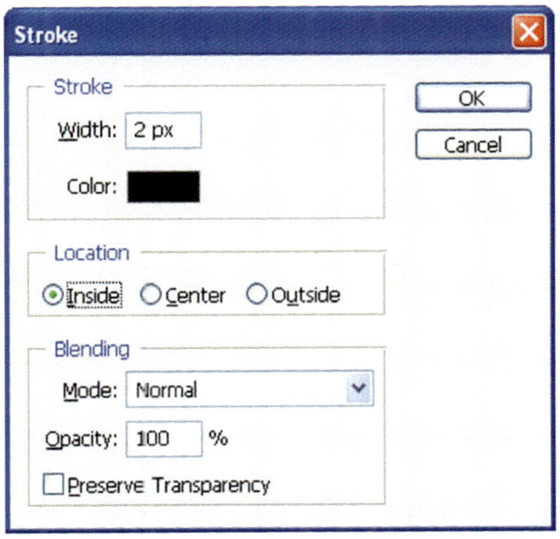

Step 12: Refine the pavement scoring.

Step 12: Refine the pavement scoring.

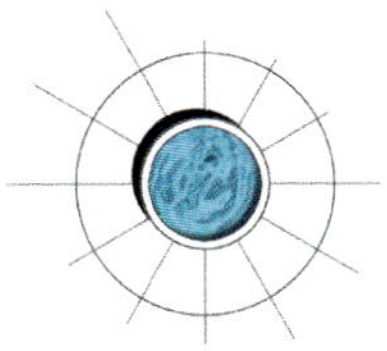

- Turn off the layer *Brush 600* by clicking on the [eye] icon on the layer tab.
- Click on the layer *Brush 300* to choose it.
- **Select > All**
- With the Move Tool, hit the [up arrow], then hit the [down arrow].
- Click on the layer *Scoring* to choose it.
- Hit the [Delete] key to erase the scoring pattern within your selection.

Step 13: Add color to the pavement.

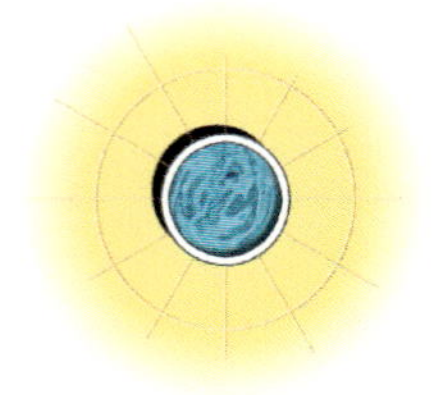

Step 13: Add color to the pavement.

- Paint the pavement.
    - Change the foreground color to tan (`#FFE38C`).
    - Create a new layer and name it ***Pavement***.
    - Choose a large, soft paintbrush for the Brush Tool and simply touch the canvas at the center point of the fountain.
        - `Master Diameter = 800 px`
        - `Hardness = 0%`
- Refine the pavement scoring pattern.
    - Click on the layer ***Scoring*** to choose it.
    - Right-click the layer tab and select "Blending Options..."
    - In the Layer Style dialog box that appears, check the "Color Overlay" checkbox.
    - Change the default color from red to brown.
        - Click on the red color box to the right of the Blend Mode drop-down list.
        - Change the color to brown (`#9E4A00`).
        - Click the [OK] button.
    - Click the [OK] button for the Layer Style dialog box.
    - Drag the layer ***Scoring*** to the "Create a new layer" icon.
    - With the layer ***Scoring copy***, repeat the steps above; however, change the color to white (`#FFFFFF`).
    - With the Move Tool, shift your copied layer slightly.

Step 14: Add accents and details.

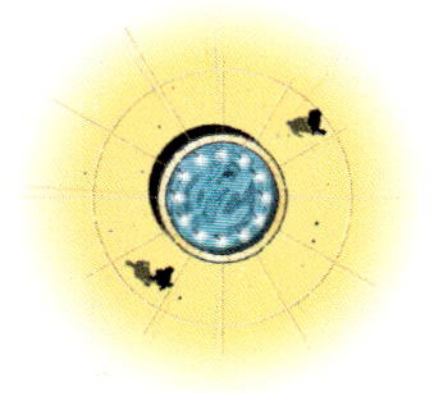

Step 14: Add accents and details.

- Add accents to the drawing.
    - Create a new layer and name it ***Accents***.
    - Using various brush sizes and colors, add accents and details to the drawing.
    - Adding people to your drawing will help give your drawing scale.
        - My preference is to draw people abstractly. Since this drawing is intended to illustrate a fountain design, you do not want the people to be the focus of your drawing.

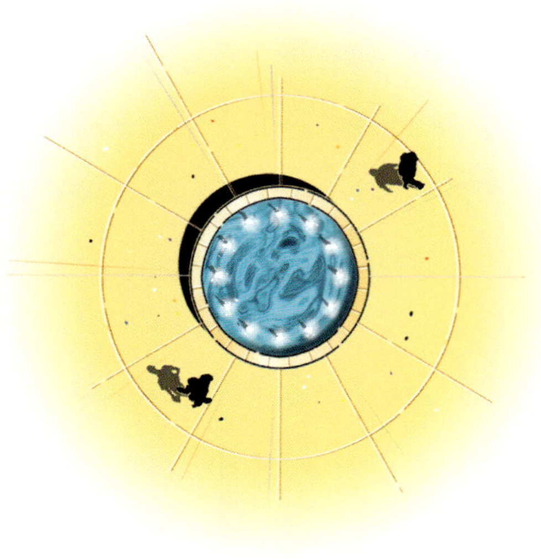

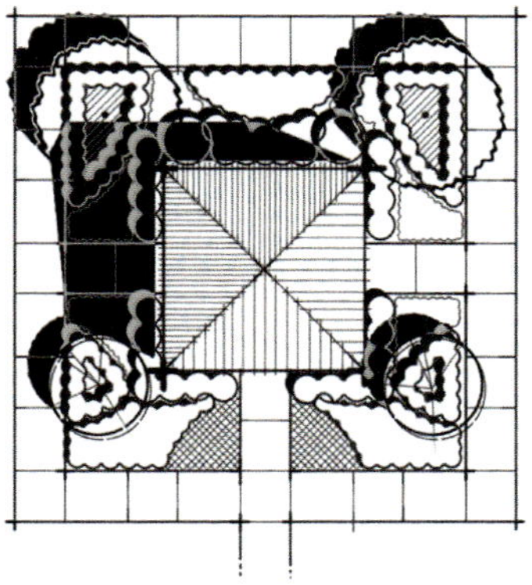

Master Plan Graphics | Inverting a Shadow

In this exercise you will learn to invert your drawing within the shadows. The principal technique illustrated is X-Ray Vision, though the following techniques are all evident in the final drawing:

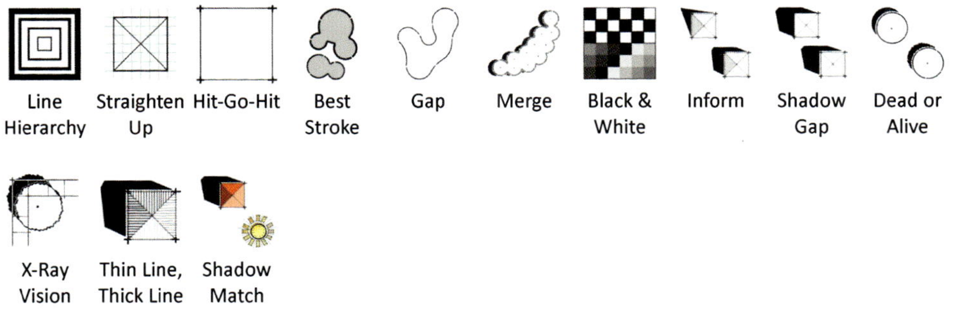

This drawing was originally drawn on a canvas with a resolution of 200 pixels per inch. Afterwards, it was scaled down to fit within these pages.

Step 1: Begin with a black line drawing.

Assume you begin with a simple black line drawing. Shadows have not been added yet, so all elements on the ground plane are still visible.

Step 1: Begin with a black line drawing.

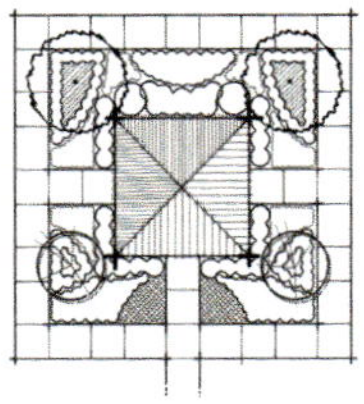

Step 2: Adding shadows.

Now consider what happens next. After adding shadows to the shrubs, trees, and building, much of the drawing is obscured. (See the figure on the right.) One way to solve this problem is to simply reduce the layer opacity of the shadows. However, the drawing begins to look washed-out and to take on a monochrome appearance rather than a black line appearance.

Step 2: Adding shadows.

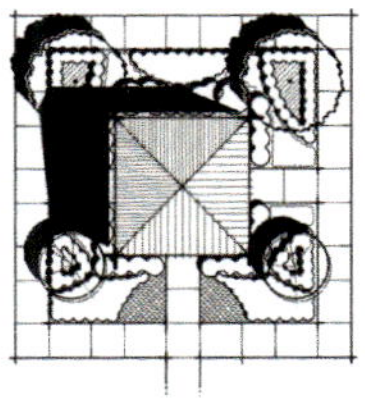

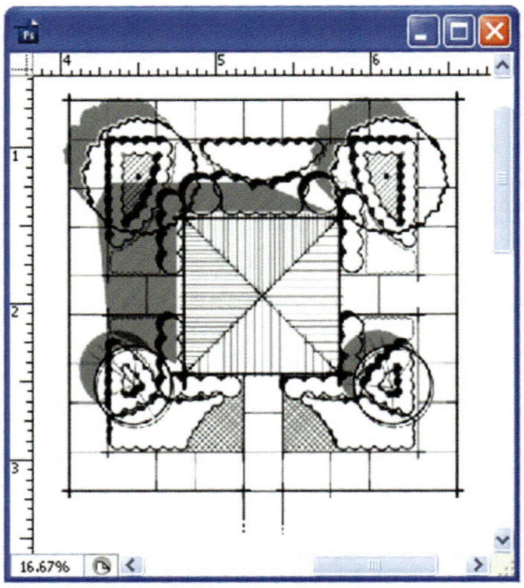

Figure 10-4: This screen capture illustrates what your drawing would look like if you reduced the opacity of the shadows to 50 percent.

Step 3: Invert a copy of the drawing.

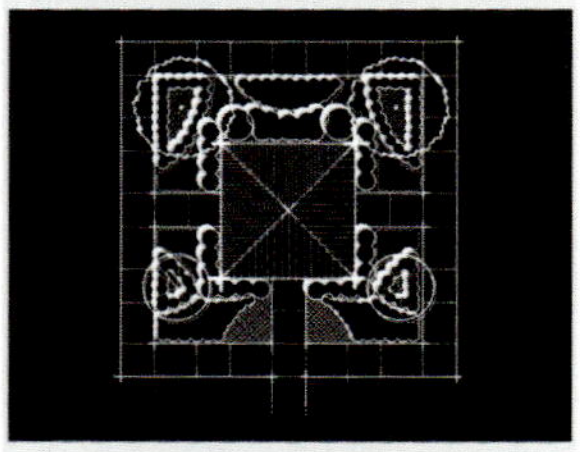

Step 3: Invert a copy of the drawing.

Before you can invert the drawing, you will need to consolidate some of the line work into one layer. Afterwards, you can insert this inverted layer within the shadows.

- Consolidate the line work into one layer.
  - While holding down the [Ctrl] key, click on all the layers you would like to consolidate.
    - This would include all the line work, excepting the shadows of the large trees and the building.
  - Drag these highlighted layers to the "Create a new layer" icon.
  - Your copied layers will now be selected. Right-click the highlighted layers and select "Merge Layers..." from the pop-up dialog box.
  - Rename the layer *Inverted Line Work*.
- Invert the merged line work.
  - Click on the layer *Inverted Line Work* to choose it.
  - **Image > Adjustments > Invert**

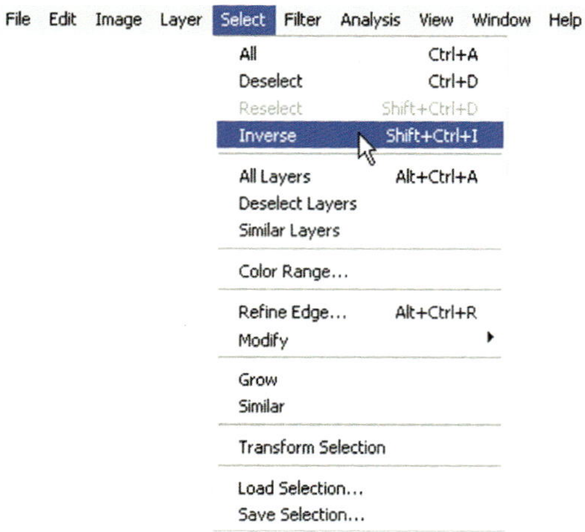

Step 4: Refine the shadows.

Now that you have an inverted copy of the line work, you will want to trim (or erase) everything but the area that appears under the shadows of the large trees and the building. To do this, you will select the areas the shadows occupy, invert your selection, and then erase.

- Select the area you want to trim.
  - With the Magic Wand Tool, select the shadows for the large trees and the building.
    - Unless all the shadows are on the same layer (which is highly unlikely), you will have to select each shadow individually.
    - To add to your current selection, hold down the [Shift] key when clicking on new areas.
    - To remove from your current selection, hold down the [Alt] key when clicking on areas to remove.
  - Now that you have selected the areas of the inverted drawing that you want to keep (that is, the areas in the large shadows), select the opposite areas so that you can remove them.
    - **Select > Inverse**
- Trim the inverted line work.
  - Click on the layer ***Inverted Line Work*** to choose it.
  - Hit the [Delete] key to erase the current selection.

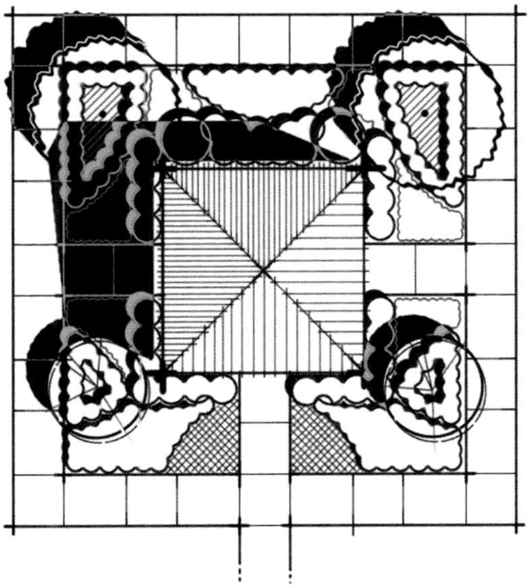

Step 4: Refine the shadows.

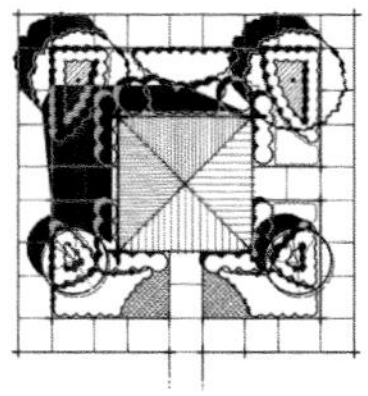

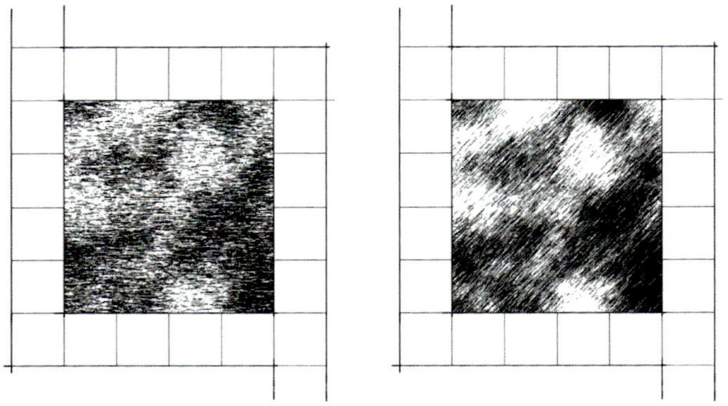

Master Plan Graphics | Hatches

In this exercise you will draw hatches that you might use to represent groundcovers. The techniques used in this example include the following:

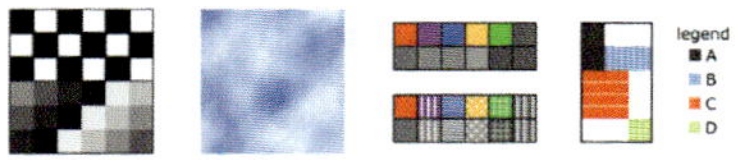

Black & White | Cloud Color | Indepen-dence | Legendary Labeling

This drawing was originally drawn on a canvas with a resolution of 200 pixels per inch. Afterwards, it was scaled down to fit within these pages.

Step 1: Paint the area for the hatch.

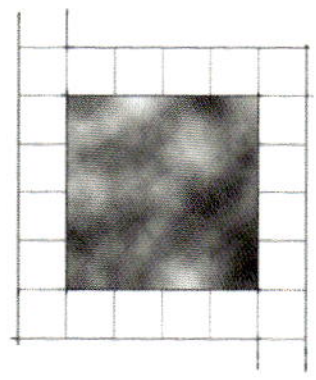

Step 1: Paint the area for the hatch.

Throughout the following exercises, you will be hatching within a drawing of a concrete path. This path was drawn by simply painting over guidelines defined every one-half inch.

- Select the area to paint.
  - Using the Rectangular Marquee Tool, select the area to paint using the guidelines.

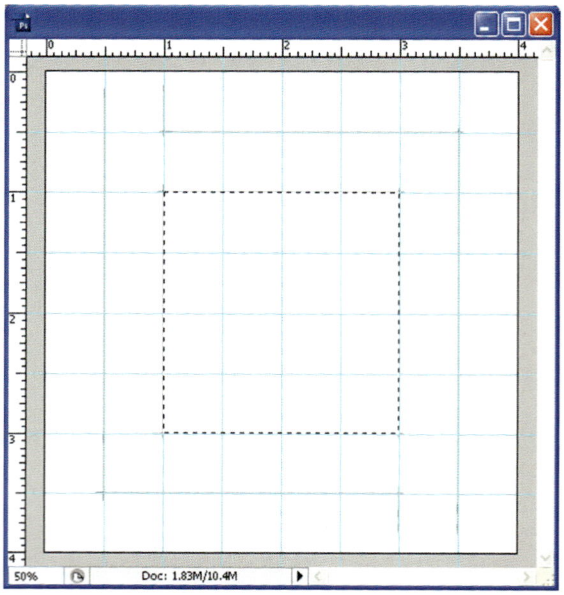

- Paint the selected area.
  - Create a new layer and name it *Hatch*.
  - Be sure that the foreground color is white (`#FFFFFF`) and the background color is black (`#000000`).
  - **Filter > Render > Clouds**

Step 2: Refine the hatch.

Step 2: Refine the hatch.

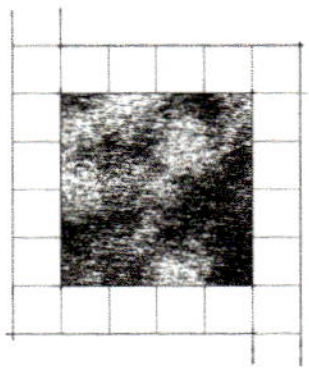

- Refine the hatch by applying a filter.
  - **Filter > Pixelate > Mezzotint...**
    - `Type = Short Lines`
  - Click the [OK] button.

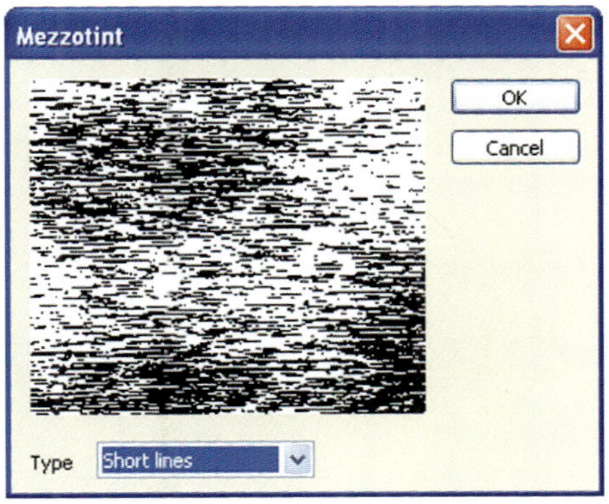

Step 2(b): Alternative refinement.

Step 2(b): Alternative refinement.

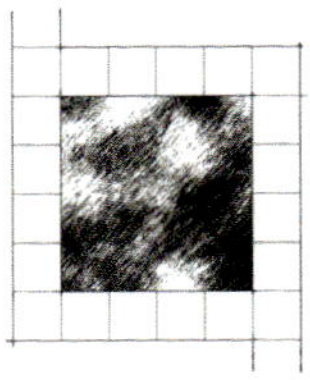

As an alternative to the previous filter, you can refine the hatch using the following filter.

- Refine the hatch by applying a filter.
  - **Filter > Sketch > Graphic Pen...**
    - `Stroke Length = 15`
    - `Light/Dark Balance = 50`
    - `Stroke Direction = Right Diagonal`
  - Click the [OK] button.

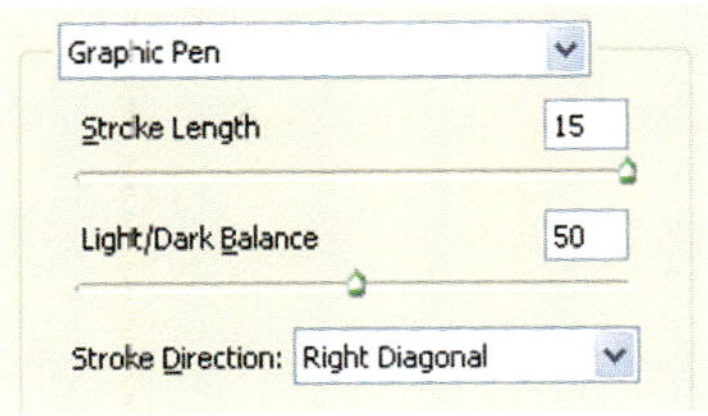

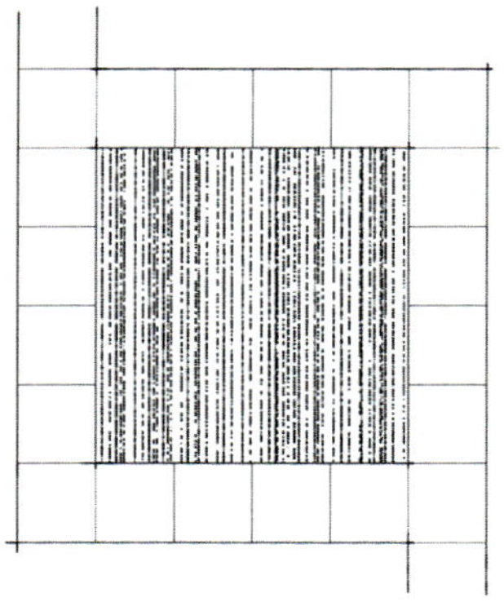

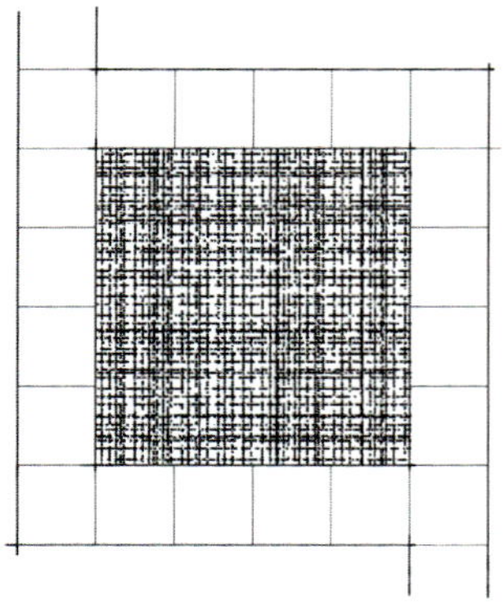

Master Plan Graphics | Hatches

In this exercise you will draw hatches that you might use to represent groundcovers. The techniques used in this example include the following:

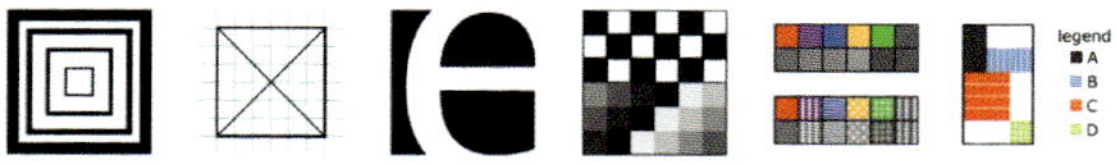

Line Hierarchy | Straighten Up | Erase | Black & White | Indepen- dence | Legendary Labeling

This drawing was originally drawn on a canvas with a resolution of 200 pixels per inch. Afterwards, it was scaled down to fit within these pages.

Step 1: Draw thin, vertical lines.

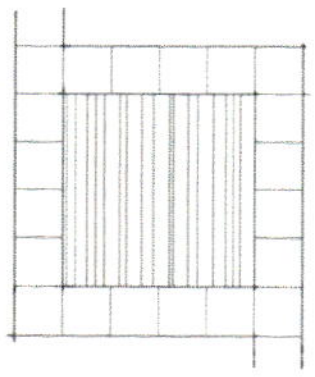

Step 1: Draw thin, vertical lines.

- Select the area to paint, as you did in the previous example.
    - Using the Rectangular Marquee Tool, select the area to paint using the guidelines.
- Draw thin, vertical lines.
    - Create a new layer and name it ***Hatch A***.
    - Choose a paintbrush for the Brush Tool and paint vertical lines within your selection.
        - `Master Diameter = 1 px`
        - `Hardness = 100%`
            - To draw straight lines, hold down the [Shift] key between mouse clicks.

Step 2: Draw more thin, vertical lines.

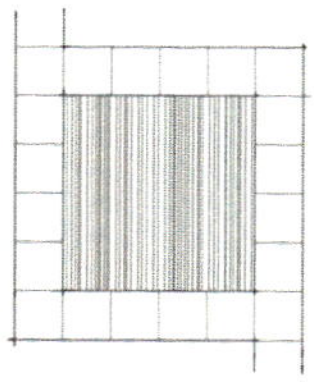

Step 2: Draw more thin, vertical lines.

- Draw more thin, vertical lines.
    - Create a new layer and name it ***Hatch B***.
    - Using the same paintbrush, draw additional thin, vertical lines.
    - Repeat this step, continuing to draw vertical lines and creating new layers ***Hatch C***, ***Hatch D***, etc.
        - Keep creating new layers until you are satisfied that enough vertical lines have been drawn.
        - By separating the lines into distinct layers, you will be able to create gaps in the lines more easily in the next step.

Step 3: Add gaps to the lines.

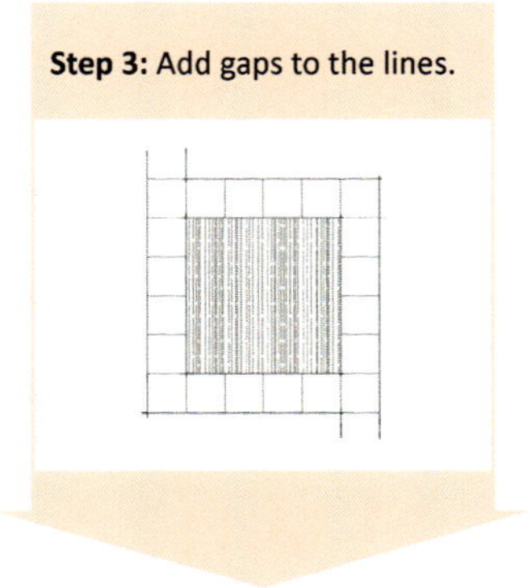

- Create gaps in the lines.
  - Click on the layer *Hatch A* to choose it.
  - Choose a brush for the Eraser Tool and erase from the vertical lines to create gaps.
  - Repeat for the other layers you created.
- Consolidate the layers of thin lines.
  - For each layer you created in the previous step, click on the layer while holding down the [Ctrl] key.
  - Right-click the layers you chose and select "Merge Layers..." from the pop-up dialog box.
  - Rename the layer *Hatch*.

Step 4: Refine the hatch.

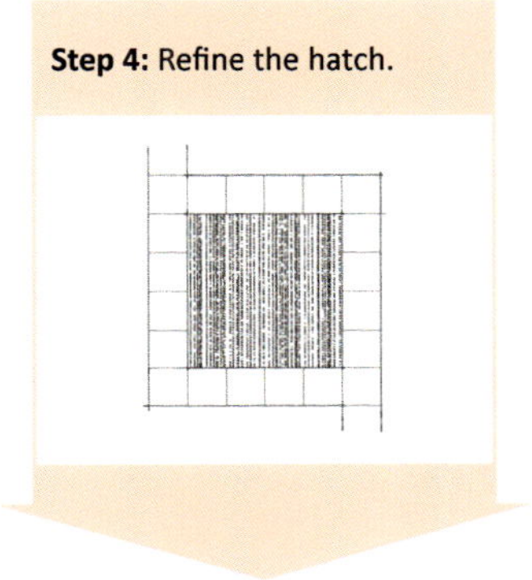

- Refine the hatch by applying a filter.
  - **Filter > Pixelate > Pointillize...**
    - `Cell Size = 5`
  - Click the [OK] button.

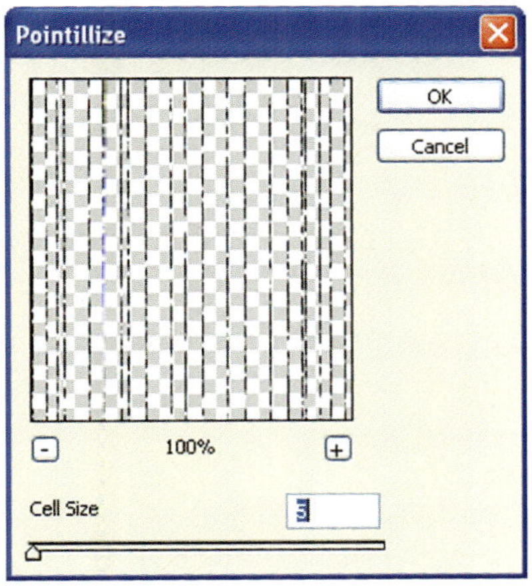

- Thicken the lines.
  - Click on the layer *Hatch* to choose it.
  - Right-click the layer tab and select "Blending Options..."
  - In the Layer Style dialog box that appears, check the "Stroke" checkbox.
    - `Size = 1 px`
    - `Location = Outside`
    - `Color = Black (#000000)`
  - Click the [OK] button.

Step 4(b): Alternative refinement.

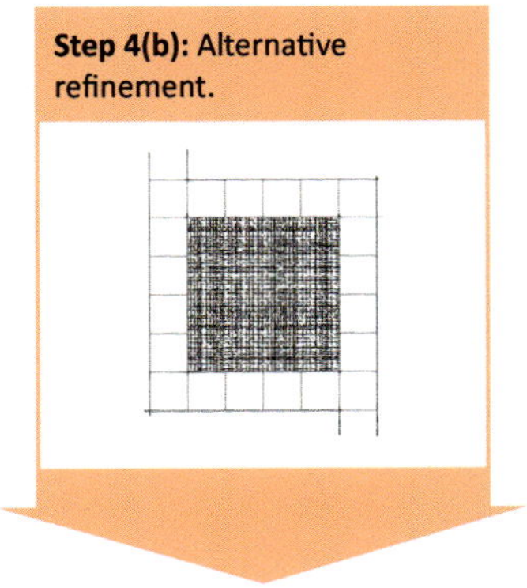

- An alternative refinement would be to copy the hatch from the previous step and rotate it to create a crosshatch.
  - Click on the layer *Hatch A* to choose it.
  - Drag the layer to the "Create a new layer" icon.
  - **Edit > Transform > Rotate 90 CW**

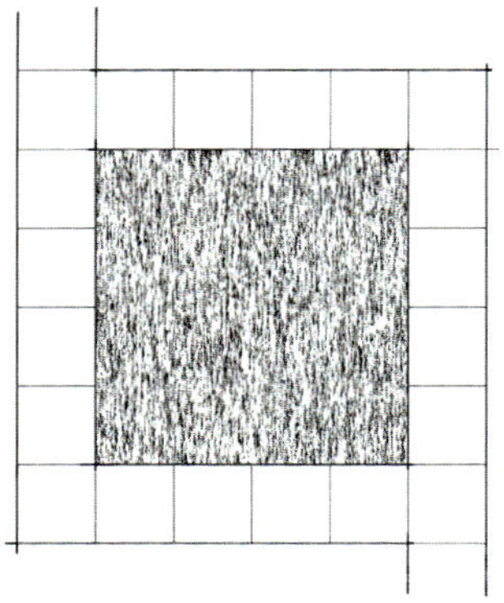

Master Plan Graphics | Hatch

In this exercise you will draw a hatch that you might use to represent groundcovers. The techniques used in this example include the following:

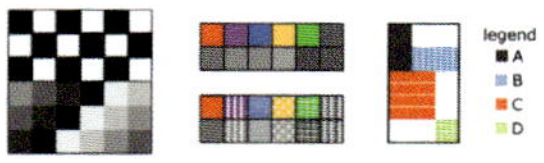

Black & White | Indepen-dence | Legendary Labeling

This drawing was originally drawn on a canvas with a resolution of 200 pixels per inch. Afterwards, it was scaled down to fit within these pages.

Step 1: Paint and refine the hatch.

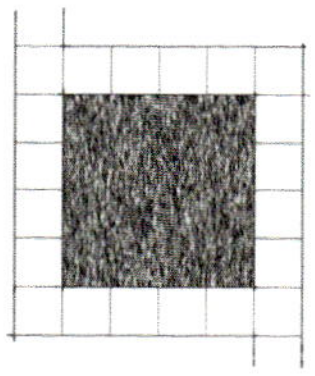

Step 1: Paint and refine the hatch.

- Select the area to paint, as you did in the previous examples.
  - Using the Rectangular Marquee Tool, select the area to paint using the guidelines.
- Paint the selected area.
  - Create a new layer and name it *Hatch*.
  - Change the foreground color to white (`#FFFFFF`).
  - **Edit > Fill**
  - Click the [OK] button.
    - It may seem silly to paint white on a white background; but, unless you paint something on the canvas, you will not be permitted to alter it with a filter. After all, you can't refine "nothing."
- Create the hatch by applying a filter.
  - **Filter > Render > Fibers...**
    - `Variance = 64`
    - `Strength = 64`
  - Click the [OK] button.

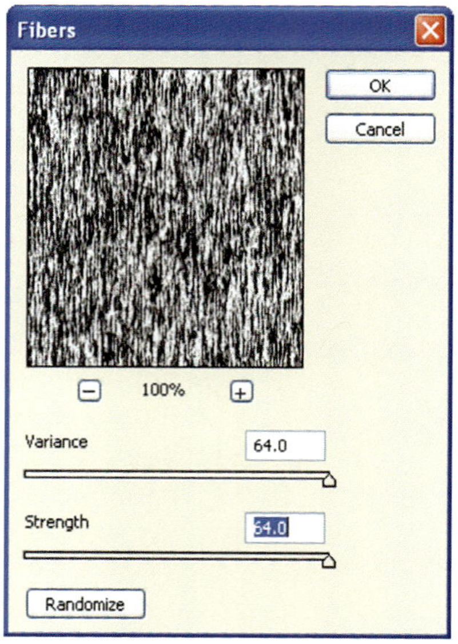

Step 2: Lighten the hatch.

- Lighten the hatch by adjusting its brightness.
  - **Image > Adjustments > Brightness and Contrast...**
    - `Brightness = 150`
    - `Contrast = 0`
  - Click the [OK] button.

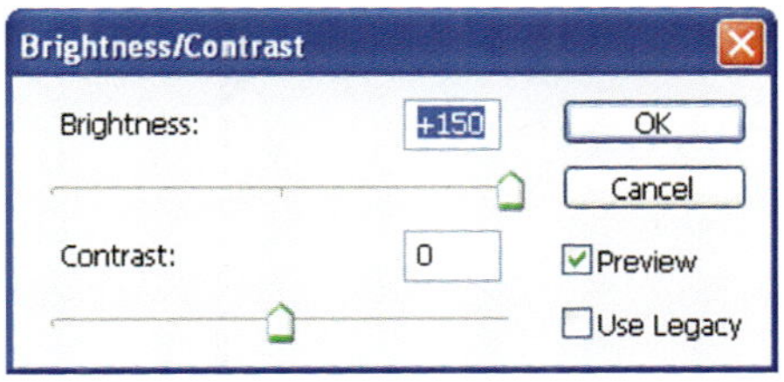

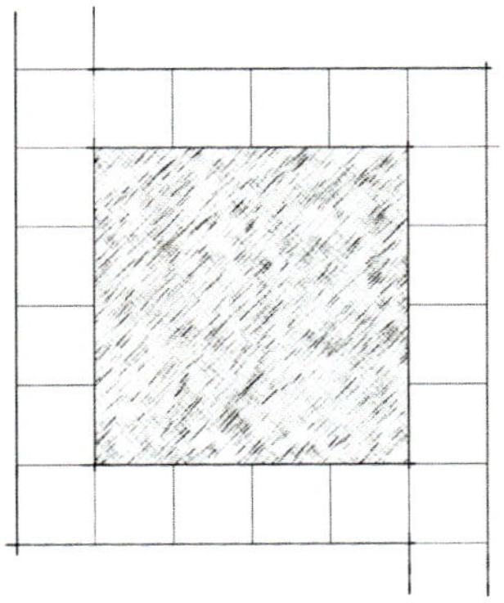

Step 2: Lighten the hatch.

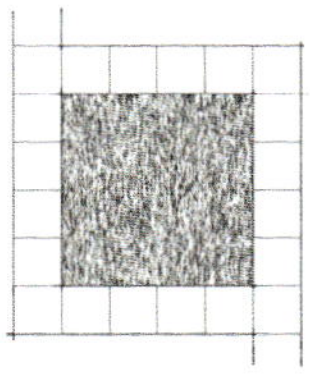

Master Plan Graphics | Hatch

In this exercise you will draw a hatch that you might use to represent groundcovers. The techniques used in this example include the following:

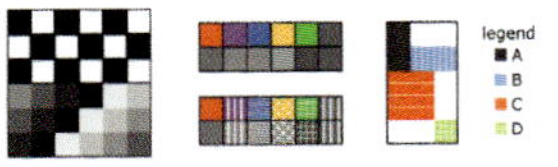

Black & White | Indepen-dence | Legendary Labeling

This drawing was originally drawn on a canvas with a resolution of 200 pixels per inch. Afterwards, it was scaled down to fit within these pages.

Step 1: Paint and refine the hatch.

Like the previous example, you will begin by painting a white (but, not empty) background and then create your hatch by applying various filters.

- Paint a white background just as you did in the previous example.

Step 1: Paint and refine the hatch.

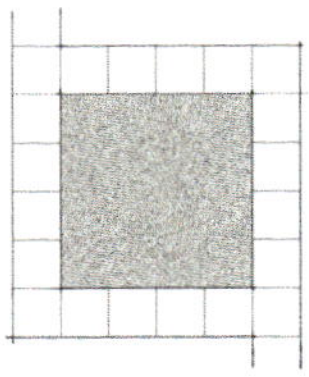

- Create the hatch by applying a filter.
  - **Filter > Noise > Add Noise...**
    - `Amount = 50%`
    - `Distribution = Gaussian`
    - `Monochromatic = checked`
  - Click the [OK] button.

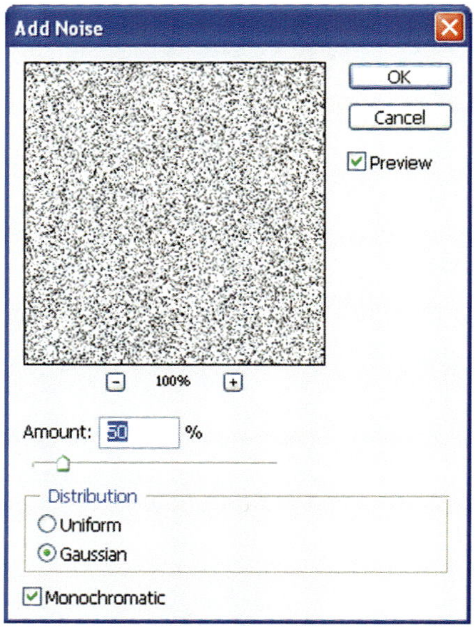

Step 2: Refine the hatch.

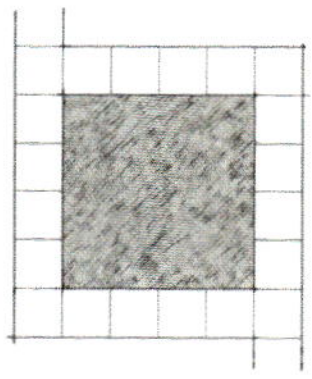

Step 2: Refine the hatch.

- Refine the hatch by applying a filter.
  - **Filter > Artistic > Colored Pencil...**
    - `Pencil Width = 1`
    - `Stroke Pressure = 15`
    - `Paper Brightness = 0`
  - Click the [OK] button.

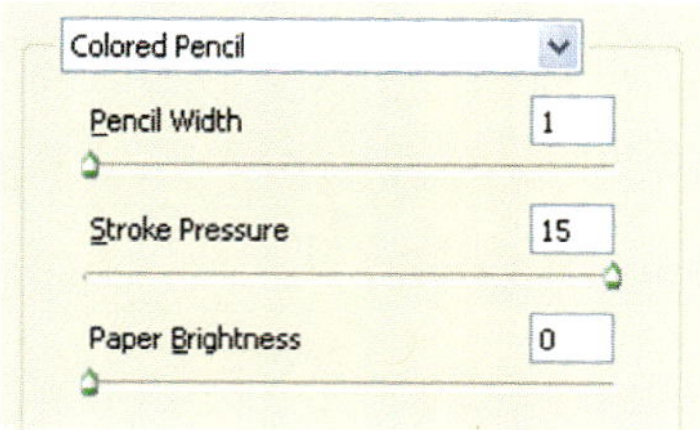

Step 3: Lighten the hatch.

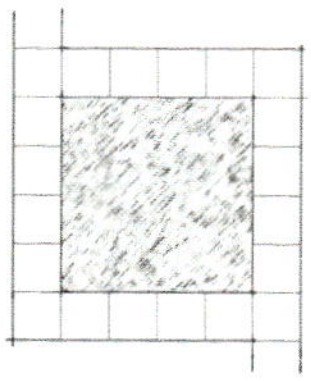

Step 3: Lighten the hatch.

- Lighten the hatch by adjusting its brightness and contrast.
  - **Image > Adjustments > Brightness and Contrast...**
    - `Brightness = 50`
    - `Contrast = 100`
  - Click the [OK] button.

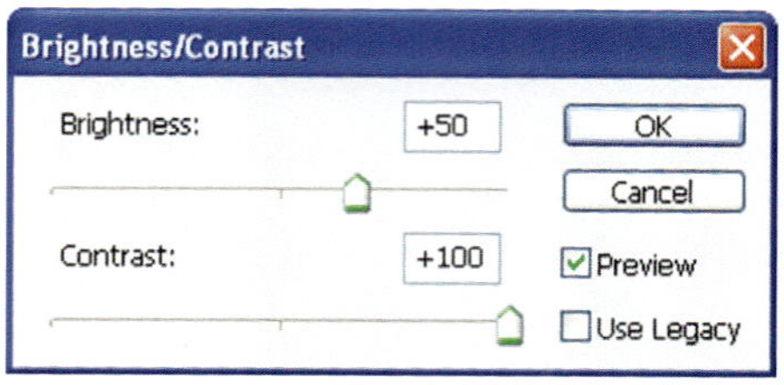

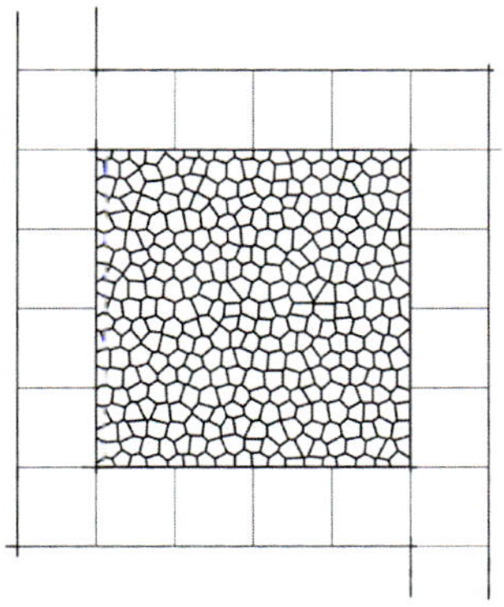

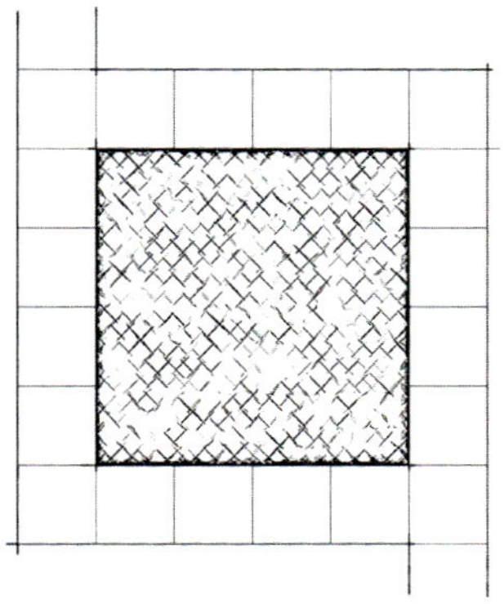

Master Plan Graphics | Hatches

In this exercise you will draw some hatches that you might use to represent groundcovers. The techniques used in this example include the following:

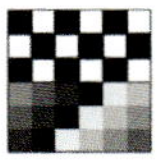

Black & White

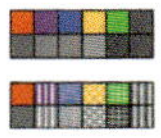

Indepen-dence

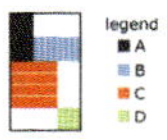

Legendary Labeling

This drawing was originally drawn on a canvas with a resolution of 200 pixels per inch. Afterwards, it was scaled down to fit within these pages.

Step 1: Paint and refine the hatch.

Step 1: Paint and refine the hatch.

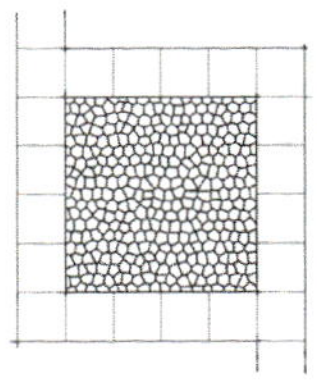

Like the previous example, you will begin by painting a white (but, not empty) background and then create your hatch by applying various filters. In fact, you are going to build six unique hatches using this step as the foundation for all of them.

- Select the area to paint, as you did in the previous examples.
  - Using the Rectangular Marquee Tool, select the area to paint using the guidelines.
- Paint a white background within your selection.
  - Create a new layer and name it *Hatch*.
  - Change the foreground color to white (`#FFFFFF`).
  - **Edit > Fill**
  - Click the [OK] button.
- Create a hatch by applying a filter.
  - **Filter > Texture > Stained Glass...**
    - `Cell Size = 15`
    - `Border Thickness = 1`
    - `Light Intensity = 0`
  - Click the [OK] button.

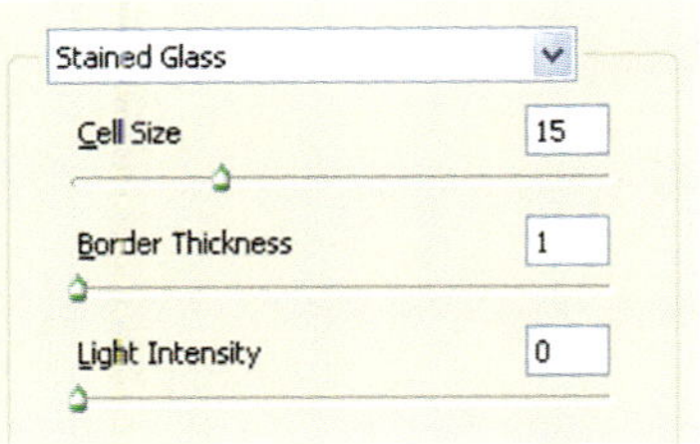

Step 2: Refine the hatch.

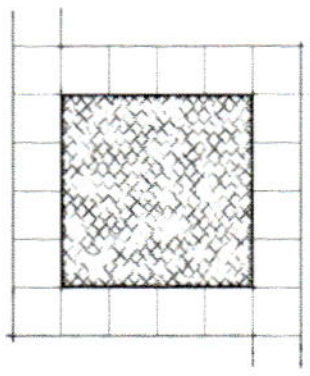

Step 2: Refine the hatch.

Like the next five hatches, this hatch is created by applying another filter to the hatch made in the last step (with the Stained Glass filter).

- Create a new hatch by applying a filter to the current hatch.
  - **Filter > Brush Strokes > Colored Pencil...**
    - `Pencil Width = 15`
    - `Stroke Pressure = 15`
    - `Paper Brightness = 50`
  - Click the [OK] button.

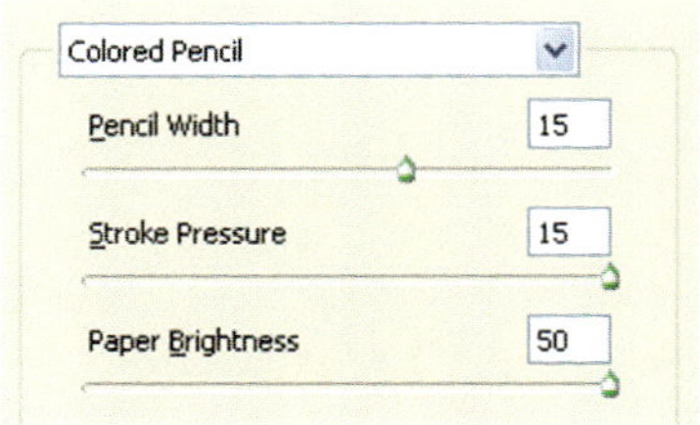

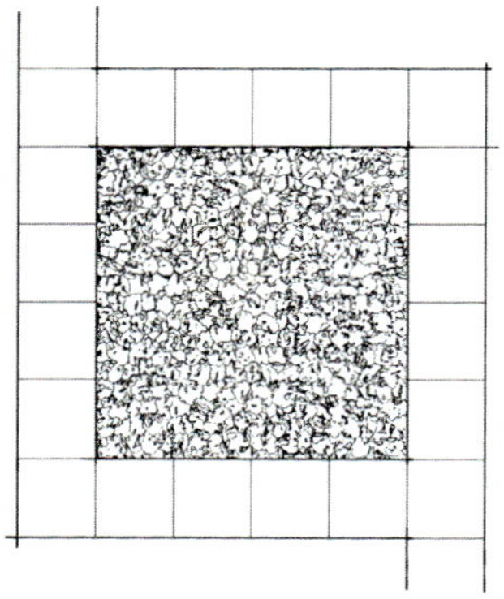

Step 2(b): Alternative refinement.

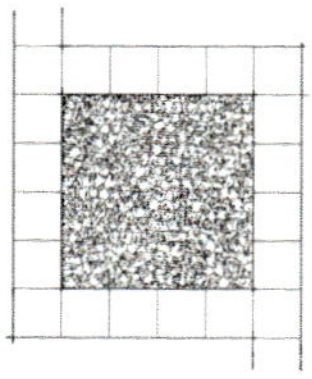

Step 2(b): Alternative refinement.

As an alternative to the last step, create a new hatch by applying a different filter to the original hatch (created from the Stained Glass filter).

- Create a new hatch by applying a different filter.
  - **Filter > Distort > Ocean Ripple...**
    - `Ripple Size = 9`
    - `Ripple Magnitude = 9`
  - Click the [OK] button.

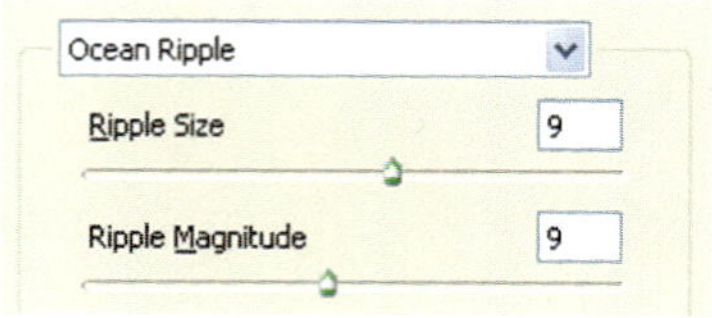

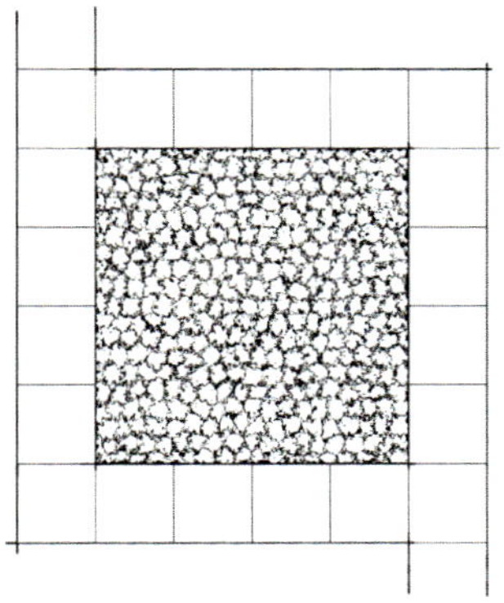

Step 2(c): Alternative refinement.

- Create a new hatch by applying a different filter.
  - **Filter > Brush Strokes > Spatter...**
    - `Spatter = 10`
    - `Smoothness = 5`
  - Click the [OK] button.

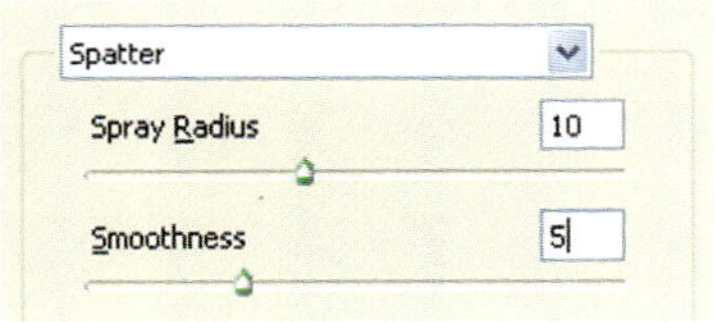

Step 2(c): Alternative refinement.

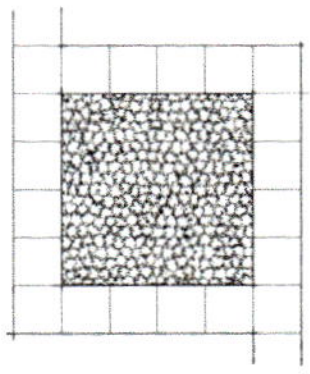

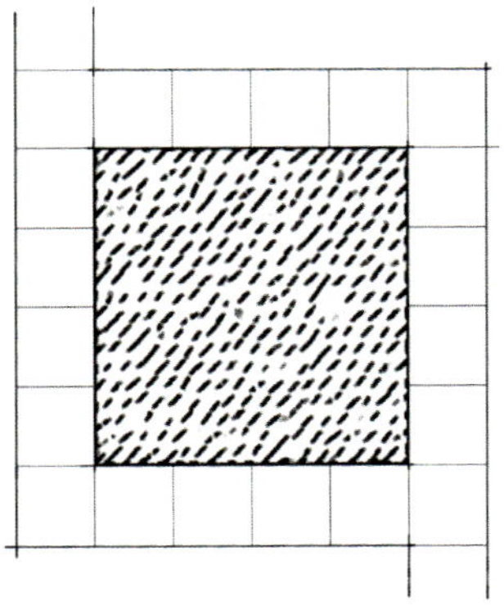

Step 2(d): Alternative refinement.

- Create a new hatch by applying a different filter.
  - **Filter > Brush Strokes > Sumi-e...**
    - `Stroke Width = 10`
    - `Stroke Pressure = 2`
    - `Contrast = 16`
  - Click the [OK] button.

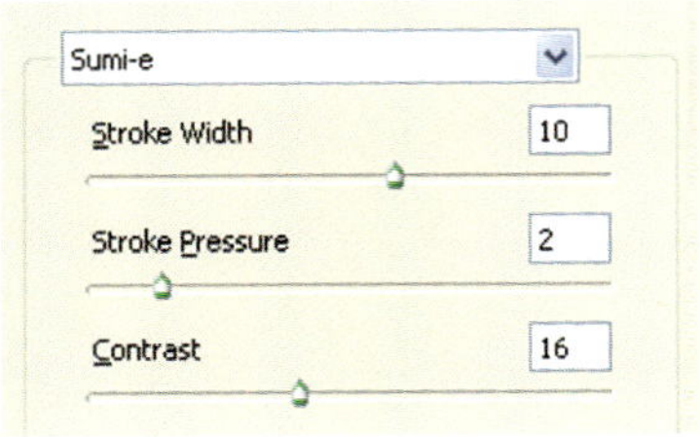

Step 2(d): Alternative refinement.

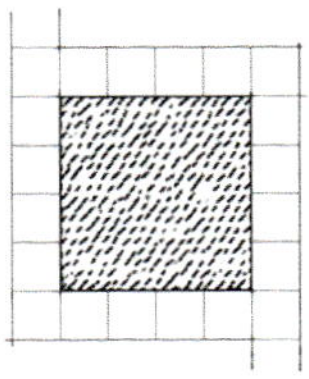

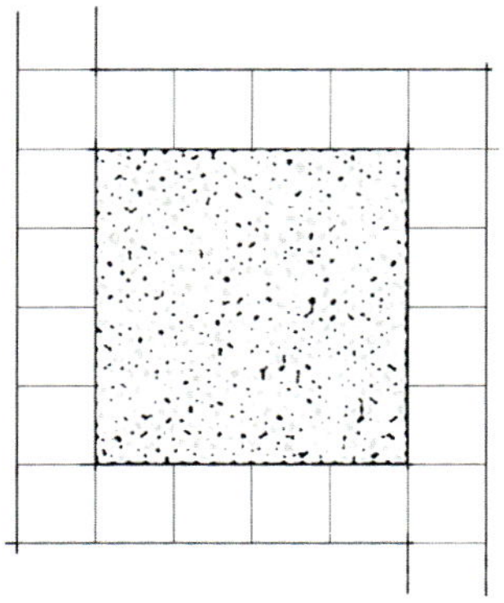

Step 2(e): Alternative refinement.

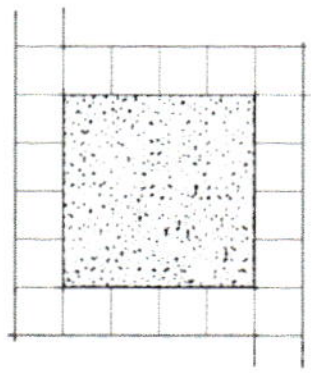

Step 2(e): Alternative refinement.

- Create a new hatch by applying a different filter.
  - **Filter > Artistic > Sponge...**
    - `Brush Size = 2`
    - `Definition = 12`
    - `Smoothness = 5`
  - Click the [OK] button.

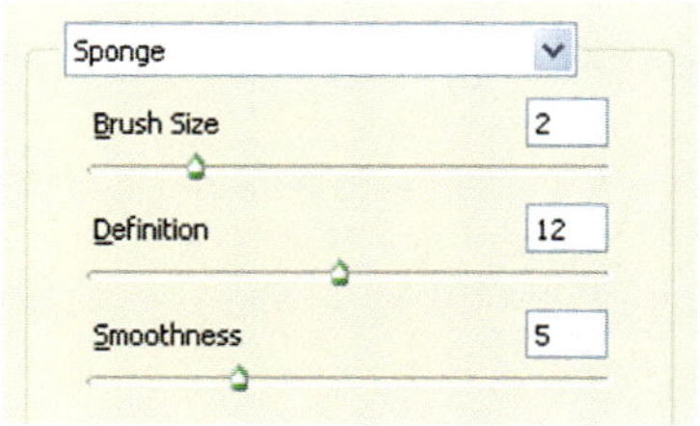

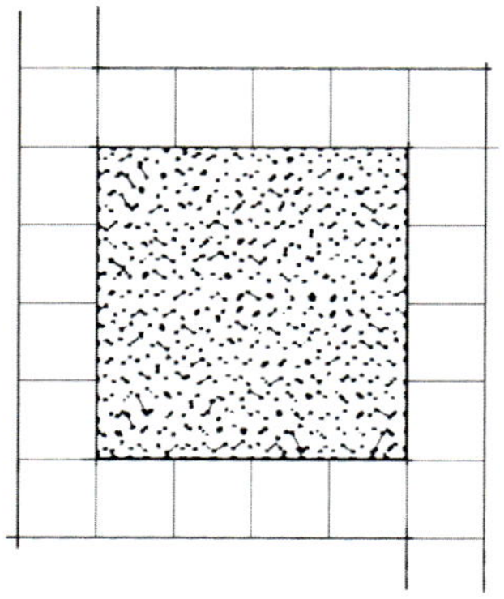

Step 2(f): Alternative refinement.

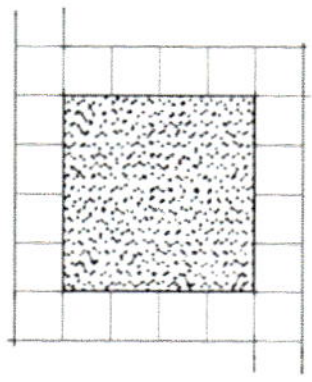

Step 2(f): Alternative refinement.

- Create a new hatch by applying a different filter.
  - **Filter > Artistic > Watercolor...**
    - `Brush Detail = 9`
    - `Shadow Intensity = 1`
    - `Texture = 2`
  - Click the [OK] button.

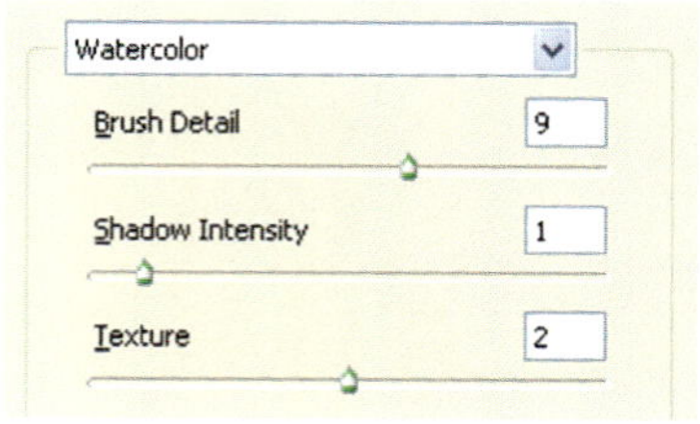

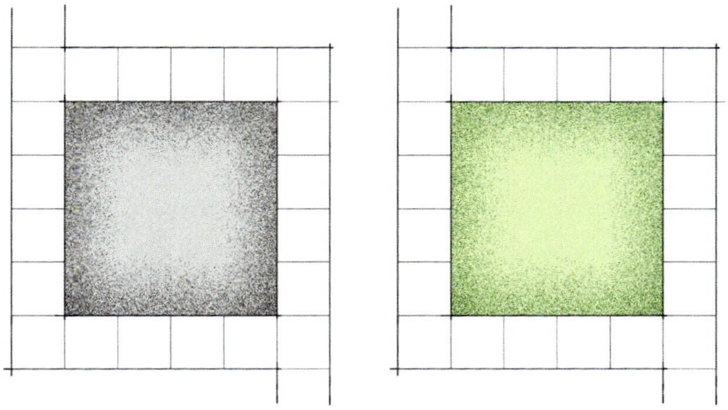

Master Plan Graphics | Turf

In this exercise you will draw some hatches that you might use to represent turf or grass. The techniques used in this example include the following:

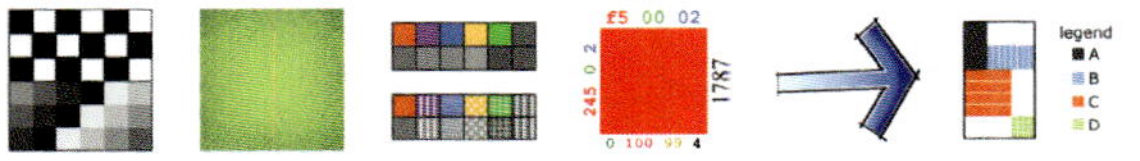

Black & White | Noisy Color | Indepen-dence | Color Palette | Light Then Dark | Legendary Labeling

This drawing was originally drawn on a canvas with a resolution of 200 pixels per inch. Afterwards, it was scaled down to fit within these pages.

Step 1: Paint the area for the turf.

- Select the area to paint, as you did in the previous examples.
  - Using the Rectangular Marquee Tool, select the area to paint using the guidelines.
- Paint a light green background within your selection.
  - Create a new layer and name it *Turf*.
  - Change the foreground color to light green (`#E0FFB5`).
  - **Edit > Fill**
  - Click the [OK] button.
  - Change the foreground color to olive green (`#686B00`).
  - Change the background color to light green (`#E0FFB5`).
  - Click on the layer ***Turf*** to choose it.
  - **Select > All**
  - With the Move Tool, hit the [up arrow] on your keyboard, then hit the [down arrow].
  - **Edit > Stroke**
    - `Width = 1 px`
    - `Location = Inside`
- Click the [OK] button.

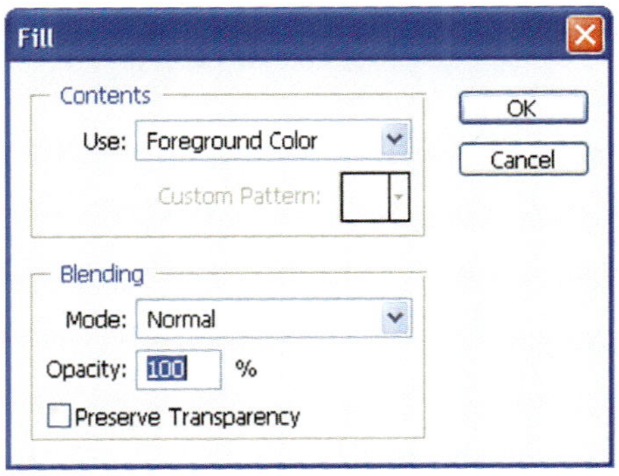

Step 1: Paint the area for the turf.

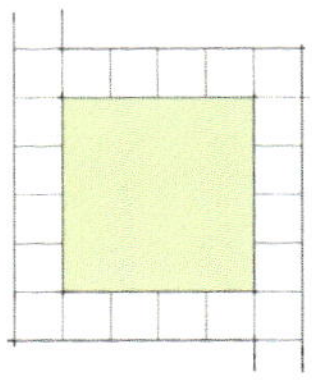

Step 2: Shade the turf.

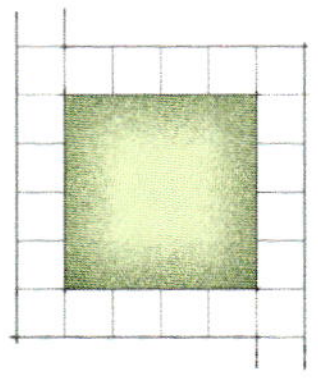

Step 2: Shade the turf.

- Shade the turf by applying a filter.
  - **Filter > Brush Strokes > Spatter...**
    - `Spray Radius = 25`
    - `Smoothness = 1`
  - Click the [OK] button.

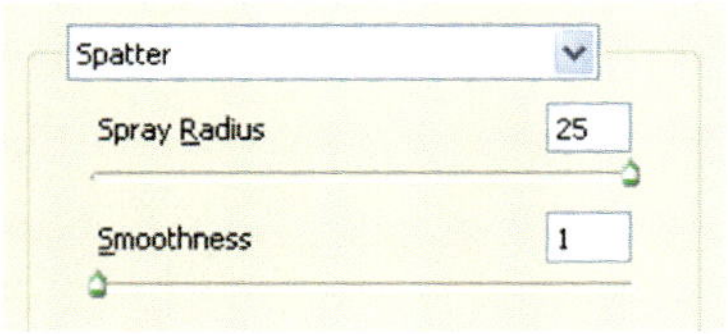

Step 3: Refine the texture.

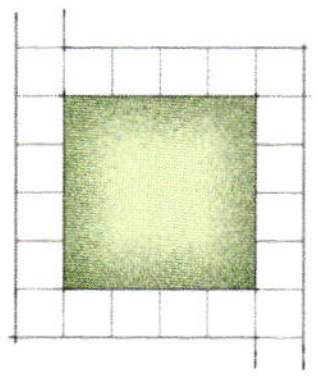

Step 3: Refine the texture.

- Refine the texture of the turf by applying a filter.
  - **Filter > Noise > Add Noise...**
    - `Amount = 5%`
    - `Distribution = Gaussian`
    - `Monochromatic = checked`
  - Click the [OK] button.

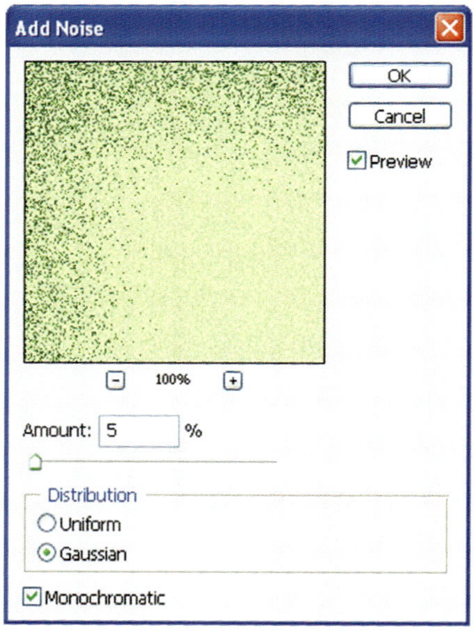

Step 4: Alternative refinement.

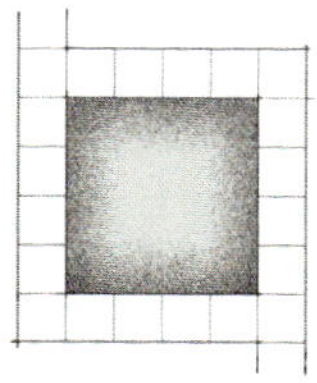

Step 4: Alternative refinement.

- If you prefer not to use color, then you can remove it.
  - Click on the layer *Turf* to choose it.
  - With the Move Tool, hit the [up arrow] on the keyboard, then hit the [down arrow].
  - **Image > Adjustments > Desaturate**

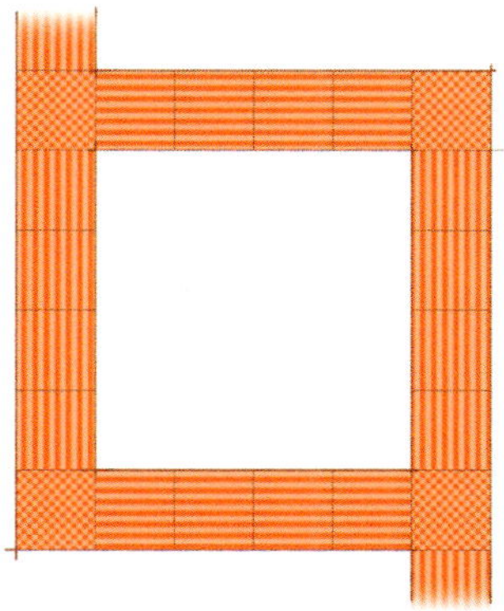

Master Plan Graphics | Brick Paving

In this exercise you will draw some hatches that you might use to represent brick paving. The techniques used in this example include the following:

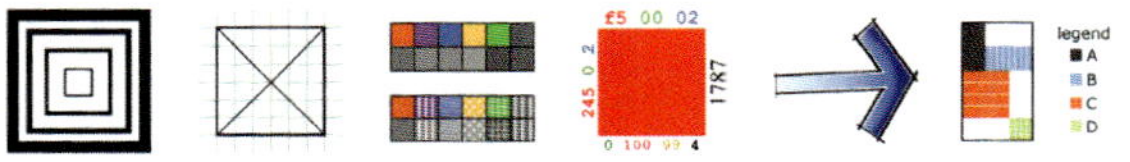

Line Hierarchy | Straighten Up | Indepen-dence | Color Palette | Light Then Dark | Legendary Labeling

This drawing was originally drawn on a canvas with a resolution of 200 pixels per inch. Afterwards, it was scaled down to fit within these pages.

Step 1: Paint the area for brick paving.

Step 1: Paint the area for the brick paving.

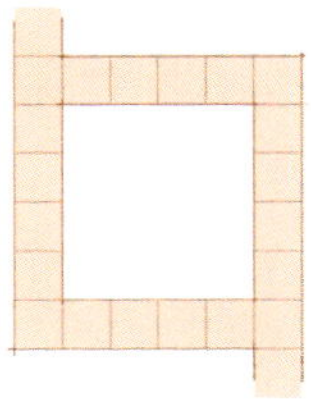

- Select the area to paint, as you did in the previous examples.
  - Using the Rectangular Marquee Tool, select the area to paint using the guidelines.
- Paint a light green background within your selection.
  - Create a new layer and name it *Brick Paving*.
  - Change the foreground color to light red (`#FFD9C7`).
  - **Edit > Fill**
  - Click the [OK] button.

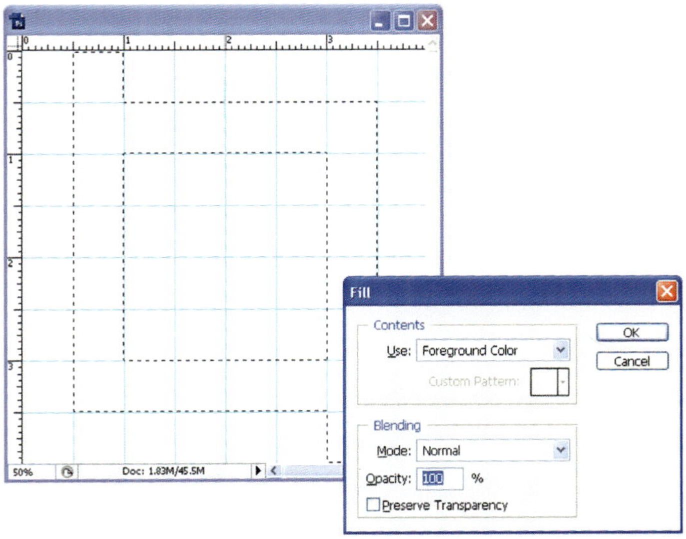

Step 2: Hatch the vertical segments of the path.

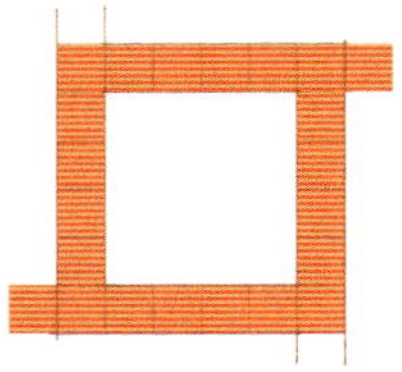

Step 2: Hatch the vertical segments of the path.

This step is a little unconventional. We would like the bricks to be aligned in the direction of the path; however, the filter will only allow us to create horizontal rows. Therefore, we are going to have to rotate our drawing, render the pavers, and then rotate it back.

- Copy and rotate the layer we want to hatch.
  - Click on the layer ***Brick Paving*** to choose it.
  - Drag the layer to the "Create a new layer" icon.
  - Rename this copied layer ***Brick Paving Vertical***.
  - **Edit > Transform > Rotate 90 CW**
- Draw the paving pattern using a filter.
  - Change the background color to dark red (`#ED5100`).
  - Change the foreground color to red (`#FF8257`).
  - **Filter > Sketch > Halftone Pattern...**
    - `Size = 3`
    - `Contrast = 0`
    - `Pattern Type = Line`
  - Click the [OK] button.

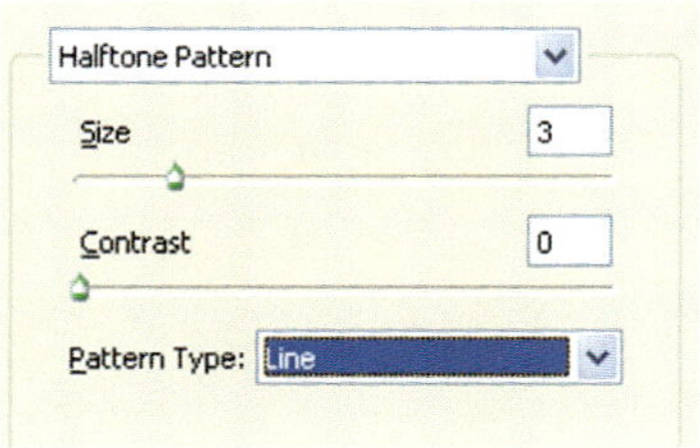

Step 3: Hatch the horizontal segments of the path.

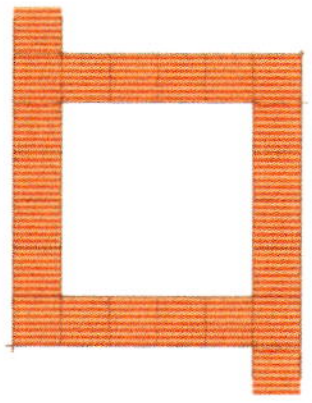

Step 3: Hatch the horizontal segments of the path.

- Rotate the vertical paving back.
  - Click on the layer ***Brick Paving Vertical*** to choose it.
  - **Edit > Transform > Rotate 90 CCW**
- Draw the paving pattern using a filter, as before.
  - Click on the layer ***Brick Paving*** to choose it.
  - **Filter > Sketch > Halftone Pattern...**
    - `Size = 3`
    - `Contrast = 0`
    - `Pattern Type = Line`
  - Click the [OK] button.
- Trim the unwanted portions.
  - Click on the layer ***Brick Paving Vertical*** to choose it.
  - Using the Rectangular Marquee Tool, select areas from the paving pattern you want to erase.
    - You are trying to reveal the horizontal paving from underneath.

Step 4: Paint the paving intersections.

Step 4: Paint the paving intersections.

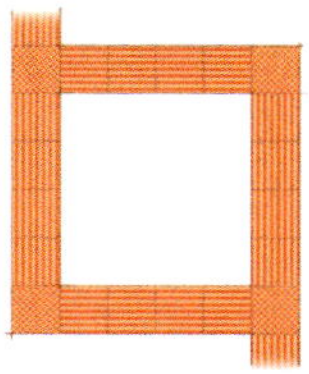

- Select the areas within the paving where the paths intersect.
  - Create a new layer and name it *Brick Paving Intersections*.
  - Using the Rectangular Marquee Tool and relying on the guidelines, select areas from the paving pattern that you want to paint.
    - You won't need tc fill these areas with a solid color as I have, below. Often, I will do this prior to adding a hatch to verify that I am painting where I intend.

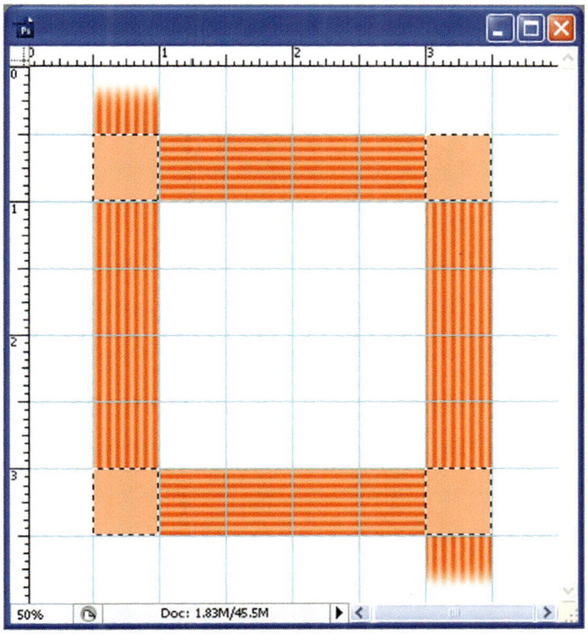

- Paint the intersections.
  - **Filter > Sketch > Halftone Pattern...**
    - `Size = 3`
    - `Contrast = 0`
    - `Pattern Type = Dot`
  - Click the [OK] button.

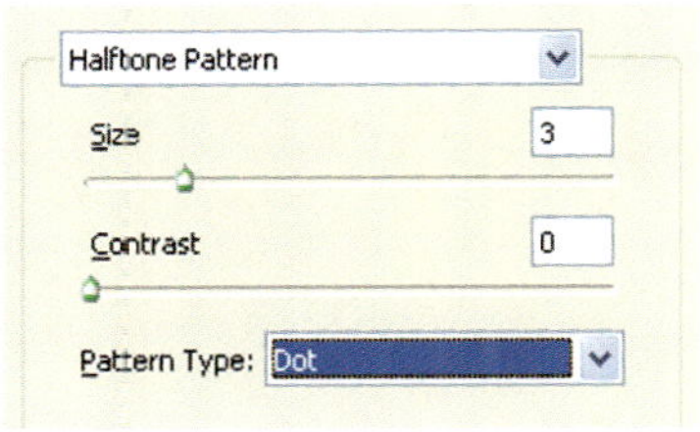

- Change the color of the overlapping line work from black to dark red.
  - Click on the layer with the path line work to choose it.
  - Right-click this layer and select "Blending Options..." from the pop-up menu.
  - Click on the "Color Overlay" tab on the Layer Style dialog box.
    - Click on the red box to the right of the Blend Mode drop-down list.
    - Change the color to dark red (`#A33100`).
    - Click the [OK] button.
  - Click the [OK] button to submit the changes to the color overlay.

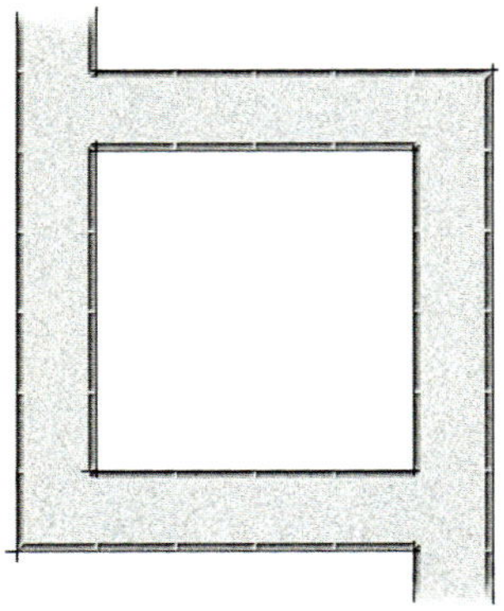

Master Plan Graphics | Crushed Rock

In this exercise you will draw some hatches that you might use to represent a path of crushed rock. The techniques used in this example include the following:

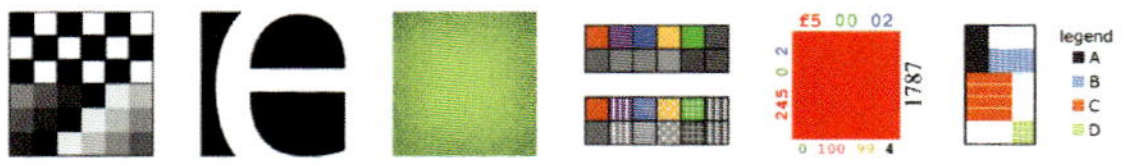

Black & White | Erase | Noisy Color | Indepen-dence | Color Palette | Legendary Labeling

This drawing was originally drawn on a canvas with a resolution of 200 pixels per inch. Afterwards, it was scaled down to fit within these pages.

Step 1: Paint the path.

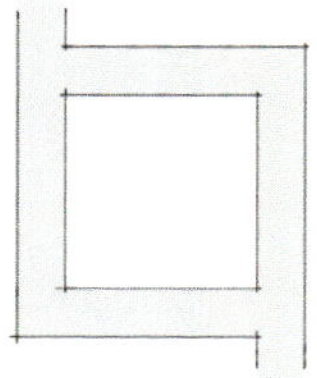

Step 1: Paint the path.

- Select the area to paint, as you did in the previous examples.
  - Using the Rectangular Marquee Tool, select the area to paint using the guidelines.
- Paint a light gray background within your selection.
  - Create a new layer and name it *Walking Path*.
  - Change the foreground color to light gray (`#E3E3E3`).
  - **Edit > Fill**
  - Click the [OK] button.

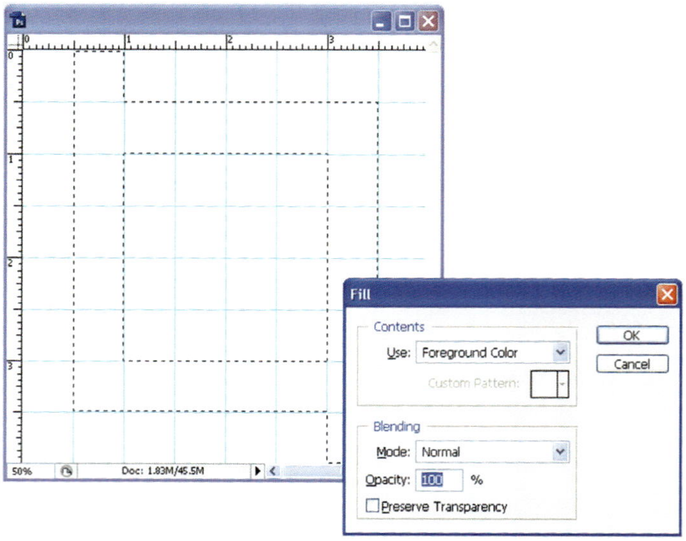

Step 2: Add texture.

- Refine the texture of the walking path by applying a filter.
    - **Filter > Noise > Add Noise...**
        - `Amount = 15%`
        - `Distribution = Gaussian`
        - `Monochromatic = checked`
    - Click the [OK] button.

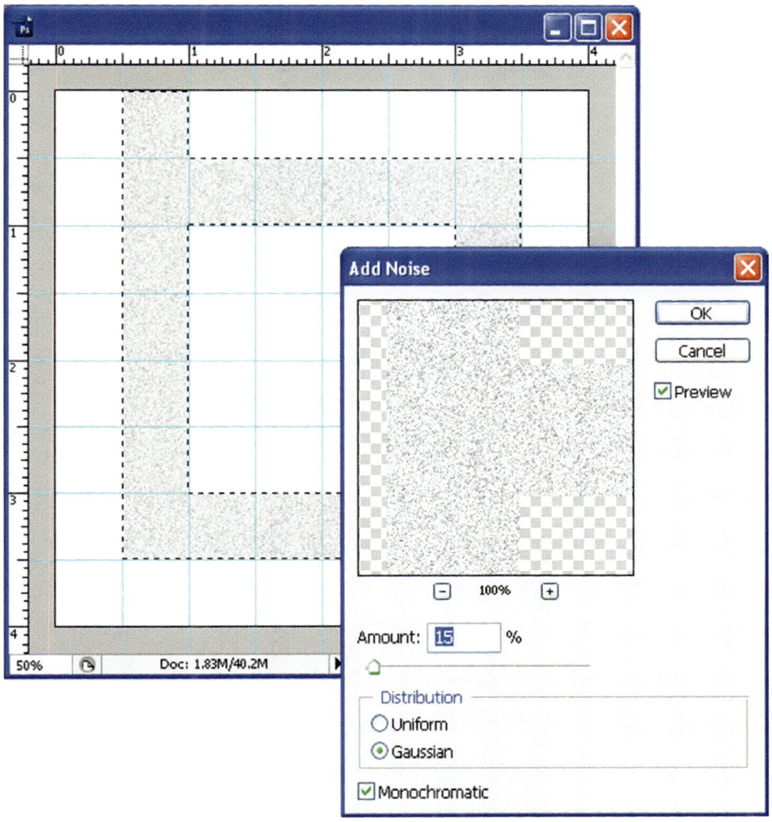

Step 2: Add texture.

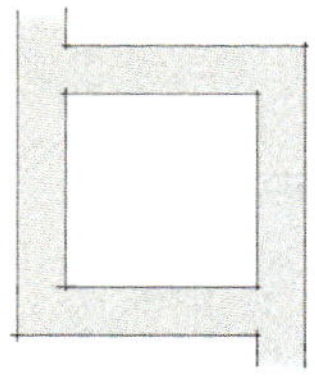

Step 3: Add an edge to the walking path.

- Paint an edge around the walking path.
    - Change the foreground color to a darker gray (`#8F8F8F`).
    - Create a new layer and name it *Edge*.
    - **Edit > Stroke...**
        - `Width = 10 px`
        - `Location = Inside`
    - Click the [OK] button.
- Break up the edge.
    - Choose a thin brush for the Eraser Tool and erase the edge along the guidelines.
        - `Master Diameter = 1 px`
        - `Hardness = 100%`
            - Basically, you are trying to represent the walking path edge as being made up of blocks of granite or similar curbing.

Step 3: Add an edge to the walking path.

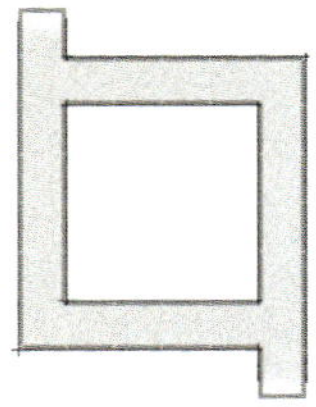

Step 4: Refine the path edge.

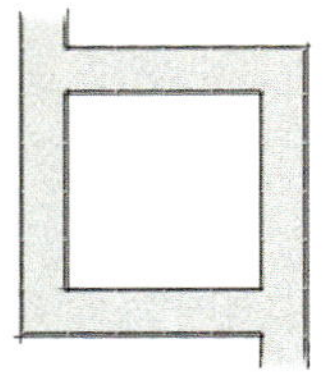

Step 4: Refine the path edge.

- Give the curbing along the path edge a three-dimensional look.
    - Click on the layer ***Edge*** to choose it.
    - Right-click this layer and select "Blending Options..." from the pop-up menu.
    - Click on the "Outer Glow" tab on the Layer Style dialog box.
        - `Blend Mode = Screen`
        - `Opacity = 75%`
        - `Noise = 0%`
        - Click the [OK] button.
    - Click the [OK] button to submit the changes to the color overlay.

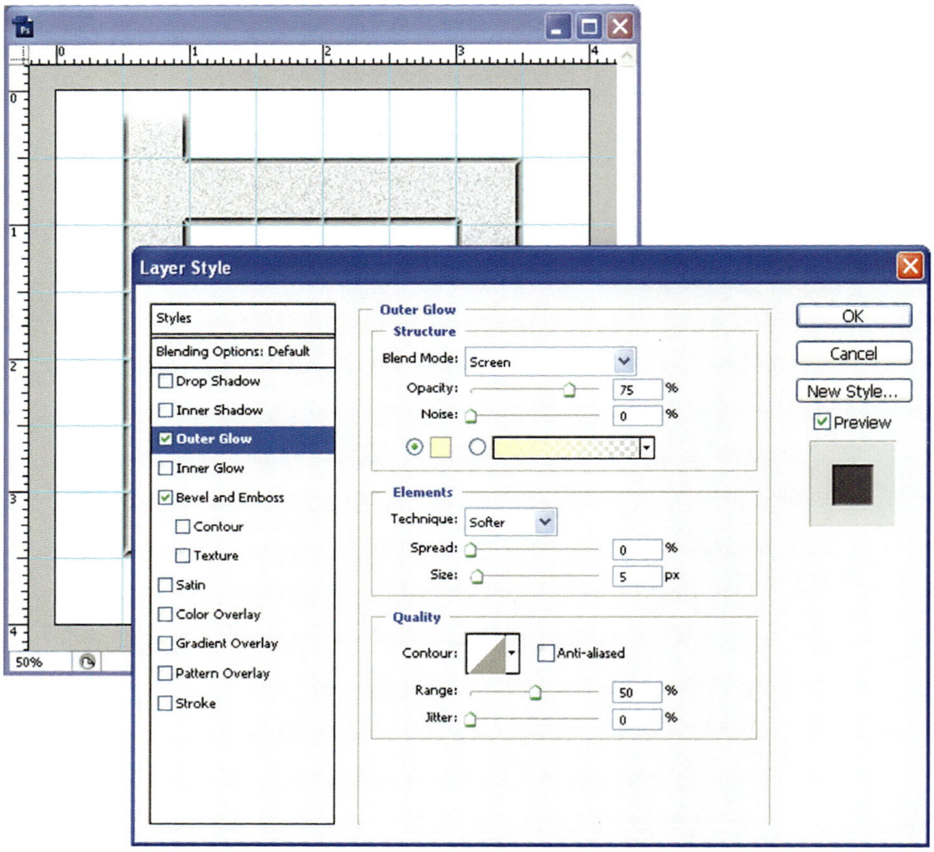

- With the Layer Style dialog box still open, click on the "Bevel and Emboss" tab.
    - `Style = Inner Bevel`
    - `Technique = Smooth`
    - `Direction = Up`
    - `Size = 5 px`
    - `Soften = 0 px`
    - `Angle = -45 degrees`
    - `Altitude = 30 degrees`
    - Click the [OK] button.
- Click the [OK] button to submit the changes to the outer glow and bevel.

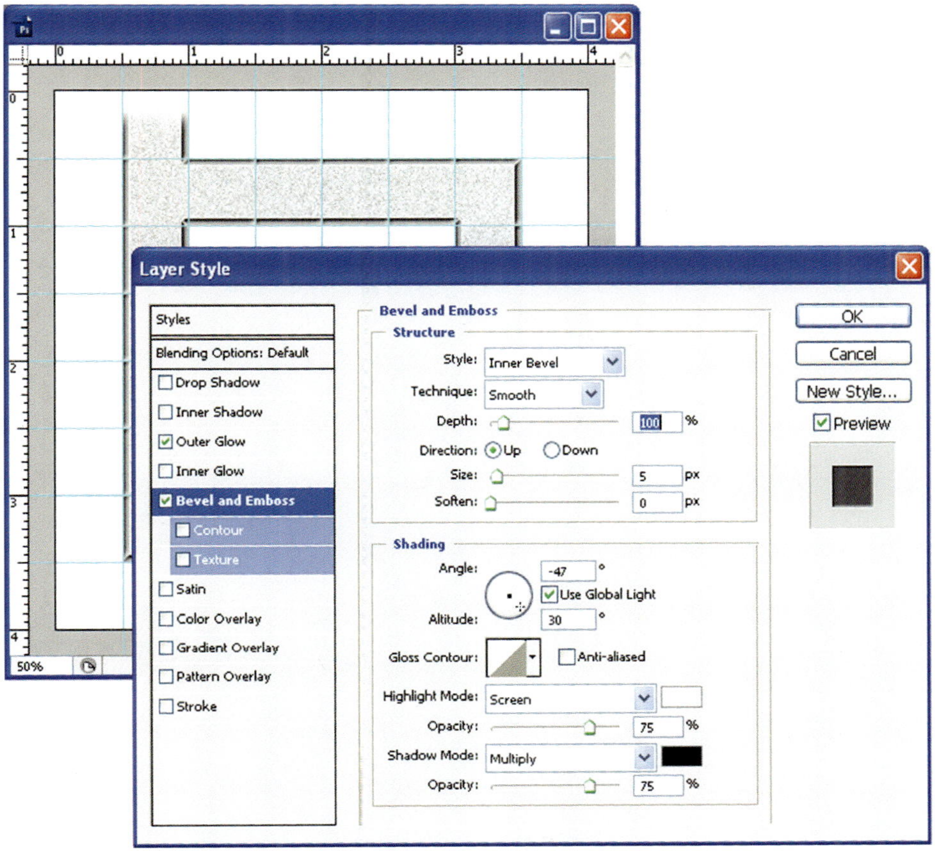

Step 5: Add texture to the curbing.

- Refine the texture of the curbing by applying a filter.
  - **Filter > Noise > Add Noise...**
    - `Amount = 15%`
    - `Distribution = Gaussian`
    - `Monochromatic = checked`
  - Click the [OK] button.

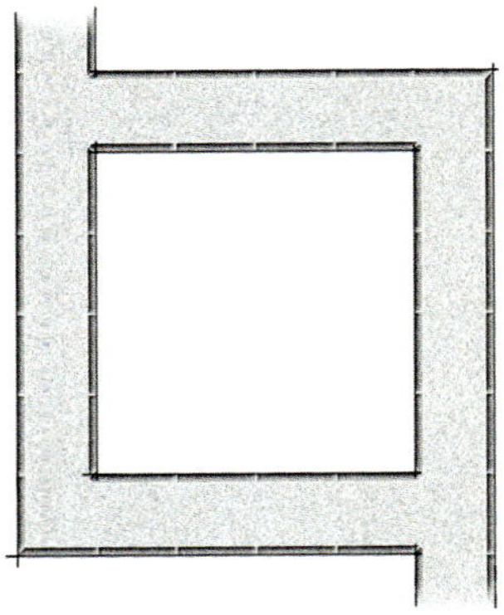

Step 5: Add texture to the curbing.

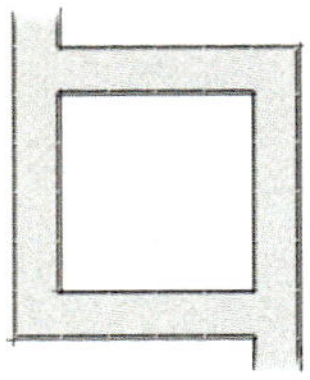

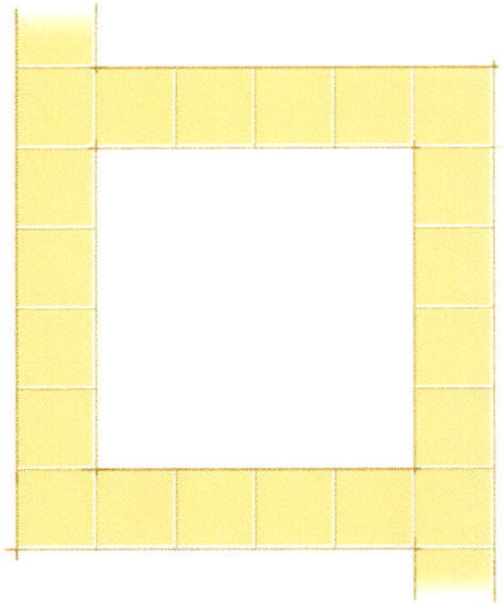

Master Plan Graphics | Concrete

In this exercise you will draw some hatches that you might use to represent a concrete walk. The techniques used in this example include the following:

Line Hierarchy

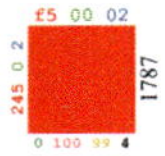

Color Palette

This drawing was originally drawn on a canvas with a resolution of 200 pixels per inch. Afterwards, it was scaled down to fit within these pages.

Step 1: Paint the concrete path.

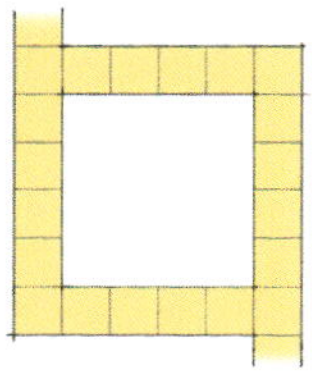

Step 1: Paint the concrete path.

- Select the area to paint, as you did in the previous examples.
  - Using the Rectangular Marquee Tool, select the area to paint using the guidelines.
- Paint a light tan background within your selection.
  - Create a new layer and name it *Concrete Path*.
  - Change the foreground color to light tan (`#FFE38C`).
  - **Edit > Fill**
  - Click the [OK] button.

Step 2: Change the color of the paving pattern.

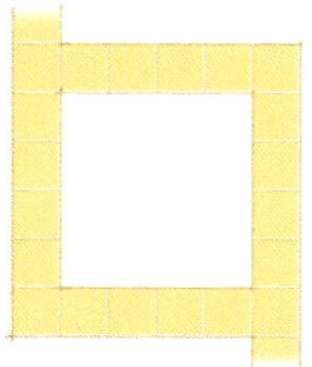

Step 2: Change the color of the paving pattern.

- Copy and change the color of the line work to give the paving pattern a 3-D look.
  - Click on the layer with the path line work to choose it.
  - Right-click this layer and select "Blending Options..." from the pop-up menu.
  - Click on the "Color Overlay" tab on the Layer Style dialog box.
    - Click on the red box to the right of the Blend Mode drop-down list.
    - Change the color to dark tan (`#C47C00`).
    - Click the [OK] button.
  - Click the [OK] button to submit the changes to the color overlay.
  - Copy the layer with the path line work.
  - Repeating the steps above, change the color to white (`#FFFFFF`).
  - With the Move Tool, shift the copied line work.

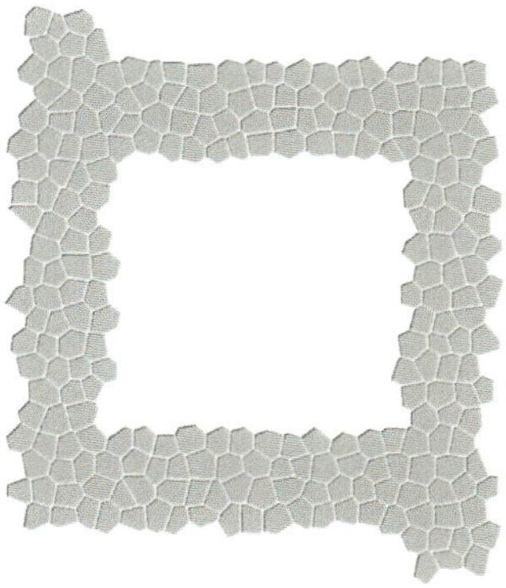

Master Plan Graphics | Flagstone

In this exercise you will draw some hatches that you might use to represent a flagstone walk. The techniques used in this example include the following:

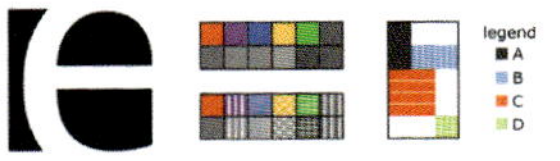

Erase | Indepen-dence | Legendary Labeling

This drawing was originally drawn on a canvas with a resolution of 200 pixels per inch. Afterwards, it was scaled down to fit within these pages.

Step 1: Paint a stained glass hatch.

- Select the area to paint, as you did in the previous examples.
    - Using the Rectangular Marquee Tool, select the area to paint using the guidelines.
- Paint the selected area.
    - Create a new layer and name it *Hatch*.
    - Change the foreground color to white (`#FFFFFF`).
    - **Edit > Fill**
    - Click the [OK] button.
- Create a new hatch by applying a different filter.
    - **Filter > Texture > Stained Glass...**
        - `Cell Size = 15`
        - `Border Thickness = 1`
        - `Light Intensity = 0`
    - Click the [OK] button.

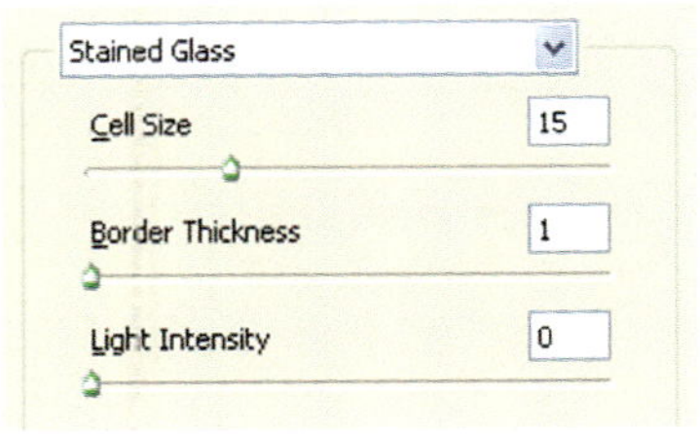

Step 1: Paint a stained glass hatch.

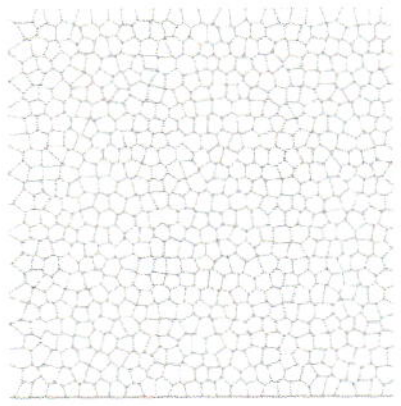

Step 2: Paint the stones within the hatch.

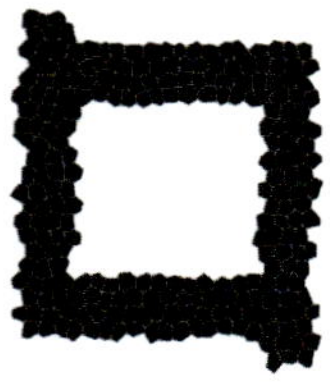

Step 2: Paint the stones within the hatch.

- Select where to paint.
  - Using the Magic Wand Tool, select the empty spaces within the hatch that are within your path.
    - `Tolerance = 10`
    - `Contiguous = checked`
  - Too add to the selection, hold down the [Shift] key when clicking the mouse. To remove from the selection, hold down the [Alt] key when clicking the mouse.

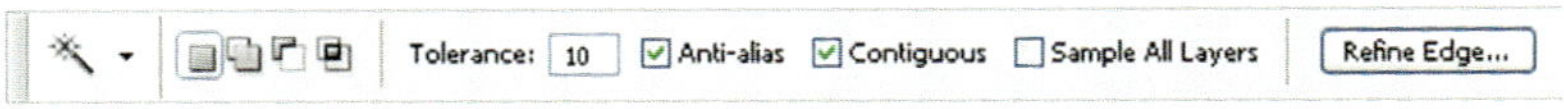

- Paint within the hatch.
  - Create a new layer and name it ***Flagstone***.
  - Change the foreground color to black (`#000000`).
  - **Edit > Fill**
  - Click the [OK] button.

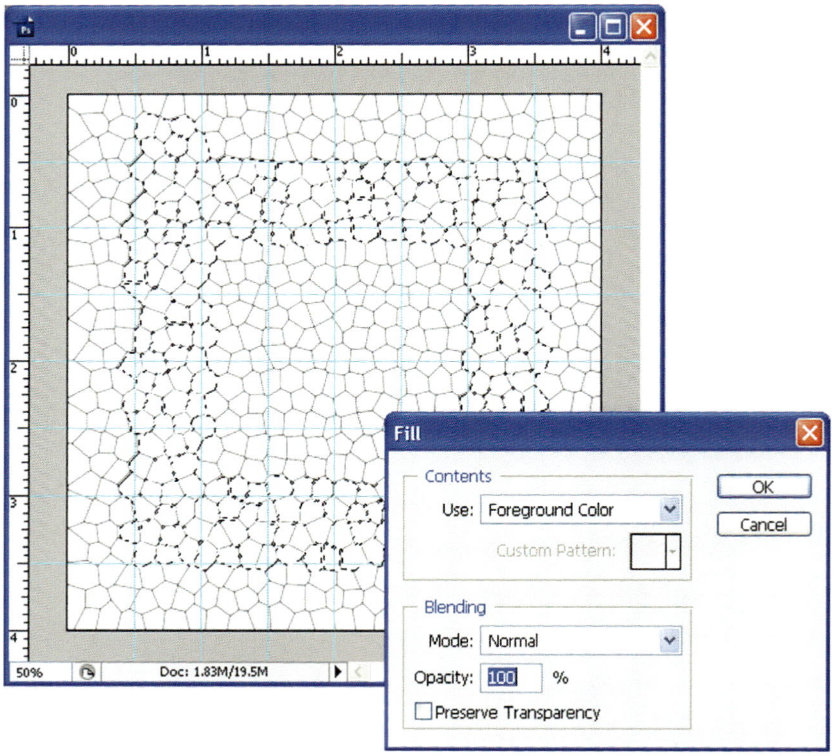

Step 3: Refine the flagstone.

Step 3: Refine the flagstone.

- Give the flagstone a three-dimensional look.
  - Click on the layer ***Flagstone*** to choose it.
  - Right-click this layer and select "Blending Options..." from the pop-up menu.
  - Click on the "Inner Glow" tab on the Layer Style dialog box.
    - `Blend Mode = Screen`
    - `Opacity = 75%`
    - `Noise = 0%`
    - Click the [OK] button.

- While the Layer Style dialog box is still open, click on the "Bevel and Emboss" tab.
    - `Style = Inner Bevel`
    - `Technique = Smooth`
    - `Direction = Up`
    - `Size = 5 px`
    - `Soften = 0 px`
    - `Angle = -45 degrees`
    - `Altitude = 30 degrees`
    - Click the [OK] button.
- While the Layer Style dialog box is still open, click on the "Color Overlay" tab.
    - Click on the red box to the right of the Blend Mode drop-down list.
    - Change the color to gray (`#BDBDBD`).
    - Click the [OK] button.
- Click the [OK] button to submit the changes to the inner glow, bevel and emboss, and color overlay.

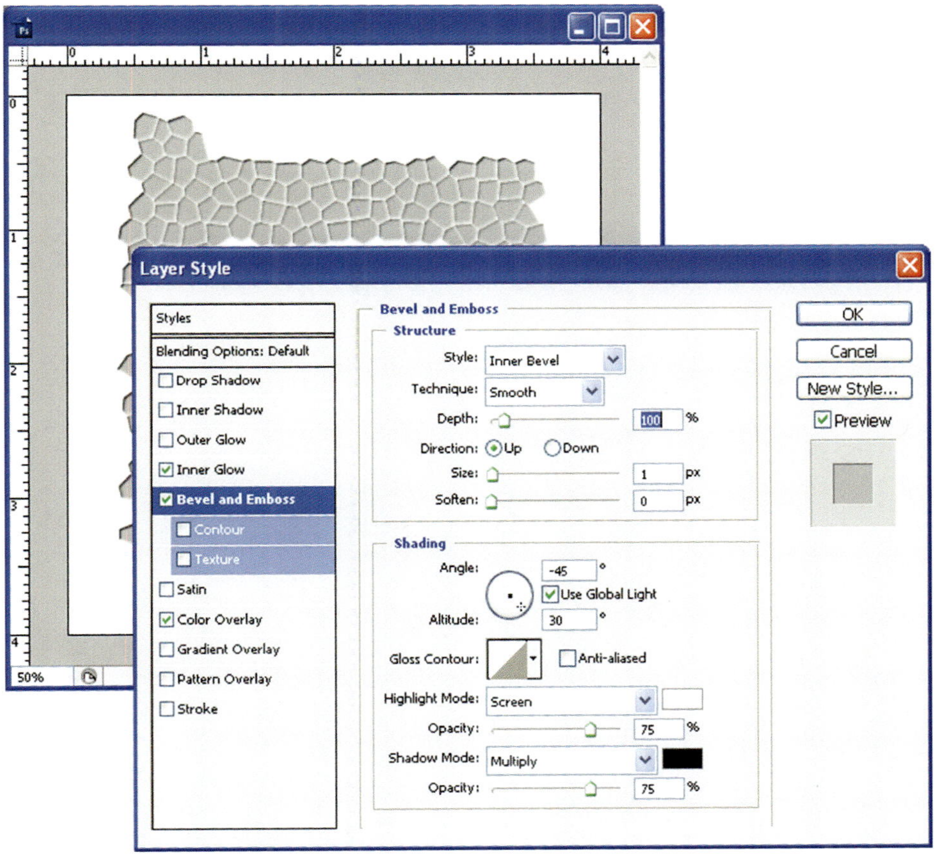

BIBLIOGRAPHY

Adobe Creative Team, editor. *Adobe Illustrator CS3 classroom in a book.* Addison-Wesley; 2007.

Adobe Creative Team, Walthers von Alten J, editors. *Adobe Photoshop CS3 classroom in a book.* Addison-Wesley; 2007.

Bertauski T. *Plan graphics for the landscape designer.* 2nd ed. Upper Saddle River (NJ): Pearson Education; 2007.

Burke PS. *Mastering InDesign CS3 for print design and production.* New York: Wiley; 2007.

Calabria A, Buitrago J. *Computer graphics for landscape architects: an introduction.* Clifton Park (NY): Delmar; 2009.

Covey, SR. *The seven habits of highly effective people.* Simon-Schuster; 2004.

Ching FDK. *Architectural graphics.* 4th ed. New York: Wiley; 2003.

Ching FDK. *Architecture: form, space, and order.* 2nd ed. New York: Van Nostrand Reinhold; 1996.

Cornwall C, Horiuchi A, Lehman C. *National Oceanic and Atmospheric Administration Earth System Research Laboratory: Solar position calculator.*
Available at http://www.srrb.noaa.gov/highlights/sunrise/azel.html. Accessed 2009 Feb 21.

Doyle ME. *Color drawing: design drawing skills and techniques for architects, landscape architects, and interior designers.* 2nd ed. New York: Wiley; 1999.

Green T, Stiller D. *Foundation Flash CS3 for designers.* New York: Apress; 2007.

Harris CW, Dines NT, editors. *Time-saver standards for landscape architecture: design and construction data.* 2nd ed. New York: McGraw-Hill; 1998.

Houle A. *MyInkBlog: Creating a realistic water texture in Photoshop.*
Available: http://www.myinkblog.com/2008/05/31/creating-a-realistic-water-texture-in-photoshop/. Accessed 5 March 2009.

Hopper LJ, editor. *Landscape architectural graphic standards.* New York: Wiley; 2007.

ISO 128-20:1996. *Technical drawings—General principles of presentation—Part 20: Basic conventions for lines.* International Organization for Standardization; 1996.

Lin MW. *Drawing and designing with confidence: a step-by-step guide.* New York: Wiley; 1993.

Meehan L. *Creative Photoshop landscape techniques.* New York: Lark; 2006.

Penley S. *Penley.* Athens (GA): Longstreet; 2005.

Phillips B, D'Orso M. *Body for life.* New York: Harper Collins; 1999.

Reid GW. *Landscape graphics.* New York: St. Martin's Press; 2002.

Reuter DD. *Computer graphics for architects, engineers, and environmental designers.* New York: Allworth Press; 2002.

Stanley A. *Next generation leader: five essentials for those who will shape the future.* Sisters (OR): Multnomah; 2003.

Sullivan C. *Drawing the landscape.* 2nd ed. New York: Wiley; 1997.

S

T

U

V

W

X